William Alexander Clouston

Wine and Walnuts

Or, the gossip of great writers. A book of anecdote, laconic sayings, and gems of

thought in prose and verse

William Alexander Clouston

Wine and Walnuts
Or, the gossip of great writers. A book of anecdote, laconic sayings, and gems of thought in prose and verse

ISBN/EAN: 9783337328719

Printed in Europe, USA, Canada, Australia, Japan

Cover: Foto ©Thomas Meinert / pixelio.de

More available books at **www.hansebooks.com**

WINE AND WALNUTS

OR,

The Gossip of Great Writers.

A BOOK OF ANECDOTE, LACONIC SAYING
AND GEMS OF THOUGHT,

In Prose and Verse.

EDITED BY

W. A. CLOUSTON.

London:

WARD, LOCK & TYLER.

WARWICK HOUSE, PATERNOSTER ROW, E.C.

PREFACE.

THE following compilation is designed to form a handy volume of curious and entertaining selections which do not properly fall within the province of "Popular Readings," "Elegant Extracts," etc.; many of them, indeed, are gleanings from the by-ways of Literature, and are probably known to few general readers.

The Editor ventures to hope that the present selection will prove acceptable to a large class who have little or no time or disposition to devote themselves to a regular course of literary study; and that, to such readers, this little book may furnish some amusement and even instruction.

W. A. C.

CONTENTS.

Contents.

CURIOUS NOTES ON NATURE AND ART—

LITERARY GEMS, OLD AND NEW—

PAGE

LITERARY
CURIOSITIES AND ECCENTRICITIES.

CURIOSITIES OF CHARACTER.

LUTHER AT HOME.

IT was a delightful thing to spend an evening with him. His broad, beneficent nature expanded into the sunniest, playfullest kindliness. His talk was full of wisdom, of humour, of genuine insight. Nature, art, humanity, philosophy, theology,—he was at home in them all. Floods of light came forth from him in single utterances, given freely, without effort. It is something more than curious to find him at one of these fireside conversations laughing at the absurdity of the Copernican system of astronomy, curious to go back so far as to find the first man of his generation counting for fancy what the merest child now knows to be fact. It is seldom you find such things, however. His mind was open as a child's for truth. It is most exhilarating to be beside him when he first discovered, studying the Greek language, after the Reformation had begun, that *metanoia* did not mean *penances*, but a *change of life*.

You know, amongst other courageous things he did, that he cast off the monk's cowl and married a nun. Catherine de Bora was her name. She had to beg her bread from door to door after her husband's death. With his wife he lived a noble domestic life, and yet an everyday one. How playfully he bantered her, laughed at her attempts to fathom the deep thoughts of her husband. "My Eve," he called her—"my Kit—my lord Kit—my rib Kit—that most learned dame, Catherine Luther de Bora. Ah, Kit, thou shouldst never preach ! If thou wouldst only say the Lord's prayer always before beginning, thy lectures would be shorter." In the history of his married life you will not miss acts of the highest benevolence, of hospitality afforded to those who could not return it, of just dealing with old servants. Luther and she were often very poor. The princes took his preaching, but left him to live as he might. He never would take money for his writings : the booksellers got all the profit. At one time he took to turning wood for a little money ; at another, to gardening. Yet, in the midst of all this hardship, when he had not a coin for himself, he would take the silver drinking cups he had got as keepsakes from the princes, and give them to poor students.—*Noble Traits of Kingly Men.*

SHELLEY'S STRANGE FANCY.

ONE evening, Lord Byron and Mr. Percy Bysshe Shelley, two ladies, and another gentleman, after having perused a German work called "Phantasmagoria," began relating ghost stories ; when his lordship having recited the beginning of "Christabel," then unpublished, the whole took so strong a hold of Mr. Shelley's mind, that he suddenly started up and ran out of the room. The physician and Lord Byron followed, and discovered him leaning against a mantel-piece, with the cold drops of perspiration trickling down his face. After having given him something to refresh him, upon inquiring into the cause of his alarm, they found that his wild imagination having pictured to him the bosom of one of the ladies with eyes (which was reported of a lady in the neighbourhood where he lived), he was obliged to leave the room in order to destroy the impression.—*Preface to the Vampire.*

In reference to the above incident, Byron, in a letter to Murray the publisher, dated May, 1819, writes :—The story of Shelley's agitation is true. I can't tell what seized him, for he don't want courage. He was once out with me in a gale of wind in a small boat, right under the rocks between Meillerie and St. Gingo. We were five in the boat : a servant, two boatmen, and ourselves. The sail was mismanaged, and the boat was filling fast. He can't swim. I stripped off my coat, made him strip off his, and take hold of an oar, telling him that I thought (being an expert swimmer) I could save him, if he would not struggle when I took hold of him, unless we got smashed against the rocks, which were high and sharp, with an awkward surf on them at that minute. We were then about a hundred yards from the shore, and the boat in peril. He answered me with the greatest coolness, that he had no notion of being saved, and that I would have enough to do to save myself ; and begged not to trouble me. Luckily, the boat righted, and, baling, we got round a point into St. Gingo, where the inhabitants came down and embraced the boatmen on their escape, the wind having been high enough to tear up some huge trees from the Alps above us, as we saw next day. And yet the same Shelley, who was as cool as it was possible to be in such circumstances (of which I am no judge myself, as the chance of swimming naturally gives self-possession when near shore), certainly had the fit of fantasy, which Polidore describes, though not exactly as he describes it.—*Byron's Letters.*

AN ECCENTRIC CLERGYMAN.

THE Rev. Thomas Priestly, who died in 1814, was a brother of the celebrated Dr. Priestly, and minister of the dissenting chapel in Cannon

Street, Manchester, from the pulpit of which he uttered many eccentricities, which have been attributed erroneously to other preachers. Observing one of his congregation asleep, he called to him (stopping in his discourse for the purpose), "Awake! I say, George Ramsay, or I'll mention your name." He had an unconquerable aversion to candles which exhibited long burned wicks, and often in the midst of his most interesting discourses, in the winter evenings, he would call out to the man appointed for that purpose, " Tommy ! Tommy ! top those candles." He was a man of great humour, which he even carried into the pulpit. He was the preacher, though others have borne the credit or odium of the circumstance, who pulled out of his pocket a half-crown, and laid it down upon the pulpit cushion, offering to bet with St. Paul, that the passage where he says "he could do all things," was not true ; but reading on, "by faith," put up his money, and said, " Nay, nay, Paul, if that's the case I'll not bet with thee."

"PRESERVED" LADIES.

AMONGST the curiosities and objects of interest to be seen by visitors to the Museum of the College of Surgeons, at Lincoln's Inn Fields, there is the body of a woman preserved in spirits in a glass case. It is the body of the wife of an eccentric quack doctor, Martin van Butchel, who died at his residence in Mount Street, Grosvenor Square, London, on the 30th October, 1814, in his eightieth year. This odd personage had been originally a surgical-instrument maker of considerable note, but relinquished that respectable profession for the more than questionable occupation of an empirical practitioner. Every afternoon Van Butchel took a "constitutional" in Hyde Park, mounted on a little white pony, to whose head was attached an ingenious contrivance by which a pair of blinkers could be instantaneously drawn over its eyes, to prevent the pony from "shying" at any uncommon object. His personal appearance was rendered the more remarkable, at a period when shaving was so generally practised, by his wearing a magnificent beard of twenty years' growth, which an Oriental might well have envied. According to popular tradition, the body of Van Butchel's spouse was thus embalmed and kept in his surgery, "for the purpose of securing a handsome income, which he only was to enjoy whilst his 'rib' remained above ground." This crafty plan of the quack doctor was well known among his acquaintance, and suggested a clever jocular "Epitaph on Mary Van Butchel," of which the following are the concluding lines :

> " O fortunate and envied man,
> To keep a wife beyond life's span !
> Whom you can ne'er have cause to blame ;
> Is ever constant and the same ;
> Who, qualities most rare, inherits
> A wife that's dumb—yet full of spirits !"

This "lady in a glass case" reminds me of another and more distinguished female personage, whose embalmed body the gallant secretary and garrulous diarist, Mr. Samuel Pepys, had the pleasure to kiss in Westminster Abbey. He has recorded the whimsical incident as follows :—"To Westminster Abbey, and saw, by particular favour, the body of Queen Catherine of Valois. I had the upper part of the body in my hands, and *I did kisse her mouth*, reflecting upon it that *I did kisse a queen*, and that this was my birthday, 36 years old, and that *I did kisse a queen.*" Mr. Pepys apparently did not deem a living dog better than a dead lion ; in other words, he did not consider that the "rud-red" lips of his own pretty Mistress Elizabeth, or, for the matter of that, the cherry lips of one of the tripping milkmaids he admired on a May-day, when on the way "to the office," were to be preferred to those of Catherine of Valois, "dead, and buried, and embalmed."—*W A. Clouston.*

FOOTE'S MAD PRANKS.

AT college, while under the care of the provost Dr. Gower, Foote's reckless conduct drew down upon him severe lectures from the learned provost, who does not however appear to have administered them with much judgment, interlarding his objurgations with many sesqui-pedalian words and phrases. On such occasions Foote would appear before his preceptor with a huge folio dictionary under his arm, and on any peculiarly hard word being used, would beg pardon with much formality for interrupting him ; turn up his book, as if to find out the meaning of the learned term which had just been uttered, and then, closing it, would say with the utmost politeness, "Very well, sir ; now please go on."

Another of his tricks was setting the bell of the college church ringing at night, by tying a wisp of hay to the bell-rope which hung down low enough to be within reach of some cows that were turned out to graze in a neighbouring lane. The mishap of Dr. Gower and the sexton, who caught hold of the peccant animal whilst in search of the author of the mischief, and imagined they had made a prisoner of him, provided a rich store of amusement for many days to the denizens of Oxford.

The following is Dr. Johnson's declaration regarding him, as related to Boswell :—"The first time I was in company with Foote was at Fitzherbert's. Having no good opinion of the fellow, I was resolved not to be pleased ; and it is very difficult to please a man against his will. I went on eating my dinner, pretty sullenly, affecting not to mind him ; but the dog was so very comical that I was obliged to lay down my knife and fork, throw myself back in my chair, and fairly laugh it out. Sir, he was irresistible." On another occasion he thus contrasts him with Garrick : "Garrick, sir, has some delicacy of feeling ; it is possible to put him out ; you may get the better of him ; but Foote is the most *incompressible* fellow that I ever knew : when you have driven him into a corner and think you are sure of him, he runs between your legs, or jumps over your head, and makes his escape."

Having made a trip to Ireland, he was asked on his return what impression was made on him by the Irish peasantry ; and replied, they gave him great satisfaction, as they settled a question which had long agitated his own mind : and that was, What became of the cast-off clothes of the English beggars ?—*Chambers' Book of Days.*

HOW TO INSURE LONG LIFE.

ARNOLD DE VILLENEUVE, who flourished in the thirteenth century, is said, according to Dr. Mackay, to have left the following receipt for insuring a length of years considerably surpassing the period which is generally supposed to be green old age. The person wishing to prolong his life almost indefinitely must rub himself well two or three times a week with the juice or marrow of cassia. Every night on going to bed he must put on his head a plaster composed of a certain quantity of oriental saffron, red rose leaves, sandal wood, aloes, and amber liquefied in oil of roses, and the best white wax. In the morning he must take it off and inclose it carefully in a leaden box till the next night, when it must be again applied. If he be of a sanguine temperament, he is to take sixteen chickens ; if phlegmatic, twenty-five ; and if melancholy, thirty : these he is to put in a yard where the air and water are pure. Upon these he is to feed, eating one a day. But these chickens have to be fattened by a peculiar method, which will impregnate their flesh with the qualities that are to produce longevity to the eater : for, being deprived of all other nourishment till they are almost dying of hunger, they are to be fed upon broth made of serpents and vinegar, thickened with wheat and bran. After two months of such diet, they will be fit for the intending Methuselah's table, and are to be washed down with good hock or claret. Fancy living for a few centuries on eternal chickens ! Possibly the serpents and vinegar might render that domestic fowl palatable for fifty years or so, but surely it would produce a most unhealthy manner in time. Besides, the experimentalist would have to catch his serpents, and a single bite might interfere unpleasantly with the theory. On the whole, I am inclined to think that we do pretty well as we are ; and if we desire to live reasonably long, we shall achieve our end by the simpler rules of common sense.—*" Free Lance " in London Society.*

A COLLECTOR OF CORKS.

NOT very long ago, a poverty-stricken old man drew his last breath in a miserable attic in Paris, who left little else behind him save a heap of corks, souvenirs of long past—

> " Reckless days and reckless nights,
> Unholy songs, and tipsy fights ; "

for he had been rich and gay once upon a time, and might have sung with Captain Morris—

"In life I've rung all changes through,
 Run every pleasure down !"

It had been a life-long custom with him to preserve every cork drawn
for the delectation of himself and his friends, and inscribe upon it the
date of drawing and the particular occasion upon which the bottle was
opened ; so his cupboard of corks was actually a record of his life.
Upon a champagne cork was written : "Bottle emptied 12th May,
1843, with M. B——, who wished to interest me in a business by which
I was to make ten millions. This affair cost me fifty thousand francs.
M. B—— escaped to Belgium—a caution to amateurs !" Upon
another was written : "Cork of Cyprus wine ; of a bottle emptied on
the 4th of December, 1850, with a dozen fast friends. Of these I
have not found one to help me in the day of my ruin : their names
are annexed below."

AN ENTHUSIASTIC NATURALIST.

AN accident which happened to two hundred of my original drawings nearly put a stop to my researches in ornithology. I shall relate
it, merely to show how far enthusiasm (for by no other name can I
call the persevering zeal with which I laboured) may enable the observer of nature to surmount the most disheartening obstacles. I left
the village of Henderson in Kentucky, situated on the bank of the
Ohio, where I resided several years, to proceed to Philadelphia on
business. I looked to all my drawings before my departure, placed
them carefully in a wooden box, and gave them in charge to a relative,
with instructions to see that no injury should happen to them. My absence
was of several months ; and when I returned, after having enjoyed the
pleasures of home for a few days, I inquired after my box, and what I
was pleased to call my treasure. The box was produced and opened,
but—reader, feel for me !—a pair of Norway rats had taken possession of the whole, and had reared a young family amongst the gnawed
bits of paper which, but a few months before, represented nearly a
thousand inhabitants of air ! The burning heat which instantly rushed
through my brain was too great to be endured without affecting my
whole nervous system. I slept not for several nights, and the days
and nights passed like days of oblivion, until, the animal power
being recalled into action through the strength of my constitution, I
took up my gun, my note-book, and my pencils, and went forth to the
woods as gaily as if nothing had happened. I felt pleased that I
might now make much better drawings than before, and ere a period
not exceeding three years had elapsed, I had my portfolio filled again.
—*Audubon's American Ornithology.*

"PASSING RICH ON EIGHTEEN POUNDS A YEAR."

A CLERGYMAN of the name of Matheson was minister of Patter-
dale, in Westmoreland, sixty years, and died lately at the age of ninety.
During the early part of his life his benefice only brought him twelve

pounds a year ; it was afterwards increased (perhaps by Queen Anne's Bounty) to eighteen, which it never exceeded. On this income he married, brought up four children, and lived comfortably with his neighbours, educated a son at the university, and left upwards of one thousand pounds behind him. With that singular simplicity and in-attention to forms which characterize a country life, he himself read the burial service over his mother, he married his father to a second wife, and afterwards buried him also. He published his own banns of marriage in the church, with a woman whom he had formerly chris-tened, and he himself married all his four children.—*European Magazine,* 1814.

JOANNA SOUTHCOTT.

POPULAR credulity in the most preposterous pretensions of religious impostors or fanatics is strikingly exemplified in the case of Joanna Southcott, whose followers at the beginning of the present century are said to have numbered over one hundred thousand,—most of whom, however, were of the ignorant classes. This woman is supposed to have been born of humble parentage, about 1750, and she was for many years a domestic servant at Exeter. When about forty years ot age she seems to have commenced her career as a " prophetess," and boldly declared herself to be the woman mentioned in the twelfth chapter of Revelation. Though very illiterate, she scribbled a vast quantity of rubbish, which she called prophecies and fulfilments ot prophecy, and drove a thriving trade in the sale of "seals," or sealed packets, at half a guinea each, which were to secure eternal salvation to the fortunate possessor ; and as her followers continued to in-crease, she predicted that she was to become pregnant in the same miraculous manner as the Virgin Mary, and this was to take place in her sixty-fifth year. What lent some colour to this extraordinary "pro-phecy," was the circumstance that after she had passed her grand climacteric, her person did really exhibit apparent symptoms of preg-nancy. Her " Books of Wonders " were freely advertised in the news-papers of the day, as will be seen from the following advertisement taken from a morning newspaper published in 1814 :—

" The Coming of Shiloh.—In a third Book of Wonders is announced, that Shiloh will be born this year, who is to gather the Jews, Gen. xlix. 10 ; and that all may bless the day the child is born, that do not treat the babe with scorn. That Shiloh is the branch mentioned by Isaiah in the eleventh chapter : 'A branch shall grow out of his roots ;' and by Zech. vi. 12 : ' Behold the man whose name is The BRANCH ; and he shall grow up out of his place, and he shall build the temple of the Lord : and he shall bear the glory, and shall sit and rule upon his throne, etc. And it is said that Joanna Southcott will, in the sixty-fifth year of her age (which is this year), conceive and bring forth this child in the same marvellous manner that the Virgin Mary did the Child Jesus ; and that, by the fulfilment of this prophecy, the truth of her mission and the truth of the gospel will be proved. In this book is strong argument from Scripture and reason, calculated to remove the differences between Jews and Christians and it proves that the office of Shiloh, The Branch, was not fulfilled by Jesus Christ at His first coming, for the Jews were then scattered and not gathered, so that there could be no fulfilment of Jacob's prophecy then.   My countrymen ! you who are desirous of knowing the truth, will read this book, and judge of yourselves, that you may be prepared to receive Shiloh, the Prince of Peace."

Lord Byron, in a letter to Murray his publisher, dated September 2nd, 1814, calls Joanna " this new (old) virgin of spiritual impregnation ; " and " longs to know what she will produce ;" and in another letter he expresses a fear that these matters will lend a hand to profane scoffers.

The following is extracted from a magazine of the same date :—

"Joanna Southcott's miraculous conception, and the cot made by Siddons of Aldersgate Street, for the 'new Messiah,' are become almost as general a topic of conversation as the late Jubilee.   In one of the prophetess's recent publications, entitled the ' Book of Wonders, the ' Coming of Shiloh ' is thus announced : ' This year, in the sixty-fifth year of thy age, thou shalt have a Son by the power of the Most High, which if they receive as their Prophet, Priest, and King, then I will restore them to their own land, and cast out the heathens for their sakes, as I cast out them when they cast out me, by rejecting me as their Saviour, Prince, and King, for which I said I was born, but not at that time to establish my kingdom.'   In consequence of this announcement, the followers of Joanna are making all sorts of preparations, and she has been literally overwhelmed with presents. Laced caps, embroidered bibs, and worked robes, a mohair mantle which cost £150, splendid silver pap-spoons and caudle-cups (one shaped like a dove) have been poured in upon her, till she at length determined to receive no more.   The word ' Shiloh ' is drawn in gold Hebrew characters on the cot, and over a canopy the inscription, ' A freewill offering of Faith to the promised Seed.'"

As the time of Joanna's predicted miraculous accouchement drew near, her house in London was besieged day and night by crowds of her credulous followers ; but they waited in vain.   Poor Joanna herself ultimately had misgivings as to the genuineness of her " mission," and declared that " if she had been deceived, she had herself been the sport of some spirit either of good or evil."   She died on the 27th December, 1814, but many of her disciples would not believe that she was really dead, and kept her body unburied until it was far advanced in decomposition.   A *post-mortem* examination of her body was made, and the prophetess was found to have died of *dropsy !*   A section of her more fanatical followers believed that she would again appear in the flesh to fulfil her " mission ;" and some of her male disciples vowed they would not shave their beards till her resurrection.   It is supposed that the last of a small band of believers in her pretensions died this year (1875).--*W. A. Clouston.*

A VERY ANCIENT FAMILY.

THE famous Lord Chesterfield had a relation, a Mr. Stanhope, who was exceedingly proud of his pedigree, which he pretended to trace to a ridiculous antiquity. Lord Chesterfield was one day walking through an obscure street in London, where he saw a miserable daub of Adam and Eve in Paradise. He purchased this painting, and having written on the top of it, "*Adam de Stanhope, of Eden, and Eve his wife,*" he sent it to his relation, as a valuable old family portrait.

ZOZIMUS, THE DUBLIN BALLAD SINGER.

ABOUT thirty years ago a tall blind man used to stand at the corner of Essex Bridge, Dublin, singing and reciting ballads, which, if not remarkable for wit, were more or less attractive to his audience from their singularity. This Homeric beggar possessed some of the sturdiness of Edie Ochiltrie, and had a certain pride in his calling, and in. the fact of his being looked up to as king of street minstrels. Even now, in Ireland, the street minstrel pursues his occupation in a more interesting fashion than that in which the same business is carried on by the fellows who chant vulgar ribaldry in our lanes or public parks ; but in the days when Zozimus flourished, the craft had retained an importance derived from its connection with the political history of the country. It is well known that Swift employed the Dublin ballad-singers to chant and hawk about some of his rhyming squibs ; and several of the chief opponents of the Union engaged the ragged followers of the gay science in a musical crusade against the Castle authorities.

The poet Zozimus derived his name from the fact of his having composed a lyric on the discovery of the desert of St. Mary of Egypt by a pious ecclesiastic called Zozimus. His biographer informs us that he was usually dressed in a heavy, coarse, long-tailed coat, and a very much worn hat, with exceedingly strong shoes. He recited or declaimed pieces of a sacred turn, interspersed with odd " asides " to the crowd, and always introducing himself with a sort of prologue :

> " Ye sons and daughters of Erin attend ;
> Gather round poor Zozimus, yer friend.
> Listen, boys, until yez hear
> My charming song."

One of his most striking and effective readings was that of a romantic version of the story of Moses in the bulrushes. This he always prefaced by inquiring, " Is there a crowd about me now ? Is there any blackguard heretic listenin' to me ? " Having been satisfied on these points, Zozimus is reported to have delivered a series of stanzas, of which the following may serve as a specimen :—

> " In Egypt's land, upon the banks of Nile,
> King Pharaoh's daughter went to bathe in style ;
> She tuk her dip, then walked unto the land,
> And, to dry her royal pelt, she ran along the strand.

A bulrush tripped her, whereupon she saw
A smiling baby in a wad of straw ;
She tuk it up, and said, in accents mild,
'*Tare an' agers, girls ! which av yez owns this child ?*'"

Zozimus could sing of his garret as gaily as Béranger,—

" Gather round me, boys ! will yez
Gather round me ?
And hear what I have to say,
Before ould Sally brings me
My bread and jug of tay.
I live in Fiddle Alley,
Off Blackpits near the Comb,
With my poor wife, called Sally,
In a narrow, dirty room."

The poet, living in the O'Connell era, was a great admirer of the agitator, and celebrated O'Connell's election to the mayoralty with much enthusiasm. Zozimus died on Friday, April 3, 1846. A priest, who went to visit him, found the bard in a miserable room, lying on a straw pallet, and surrounded by a horde of ballad singers, to whom it seems he was teaching the doggrel that was no longer of much use to him. " How are you, Mike ?" said the priest. " I'm dictatin'," was the characteristic reply of the minstrel. He had a grand wake and a funeral, which no doubt Zozimus would have enjoyed, but for the inactive part he was compelled to take in it.—*Pall Mall Gazette.*

SOUWORROW, THE RUSSIAN GENERAL.

IT has been generally considered as a mark of a great mind in a soldier successfully to attempt hazardous things on his own responsibility ; that is, without orders, or contrary to their spirit. Souworrow did more, for he dared to violate the positive orders of his commander, and staked his life upon the issue of an enterprise, not only expressly forbidden, but extremely perilous, and seemingly desperate. While yet a major, he commanded an outpost in sight of the enemy who was daily growing stronger, and he requested permission to attack him, going so far as to pledge himself for the success. The commander-in-chief thinking it rash and impracticable on account of the enemy's great superiority, forbade the attempt under pain of death ; and made the chagrin of Souworrow, who was conscious of his own better judgment, quite insupportable. Foreseeing that the enemy's numerical superiority, constantly increasing, would shortly deprive him of the opportunity of striking the meditated blow, he invited his brother officers to a supper, and by flattering them with the certain prospect of glory, while the deadly prohibition was confined to his own breast, that he alone might suffer in case of failure, he prevailed on them to join in the attack, and they mustered a force of 1000 strong from the junction of different outposts under the command of Souworrow. Justly calculating that the enemy, being five times stronger, had too much confidence to expect or to be prepared for an attack from so weak a body, Souworrow fell upon him at night, defeated him with great slaughter, obtaining a decisive victory, which he thus reported : — "As a soldier, I deserve death for disobeying my orders ; as a Russian, I have done my duty ; the enemy is no more." The commander-in-chief was thunderstruck on reading this dispatch, yet so pleased with the boldness of Souworrow's genius, and the brilliant result of his conduct, that not knowing how to decide himself, he stated the whole to the empress, and sent her the original dispatch. Her majesty immediately returned the following answer, addressed to Souworrow :— "As a soldier, I leave you to the mercy of the commander-in-chief ; as a Russian, I congratulate you as my lieutenant-colonel." From this time was Souworrow's rise regular and progressive ; and the impression he made on the empress was never effaced.

THE POET POPE.

IT is not probable, indeed, that a woman would have fallen in love with him as he walked along the Mall, or in a box at the opera, nor from a balcony, nor in a ballroom ; but in society he seems to have been as amiable as unassuming, and, with the greatest disadvantages of figure, his head and face were remarkably handsome, especially his eyes. He was adored by his friends—friends of the most opposite dispositions, ages, and talents : by the old and wayward Wycherley, by the cynical Swift, the rough Atterbury, the gentle Spence, the stern attorney-bishop Warburton, the virtuous Berkeley, and the "cankered Bolingbroke." Bolingbroke wept over him like a child ; and Spence's description of his last moments is at least as edifying as the more ostentatious account of the deathbed of Addison. The soldier Peterborough and the poet Gay, the witty Congreve and the laughing Rowe, the eccentric Cromwell and the steady Bathurst, were all his intimates. The man who could conciliate so many men of the most opposite description, not one of whom but was a remarkable or a celebrated character, might well have pretended to all the attachment which a reasonable man would desire of an amiable woman.—*Byron.*

PALEY'S "PUDDENS."

AFTER Paley's preferment to the archdeaconry, he dined with a large number of clergymen at his first visitation, all of whom were in eager expectation to hear the improving conversation of the great man. The latter remained silent till the second course was served. He then opened his lips, and every one listened with rapt attention to what the archdeacon would deign to say. His remark was: "I don't think these *puddens* are much good unless the seeds are taken out of the raisins." On another occasion Paley gave utterance to a speech such as we might have expected, as a joke, from Sydney Smith. Feeling annoyed by a draught of air behind him, he said, "Shut that window behind me, and open one lower down, behind one of the curates."

AN ECCENTRIC OLD LADY.

IN the "Monthly Obituary" of the *European Magazine* for September, 1814, the following particulars are given regarding an eccentric female personage, then recently deceased:—

"Lately, at Gray's Alms Houses, Taunton, Hannah Murton, a maiden lady. She vowed, several years ago, that no HE FELLOW should ever touch her, living or dead. In pursuance of this resolution, she purchased a coffin, in which, whenever she felt serious illness, she immediately deposited herself—thus securing the gratification of her peculiar sensibility. The coffin was not, however, exclusively appropriated to the reception of her mortal remains, but served also as her wardrobe, and the depository of her bread and cheese."

This narrative of the aged spinster's "peculiar sensibility" is tantalizingly incomplete; one is curious to know whether, after all, she died in her coffin!

IRISH CAR-DRIVERS.

ONE of the richest characters of the class, we encountered on the road from Ross to Wexford; he told us how he got his first situation:—

"The masther had two beautiful English horses, and he wanted a careful man to drive them; he was a mighty pleasant gintleman, and loved a joke. Well, there was as many as fifteen after the place, and the first that wint up to him, ' Now, my man,' says he, 'tell me,' says he, 'how near the edge of a precipice you would undertake to drive my carriage?' So the boy considered, and he says, says he, ' Within a foot, plase yer honour, and no harm.' ' Very well,' says he, 'go down, and I'll give ye yer answer by-and-by.' So the next came up, and said he'd be bound to carry 'em within half a foot; and the next said five inches; and another, a dandified chap intirely, was so mighty nice, that he would drive it within ' three inches and a half, he'd go bail.' Well, at last my turn came, and when his honour axed me how nigh I would drive his carriage to a precipice, I said, says I, ' Plase yer honour, *I'd keep as far off it as I could.*' ' Very well, Mr. Byrne,' says he, 'you're my coachman,' says he. Och, the roar there was in the kitchen when I wint down and tould the joke!"—*Mr. and Mrs. Hall's Ireland.*

"MERRY ANDREW."

ANDREW BORDE was one of those eccentric geniuses who live in their own sphere, moving on principles which do not guide the routine of society. He was a Carthusian friar; his hair-shirt, however, could never mortify his unvarying facetiousness; but if he ever rambled in his wits, he was a wider rambler, even beyond the boundaries of Christendom, "a thousand or two and more myles;" an extraordinary feat in his day. He took his degree at Montpellier, was incorporated at Oxford, and admitted into the College of Physicians in London, and was among the physicians of Henry VIII. His facetious genius could not conceal the real learning and the practical knowledge which he derived from personal observation. Borde has received hard measure from our literary historians. This ingenious scholar has been branded by Warton as a mad physician. To close the story of one who was all his days so facetious, we find that this Momus of philosophers died in the Fleet. This was the fate of a great humorist, neither wanting in learning nor genius. It is said that such was his love of the "commonwealth," that he sometimes addressed them from an open stage, in a sort of gratuitous lecture, as some amateurs of our own days have delighted to deliver, and from whence has been handed down to us the term of "Merry Andrew."—*Disraeli's Amenities oj Literature.*

A RETORT BY DANTE.

WHEN Dante was at the court of Signore della Scala, then sovereign of Verona, that prince said to him one day, " I wonder, Signor Dante, that a man so learned as you are, should be hated by all my court ; and this fool," pointing to his favourite buffoon, who stood by him, " should be by all beloved." Dante, highly piqued at this comparison, replied, " Your excellency would wonder less, if you considered that we like those best who most resemble ourselves."

BURNS IN EDINBURGH.

IT was not in the debating club of Tarbolton alone, about which so much nonsense has been prosed, that he had learned eloquence ; he had been long giving chosen and deliberate utterance to all his bright ideas and strong emotions; they were all his own, or he had made them his own by transfusion ; and so, therefore, was his speech. Its fount was in genius, and therefore could not run dry—a flowing spring that needed neither to be "fanged" nor pumped. As he had the power of eloquence, so had he the will, the desire, the ambition, to put it forth ; for he rejoiced to carry with him the sympathies of his kind, and in his highest moods he was not satisfied with their admiration without their love. There never beat a heart more alive to kindness. To the wise and good, how eloquent his gratitude ! to Glencairn, how imperishable ! This exceeding tenderness of heart often gave such pathos to his ordinary talk, that he even melted commonplace people into tears ! Without scholarship, without science, with not much of what is called information, he charmed the first men in a society equal in all these to any at that time in Europe.—*Professor Wilson.*

A DREADFUL ALTERNATIVE.

THE servant maid of the celebrated lyric poet Le Brun appearing one day before him with all his manuscripts in her hands, threatened to consign all his glory to the flames if he did not marry her. Le Brun, frightened at the imminent danger in which his verses were of being reduced to ashes, and of thus losing his hopes of immortality, sent for a lawyer immediately, and married her.

CHEERFULNESS OF MEN OF GENIUS.

MEN of truly great powers of mind have generally been cheerful, social, and indulgent; while a tendency to sentimental whining or fierce intolerance may be ranked among the surest symptoms of little souls and inferior intellects. In the whole list of our English poets we can only remember Shenstone and Savage—two, certainly, of the lowest— who were querulous and discontented. Cowley, indeed, used to call himself melancholy; but he was not in earnest, and at any rate was full of conceits and affectations, and has nothing to make us proud of him. Shakspeare, the greatest of them all, was evidently of a free and joyous temperament; and so was Chaucer, their common master. The same disposition appears to have predominated in Fletcher, Jonson, and their great contemporaries. The genius of Milton partook something of the asperity of the party to which he belonged, and of the controversies in which he was involved; but, even when "fallen on evil days and evil tongues," his spirit seems to have retained its serenity as well as its dignity; and in his private life, as well as in his poetry, the majesty of a high character is tempered with great sweetness, genial indulgence, and practical wisdom. In the succeeding age our poets were but too gay; and though we forbear to speak of living authors, we know enough of them to say with confidence, that to be miserable is not now, any more than heretofore, the common lot of those who excel.—*Jeffrey.*

ST. SIMEON STYLITES, HERMIT OF THE PILLAR.

IN the monastery of Heliodorus (a man sixty-five years of age, who had spent sixty-two years so abstracted from the world that he was ignorant of the most obvious things in it) the monks ate but once a day; Simeon joined the community, and ate but once a week. Heliodorus required Simeon to be more private in his mortifications; "with this view," says Butler, "judging the rough rope of the well, made of twisted palm-tree leaves, a proper instrument of penance, Simeon tied it close about his naked body, where it remained, unknown both to the community and his superior, till such time as it having ate into his flesh, what he had privately done was discovered by the effluvia proceeding from the wound." Butler says that it took three days to disengage the saint's clothes, and that "the incisions of the physicians, to cut the cord out of his body, were attended with such anguish and pain, that he lay for some time as dead." After this he determined to pass the whole forty days of Lent in total abstinence, and retired to a hermitage for that purpose. Bassus, an abbot, left with him ten loaves and water, and coming to visit him at the end of the forty days, found both loaves and water untouched, and the saint stretched on the ground without signs of life. Bassus dipped a sponge in water, moistened his lips, gave him the eucharist, and Simeon by degrees swallowed a few lettuce leaves and other herbs. He passed twenty-six Lents in the same manner. In the first part of a Lent he prayed standing; growing weaker, he prayed sitting; and towards the end, being almost exhausted, he prayed lying on the ground. At the end of three years he left his hermitage for the top of a mountain, made an inclosure of loose stones, without a roof, and having resolved to live exposed to the inclemencies of the weather, he fixed his resolution by fastening his right leg to a rock with a great iron chain. Multitudes thronged to the mountain to receive his benediction, and many of the sick recovered their health. But as some were not satisfied unless they touched him in his inclosure, and Simeon desired retirement from the daily concourse, he projected a new and unprecedented manner of life. He erected a pillar six cubits high (each cubit being eighteen inches) and dwelt on it four years; on a second of twelve cubits high he lived three years; on a third of twenty-two cubits high, ten years; and on a fourth of forty cubits, or sixty feet high, which the people built for him, he spent the last twenty years of his life. This occasioned him to be called *Stylites*, from the Greek word *stylos*, a pillar. This pillar did not exceed three feet in diameter at the top, so that he could not lie extended on it; he had no seat with him; he only stooped or leaned to take a little rest, and bowed his body in prayer so often that a certain person who counted these positions found that he made one thousand two hundred and forty-four reverences in one day, which if he began at four o'clock in the morning and finished at eight o'clock at night, gives a bow to every three-quarters of a minute; besides which he exhorted the people twice a day. His garments were the skins of beasts, he wore an iron collar round his neck, and had a horrible ulcer in his foot. During his forty days' abstinence throughout Lent, he tied himself to a pole. He treated himself as the outcast of the world and the worst of sinners, worked miracles, delivered prophecies, had the sacrament delivered to him on the pillar, and died bowing upon it, in the sixty-ninth year of his age, after having lived upon pillars for six-and-thirty years. His corpse was carried to Antioch, attended by the bishops and the whole country, and worked miracles on its way.—*Hone's Every-Day Book.*

DR. BARROW AND THE EARL OF ROCHESTER.

MEETING at court one day Rochester with mock politeness thus accosted the witty divine : "Doctor, I am yours to my shoe-tie;" to which Barrow rejoined, "My lord, I am yours to the ground;" followed by Rochester with, "Doctor, I am yours to the centre;" to which the doctor returned, "My lord, I am yours to the antipodes." Rochester, scorning to be foiled by a piece of musty divinity, as he termed Barrow, replied, "Doctor, I am yours to the lowest pit of h—l;" whereupon Barrow, turning on his heel, quietly observed, "*There*, my lord, I leave you !"

THE OLD ENGLISH HOUSEWIFE.

NEARLY two centuries and a half ago, Gervase Markham wrote a very useful and entertaining tract entitled, "The English Housewife, containing the inward and outward virtues which ought to be in a complete woman.   As her skill in physic, surgery, cookery, extraction of oyles, banquetting stuffe, ordering of great feasts, preserving of all sorts of wines, conceited secrets, distillations, perfumes, ordering of wool, hemp, flax, making cloth, and dyeing;—the knowledge of dayries, office of malting oates, their excellent uses in a family, of brewing, baking, and all other things belonging to a household."

LORD AND LADY BYRON.

WRITING of Lady Byron before marriage, Mr. Harness says, "Miss Milbank was not without a certain amount of prettiness or cleverness ; but her manner was stiff and formal, and gave one the idea of being self-willed and self-opinionated. She was almost the only young, pretty, well-dressed girl we ever saw who carried no cheerfulness along with her.   I seem to see her now, moving slowly along her mother's draw- ing-room, talking to scientific men and literary women, without a trace of emotion in her voice, or the faintest glimpse of a smile upon her countenance. A lady who had been on intimate terms with her from their mutual childhood, once said to me, 'If Lady Byron has a heart, it is deeper seated and harder to get at than anybody else's heart I have ever known.'"

As a contribution to the Byron controversy, the evidence given by Mr. Harness as to Byron's peculiar idiosyncrasy is not without im- portance :—" Byron had one pre-eminent fault,—a fault which must be considered as deeply criminal by every one who does not, as I do, be- lieve it to have resulted from monomania.   He had a morbid love of a bad reputation.   There was hardly an offence of which he would not, with perfect indifference, accuse himself."

After reading the story set afloat by Mrs. Stowe, Mr. Harness pro- fessed himself utterly shocked that such a scandal should have been circulated by a lady, and utterly incredulous as to its possessing any real basis.   " He said that he had heard the charge long before ; that it arose out of the publication of ' Manfred,' but that it was as untrue as it was revolting.   He reiterated what he had before said of Byron's love of romancing and of exaggerating his dissipations, and that he was encouraged to such rhapsodies by the serious interpretation his wife put upon them."   " She took seriously every word he uttered, weighed it in her precise balance, and could not refrain from express- ing her condemnation of his principles and her abhorrence of his language.   This fanned the flame, increased his irritation, or added zest to his amusement.   Whatever crime she accused him of, he was not only ready to admit, but to trump by the confession of some greater enormity."   Probably the solution of many of the puzzles which occur in Byron's career lies in the remark Mr. Harness makes as the result of deliberate consideration, and with full knowledge of the circumstances of the case,—" There can be no doubt that Byron was a little maddish."--*Literary Life of Rev. Mr. Harness.*

A MAN OF GREAT IDEAS.

SENECIO was a man of a turbid and confused wit, who could not endure to speak any but mighty words and sentences, till this humour grew at last into so notorious a habit or disease as became the sport of the whole town. He would have no servants but huge, massy fellows ; no plate nor household stuff, but thrice as big as the fashion. You may believe me, for I speak it without raillery, his extravagancy came at last into such a madness, that he would not put on a pair of shoes, each of which was not big enough for both his feet. He would eat nothing but what was great, nor touch any fruit but horse plums and pound pears. He kept a mistress that was a very giantess, and made her walk too always in chioppins, till at last he got the surname of *Senecio Grandio.—Cowley's Essays.*

DESCRIPTION OF A "FAIR AND HAPPY MILKMAID."

A FAIR and happy milkmaid is a country wench that is so far from making herself beautiful by art, that one look of hers is able to put all face physic out of countenance. She knows a fair look is but a dumb orator to commend virtue, therefore minds it not. All her excellencies stand in her so silently, as if they had stolen upon her without her knowledge. The lining of her apparel (which is herself) is far better than outsides of tissue ; for though she be not arrayed in the spoil of the silkworm, she is decked in innocency, a far better wearing. She doth not, with lying long abed, spoil both her complexion and conditions. Nature hath taught her too immoderate sleep is rust to the soul : she rises therefore with chanticleer, her dame's cock, and at night makes the lamb her curfew. Her breath is her own, which scents all the year long of June, like a new-made haycock. She makes her hand hard with labour, and her heart soft with pity ; and when winter evenings fall early, sitting at her merry wheel, she sings a defiance to the giddy wheel of fortune. She doth all things with so sweet a grace, it seems ignorance will not suffer her to do ill, being her mind is to do well. She bestows her year's wages at next fair ; and in choosing her garments, counts no bravery in the world like decency. The garden and beehive are all her physic and chirurgery, and she lives all the longer for it. She dares go alone and unfold sheep in the night, and fears no manner of ill, because she means none : yet, to say the truth, she is never alone, for she is still accompanied with old songs, honest thoughts, and prayers, but short ones ; yet they have their efficacy, in that they are not palled with ensuing idle cogitations. Lastly, her dreams are so chaste that she dare tel them : only a Friday's dream is all her superstition ; that she conceals for fear of anger. Thus lives she ; and all her care is that she may die in the spring-time, to have store of flowers stuck upon her winding-sheet. —*Sir Thomas Overbury.*

CURIOSITIES OF CRITICISM.

THE UNIVERSALITY OF SHAKSPEARE'S GENIUS.

MORE full of wisdom and ridicule and sagacity than all the moralists and satirists in existence, he is more wild, airy, and inventive, and more pathetic and fantastic, than all the poets of all regions and ages of the world ; and has all the elements so happily mixed up in him, and bears his high faculties so temperately, that the most severe reader cannot complain of him for want of strength or of reason, nor the most sensitive for defect of ornament or ingenuity. Everything in him is in unmeasured abundance and unequalled perfection ; but everything so balanced and kept in subordination as not to jostle or disturb, or take the place of another. The most exquisite poetical conceptions, images, and descriptions, are given with such brevity, and introduced with such skill, as merely to adorn without loading the sense they accompany. Although his sails are purple, and perfumed, and his prow of beaten gold, they waft him on his voyage, not less, but more rapidly and directly, than if they had been composed of baser materials. All his excellencies, like those of Nature herself, are thrown out together ; and instead of interfering with, support and recommend each other. His flowers are not tied up in garlands, nor his fruits crushed into baskets, but spring living from the soil, in all the dew and freshness of youth ; while the graceful foliage in which they lurk, and the ample branches, the rough and vigorous stem, and the wide spreading roots on which they depend, are present along with them, and share in their places the equal care of their Creator.— *Jeffrey.*

Shakspeare was the man who, of all modern and perhaps ancient poets, had the largest and most comprehensive soul. All the images of nature were still present to him, and he drew them not laboriously, but luckily. When he describes anything, you more than see it,—you feel it too. Those who accuse him to have wanted learning give him the greater commendation : he was naturally learned ; he needed not the spectacles of books to read nature ; he looked inwards, and found her there.—*Dryden.*

OPINIONS ON THOMAS CARLYLE.

CARLYLE is like pickles ; only a little of him can be tasted, with any relish, at a time.—*Dr. Mackay.*

The ingenious Tom Carlyle.—*Jas. Hogg.*

Mr. Carlyle formerly wrote for the *Edinburgh Review;* a man of talents, though absurdly overpraised by some of his admirers. I believe, though I do not know, that he ceased to write, because the oddities of his diction, and his new words, compounded *à la Teutonique,* drew such strong remonstrances from Napier.—*Macaulay to Leigh Hunt.*

Although Mr. Carlyle first propounded his views of hero-worship in a series of lectures, yet it is easy to discern from his studied—sometimes painfully studied—style of writing, that he is not well-adapted for an orator. We once heard him deliver a few sentiments at a public meeting ; but he spoke, and that was all. The words that came uppermost did not please him, and he waited for others. Although he did what the best orators have been defined to do, though he " thought upon his legs," he did not think aloud ; and the intervals between his silent thoughts and the expression of them were too long and too frequent for the patience of a mixed auditory. Yet the few sentences he did utter were aphorisms full of wisdom.—*R. Chambers.*

We shall regard it as one of the most melancholy evidences of the decline of all pure and healthful literature, if the writings of Mr. Carlyle continue to have an enduring hold upon the popular mind.—*Church of England Quarterly Review.*

A man who, though no systematic philosopher, has probably done more to spiritualize philosophy in England than any other modern writer.—*J. R. Morell.*

Thomas Carlyle I excuse ; he is entitled to be crazy, being a man of genius.

North. And of virtue ; as Cowper said of his brother, "a man of morals and of manners too."

Tickler. But oh, sir, the impudent stupidity of some of the subscribers to that Signet Seal !

North. Hopeless of achieving mediocrity in any of the humbler walks of their native literature, the creatures expect to acquire character by acquaintance with the drivel of German dotage ; and going at once to the fountain head, gabble about Goethe, "the Master"! Yes, I beseech you, Hal, look at the flunkies !—*Noctes Ambrosianæ.* —*Russell's Book of Authors.*

HOGARTH AS A SATIRIST.

I INCLUDE the great name of Hogarth among our satirists, upon the strength of Charles Lamb's text, in his perfectly admirable essay upon that extraordinary artist :—" His graphic representations," Lamb says, " are indeed books ; they have the teeming, fruitful, suggestive meaning of words. Other pictures we look at—his prints we read." I would say, not so much—certainly not more—is Hogarth the artist, the penciller of the ludicrous, the incongruous, and the buffoonery in life's scene, as he is of the serious, the pathetic, and even the terrible. Lamb has, with fine critical tact, traced a parallel between the " Rake's Progress " and the "Timon of Athens" of Shakspeare. And if we read any of the painter's scenes of a life, we shall find as many incidents brought together, as many deep feelings expressed, and as many thoughts indicated and suggested, as in a first-rate drama or novel.

His by-plays, his asides, his subordinate points, display almost as much genius as the broad action of his leading characters. As, for instance, in the last scene of "The Harlot's Progress," amid the exhibition of shocking insensibility in the faces of the wretches assembled round the coffin of the poor dead outcast, that figure of the little boy, dressed in a mourning cloak and funeral weepers, who is to make one in the procession, calmly winding up his peg-top ; as Lamb says, "the only thing in that assembly not a hypocrite." Again, for a satirical incident, that one often noticed in the marriage scene of " The Rake's Progress " of the church poor-box, with a spider's web over the lid, and the commandments over the communion-table cracked across. In the settlement scene of the "Marriage à-la-Mode," the bride abstractedly drawing her handkerchief to and fro through her ring ; it is evident from her manner that the mystic symbol of union may as well be there as on her finger or anywhere else. The morning after the masquerade ; the candles in the ante-room, with long wicks swaled down to the sockets, and the footman yawning his head half off ; and the steward going out shrugging his shoulders, with one receipt upon the file. These three great histories (with that of the " Idle and Industrious Apprentice "), for they are "great ";—great in invention, great in design, great in execution, and great in detail, in wit, humour, satire, pathos, and horror ; these elaborate series of so many lives,—are like pictorial telegraphs, biographies in hieroglyphic ; whole years are suddenly condensed, like events in a dream, that would occupy hours to relate, but have passed over the mental retina in a few seconds. It may appear an extravagant confession, but I never recur to these high productions without coming to the conclusion that, after the great poets of our nation, I think I should wish to have been Hogarth ; first, for his genius, and then for the profound moral lessons he has read to his fellow-men.—*Charles Cowden Clarke.*

CARLYLE ON KING DAVID.

On the whole we make too much of faults ; the details of the business hide the real centre of it. Faults ? The greatest of faults, I should say, is to be conscious of none. Readers of the Bible, above all, one would think, might know better. Who is called there "the man according to God's own heart"? David, the Hebrew king, had fallen into sins enough ; blackest crimes ; there was no want of sins. And thereupon the unbelievers sneer, and ask, Is this your man according to God's own heart? The sneer, I must say, seems to me but a shallow one. What are faults, what are the outward details of life, if the inner secret of it, the remorse, temptations, true, often baffled, never-ended struggle of it be forgotten? "It is not in man that walketh to direct his steps." Of all acts, is not, for a man, repentance the most divine ? The deadliest sin, I say, were that same supercilious consciousness of no sin—that is death ; the heart so conscious is divorced from sincerity, humility, and fact ; is dead ; it is pure, as dead dry sand is pure. David's life and history, as written for us in those Psalms of his, I consider to be the truest emblem ever given of a man's moral progress and warfare here below. All earnest souls will ever discern in it the faithful struggle of an earnest human soul towards what is good and best. Struggle often baffled, sore baffled, down as into entire wreck ; yet a struggle never ended ; ever with tears, repentance, true unconquerable purpose, begun anew. Poor human nature ! Is not a man's walking, in truth, always that : "a succession of falls"? Man can do no other. In this wild element of a life he has to struggle onwards ; now fallen, deep abased ; and ever with tears, repentance, with bleeding heart, he has to rise again, struggle again still onwards. That his struggle be a faithful unconquerable struggle : that is the question of questions.

SHAKSPEARIAN NOTES.

SIR THOMAS MORE, in his History of Richard III., written in 1513, gives an account of Jane Shore, the celebrated courtesan, in which, after relating some of her many acts of kindness and favour, not only towards people of her original rank in life, but towards disgraced courtiers, etc., he makes the following fine reflection :—" For men use, if they have an evil turn, to write it in marble ; and whoso doth us a good turn, we write it in dust." These words of Sir Thomas More probably suggested to Shakspeare the proverbial observation in Henry VIII., Act iv., Sc. 2 :—

" Men's evil manners live in brass, their virtues
  We write in water."

Shakspeare, in his play of Richard III., follows More's history of that reign, and therefore could not but see this passage.

The distich which Shakspeare has put into the mouth of his madman in King Lear, Act iii., Sc. 4—

" Mice and rats and such small deer,
  Have been Tom's food for seven long year "—

has excited the attention of the critics. Instead of *deer* one of them would substitute *gear*, and another, *cheer*. But the ancient reading is established by the old romance of Sir Bevis, which Shakspeare had doubtless often heard sung to the harp. This distich is part of a description there given of the hardships suffered by Bevis, when confined for seven years in a dungeon :—

" Rattes and myse and such small dere
  Was his meate that seven yeare."
  Percy's Reliques of Ancient Poetry.

LITERARY MERITS OF THE BIBLE.

I HAVE carefully and regularly perused these Holy Scriptures, and am of opinion that the volume, independently of its Divine origin, contains more sublimity, purer morality, important history, and finer strains of eloquence than can be collected from all other books, in whatever language they may have been written.—*Sir Wm. Jones.*

THE FOUR GREAT ENGLISH POETS.

THE four greatest names in English poetry are almost the four first we come to : Chaucer, Spenser, Shakspeare, and Milton. There are no others that can really be put in competition with these. The last two have had justice done them by the voice of common fame. Their names are blazoned in the very firmament of reputation ; while the first two (though "the fault has been more in their stars than in themselves that they are underlings") either never emerged far above the horizon, or were too soon involved in the obscurity of time. In comparing these four writers together, it might be said that Chaucer excels as the poet of manners, or of real life ; Spenser as the poet of romance ; Shakspeare as the poet of nature (in the largest use of the term) ; and Milton as the poet of morality. Chaucer most frequently describes things as they are ; Spenser, as we wish them to be ; Shakspeare, as they would be ; and Milton, as they ought to be. As poets, and as great poets, imagination, that is, the power of feigning things according to nature, was common to them all ; but the principle, or moving power, to which this faculty was most subservient in Chaucer, was habit or inveterate prejudice ; in Spenser, novelty and the love of the marvellous ; in Shakspeare, it was the force of passion, combined with every variety of possible circumstances ; and in Milton combined only with the highest. The characteristic of Chaucer is intensity ; of Spenser remoteness ; of Milton elevation ; of Shakspeare everything. It has been said by some critic that Shakspeare was distinguished from the other dramatic writers of his day only by his wit ; that they had all his other qualities but that ; that one writer had as much sense, another as much fancy, another as much knowledge of character, another the same depth of passion, and another as great power of language. This statement is not true ; nor is the inference from it well-founded, even if it were. This person does not seem to have been aware that, upon his own showing, the great distinction of Shakspeare's genius was its virtually including the genius of all the great men of his age, and not his differing from them in one accidental particular. The striking peculiarity of Shakspeare's mind was its generic quality, its power of communication with all other minds, so that it contained a universe of thought and feeling within itself, and had no one peculiar bias or exclusive excellence more than another. He was just like any other man, but that he was like all other men. He was the least of an egotist that it was possible to be. He was nothing in himself ; but he was all that others were, or that they could become. He not only had in himself the germs of every faculty and feeling, but he could follow them by anticipation, intuitively, into all their conceivable ramifications, through every change of fortune, or conflict of passion, or turn of thought.—*Hazlitt's Lectures on the English Poets.*

OUR FRIENDS IN FICTION.

THEY used to call the good Sir Walter the " Wizard of the North."
What if some writer should appear who can write so *enchantingly*
that we shall be able to call into actual life the people whom he
invents ? What if Mignon and Margaret and Goetz von Berlichingen
are alive now (though I don't say they are visible), and Dugald
Dalgetty and Ivanhoe were to step in at that open window by the little
garden yonder ? Suppose Uncas and our noble old Leather Stocking
were to glide in silent ? Suppose Athos, Porthas, and Aramis should
enter, with a noiseless swagger, curling their moustaches ? And
dearest Amelia Booth, on Uncle Toby's arm ; and Tittlebat Titmouse,
with his hair dyed green ; and all the Crummles company of comedians,
with the Gil Blas troop ; and Sir Roger de Coverley ; and the greatest
of all crazy gentlemen, the Knight of La Mancha, with his blessed
squire ? I say to you, I look rather wistfully towards the window,
musing upon these people. Were any of them to enter, I think I
should not be very much frightened. Dear old friends, what pleasant
hours I have had with them ! We do not see each other very often,
but when we do, we are ever happy to meet.—*Thackeray's Roundabout
Papers.*

CHARACTER OF FALSTAFF.

FALSTAFF'S wit is an emanation of a fine constitution, an exuberation
of good-humour and good-nature ; an overflowing of his love of
laughter and good fellowship ; a giving vent to his heart's ease and
over-contentment with himself and others. He would not be in character if he were not so fat as he is ; for there is the greatest keeping in
the boundless luxury of his imagination, and the pampered self-indulgence of his physical appetites. He manures and nourishes his mind
with jests, as he does his body with sack and sugar. He carves out
his jokes as he would a capon or a haunch of venison, where there is
cut and come again ; and pours out upon them the oil of gladness.
His tongue drops fatness, and in the chambers of his brain "it snows
of meat and drink." He keeps up perpetual holiday and open house,
and we live with him in a round of invitations to a rump and a dozen.
Yet we are not to suppose that he was a mere sensualist. All this is
as much in imagination as in reality. His sensuality does not engross
and stupefy his other faculties, but " ascends me into the brain, clears
away all the dull crude vapours that environ it, and makes it full of
nimble, fiery, and delectable shapes." His imagination keeps up the
ball after his senses have done with it. He seems to have even a
greater enjoyment of the freedom from restraint, of good cheer, of his
ease, of his vanity, in the ideal exaggerated description which he gives
of them than in fact. He never fails to enrich his discourse with
allusions to eating and drinking ; but we never see him at table. He
carries his own larder about with him, and he is himself " a tun of
man." His pulling out the bottle on the field of battle is a joke to
show his contempt for glory accompanied with danger, his systematic
adherence to his Epicurean philosophy in the most trying circum-

stances. Again, such is his deliberate exaggeration of his own vices, that it does not seem quite certain whether the account of his hostess's bill, found in his pocket, with such an out-of-the-way charge for capons and sack, with only one halfpenny worth of bread, was not put there by himself as a trick to humour the jest upon his favourite propensities, and as a conscious caricature of himself. He is represented as a liar, a braggart, a coward, a glutton, etc., and yet we are not offended, but delighted with him ; for he is all these as much to amuse others as to gratify himself. He openly assumes all these characters to show the humorous part of them. The unrestrained indulgence of his own ease, appetites, and convenience has neither malice nor hypocrisy in it. In a word, he is an actor in himself almost as much as upon the stage, and we no more object to the character of Falstaff in a moral point of view, than we should think of bringing an excellent comedian, who should represent him to the life, before one of the police offices.— *Hazlitt's Characters of Shakspeare.*

A GREAT BOOK, A GREAT EVIL.

THE smallness of the size of a book is always its own commendation, as, on the contrary, the largeness of a book is its own disadvantage, as well as a terror of learning. In short, a big book is a scarecrow to the head and pocket of the author, student, buyer, and seller, as well as a harbour of ignorance. Small books seem to pay a deference to the reader's quick and great understanding ; large books to mistrust his capacity, and to confine his time as well as his intellect.—*Holkot's Philobiblion.*

BYRON ON SHERIDAN AND COLMAN.

IN 1815 I had occasion to visit my lawyer in Chancery Lane ; he was with Sheridan. After mutual greetings, etc., Sheridan retired first. Before recurring to my own business, I could not help inquiring what of Sheridan. " Oh," replied the attorney, " the usual thing ! to stave off an action from his wine merchant, my client." " Well," said I, " and what do you mean to do?" " Nothing at all for the present. Would you have me proceed against old Sherry? What would be the use of it?" And here he began laughing, and going over Sheridan's good gifts of conversation. Now, from personal experience I can vouch that my attorney is by no means the tenderest of men, or particularly accessible to any kind of impression out of the statute or record ; and yet Sheridan, in half an hour, had found the way to soften and seduce him in such a manner, that I almost think he would have thrown his client (an honest man, with all the laws and some justice on his side) out of the window, had he come in at that moment. Such was Sheridan : he could soften an attorney ! There has been nothing like it since the days of Orpheus.

He told me that on the night of the grand success of his " School for Scandal " he was knocked down and put into the watch-house, for making a row in the street and being found intoxicated by the watchmen. When dying he was requested to undergo "an operation." He replied that he had already submitted to two, which were enough for one man's lifetime. Being asked what they were, he answered, " having his hair cut, and sitting for his picture."

I have met George Colman occasionally, and thought him extremely pleasant and convivial. Sheridan's humour, or rather wit, was always saturnine, and sometimes savage ; he never laughed (at least that I saw, and I watched him), but Colman did. If I had to choose, and could not have both at a time, I should say, " Let me begin the evening with Sheridan, and finish it with Colman." Sheridan for dinner, Colman for supper ; Sheridan for claret or port, but Colman for everything, from the madeira and champagne at dinner, the claret with a layer of port between the glasses, up to the punch of the night, and down to the grog, or gin-and-water of daybreak ; all these I have threaded with both the same. Sheridan was a grenadier company of life-guards, but Colman a whole regiment, of light infantry to be sure, but still a regiment.—*Byron's Journals, Letters, etc.*

POETICAL PORTRAITS.

SHAKSPEARE.
His was the wizard spell,
The spirit to enchain ;
His grasp o'er Nature fell ;
Creation owned his reign.

MILTON.
His spirit was the home
Of aspirations high ;
A temple, whose huge dome
Was hidden in the sky.

THOMSON.
The seasons as they roll
Shall bear his name along ;
And, graven on the soul
Of Nature, live thy song !

GRAY.
Soaring on pinions proud,
The lightnings of his eye
Scar the black thunder cloud;
He passes swiftly by.

BURNS.
He seized his country's lyre
With ardent grasp and strong,
And made his soul of fire
Dissolve itself in song.

SOUTHEY.

Where Necromancy flings
    O'er Eastern lands her spell,
Sustained on Fable's wings,
    His spirit loves to dwell.

COLERIDGE.

Magician, whose dread spell,
    Working in pale moonlight,
From Superstition's cell
    Invokes each satellite.

WORDSWORTH.

He hung his harp upon
    Philosophy's pure shrine;
And, placed by Nature's throne,
    Composed each placid line.

CAMPBELL.

With all that Nature's fire
    Can lend to polished art,
He strikes his graceful lyre
    To thrill or warm the heart.

SCOTT.

He sings, and lo! Romance
    Starts from its mouldering urn,
While Chivalry's bright lance
    And nodding plumes return.

WILSON.

His strain, like holy hymn,
    Upon each ear doth float,
Or voice of cherubim
    In mountain vale remote.

HEMANS.

To bid the big tear start
    Unchallenged from its shrine,
And thrill the quivering heart
    With pity's voice, are thine.

SHELLEY.

A solitary rock
    In a far distant sea,
Rent by the thunder's shock,
    An emblem stands of thee.

HOGG.

Clothed in the rainbow's beam,
    'Mid strath and pastoral glen,
He sees the fairies gleam
    Far from the haunts of men.

BYRON.

Black clouds his forehead bound,
And at his feet were flowers ;
Mirth, Madness, Magic, found
In him their keenest powers.

MOORE.

Crowned with perennial flowers,
By wit and genius wove,
He wanders through the bowers
Of Fancy and of Love.

Robert Macnish.

DIFFERENCE BETWEEN TASTE AND GENIUS.

TASTE and genius are two words frequently joined together, and therefore, by inaccurate thinkers, confounded. They signify, however, two quite different things. The difference between them can be clearly pointed out, and it is of importance to remember it. Taste consists in the power of judging ; genius in the power of executing. One may have a considerable degree of taste in poetry, eloquence, or any of the fine arts, who has little or hardly any genius for composition or execution of any of these arts ; but genius cannot be found without including taste also. Genius therefore deserves to be considered as a higher power of the mind than taste. Genius always imports something inventive or creative, which does not rest in mere sensibility to beauty where it is perceived, but which can, moreover, produce new beauties, and exhibit them in such a manner as strongly to impress the minds of others. Refined taste forms a good critic ; but genius is further necessary to form the poet or the orator.—*Blair's Lectures.*

THE USES OF FICTION.

EVEN the nobler tenets of morality are comparatively less interesting, in an insulated and didactic state, than when they are blended with strong imitations of life, where passion, character, and situation bring them deeply home to our attention. Fiction is, on this account, so far the soul of poetry, that without its aid as a vehicle, poetry can only give us morality in an abstract and comparatively uninteresting shape. But why does fiction please us ? Surely not because it is false, but because it seems to be true ; because it spreads a wider field and a more brilliant crowd of objects to our moral perception than reality affords. Morality (in a high sense of the term, and not speaking of it as a dry science) is the *essence of poetry*. We fly from the injustice of this world to the poetical justice of fiction, where our sense of right and wrong is either satisfied, or where our sympathy, at least, reposes with less disappointment and distraction than on the characters of life itself. Fiction, we may indeed be told, carries us into "a world of gayer tint and grace," the laws of which are not to be judged by solid observations on the real

world.   But this is not the case,—for moral truth is still the light of
poetry, and fiction is only the refracting atmosphere which diffuses it ;
and the laws of moral truth are as essential to poetry as those of physical truth (anatomy and optics for instance) are to painting. Allegory,
narration, and the drama make the last appeal to the ethics of the
human heart.   It is therefore unsafe to draw a marked distinction
between morality and poetry, or to speak of " solid observations on
life " as of things in their nature unpoetical ; for we *do* meet in poetry
with observations on life, which, for the charm of their solid truth, we
should exchange with reluctance for the most ingenious touches of fancy.
—*Campbell's Specimens of British Poets.*

THE GENIUS OF GOLDSMITH.

ONE should have his own pen to describe him as he ought to be
described. Amiable, various, and bland, with careless, inimitable grace,
touching on every kind of excellence, with manners unstudied, but a
gentle heart, performing miracles of skill from pure happiness of nature,
and whose greatest fault was ignorance of his own worth. As a poet,
he is the most flowing and elegant of our versifiers since Pope, with traits
of artless nature which Pope had not ; and with a peculiar felicity in
his turns upon words, which he constantly repeated with delightful
effect, such as,—

> ————" His lot though small,
> He sees that little lot, the lot of all."

*   *   *   *

" And turned and looked, and turned to look again."

As a novelist, his " Vicar of Wakefield " has charmed all Europe.
What reader is there in the civilized world who is not the better for the
story of the washes which the worthy Dr. Primrose demolished so deliberately with the poker—for the knowledge of the guinea which the
Miss Primroses kept unchanged in their pockets—the adventure of the
picture of the Vicar's family which could not be got into the house—
and that of the Flamborough family, all painted with oranges in their
hands—or for the story of the case of shagreen spectacles and the cos-
mogony ?

As a comic writer, his Tony Lumpkin draws forth new powers from
Mr. Liston's face. That alone is praise enough for it. Poor Goldsmith ! How happy he has made others ! how unhappy he was in
himself ! He never had the pleasure of reading his own works. He
only had the satisfaction of good-naturedly relieving the necessities of
others, and the consolation of being harassed to death with his own ! He
is the most amusing and interesting person in one of the most amusing
and interesting books in the world, " Boswell's Life of Johnson." His
peach-coloured coat shall always bloom in Boswell's writings, and his
fame survive in his own ! His genius was a mixture of originality and
imitation. He could do nothing without some model before him ; and
he could copy nothing that he did not adorn with the graces of his own

mind. Almost all the latter part of the "Vicar of Wakefield," and a good deal of the former, is taken from "Joseph Andrews," but the circumstances I have mentioned above are not.

The finest things he has left behind him in verse are his character of a country schoolmaster, and that prophetic description of Burke in the "Retaliation." His moral essays in "The Citizen of the World" are as agreeable chit-chat as can be conveyed in the form of didactic discourses.—*Hazlitt.*

FADING BEAUTY AND HER MIRROR.

THE general idea of a beautiful woman relinquishing her looking-glass on discovering that her charms begin to wane, presents a picture that has in it both a shade of sadness and a touch of satire. Apart from its mechanical uses, her looking-glass, it must be confessed, is no unimportant element in a woman's life ; and it may be said to be a necessary help to her attaining that complete self-knowledge at which all should aim. It is right that a beautiful woman should know whether she is beautiful or not. Socrates is said to have enjoined all young persons to look often into their glass, to ascertain if they were good-looking, that, if they were so, they might strive to make their mental attainments correspond ; and if they were not so, then that they might endeavour by the superior accomplishments of their minds to compensate for their personal shortcomings. The fondness for this species of self-contemplation seems to be strong in the sex in general. Novelists describe the village coquette as delighting to admire her face in a small fragment of looking-glass ; and in one of Southey's books we are told of the poor Portuguese nuns who had never seen the reflection of themselves from the time of entering their place of seclusion, until the nunneries were thrown open by the effects of the French invasion. The first impulse of them all was to fly to a looking-glass, that they might see their own faces,—a sight which to most of them would seem strange indeed, and would inflict the same kind of pain that Lais was determined to avoid. Ovid somewhere tells of a lady,—

"The time will come when this your old delight,
Your mirror, will present no pleasant sight."

This era, at which a woman's looking-glass becomes distasteful to her, must bring with it a severe trial and a crisis in her character. In a light French comedy, a handsome and gay widow is one day found by her friends and admirers to be in a very wayward mood, the explanation of which, on careful inquiry, is found to be that she had that morning observed in her glass the first wrinkle that had visited her face. It must require in the case of an established beauty no small degree of good humour, good sense, and strength of mind, to submit cheerfully to the change thus commencing ; and it will be well for her if she has already followed the advice that Ovid gives to a young woman :—

"Build up the mind to prop frail beauty's power ;
The mind alone lasts to life's latest hour."

The beauty who thus passes into the list of has-beens may, however, console herself with the sentiment expressed by a clever wit to a plain-looking woman who was taunting by that epithet a veteran belle, that " the *Has-beens* were at least better than the *Never-was-es.*"—*Lord Neaves, The Greek Anthology.*

DR. JOHNSON'S LITERARY CONTEMPORARIES.

WHEN Johnson arrived in London in the year 1737, with his tragedy of "Irene " and very little coin in his pocket, accompanied by his quondam pupil David Garrick, the second monarch of the House of Hanover had been seated on the English throne for ten years—in other words, George the Second was king, Sir Robert Walpole was premier, actively opposed by Lord Chesterfield and his clique, and the country was in a state of great prosperity. It may prove somewhat interesting to our readers if we attempt to furnish a little information on the state of literature in England about the period when the penniless schoolmaster from Edial, with his slipshod dress, with his gaunt, twitching body, in which the bones were hideously prominent (for Johnson had not then become the " tun of man " he was in after-years), entered the Great City to win his spurs in the arena of letters.

Most of the " old set "—the brilliant writers who flourished in the latter part of the seventeenth and beginning of the eighteenth centuries —were dead. Dryden—" glorious John "—had been dead eight years, and the philosopher Locke five years, before Johnson was born. Burnet, Newton, Wycherly, Congreve, Rowe, Matt. Prior, Addison, Steele, Parnell, Gay, had all gone to their rest before the year 1737.

The poet laureate was Colley Cibber, upon whom Johnson wrote the biting epigram,—

> " Augustus still survives in Maro's strain,
> And Spenser's verse prolongs Eliza's reign ;
> Great George's acts let tuneful Cibber sing,
> For Nature formed the poet for the king."

Pope was in the zenith of his fame, and his villa at Twickenham was the rendezvous of the most illustrious men of letters and statesmen of the period. Bolingbroke was residing in France. Swift's political pamphlets, his " Drapier's Letters," " Gulliver's Travels," " Tale of a Tub," and the " Miscellanies," the joint production of himself, Pope, and Dr. Arbuthnot, had all been published, and the satirical and witty Dean was a sour, half-insane recluse at his house in Dublin. Thomson's " Seasons," " Castle of Indolence," plays, etc., had many years before gained him deserved renown ; and the poet, who had grown " more fat than bard beseems," was living in comfortable and dignified retirement at Richmond. Young was a middle-aged man, but had not yet penned his " Night Thoughts," although he was known as a poet of considerable genius from his " Love of Fame," a satire produced in early youth, and other poems. Hogarth was steadily working his way by pencil and burin towards celebrity. He had long before abandoned the not very remunerative occupation of engraving arms, crests, etc., upon silver plate; had designed his magnificent illustrations to "Hudibras," and his "Harlot's Progress" and "Rake's Progress" had been published, and were being remorselessly pirated by unprincipled book and print sellers. Dyer's poem, "Grongar Hill," had appeared, and rendered the author justly celebrated. Glover had written his epic poem "Leonidas," which was very popular. Fielding was but a young man, known to the world chiefly as the author of some plays which had indifferent success. His first production, however, "Love in several Masques" (written at the early age of 20), although it followed "The Provoked Husband,"— a play that had a "run" like some of our modern sensation pieces,— was very well received. A good story is told by Murphy, which is highly characteristic of young Fielding's reckless disposition. A play of his was being performed for the first time, and Garrick, who anticipated an unfavourable result, ventured to propose to the author some alterations in the character he had to play. "No, d——n them," replied careless Harry, "if the scene is not good let them find it out!" In the course of the performance, Fielding was enjoying a bottle of champagne and a pipe, when the hisses and cat-calls of the audience greeted him as he sat in the green-room. "What is the matter, Garrick?" inquired he of the actor, who appeared in a state of great agitation. "What are they hissing now?" "Why, the scene I begged you to retrench I knew would not do, and they have so frightened me that I shall not recollect myself again the whole night." "Oh," coolly replied the author, "they *have* found it out, have they?" The "History of Jonathan Wild the Great," an entertaining romance, the subject of which, as Fielding himself once observed, is not so much a rogue as roguery, was the only work of any importance he had yet published. "Tom Jones," "Joseph Andrews," and "Amelia," still slumbered in the chambers of his fertile brain. Smollett, the rival of Fielding in fiction, was a lad of sixteen studying medicine; and his seafaring experiences were yet to be acquired, in the capacity of surgeon's mate, before he flashed "Roderick Random" on the world. Sterne was a student at Jesus College, Cambridge; and the very remarkable "Shandy" family were not heard of till many a long year afterwards. David Hume was a young man of about Johnson's own age. He had tried commercial pursuits at Bristol, but his passion for literature rendered the dull routine of business distasteful. He was not yet known as an author, although he had written an "Essay on Human Nature," which, notwithstanding his remarkable views, failed to attract any notice from the most bigoted and orthodox—in his own words, "it fell still-born from the press." Edmund Burke, the orator and essayist, was a small boy creeping "like snail unwillingly to school." Oliver Goldsmith had "had the small-pox," and was a schoolboy of ten at Elphin in Roscommon. Sir Joshua Reynolds, the fast friend of Johnson and Goldsmith in later years, was a youth of fifteen. Collins was a scholar at Winchester College; and Gray a student at Cambridge University. Shenstone's poetry was yet unwritten. The fiercely pugnacious, satirical Churchill had hardly shed his milk teeth—the young cub!

The "English Aristophanes," Samuel Foote, was a boy of fifteen studying law, which, however, he soon relinquished for the stage. Armstrong's "Art of Preserving Health"—a didactic poem but little read now-a-days—had not appeared, but he was known to the literary world as the author of a humorous essay on the empirical practice in London, and a poem entitled "The Enemy of Love." Akenside was a youth at Edinburgh College ; the Wartons were schoolboys ; Horace Walpole was still at Cambridge ; Edward Gibbon, the illustrious author of "The Decline and Fall," was only born this year ; and the prince of biographers, even James Boswell, was yet to be born, when Samuel Johnson first set foot in the metropolis.—*W A. Clouston.*

THE POETRY OF WALTER SCOTT.

SCOTT, cradled in ballad-land, became the most zealous as well as the ablest of ballad editors in collecting materials for the " Minstrelsy of the Scottish Border," thinking, as it was said, "of little but the queerness and the fun he was making for himself" for the work of his life. He was also in no small degree making at the same time the public taste to which that work was to be submitted. In fulness of time the " Lay of the Last Minstrel" was born to fascinate a world, athwart which the genius of Burns had lately flashed, but in which Hayley was probably the most popular poet, and the laurels of Dryden certainly wreathed the brow of Pye ! Few critics will question the supremacy of Scott, at least in our language, in the field of metrical romance. Opinion may vary as to the rank to be assigned to that class of composition. Other poets have soared higher into the empyrean of thought, or have dived deeper into the mystery of life. But none has ever told his tale with greater breadth of light and shade, or hurried his reader along with a more genial vivacity ; none has ever lit up the banquet-hall or the battle-field with more of Homeric fire, or adorned his action with a more exquisite transcript of the scenery of nature. It is in virtue of these qualities that a great poet holds as his own for ever the ground, historical or topographical, which his wand has once touched ; and conquests of this kind are, in one sense, a measure of his power. In this sphere Scott is certainly the greatest of peaceful and beneficent conquerors in the world of letters.—*Sir W. Stirling Maxwell, at the Scott Centenary Banquet, Edinburgh,* 1871.

THE PRINCE OF NOVELISTS.

HENRY FIELDING, upon whom we place the distinction of being England's first great novelist, has for a century past been the constant subject of criticism. His surpassing merits have compelled even his most pronounced foes to assign him a lofty place in the art which he adorned. Attempts to depreciate his genius, because the moral backbone was lacking in some of his characters, have been repeatedly made, but with no permanent effect upon his renown. For ourselves, we affirm, at the outset, that we consider him the Shakspeare of novelists.

By this, of course, it will be understood we do not imply that the sum of his genius was in any way comparable to that of the illustrious dramatist ; but that he achieved his results in the same way. He was the great artist in fiction, because he was the great observer and interpreter of human nature. The novel will never be able to assume a position of equal importance with the drama, because of its comparative defectiveness of construction. But to such perfection as it is capable of being brought, Fielding almost attained. It is, then, for the reason of the similarity of his method to that of Shakspeare, that we have ventured to award him the highest title of eminence.   .
Byron gave it as his belief that " Fielding was the prose Homer of human nature ; " the far-seeing Goethe was delighted with his art ; and Gibbon demonstrated his literary sagacity by the following eloquent eulogium :—" Our immortal Fielding was of the younger branch of the Earls of Denbigh, who drew their origin from the Counts of Hapsburgh, the lineal descendants of Eltrico, in the seventh century Dukes of Alsace. Far different have been the fortunes of the English and German divisions of the family of Hapsburgh : the former, the knights and sheriffs of Leicestershire, have slowly risen to the dignity of a peerage ; the latter, the Emperors of Germany and Kings of Spain, have threatened the liberties of the old, and invaded the treasures of the new, world. The successors of Charles V. may disdain their brethren in England ; but the romance of ' Tom Jones,' that exquisite picture of human manners, will outlive the palace of the Escurial and the Imperial Eagle of Austria."   .   We have no writer to whom we can point who excels Fielding in the art of setting out his characters by means of strong broad lights and shadows. The drawing is masterly and accurate, and nothing deters him from telling the whole truth. He is full of a sublime candour. His narrative is no mere record of events, but personal history of the most effective description. Whoever comes in the way of his pencil, must submit to the most rigorous and unflinching representation.—*Macmillan's Magazine.*

THE OLD SCOTTISH BALLADS.

FOR the true carelessness of song-writing we must go back to an earlier time, in which the happy persons who found themselves capable of stringing rhymes together for the amusement of their neighbours, did not immediately begin to make a profession of it, and become thereafter the slaves of the public and the hunted of the critics. They sang their songs in their own way. They were pathetic, or merry, or scornful, just as it pleased them. When they had some little story to tell, they told it briefly, so that people should remember it ; and when they had no story to tell, they remained silent, and earned their living at the plough, or at the loom, or at the shoemaker's bench. The fortunate result for us is, that a collection of songs written by a song-loving people, gathered from all periods of its history, and brought together independently of any theory or prejudice to be satisfied, contains an astonishing amount of what may be called the rough material of poetry.

Here are no painful discussions about the various emotions, but the emotions themselves, uttered in the simplest, briefest, and most direct fashion possible, convincing one of their genuineness by the rude artlessness of the lines, and going straight to the heart in consequence. Here is no "damnable iteration" of a particular mood. The songs that are written in the song-writing period of a people's life are as various as that life itself is. The busy coming and going of the world as it exists is displayed in them—its political hopes and triumphs, its humorous stories, its pathetic fireside tales, its universal, thoughtless, unconscious delight in the mere activity of living. They commend themselves to all moods and to all circumstances with a charming inconsistency, for a man is not always praying, or always joyful, or always broken-hearted. Here is a merry song about drinking; and here is one that tells of fell slaughter in battle; and here is one that praises a comely lass; and here is yet another, we regret to say, making fun of over-solemn ministers of religion, in no very modest or charitable fashion. Each of these utterances, it is easy to see, has been the honest expression of the song-writer's sentiment for the moment. He fears no critics; he does not even clamour for a public; he sings his songs, Autolycus-like, to cheer the hard ways of the world, and those may listen who choose.

As for the sentiments which these songs convey, they are as varied and contradictory as human life itself is, even when they propose to give homely and shrewd advice. In many of them an honest contempt for the law is visible, and an unholy triumph when some notorious freebooter has been successful. When at length he is brought to the gallows, there is no craven submission attributed to him. Macpherson is made to say—

> "Untie these bands frae aff my hands,
> And bring to me my sword,
> And there's no man in all Scotland
> But I'll brave him at his word."

And the old ballad that bewails the fate of Gilderoy, who was executed at Edinburgh in 1638, exclaims :—

> "Wae worth the loon that made the laws
> To hang a man for gear !
> To reave of life for ox or ass,
> For sheep, or horse, or meer !
> Had not the laws been made so strick,
> I ne'er had lost my joy ;
> Wi' sorrow ne'er had wet my cheek
> For my dear Gilderoy !"

But the songs which throw the strongest light on the manners and customs of the Scottish peasantry of bygone times are those that are of a humorous and jovial character, describing odd incidents in court-ship, in domestic management, and so forth, all with marked and appropriate characters introduced. We meet with figures that become as familiar as our own friends to us, through the medium of a few happy lines of description. We know the Laird of Cockpen, and old John Anderson; we can picture the persistent wooing of Duncan Gray, and the scorn of Maggie Lauder when she was asked her name by the travelling piper. There is a great bluntness of speech among these people. The elderly maiden of ungainly presence goes over all her worldly possessions, her cattle, and housing, and linen, and so on, and then bids her lover say at once whether he means to marry her or not. There is an equal frankness of conduct; if the lass of the mill can only get out without awakening her father (who has doubtless a gun loaded with small shot for the reception of young men who come tapping at window-panes), she is free to go down to the corn-rigs with her sweetheart, and spend the best part of a moonlight night in wandering about the country. As for the drinking songs, they have such an amazing good humour in them that it is clear they were not written after one of the bouts which they describe so vividly. These devil-may-care lyrics were never written by a man with a headache; if they were, he was probably philosopher enough to foresee that the ailment would be but temporary, and to laugh and have his joke all the same. Now-a-days the result of a headache on one of our painfully-conscientious and introspective poets would doubtless be different. We should probably have as the result an agonizing dissection of the emotions of a suicide, with some discourteous allusions to revealed religion, and an intimation that the world was only fit for the judgment that overtook Sodom and Gomorrah.—*Daily News.*

SHELLEY ON POETRY.

POETRY is the record of the best and happiest moments of the happiest and best minds. We are aware of evanescent visitations of thought and feeling, sometimes associated with place and person, sometimes regarding our own mind alone, and always arising unforeseen, and departing unbidden, but elevating and delightful beyond all expression; so that even in the desire and regret they leave, there cannot but be pleasure, participating as it does in the nature of its object. It is, as it were, the interpretation of a diviner nature through our own; but its footsteps are like those of a wind over the sea, which the morning calm erases, and whose traces remain only as on the wrinkled sand which paves it. These, and corresponding conditions of being, are experienced principally by those of the most delicate sensibility and the most enlarged imagination; and the state of mind produced by them is at war with every base desire. The enthusiasm of virtue, love, patriotism, and friendship, is essentially linked with such emotions; and whilst they last, self appears as what it is, an atom of the universe. Poets are not only subject to these experiences as spirits of the most refined organization, but they can colour all that they combine with the evanescent hues of this ethereal world; a word, a trait in the representation of a scene or passion, will touch the enchanted chord, and re-animate in those who have ever experienced these emotions, the sleeping, the cold, the buried image of the past. Poetry thus makes immortal all that is best and most beautiful in the world ; it arrests the vanishing apparitions which haunt the interlunations of life, and veiling them, or in language or in form, sends them forth among mankind, bearing sweet news of kindred joy to those with whom their sisters abide—abide, because there is no portal of expression from the caverns of the spirit which they inhabit into the universe of things. Poetry redeems from decay the visitations of the divinity in man.

WORDSWORTH'S POETRY.

WORDSWORTH was a wise and happy man, a thinker and a dreamer, who read and walked.   He was from the first in tolerably easy circumstances, and had a small fortune.   Happily married, amidst the favours of Government and the respect of the public, he lived peacefully on the margin of a beautiful lake, in sight of noble mountains, in the pleasant retirement of an elegant house, amidst the admiration and attentions of distinguished and chosen friends, engrossed by contemplations which no storm came to distract, and by poetry which was produced without any hindrance.   In this deep calm he listens to his own thoughts ; the peace was so great within him and around him, that he could perceive the imperceptible.   " To me, the meanest flower that blows can give thoughts that do often lie too deep for tears."   He saw a grandeur, a beauty, a teaching in the trivial events which weave the woof of our most commonplace days.   He needed not, for the sake of emotion, either splendid sights or unusual actions.   The dazzling glare of lamps, the pomp of the theatre, would have shocked him ; his eyes were too delicate, accustomed to quiet and uniform tints.   He was a poet of the twilight.   Moral existence in commonplace existence, such was his object—the object of his choice.   His paintings are cameos with a grey ground, which have a meaning ; designedly he suppresses all which might please the senses, in order to speak solely to the heart.   Out of this character sprang a theory—his theory of art, altogether spiritualistic, which, after repelling classical habits, ended by rallying Protestant sympathies, and won for him as many partisans as it had raised enemies.   Since the only important thing is moral life, let us devote ourselves solely to nourishing it.   The reader must be moved genuinely, with profit to his soul ; the rest is indifferent ; let us, then, show him objects moving in themselves, without dreaming of clothing them in a beautiful style.   Let us strip ourselves of conventional language and poetic diction.   Let us neglect noble words, scholastic and courtly epithets, and all the pomp of factitious splendour, which the classical writers thought themselves bound to assume, and justified in imposing.   In poetry, as elsewhere, the grand question is, not ornament, but truth.   Let us leave show and seek effect.   Let us speak in a bare style, as like as possible to prose, to ordinary conversation, even to rustic conversation, and let us choose our subjects at hand, in humble life.   Let us take for our characters an idiot boy, a shivering old peasant woman, a hawker, a servant stopping in the street. It is the truth of sentiment, not the dignity of the folks, which makes the beauty of a subject ; it is the truth of sentiment, not the dignity of the words, which makes the beauty of poetry. What matters that it is a villager who weeps, if these tears enable me to see the maternal sentiment ? What matters that my verse is a line of rhymed prose, if this line displays a noble emotion ? Men read that they may carry away emotion, not phrases; they come to us to look for moral culture, not pretty ways of speaking. And thereupon Wordsworth, classifying his poems according to the different faculties of men, and the different ages of life, undertakes to lead us through all compartments and degrees of inner education, to the convictions and sentiments which he has himself attained. All this is very well, but on condition that the reader is in Wordsworth's position ; that is, essentially a philosophical moralist, and an excessively sensitive man. —*Taine's History of English Literature.*

A MODERN ENGLISH ESSAYIST.

HAZLITT was a poet more than a critic. His mind had not the exquisite critical balance, but belonged to the advocate rather than the judge. He was an intensity. What he liked, that he loved ; what he despised or disliked, he hated. But he was a poet. His eye speedily detected anything beautiful, and with the same unerring eye he selected it and brought it out ; whilst, with the love he had for it, he gave it honour. His criticisms are so rich in thought and language that they not only point out the beauties they treat of, but are substantive beauties in themselves. He often rises to high eloquence, and uses painted words to bring his pictures before our eyes, though his thoughts are sometimes clothed in too gay rhetoric. It was an occasional redundancy of ornament that brought on Hazlitt the on-slaught of the *Quarterly Review* in the article on the " Round Table." Reading that article in these days, one is sensible that the recoil on the *Quarterly* is harder than the blow to Hazlitt. Those were the days when, on both sides, men of genius were liable to depreciation by their rivals. A healthier tone has since been given to the reviews, and it belongs only to a few of the lower press of to-day to make freedom of opinion a crime and reason for abuse. In his essay " On going a Journey," we see Hazlitt's love of the beautiful in nature, and how he must be alone to worship it in " that undisturbed silence of the heart which alone is eloquence." " I want," he says, " to see my vague notions float like the down of the thistle before the breeze, and not to have them entangled in the briars and thorns of controversy."

Hazlitt had that generous appreciation of genius in others which belongs generally to the highest class of minds—which caused Goethe to hold out the hand of fellowship to all rising talent, and Johnson to stand by Goldsmith. His powers of analysis were very great, and yet he could reconstruct and generalize, so that the picture as a whole gained in his hands by his powers of dissection. His love of beauty in everything enabled him to detect it with a certainty and an admiration which gave an extraordinary virtue and charm to his criticism.— *Temple Bar.*

DR. JOHNSON'S STYLE.

I OWN I like not Johnson's turgid style,
That gives an inch the importance of a mile ;
Casts of manure a wagon-load around,
To raise a simple daisy from the ground ;
Uplifts the club of Hercules—for what ?
To crush a butterfly, or brain a gnat.
Creates a whirlwind, from the earth to draw
A goose's feather, or exalt a straw ;
Sets wheels on wheels in motion—such a clatter,
To force up one poor nipperkin of water ;
Bids ocean labour with tremendous roar,
To heave a cockle-shell upon the shore.
Alike in every theme his pompous art,
Heaven's awful thunder, or a rumbling cart !

Peter Pindar (*Dr. Wolcot*).

SIR WALTER SCOTT ON THE POET BURNS.

As to Burns, I may truly say, " Virgilium vidi tantum." I was a lad of fifteen in 1786-7, when he came first to Edinburgh, but had sense enough to be much interested in his poetry, and would have given worlds to know him ; but I had very little acquaintance with the literary people, and still less with the gentry of the west country—the two sets that he most frequented. Mr. Thomas Grierson was at that time a clerk of my father's. He knew Burns, and promised to ask him to his lodgings to dinner, but had no opportunity to keep his word, otherwise I might have seen more of this distinguished man. As it was, I saw him one day at the late venerable Professor Ferguson's, where there were several gentlemen of literary reputation, among whom I remember the celebrated Mr. Dugald Stewart. Of course, we youngsters sat silent,—looked, and listened. The only thing I remember was remarkable in Burns' manner, was the effect produced upon him by a print of Banbury's, representing a soldier lying dead on the snow, his dog sitting in misery on the one side, on the other his widow with a child in her arms. These lines were written beneath :—

" Cold on Canadian hills, or Minden's plain,
Perhaps that parent wept her soldier slain,
Bent o'er her babe, her eye dissolved in dew,
The big drops, mingling with the milk he drew,
Gave the sad presage of his future years,—
The child of misery baptized in tears."

Burns seemed much affected by this print, or rather the ideas which it suggested to his mind. He actually shed tears. He asked whose the lines were ; and it chanced that but myself, nobody remembered that they occur in a half-forgotten poem of Langhorne's, called by the unpromising title of the "Justice of the Peace." I whispered my information to a friend present, who mentioned it to Burns, who rewarded me with a look and a word, which, though it of mere civility, I then received, and still recollect, with very great pleasure.

His conversation expressed perfect self-confidence, without the slightest presumption. Among the men who were the most learned of their time and country, he expressed himself with perfect firmness, but without the least intrusive forwardness ; and when he differed in opinion, he did not hesitate to express it firmly yet modestly. I do not remember any part of his conversation distinctly enough to be quoted, nor did I see him again, except in the street, where he did not recognise me, as I could not expect he should.—*Lockhart's Life of Scott.*

TRUE HEROISM.

LET us say, then, that true heroism must involve self-sacrifice. Those stories certainly involve it, whether ancient or modern, which the hearts, not of philosophers merely, or poets, but of the poorest and most ignorant, have accepted instinctively as the highest form of moral beauty—the highest form, and yet one possible to all. Grace Darling rowing out into the storm toward the wreck. The "drunken private of the Buffs," who, prisoner among the Chinese, and commanded to prostrate himself and kotoo, refused in the name of his country's honour—" He would not bow to any Chinaman on earth;" and so was knocked on the head, and died surely a hero's death. Those soldiers of the *Birkenhead*, keeping their ranks to let the women and children escape, while they watched the sharks who in a few minutes would be tearing them limb from limb. Or, to go across the Atlantic—for there are heroes in the Far West—Mr. Bret Harte's "Flynn of Virginia," on the Central Pacific Railway (the place is shown to travellers) who sacrificed his life for his married comrade :—

> " Thar, in the drift,
> Back to the wall,
> He held the timbers
> Ready to fall.
> Then in the darkness
> I heard him call—
> ' Run for your life, Jake !
> Run for your wife's sake !
> Don't wait for me.'

> " And that was all
> Heard in the din—
> Heard of Tom Flynn,
> Flynn of Virginia."

Or the engineer, again, on the Mississippi, who, when the steamer caught fire, held, as he had sworn he would, her bow against the bank till every soul save he got safe on shore :—

> " Through the hot black breath of the burning boat
> Jim Bludso's voice was heard ;
> And they all had trust in his cussedness,
> And knew he would keep his word.
> And sure's you're born, they all got off
> Afore the smokestacks fell,—
> And Bludso's ghost went up alone
> In the smoke of the *Prairie Belle.*

> " He weren't no saint—but at Judgment
> I'd run my chance with Jim
> 'Longside of some pious gentlemen
> That wouldn't shake hands with him.
> He'd seen his duty—a dead sure thing—
> And went for it there and then :
> And Christ is not going to be too hard
> On a man that died for men."

To which gallant poem of Colonel John Hay's—and he has written many gallant and beautiful poems—I have but one demurrer : Jim Bludso did not merely do his duty, but more than his duty. He did a voluntary deed to which he was bound by no code or contract, civil or moral ; just as he who introduced me to that poem won his Victoria Cross—as many a cross, Victoria and other, has been won—by volunteering for a deed to which he, too, was bound by no code or contract, military or moral. And it is of the essence of self-sacrifice, and therefore of heroism, that it should be voluntary : a work of supererogation, at least towards society and man—an act to which the hero or heroine is not bound by duty, but which is above though not against duty.—*Charles Kingsley.*

MILTON AND SHAKSPEARE.

THE personal interest may in some cases oppress and circumscribe the imaginative faculty, as in the instance of Rousseau ; but in general the strength and consistency of the imagination will be in proportion to the strength and depth of feeling ; and it is rarely that a man even of lofty genius will be able to do more than carry his own feelings and character, or some prominent and ruling passion, into fictitious and uncommon situations. Milton has, by allusion, embodied a great part of his political and personal history in the chief characters and incidents of " Paradise Lost." He has, no doubt, wonderfully adapted and heightened them, but the elements are the same ; you trace the bias and opinions of the man in the creations of the poet.

Shakspeare (almost alone) seems to have been a man of genius, raised above the definitions of genius. " Born universal heir to all humanity," he was "as one in suffering all who suffered nothing"; with a perfect sympathy with all things, yet alike indifferent to all: who did not tamper with nature, or warp her to his own purposes; who "knew all qualities with a learned spirit," instead of judging of them by his own predilections; and was rather "a pipe for the Muse's finger to play what stop she pleased," than anxious to set up any character or pretensions of his own. His genius consisted in the faculty of transforming himself at will into whatever he chose. His originality was the power of seeing every object from the exact point of view in which others would see it. He was the Proteus of human intellect.—*Hazlitt's Table Talk.*

HORACE.

NO writer of antiquity has taken a stronger hold upon the modern mind than Horace. The causes of this are manifold, but three may be especially noted : his broad human sympathies ; his vigorous common sense ; and his consummate mastery of expression. The mind must be either singularly barren or singularly cold to which Horace does not speak. The scholar, the statesman, the soldier, the man of the world, the town-bred man, the lover of the country, the thoughtful and the careless, he who reads much and he who reads little,—all find in his pages more or less to amuse their fancy, to touch their feelings, to quicken their observation, to nerve their convictions, to put into happy phrase the deductions of their experience. His poetical sentiment is not pitched in too high a key for the imagination, but it is always so genuine that the most imaginative feel its charm. His wisdom is deeper than it seems, so simple, practical, and direct as it is in its application ; and his moral teaching more spiritual and penetrating than is apparent in a superficial study. He does not fall into the common error of didactic writers, of laying upon life more than it will bear ; but he insists that it shall at least bear the fruits of integrity, truth, honour, justice, self-denial, and brotherly charity. Over and above the mere literary charm of his works, too (and herein, perhaps, lies no small part of the secret of his popularity), the warm heart and thoroughly urbane nature of the man are felt instinctively by his readers, and draw them to him as to a friend.

Hence it is that we find he has been a manual with men the most diverse in their natures, cultures, and pursuits. Dante ranks him next after Homer. Montaigne, as might be expected, knows him by heart. Fénélon and Bossuet never weary of quoting him. La Fontaine polishes his own exquisite style upon his model ; and Voltaire calls him "the best of preachers." Hooker escapes with him to the field to seek oblivion of a hard life, made harder by a shrewish spouse. Lord Chesterfield tells us, "When I talked my best, I quoted Horace." To Boileau and Wordsworth he is equally dear. Condorcet dies in his dungeon with Horace open by his side ; and in Gibbon's militia days, "on every march," he says, "in every journey, Horace was always in my pocket, and often in my hand." And as it has been, so it is. In many a pocket, where this might be least expected, lies a well-thumbed Horace ; and in many a devout Christian heart, the maxims of the gentle, genial pagan find a place near the higher teaching of a greater Master.—*Theodore Martin.*

CARLYLE ON BOSWELL'S LIFE OF JOHNSON.

THAT loose-flowing, careless-looking work of his is a picture by one of nature's own artists ; the best possible resemblance of a reality ; like the very image thereof in a clear mirror.   Which indeed it was ; let but the mirror be *clear*, this is the great point ; the picture must and will be genuine.   How the babbling Bozzy, inspired only by love, and the recognition and vision which love can lend, epitomises nightly the words of Wisdom, the deeds and aspects of Wisdom, and so, by little and little, unconsciously works together for us a whole *Johnsoniad;* a more free, perfect, sunlit, and speaking likeness than for many centuries had been drawn by man of man ! Scarcely since the days of Homer has the feat been equalled ; indeed, in many senses, this also is a kind of heroic poem.   The fit Odyssey of our unheroic age was to be written—not sung ; of a thinker, not of a fighter ; and (for want of a Homer) by the first open soul that might offer.

As for the book itself, questionless the universal favour entertained for it is well merited.   In worth as a book we have rated it beyond any other product of the eighteenth century.   Which of us but remembers, as one of the sunny spots in his existence, the day when he opened these airy volumes, fascinating him by a true natural magic. It was as if the curtains of the past were drawn aside, and we looked mysteriously into a kindred country, where dwelt our fathers ; inexpressibly dear to us, but which had seemed for ever hidden from our eyes.—*Carlyle.*

THE POET COWLEY.

THE mind of Cowley was beautiful, but a querulous tenderness in his nature breathes not only through his works, but influenced his habits and his views of human affairs.   From his earliest days he tells us how the poetic affections had stamped themselves on his heart, " like letters cut into the bark of a young tree, which with the tree will grow proportionately."—*Disraeli's Calamities of Authors.*

ROGER ASCHAM.

THE first English author who may be regarded as the founder of our PROSE style was Roger Ascham, the venerable parent of our native literature.—*Disraeli's Calamities of Authors.*

The works of Ascham, which are collected in a single volume, remain for the gratification of those who preserve a pure taste for the pristine simplicity of our ancient writers.   His native English, that English which we have lost, but which we are ever delighted to recover, after a lapse of nearly three centuries, is still critical without pedantry, and beautiful without ornament ; and, which cannot be said of the writings of Sir Thomas Elyot and Sir Thomas More, the volume of Ascham is indispensable in every English library, whose possessor in any way aspires to connect together the progress of taste and of opinion in the history of our country.—*Disraeli's Amenities of Literature.*

CURIOSITIES OF LANGUAGE AND LITERATURE.

VALUE OF BOOKS IN THE MIDDLE AGES.

BEFORE the invention of the art of printing, books were so very valuable that the cost of a copy of the Bible was equal to the cost of building an ordinary church ; and the bequest of a Bible with annotations to a monastery was attended with certain solemn ceremonies, and procured for the generous donor a daily mass for the repose of his soul. The following is a specimen of the formalities practised in bequeathing a book in those days (the spelling is modernized):—

" I, Philip of Repyngdon, late of Lincoln, give this book, called, Peter de Aureolis, to the new library to be built within the church of Lincoln; reserving the use and possession of it to Richard Trysely, clerk, canon, and prebendary of Milton, in fee and to the term of his life ; and afterwards to be given up and restored to the said library or to the keepers of the same for the time being, faithfully and without delay. Written with my own hand, A.D. 1422."

"TOM JONES" AND THE PUBLISHERS.

[This interesting narrative is given in an edition of Fielding's Novels published about thirty years ago. The circumstances here related bear some resemblance to the difficulties encountered by the authors of " Paradise Lost" and " Robinson Crusoe" with the booksellers of their day.]

FIELDING, having finished his manuscript of " Tom Jones," and being at the time hard pressed for money, went with it to one of the second-rate booksellers, with the view of selling it for what it would fetch at the moment. He left it with this trader in the children of other men's brains, and called upon him the succeeding morning, full of anxiety both to know at how high a rate his labours were appreciated, as well as how far he might calculate upon its producing him wherewithal to discharge a debt of some twenty pounds, which he had promised to pay the next day. He had reason to imagine, from the judgment of some literary friends, to whom he had shown his manuscript, that it should at least produce twice that sum. But, alas ! when the bookseller, with a significant shrug, showed a hesitation as to publishing the work at all, even the moderate expectations with which our Cervantes had buoyed up his hopes, seemed at once to close upon him at this unexpected and distressing intimation.

"And will you give me no means of hopes?" said he, in a tone of despair.

"Very faint ones, indeed, sir," replied the bookseller; "for I have scarcely any that the book *will move.*"

"Well, sir," answered Fielding, "money I must have for it; and little as that may be, pray give me some idea of what you can afford to give for it."

"Well, sir," returned our bookseller, again shrugging up his shoulders, "I have read some part of your 'Jones,' and in justice to myself, must even think again before I name a price for it. The book will *not move;* it is not for the public; nor do I think that any inducement can make me offer you more than twenty-five pounds for it."

"And that you *will* give for it?" said Fielding, quickly.

"Really I must think again, and will endeavour to make up my mind by to-morrow."

"Well, sir," replied Fielding, "I will look in again to-morrow morning. The book is yours for the twenty-five pounds; but these must positively be laid out for me when I call. I am pressed for the money, and if you decline, must go elsewhere with my manuscript."

"I will see what I can do," replied the bookseller.

Our author, returning home from this unpromising visit, met his friend Thomson, the poet, and told him how the negotiation for the manuscript he had formerly shown him stood. The poet, sensible of the extraordinary merit of his friend's production, reproached Fielding with his headstrong bargain; conjured him, if he could do it honourably, to cancel it ; and promised him, in that event, to find him a purchaser whose purse would do more credit to his judgment. Fielding, therefore, posted away to his appointment the next morning, with as much apprehension lest the bookseller should stick to his bargain, as he had felt the day before lest he should altogether decline it. To his great joy, the ignorant trafficker in literature, either from inability to advance the money, or a want of common discrimination, returned the manuscript very safely into Fielding's hands. Our author set off, with a gay heart, to his friend Thomson, and went in company with him to Mr. Andrew Millar, a popular bookseller of that day. Mr. Millar was in the habit of publishing no work of light reading but on his wife's approbation ; the work was, therefore, left with him, and some days after, she, having perused it, bade him by no means let it slip through his fingers. Millar, accordingly, invited the two friends to meet him at a coffee-house in the Strand, where, having disposed of a good dinner and two bottles of port, Thomson at last suggested, "it would be as well if they proceeded to business." Fielding, still with no little trepidation, arising from his recent rebuff in another quarter, asked Millar what he had concluded upon giving for his work.

"I am a man," said Millar, "of few words, and fond of coming to the point; but really, after giving every consideration I am able to your novel, I do not think I can afford to give you more than *two hundred pounds* for it."

"What!" exclaimed Fielding; "two hundred pounds!"

"Indeed, Mr. Fielding," returned Millar, "indeed, I am sensible of your talent, but my mind is made up."

"Two hundred pounds!" continued Fielding, in a tone of perfect astonishment. "Two hundred pounds, did you say?"

"Upon my word, sir, I mean no disparagement to the writer or his great merit, but my mind is made up, and I cannot give more."

"Allow me to ask you," continued Fielding, "to ask you—whether —you—are—se—rious?"

"Never more so," replied Millar, "in all my life; and I hope you will candidly acquit me of every intention to injure your feelings or depreciate your abilities, when I repeat that I positively cannot afford you more than two hundred pounds for your novel."

"Then, my good sir," said Fielding, recovering himself from this unexpected stroke of good fortune, "give me your hand; the book is yours. And, waiter," continued he, "bring a couple of bottles of your best port."

Before Millar died he had cleared eighteen thousand pounds by "Tom Jones," out of which he had the generosity to make Fielding presents, at different times, of various sums, till they amounted to two thousand pounds; and he closed his life by bequeathing a handsome legacy to each of Mr. Fielding's sons.

SIGNIFICATION OF HEBREW NAMES.

IN the Hebrew tongue nearly all proper names are significant, each individual having received his name from some circumstance connected either with his birth or with his life and character. Thus Abraham signifies "the father of a great multitude;" Jacob, "the supplanter;" David, "the beloved," etc. This often gives a force to particular passages in the original Scriptures that is quite lost in the translation. We shall give an instance:—When Abigail meets David coming to avenge himself on her husband, she says, "Let not my lord, I pray thee, regard this man of Belial, even Nabal; for as his name is, so is he; Nabal is his name, and folly is with him." This has no point at all in English; it is impossible for the mere English scholar to perceive its meaning; but to the Hebrew scholar who understands that "Nabal" signifies "foolish, stupid, wicked, abandoned, impious," and that the word translated "folly" is simply the noun substantive formed from the same root, the sentence has a pungency and a zest that can at once be appreciated. A very wonderful example of something of the same kind is the following, which indeed appears to suggest matter for serious reflection. The names of the ante-diluvian patriarchs, from Adam to Noah inclusive, run thus in the Hebrew: Adam, Seth, Enos, Cainan, Mahalaleel, Jared, Enoch, Methuselah, Lamech, Noah; which names, read in their order, and literally translated, give the following English sentence:—" Man appointed wretched miserable, the blessed God shall descend teaching, his death sends to the afflicted rest."

"THE GRASSHOPPER AND THE CRICKET."

THE occasion (meeting of Hunt and Keats) that recurs with the liveliest interest was one evening when—some observations having been made upon the character, habits, and pleasant associations with that reverend denizen of the hearth, the cheerful little grasshopper of the fireside—Hunt proposed to Keats the challenge of writing then, there, and to time, a sonnet " On the Grasshopper and Cricket." No one was present but myself, and they accordingly set to. I, apart, with a book at the end of the sofa, could not avoid furtive glances every now and then at the emulants. I cannot say how long the trial lasted. I was not proposed umpire, and had no stop watch for the occasion. The time, however, was short for such a performance, and Keats won as to time. But the event of the after scrutiny was one of many such occurrences which have riveted the memory of Leigh Hunt in my affectionate regard and admiration for unaffected generosity and perfectly unpretentious encouragement. His sincere look of pleasure at the first line—

" The poetry of earth is never dead."

" Such a prosperous opening!" he said; and when he came to the tenth and eleventh lines—

" On a lone winter evening, when the frost
Has wrought a silence— "

" Ah! that's perfect! Bravo, Keats!" And then he went on in a dilatation upon the dumbness of Nature during the season's suspension and torpidity. With all the kind and gratifying things that were said to him, Keats protested to me, as we were walking home, that he preferred Hunt's treatment of the subject to his own. As neighbour Dogberry would have rejoined, " 'Fore God, they are both in a tale!" It has occurred to me, upon so remarkable an occasion as the one here recorded, that a reunion of the two sonnets will be gladly hailed by the reader.

ON THE GRASSHOPPER AND CRICKET.

The poetry of earth is never dead:
    When all the birds are faint with the hot sun,
    And hide in cooling trees, a voice will run
From hedge to hedge about the new-mown mead;
That is the Grasshopper's—he takes the lead
    In summer luxury—he has never done
    With his delights, for when tired out with fun
He rests at ease beneath some pleasant weed.

The poetry of earth is ceasing never :
  On a lone winter evening, when the frost
Has wrought a silence, from the stove there thrills
The Cricket's song, in warmth increasing ever,
  And seems, to one in drowsiness half lost,
The Grasshopper's among some grassy hills,
Dec. 30, 1816.   JOHN KEATS.

ON THE GRASSHOPPER AND THE CRICKET.

Green little vaulter in the sunny grass,
  Catching your heart up at the feel of June,
  Sole voice that's heard amidst the lazy noon,
When e'en the bees lag at the summoning brass;
And you, warm little housekeeper, who class
  With those who think the candles come too soon,
  Loving the fire, and with your tricksome tune
Nick the glad silent moments as they pass;
Oh, sweet and tiny cousins, that belong,
  One to the fields, the other to the hearth,
Both have your sunshine; both though small are strong
  At your clear hearts; and both were sent on earth
To sing in thoughtful ears this natural song—
  In doors and out, Summer and Winter, Mirth !
Dec. 30, 1816.   LEIGH HUNT.
—*Charles Cowden Clarke, in the Gentleman's Magazine.*

PARALLEL PASSAGES AND POETICAL RESEMBLANCES.
"THE MIND, THE MUSIC OF HER FACE."

LORD BYRON has been censured for a line in his " Bride of
Abydos," in which he says of his heroine, " The mind, the *music*
breathing from her face." The noble poet vindicates the expression
on the ground of its truth and appositeness. He does not seem to
have been aware (as was pointed out by Sir Egerton Brydges) that
Lovelace first employed the same illustration in a song of Orpheus
lamenting the death of his wife :—

      " Oh, could you view the melody
        Of every grace,
        And *music of her face*,
        You'd drop a tear;
      Seeing more harmony in her bright eye,
        Than now you hear."

"MUTE, INGLORIOUS MILTON."

The following lines from Shenstone's " Schoolmistress " probably
suggested to Gray the fine reflection in his " Elegy "—

  " Some mute, inglorious Milton here may rest," etc.

Mr. Disraeli has pointed out this resemblance in his "Curiosities of Literature," and it would appear well-founded:—

> " Yet, nursed with skill, what dazzling fruits appear!
> E'en now sagacious foresight points to show
> A little bench of heedless bishops here,
> And there a chancellor in embryo,
> Or bard sublime, if bard may e'er be so,
> As Milton, Shakspeare—names that ne'er shall die!
> Though now he crawl along the world so low,
> Nor weeting how the Muses soar so high,
> Wisheth, poor starveling elf! his paper kite to fly."

The palm of merit, as well as originality, seems to rest with Shenstone; for it is more natural and just to predict the existence of undeveloped powers and great eminence in the humble child at school, than to conceive they had slumbered through life in the peasant in the grave. Yet the conception of Gray has a sweet and touching pathos that sinks into the heart and memory.

"DISTANCE LENDS ENCHANTMENT."

Byron thought the original of Campbell's far-famed lines,—

> " Tis distance lends enchantment to the view,
> And robes the mountains in its azure hue,"

was to be found in the following lines from Dyer's poem, "Grongar Hill":—

> " As yon summits, soft and fair,
> Clad in colours of the air,
> Which, to those who journey near,
> Barren, brown, and rough appear;
> Still we tread the same coarse way,
> The present's still a cloudy day."

"A MAN'S A MAN FOR A' THAT."

Moore has noticed that Burns' famous lines,—

> " The rank is but the guinea stamp,
> The man's the gowd for a' that,"

may possibly have been suggested by the following passage in Wycherley's play of "The Plain Dealer":—"I weigh the man, not his title; 'tis not the king's *stamp* can make the metal better." The same sentiment occurs in "Tristram Shandy," in Sterne's "Dedication to a Great Man": "Honours, like impressions upon coin, may give an ideal and local value to a bit of base metal, but gold and silver pass all the world over, without any other recommendation than their own weight." Another part of Burns' song "A man's a man for a' that," finds a singular parallelism in Massinger's play of "The Great Duke of Florence," who says of princes that—

"They can give wealth and titles, but no virtues ;
    This is without their power."

The expression, one would suppose, had been merely paraphrased by the Scottish national bard in the lines—

"A king can mak a belted knight,
A marquis, duke, an' a' that,
But an honest man's aboon his might," etc.

But there seems to be nothing in the idea of the inherent equality o man that should render it difficult of discovery ; and we can readily believe that Burns, without crediting him with a very high degree of sagacity, or being necessitated to suppose that he borrowed from others, soon saw the truth and acted on it.

LOVERS' WISHES.

The impassioned language of love has been much the same in all ages. Shakspeare makes his *beau-idéal* of a lover, Romeo, gazing with rapture on his beloved Juliet, exclaim :—

"Oh, that I were a glove upon that hand,
    That I might touch that cheek !"

Still more beautifully is the same idea expressed in the first four lines of the following stanza, which Burns quotes from an old ballad ;—

"Oh, that my love were yon red rose,
    That grows upon the castle wa',
And I myself a drap o' dew,
    Into her bonny breast to fa' ! "
Oh, there beyond expression blest,
    I'd feast on beauty a' the night,
Sunk in her silk-saft faulds to rest,
    Till fleyed awa by Phœbus' light.

Compare these citations with this fine little poem, from the Greek, ascribed to Rufinus, and also to Dionysius the Sophist :—

"Oh that I were some gentle air,
    That when the heats of summer glow,
And lay thy panting bosom bare,
    I might upon thy bosom blow !

Oh that I were yon blushing rose,
    Which even now thy hands have prest,
That I might love in sweet repose,
    Reclining on thy snowy breast !

Oh that I were a lily fair,
    That, culled by fingers fairer still,
I might thy every movement share,
    And on thy beauty gaze my fill !"

In the above passages each poet drew his inspiration from the common fount of nature.

E

POVERTY AND LOVE.

Burns' touching verse,—

> " Oh, poortith cauld, and restless love,
>   Ye wreck my peace between ye ;
> But poortith a' I could forgi'e,
>   An' 'twerna for my Jeanie,"

finds an interesting parallel in the following translation of an anonymous Greek epigram :—

> " Two evils, Poverty and Love,
>   My anxious bosom tear ;
> The one my heart would little move,
>   But Love I cannot bear."

SLEEP.

It is interesting to note the various epithets applied by different poets to sleep. Shakspeare terms sleep " nature's soft nurse," and Scott follows closely with " the kind nurse of men," while Young opens his " Night Thoughts " with the well-known line :—

> " Tired nature's sweet restorer, balmy sleep ! "

Sir Philip Sidney, in a sonnet, calls sleep :—

> ——" the certain knot of peace,
> The baiting place of wit, the balm of woe."

In a play entitled " Valentinian," by Beaumont and Fletcher, there is a fine passage which thus begins :—

> " Care-charming Sleep, thou easer of all woes,
>   Brother to Death."

The same expressions as those last quoted are to be found in the works of an earlier poet, in one of Samuel Daniel's pleasing sonnets :—

> " Care-charmer Sleep, son of the sable night,
>   Brother to Death, in darkness born."

Dryden has, in his translation of the Æneid,—

> " Death's half-brother, Sleep."

Shelley opens " Queen Mab " with—

> " How wonderful is Death, Death and his brother Sleep."

And in Pope's Homer we have—

> "Sleep and Death, two twins of winged race."

LOVE AND RESTRAINT.

Butler thus expresses the idea that love will not be constrained :—

" Love, that's too generous t'abide
 To be against its nature tied ;
 For where 'tis of itself inclined,
 It breaks loose when it is confined,
 And like the soul, its harbourer,
 Debarred the freedom of the air,
 Disdains against its will to stay,
 But struggles out and flies away."
                    Hudibras, Part III., C. I.

These lines, beautiful as they are, seem but an amplification of
Spenser's :—

" Ne may love be compeld by maistery ;
 For, soone as maistery comes, sweet love anone
 Taketh his nimble winges, and soone away is gone.
                    Faerie Queene, Book III., C. I., St. 25.

But if the author of Hudibras was partly indebted to Spenser for the
idea, the latter seems to have deliberately stolen (" *convey* the wise it
call ! "), not only the sentiment, but almost the precise words from the
Father of English poetry :—

" Love wil nouht buen constreyned by maistré.
 Whan maistré commeth, the god of love anon
 Beteth his winges, and fare wel, he is gone."
                    Chaucer's Canterbury Tales, l. 1076.

The resemblance in this case, even in the very arrangement of the
words, is so close that it is almost impossible to acquit Spenser of
wilful plagiarism.

FORGETTING TIME.

Milton, in " Paradise Lost," Book IV., has the following well-known
lines (Eve addressing Adam) :—

" With thee conversing I forget all time,
 All seasons, and their change, all please alike."

This beautiful expression has evidently been adapted by Charles
Wesley in a hymn beginning :—

" Talk with us, God, Thyself reveal,"

of which the second verse is as follows :—

" *With Thee conversing we forget*
 All time and toil and care ;
 Labour is rest, and pain is sweet,
 If Thou, my God, art there."

The hymn-writer has not improved on the author of the great English
epic.

DEATH AND IMMORTALITY.

In one of the old visitors' books preserved at Stratford-on-Avon, Washington Irving wrote the following lines, which have been much admired :—

" Of mighty Shakspeare's birth the room we see ;
  That where he died in vain to try :
  Useless the search, for all immortal he,
  And those that are immortal never die."

The last line bears a close resemblance to that of the following translation (from Lord Neaves' " Greek Anthology ") of an epigram by Parmenio, " alluding to the story of the Pythian oracle having declared Alexander to be invincible " :—

" The rumour's false that Alexander's dead,
  Unless we hold that Phœbus told a lie :
  ' Thou art invincible,' the Pythian said,
  And those that are invincible can't die."

DEATH THE HEALER.

Longfellow has been praised by the critics for likening death to a healer of pain and sorrow, in the following lines in " Evangeline " :—

" And as she looked around, she saw how Death the consoler,
  Laying his hand upon many a heart, had healed it for ever."

This, however, is by no means original. In the " Anthology," above quoted, the same expression is to be found in an epigram by Agathias :—

" Why fear ye Death, the parent of repose,
  That puts an end to penury and pain ?
  His presence once, and only once, he shows,
  And none have seen him e'er return again.
  But maladies of every varying hue,
  In thick succession, human life pursue."

Lord Neaves observes of the above, that " Æschylus had anticipated this last idea by writing of death as the only ' healer of irremediable woes ';" and in another epigram, by Amytè, death is termed the " kind healer of our woes."

GATHERING PEBBLES.

Sir Isaac Newton, a little before he died, said : " I don't know what I may seem to the world, but as to myself, I seem to have been only like a boy playing on the sea-shore, and diverting myself now and then by finding a smoother pebble or a prettier shell than ordinary, whilst the great ocean of truth lay all undiscovered before me."—*Spence's Anecdotes.*

This remarkable saying is often quoted, but Newton was anticipated by Milton :—

> " Who reads
> Incessantly, and to his reading brings not
> A spirit and judgment equal or superior,
> (And what he brings what need he elsewhere seek ?)
> Uncertain and unsettled still remains ;
> Deep versed in books, and shallow in himself,
> Crude or intoxicate, collecting toys
> And trifles for choice matters, worth a sponge,
> As children gathering pebbles on the shore."
> *Paradise Regained*, Book IV.

But even Milton is not the only other great writer who employed the striking simile of "gathering pebbles." The following passage occurs in the essay " On Useful Studies," from the works of Jeremy Taylor :—

" Spend not your time in that which profits not ; for your labour and your health, your time and your studies, are very valuable; and it is a thousand pities to see a diligent and hopeful person spend himself in gathering cockle shells and little pebbles, in telling sands upon the shores, and making garlands of useless daisies."

THE CLAIMS OF DESCENT.

The witty Earl of Rochester has, in a poetical " Epistle from Artemesia in Town to Chloe in the Country," the following lines, which have long been " popular quotations ":—

> " The heir and hope of a great family,
> Which with strong beer and beef the country rules,
> And ever since the Conquest have been fools."

Both Pope and Savage have imitated this passage, the former, however, with little elegance :—

> Go, if your ancient but ignoble blood
> Have crept through scoundrels ever since the flood.—*Pope.*

Savage speaks of himself as

> No tenth transmitter of a foolish face.

HONOUR.

Hotspur's speech on honour, in Shakspeare's Henry IV., Part I., is a " stock" quotation :—

> " By Heaven, methinks it were an easy leap
> To pluck bright honour from the pale-faced moon ;
> Or dive into the bottom of the deep,
> Where fathom line could never touch the ground

And pluck up drownèd honour by the locks ;
So he, that doth redeem her thence, might wear
Without co-rival all her dignities."

This speech finds a curious parallel in a tragedy of the Greek poet Euripides, where the usurping Theban king, Eteocles, exclaims :—

" For honour I would mount above the stars,
Above the sun's high course, or sink beneath
Earth's deepest centre, might I so obtain
This idol of my soul, this worship power
Of regal state ; and to another never
Would I resign her, but myself engross
The splendid honour. It were base indeed
To barter for low rank a kingly crown ;
And shame it were that he who comes in arms,
Spreading o'er this brave realm the waste of war,
Should his rude will enjoy. All Thebes would blush
At my dishonour, did I, craven-like,
Shrink from the Argive spear, and to his hand
Resign my rightful sceptre."

THE SANGUINE FLOWER.

Drummond, of Hawthornden, has the following in his "Epitaph on Prince Henry" :—

" Sad violet, and that sweet flower that bears
In sanguine spots the tenor of our woes ;"

which Milton has thus imitated in his " Lycidas ":—

," Inwrought with figures dim, and on the edge
Like to that sanguine flower inscribed by woe."

PEDANTRY.

An instance of imitation in prose composition is to be found in an essay in the *Mirror*, by Henry Mackenzie, in which he can hardly be said to have merely imitated the style of Addison, but to have borrowed both sentiment and language. In an excellent essay in the *Spectator*, Addison has the following passage :—

" A man who has been brought up among books, and is able to talk of nothing else, is a very indifferent companion, and what we call a pedant. But, methinks, we should enlarge the title, and give it to every one that does not know how to think out of his profession and particular way of life."

Observe how very closely his imitator, Mackenzie, follows the above :—

" Pedantry, in the common sense of the word, means an absurd ostentation of learning, and stiffness of phraseology, proceeding from a misguided knowledge of books, and a total ignorance of men. But I have often thought, that we might extend its signification a good deal further, and, in general, apply it to that failing which disposes a person to obtrude upon others subjects of conversation relating to his own business, studies, or amusement."

Here Mackenzie has said the same thing as Addison, with this difference : Addison has expressed himself in fifty-seven words, which his imitator amplifies into seventy-three, and without any advantage to the sense. Mackenzie was a deliberate imitator of the charming literary style of Addison, and the two periodicals conducted by Mackenzie (*Mirror* and *Lounger*), published in Edinburgh during the latter part of last century, were avowedly formed on the model of the *Spectator;* but surely, in the case above cited, the author of the " Man of Feeling" has gone considerably beyond mere imitation of style.

"SWEETNESS ON THE DESERT AIR."

Disraeli, in his "Curiosities of Literature," says the following celebrated stanza in "Gray's Elegy" seems partly to be borrowed :—

> " Full many a gem of purest ray serene
> The dark unfathomed caves of ocean bear ;
> Full many a *flower* is born to blush *unseen*,
> And *waste its sweetness on the desert air.*"

Pope had said,—" Rape of the Lock," Canto. IV. :—

> " There kept my charms concealed from mortal eye,
> Like *roses* that in *deserts bloom and die.*"

Young says of Nature, " Love of Fame," Satire 5 :—

> " In distant wilds, by human eye *unseen*,
> She rears her *flowers* and spreads her velvet green ;
> Pure gurgling rills the lonely *deserts* trace,
> And *waste their music* on a savage race."

And Shenstone has, Elegy IV. :—

> " And like the *desert's lily, bloom to fade.*"

BUBBLES.

The writer of a paper in *Fraser's Magazine*, some years ago, entitled, " The Plagiarisms of Thomas Moore," sets down every resemblance between that poet and his predecessors and contemporaries as a direct theft. He occasionally finds, however, that from the number of writers who have used the same illustration, it is often difficult to say which was the model that the Irish bard had followed ; and to justify his attack on Moore, he is necessitated to charge upon each writer the crime of pilfering from the other. For example, in the following :—

> See how, beneath the moonbeam's smile,
> Yon little billow heaves its breast,

And foams and sparkles for awhile,
  And, murmuring, then subsides to rest !
Thus man, the sport of bliss and care,
  Rises on Time's eventful sea,
And having swelled a moment there,
  Then melts into eternity.—*Moore.*

On the vast ocean of his wonders here,
  We, momentary bubbles, ride ;
Till, crushed by the tempestuous tide,
  Sunk in the parent flood, we disappear.—*Fenton.*

All forms that perish other forms supply ;
  By turns we catch the vital breath, and die ;
Like bubbles on the sea of matter borne,
  They rise, they break, and to that sea return.—*Pope.*

A smoke, a flower, a shadow, and a breath,
  Are real things compared with life and death.
Like bubbles on the sea of life we pass,
  Swell, burst, and mingle with the common mass.—*S. Boyse.*

Here the idea is the same, and the expression often identical ; yet it does not follow that one writer imitated another. The comparison of time to the ocean, and of human life to the bubbles which are raised by the surge, is surely not of so hidden a character as to preclude more than one person from having suggested it.

TRACKLESS OCEAN.

In Byron's well-known apostrophe to the ocean in " Childe Harold," the line,—

" Time writes no wrinkle on thine azure brow,"

finds a parallelism in Barry Cornwall's (Bryan Waller Proctor) "Address to the Ocean," in the following :—

" Thou trackless and immeasurable main !
  On thee no record ever lived again
  To meet the hand that writ it."

THE TALISMAN.

Sir William Jones, in his preface to the Persian Grammar, says of perfection, that " it seems to withdraw itself from the pursuit of mortals in proportion to their endeavours of attaining it, like the talisman in the Arabian Tales, which a bird carried from tree to tree, as often as its pursuer approached." Observe the style in which Moore throws into verse this Eastern allusion :—

" Has Hope, like the bird in the story,
  That flitted from tree to tree,
With the talisman's glittering glory,—
  Has Hope been that bird to thee ?

On branch after branch alighting,
　The gem she did still display,
And when nearest and most inviting,
　Then waft the fair gem away."

BEAUTY AND FLOWERS.

In the following examples, one is at a loss to say which poet has stated the thought most beautifully :—

Nor did I wonder at the lilies white,
　Nor praise the deep vermilion of the rose ;
They were but sweet, sweet figures of delight,
　Drawn after thee, thou pattern of all those.—*Shakspeare*.

If any ask why roses please the sight ?
Because their leaves upon thy cheek do glow.
If any ask why lilies are so white ?
Because their blossoms in thy mind do glow.—*G. Fletcher*.

Why does azure deck the sky ?
'Tis to be like thine eyes of blue.
Why is red the rose's dye ?
Because it is thy blushes' hue.
All that's fair, by Love's decree,
Has been made resembling thee.—*Moore*.

THE MEASURE OF HAPPINESS.

" Sperone Speroni, when Francis Maria II., Duke of Rovere, proposed the question : Which was preferable, the republic or the principality ; the perfect and the not durable, or the less perfect and not so liable to change,—replied that ' Our happiness is to be measured by its quality, not by its duration, and that he preferred to live for one day like a man, than for a hundred years like a brute, a stock, or a stone.' " This same sentiment has been thus finely condensed by Addison, in his " Cato " :—

" A day, an hour, of virtuous liberty,
　Is worth a whole eternity of bondage."

In language still more glowing and eloquent, has Heber embodied the same idea :

" Swell, swell the bugle ; sound the fife ;
　To all the sensual world proclaim—
One crowded hour of glorious life
　Is worth an age without a name."

RUDDY DROPS.

Gray has a well-known line :—

" Dear as the ruddy drops that warm my heart,"

which seems to have borrowed its beauty from the address of Brutus to his wife, in Shakspeare's " Julius Cæsar " :—

> " You are my true and honourable wife,
> As dear to me as are the ruddy drops
> That visit my sad heart."

THE CHARGE OF THE LIGHT BRIGADE.

Tennyson appears to have borrowed the style of his famous " Charge of the Light Brigade,"—

> " Cannon to right of them,
> Cannon to left of them,
> Cannon in front of them,
>   Volleyed and thundered ;
> Stormed at with shot and shell,
> Boldly they rode and well,
> Into the jaws of death,
> Into the mouth of hell,
>   Rode the Six Hundred,—"

from Drayton's poem on " Agincourt " :—

> " They now to fight are gone,
> Armour on armour shone ;
> Drum now to drum did groan,
>   To hear was wonder ;
> That with the cries they make,
> The very earth did shake,
> Trumpet to trumpet spake,
>   Thunder to Thunder."

THE SUN.

In Pope's " Essay on Criticism " the following simile occurs :—

> " True expression, like the unchanging sun,
> Clears and improves whate'er it shines upon,—
> It gilds all objects, but it alters none."

Heber, in one of his majestic lyrics, applies the same simile to the sacred Volume :—

> " A glory gilds the sacred page,
> Majestic like the sun ;
> It gives a light to every age,—
> It gives, but borrows none."

TREADING ON FLOWERS.

The ancient Greek poet, Hesiod, in his beautiful description of the rise of Aphrodite from the sea, has the following highly poetical expression (according to Mr. Hookham Frere's translation) :—

" Where her delicate feet
Had pressed the sands, green herbage flowering sprang."

This pretty expression finds parallels in the writings of several of our modern poets. Thus Scott :—

" A foot more light, a step more true,
Ne'er from the heath-flower dashed the dew ;
E'en the slight harebell raised its head,
Elastic from her airy tread."—*Lady of the Lake.*

And Tennyson :—

"But light as any wind that blows,
So fleetly did she stir,
The flower she touched on dipt and rose,
And turned to look at her."

Still more to the point, which is the charm to create verdure and flower growth which pertains to Aphrodite's feet, are the following citations from Ben Jonson and Wordsworth :—

" Here she was wont to go, and here, and here,
Just where those daisies, pinks, and violets grow.
The world may find the spring by following her,
For other print her airy steps ne'er left ;
And where she went the flowers took thickest root.
As she had sowed them with her odorous foot."
Ben Jonson's " Sad Shepherd."

" Flowers laugh before thee in their beds,
And fragrance in thy footing treads."
Wordsworth's " Ode to Duty."

THE EPITHET, "TERMAGANT."

TERMAGAUNT is the name given in the old romances to the god of the Saracens, in which he is constantly linked with Mahound, or Mahomet. Thus in the legend of Syr Guy, the Soudan (sultan) swears,—

" So helpe me Mahoune of might,
And Termagaunt, my god so bright."

This word is said to be derived from the Anglo-Saxon *tyr*, very, and *magan*, mighty. As the word had so sublime a derivation, and was so applicable to the true God, how shall we account for its being so degraded ? Perhaps *Tyr Magan*, or Termagant, had been a name originally given to some Saxon idol, before our ancestors were converted to Christianity ; or had been the peculiar attribute of one of their false deities ; and therefore the first Christian missionaries rejected it as profane, and improper to be applied to the true God. Afterwards, when the irruptions of the Saracens into Europe, and the Crusades into the East, had brought them acquainted with a new species of unbelievers, our ignorant ancestors, who thought all who did not receive the Christian law were necessarily pagans and idolaters, supposed the Mohammedan creed was in all respects the same with that of their pagan forefathers, and therefore made no scruple to give the ancient name of Termagant to the god of the Saracens ; just in the same manner as they afterwards used the name of Saracen to express any kind of pagan or idolater. In the ancient romance of Merlin, the Saxons themselves that came over with Hengist, because they were not Christians, are constantly called Saracens.

However that be, it is certain that after the times of the Crusades, both Mahound and Termagaunt made their frequent appearance in the pageants and religious interludes of the barbarous ages, in which they were exhibited with gestures so frantic as to become proverbial. Thus Skelton speaks of Wolsey :—

> " Like Mahound in a play,
> No man dare him withsay."

In like manner, Bale, describing the threats used by some papist magistrates to his wife, speaks of them as " grennyng upon her like Termagauntes in a playe." Accordingly, in a letter of Edward Alleyn, the founder of Dulwich College, to his wife, who, it seems, with all her fellows (the players), had been " by my Lord Mayor's officers, made to ride in a cart," he expresses his concern that she should " fall into the hands of such termagants." Hence we may conceive the force of Hamlet's expression in Shakspeare, where, condemning a ranting player, he says, " I could have such a fellow whipped for o'erdoing Termagant ; it out-herods Herod." By degrees the word came to be applied to an outrageous, turbulent person, and especially to a violent, brawling woman, to whom alone it is now confined ; and this the rather, as, I suppose, the character of Termagant was anciently represented on the stage after the Eastern mode, with long robes or petticoats.— *Percy's Reliques of Ancient Poetry.*

BIBLICAL CURIOSITY.

THE 21st verse of the 7th chapter of Ezra contains every letter of the alphabet, and is the only one thus distinguished : " And I, even I, Artaxerxes the king, do make a decree to all the treasurers which are beyond the river, that whatsoever Ezra the priest, the scribe of the law of the God of heaven, shall require of you, it be done speedily."

THE ORTHOGRAPHY OF SHAKSPEARE'S NAME.

THERE are but five authenticated signatures of the poet now in existence ; three of which are attached to his will in Doctors' Commons, and two others to a document connected with a purchase in Blackfriars; but so indistinctly are they written, that it has been for a long time a vexed question as to how he spelt his name. The clerks spell it Shackspeare, which was probably the common pronunciation, and it has been suggested that there may have been two modes, Mr. Shackspeare in the country, and in polished circles the more stately Mr. Shakespeare. There is in the British Museum a copy of Florio's Montaigne, 1609, which bears the poet's name on a blank leaf, and in this instance the spelling is clearly Shakspere, but doubts are entertained as to the genuineness of the signature. "Venus and Adonis" and "Tarquin"—the only works published by the poet himself—have the name printed "Shake-speare." But it seems pretty certain that Sir Frederick Madden is right in stating, as he does in a letter to the Society of Antiquaries, that the poet's own signature was Shakspere. The orthography of proper names, and indeed of words in general, was very loose in Shakspeare's time, and his name is spelt in every possible way in the records of Warwickshire—such as Shaxpere, Shagspere, Shakespeare, Shakspere, etc., etc. The poet's name in the inscription in Stratford Church is spelt Shakspeare, and this circumstance no doubt led Rowe and other early editors to adopt this mode of spelling in preference to any other. In almost all important Encyclopædias and Biographical Dictionaries, the name will be found thus written, and in the town of Stratford it is the most usual variety to be met with.

When the poet's birthplace was used as a butcher's shop, a board, which is still preserved, was suspended over the door with this inscription : —

" William Shakspeare born in this house.
N.B.— A horse and taxed cart to let."

TRANSLATIONS OF THE BIBLE.

THE translation of the Bible was begun very early in this kingdom. Some part of it was done by King Alfred. Adelmus translated the Psalms into Saxon in 709 ; other parts were done by Edfrid, or Egbert, in 750 ; the whole, by Bede. In 1357, Trevisa published the whole in English. Tindal's translation appeared in 1334 ; was revised and altered in 1538 ; published with a preface of Cranmer's in 1549, and allowed to be read in churches. In 1551 another translation was published, which, being revised by several bishops, was printed with their alterations in 1560. In 1613 a new translation was published by authority, which is that in present use. There was not any translation of it into the Irish language till 1685. The pope did not give his permission for the translation of the Bible into any language until the year 1759.

CHANGES IN THE SIGNIFICATION OF WORDS.

IT is curious to observe the changes of meaning which some of our words have undergone since the days of Shakspeare. In certain instances, the modern signification is precisely the reverse of the original meaning. The word *wretch*, for example, was not formerly employed to denote a miserable or extremely vicious person, but was used as a term of soft endearment,—as will be seen from the following passage from Pepys' Diary, under date February 23, 1668 :—"This evening my wife did with great pleasure show me her stock of jewels, increased by the ring she hath made lately as my valentine's gift this year, a Turkey stone set with diamonds ; and with this, and what she had, she reckons that she hath above £150 worth of jewels of one kind or other, and I am glad of it, for it is fit the *wretch* should have something to content herself with." Shakspeare makes Othello speak fondly of Desdemona as "excellent wretch." The word *knave* did not originally signify anything disreputable, as a scoundrel or black-guard, but was merely the common term for a man-servant. In this sense it is employed in an early translation of the New Testament, where we read, " Paul, the *knave* of Jesus Christ ;" and in the fine old ballad of " Robin Hood and Guy of Gisborne"—

> " But now I have slain the *master*, he says,
> Let me go strike the *knave*."

The word *companion*, on the other hand, had formerly the meaning which we now attach to the term *fellow*, in its abusive sense ;—thus, in the play of *Othello*, we find Emilia, on discovering that some scoundrel had secretly aspersed the character of Desdemona, bitterly exclaims—

> " O Heaven ! that such *companions* thou'dst unfold ;
> And put in every honest hand a whip,
> To lash the rascal naked through the world."

The term *wench* had not originally its modern low and vulgar signi-fication, but was the appellation of young women, as *damsel* was of young ladies of quality.

CURIOSITIES OF LEGEND AND SUPERSTITION.

CATS.

THE question why the chariot of Freyja was drawn by cats, and why Holda was attended by maidens riding on cats, or themselves disguised in feline form, is easily solved. Like the lynx, and the owl of Pallas Athene, the cat owes its celestial honours above all to its eyes, that gleam in the dark like fire ; but the belief in its supernatural powers may very probably have been corroborated by the common observation that the cat, like the stormy boar, is a weatherwise animal. Pigs, as everybody knows, see the wind ; in Westphalia they smell it. Good weather may generally be expected when the cat washes herself, but bad when she licks her coat against the grain, or washes her face over her ear, or sits with her tail to the fire. In Germany, if it rains when women have a large washing on hand, it is a sign that the cats have a spite against them, because they have not treated the animals well ; an enemy to cats may reckon upon it that he will be carried to his grave in wind and rain ; and in Holland, if the weather is rainy on a wedding-day, the saying is that the bride has neglected to feed the cat. Seeing that these sly creatures know so much of the weather, and are more than suspected of having a share in making it, nothing can be more unwise than to provoke them, as English sailors know very well. They do not much like to see cats on board, but least of all do they like to see them unusually frisky, for then they say, " the cat has a gale of wind in her tail." An infallible recipe for raising a storm, is to throw a cat overboard. The presence of a dead hare on board ship is also said to bring bad weather.

Cats, though inveterate milk-stealers, very rarely rob the dairy in any but the natural way ; on the other hand, witch-cats have a great hankering after beer, a liquor into which no canny puss will dip her whiskers. Witches are adepts in the art of brewing, and therefore fond of making parties to taste what their neighbours brew. It appears that on these occasions they always masquerade as cats, and what they steal they consume on the spot. There was a countryman whose beer was all drunk up by night whenever he brewed, so that at last he resolved for once to sit up all night and watch. Well, as he was standing by his brewing copper, up came a great lot of cats, and he called to them, " Come, puss, puss ! come, warm you a bit." So they all squatted in a great ring round the fire, as if to warm themselves. After they had sat there for a while, he asked them if the water was hot. " Just on the boil," said they ; and as they spoke he dipped his long-handled pail in the wort, and soused the whole company with it. They all vanished at once ; but on the following day his wife had a terribly scalded face, and then he knew who it was that had always drunk up his beer.— *Kelly's Curiosities of Indo-European Tradition and Folk-Lore.*

THE JEWELS : A TRADITION OF THE RABBINS.

THE celebrated teacher, Rabbi Meir, sat during the whole of one Sabbath day in the public school instructing the people. During his absence from the house his two sons died, both of them of uncommon beauty, and enlightened in the law. His wife bore them to her bed-chamber, laid them upon the marriage bed, and spread a white covering over their bodies. In the evening the Rabbi Meir came home.

" Where are my two sons," he asked, " that I may give them my blessing ? I repeatedly looked round the school, and I did not see them there."

She reached him a goblet. He praised the Lord at the going out of the Sabbath, drank, and again asked—

" Where are my sons, that they too may drink of the cup of blessing ?"

" They will not be afar off," she said, and placed food before him, that he might eat.

He was in a gladsome and genial mood ; and when he had said grace after the meal, she thus addressed him : —

" Rabbi, with thy permission, I would fain propose to thee one question."

"Ask it, then, my love," he replied.

" A few days ago, a person entrusted some jewels into my custody, and now he demands them again ; should I give them back again ?"

" This is a question," said Rabbi Meir, " which my wife should not have thought it necessary to ask. What! wouldst thou hesitate or be reluctant to restore to every one his own ?"

" No," she replied ; " but yet I thought it best not to restore them without acquainting you therewith."

She then led him to the chamber, and stepping to the bed, took the white covering from the dead bodies.

" Ah ! my sons, my sons !" thus loudly lamented the father ; " my sons ! the light of my eyes, and the light of my understanding ! I was your father, but ye were my teachers in the law."

The mother turned away, and wept bitterly. At length she took her husband by the hand, and said,—

" Rabbi, didst thou not teach me that we must not be reluctant to restore that which was entrusted to our keeping ? See, the Lord gave, the Lord has taken away, and blessed be the name of the Lord !"

" Blessed be the name of the Lord !" echoed Rabbi Meir ; "and blessed be His name for thy sake too, for well it is written, 'Whoso hath found a virtuous wife, hath a greater treasure than costly pearls ; she openeth her mouth with wisdom, and in her tongue is the law of kindness.'"—*Translated by Coleridge.*

FRODI'S MILL: A NORSE LEGEND.

OF all beliefs, that in which man has, at all times of his history, been most prone to set faith, is that of a golden age of peace and plenty, which has passed away, but which might be expected to return.
. Such a period of peace and plenty, such a golden time, the Norseman could tell of in his mythic Frodi's reign, when gold, or *Frodi's meal,* as it was called, was so plentiful that golden armlets lay untouched from year's end to year's end on the king's highway, and the fields bore crops unsown. In Frodi's house were two maidens of that old giant race, Fenja and Menja. These daughters of the giant he had bought as slaves, and he made them grind his quern or handmill, Grotti, out of which he used to grind peace and gold. Even in that golden age one sees there were slaves, and Frodi, however bountiful to his thanes and people, was a hard task-master to his giant handmaidens. He kept them to the mill, nor gave them longer rest than the cuckoo's note lasted, or they could sing a song. But that

quern was such that it ground anything that the grinder chose, though until then it had ground nothing but gold and peace. So the maidens ground and ground, and one sang their piteous tale in a strain worthy of Æschylus as the other rested. They prayed for rest and pity, but Frodi was deaf. Then they turned in giant mood, and ground no longer peace and plenty, but fire and war. Then the quern went fast and furious, and that very night came Mysing the sea-rover, and slew Frodi and all his men, and carried off the quern ; and so Frodi's peace ended. The maidens the sea-rover took with him, and when he got on the high seas he bade them grind salt. So they ground ; and at midnight they asked if he had not salt enough, but he bade them still grind on. So they ground till the ship was full, and sank,—Mysing, maids, and mill, and all,—and that's why the sea is salt.—*Dr. Dasent's Popular Tales from the Norse.*

SNEEZING.

RABBINICAL writers tell us that "sneezing was a mortal sign, even from the first man, until it was taken off by the special supplication of Jacob. From whence, as a thankful acknowledgment, this salutation first began, and was after continued by the expression of Tobim Chaüm, or *vita bona*, by standers-by, upon all occasions of sneezing" (see Buxtorf, *Lex. Chald.*). Aristotle mentions the omen, "why sneezing from noon to midnight was good, but from night to noon unlucky." And the ancients, says St. Austin, "were wont to go to bed again if they sneezed while they put on their shoe." Ross, in his "Arcana Microcosmi," says :—"Prometheus was the first that wisht well to the sneezer, when the man, which he had made of clay, fell into a fit of sternutation upon the approach of that celestial fire which he stole from the sun. This gave original to that custome among the Gentiles in saluting the sneezer. They used also to worship the head in sternutation, as being a divine part and seat of the senses and cogitation."

A writer in the *Gentleman's Magazine* (April, 1777) informs us that "the year 750 is commonly reckoned the era of the custom of saying 'God bless you' to one who happens to sneeze. It is said that, in the time of the pontificate of St. Gregory the Great, the air was filled with such a deleterious influence that they who sneezed immediately expired." Pliny inferred that to sneeze to the right was considered fortunate ; to the left, and near a burial place, the reverse. Creech, in his translation of the eighteenth Idyllium of Theocritus, mentions the custom :—

"O happy bridegroom ! Thee a lucky sneeze
    To Sparta welcomed."

Again, in another Idyllium :—

"The Loves sneezed on Smichid."

It is said that when the king of Mesopotamia sneezed, loud acclamations were made in all parts of his dominions. The Persians looked

F

upon the custom as being a very happy one ; and the Siamese wished long life to all sneezers. There was, says Langley in his abridgment of Polydore Vergil,—

"A plague whereby many as they neezed dyed sodeynly, werof it grew into a custome that they that were present when any man neezed should say ' God helpe you.' A like deadly plage was sometyme in yawning, wherfore menne used to fence themselves with the sign of the crosse : bothe which customes we reteyne styl at this day."

One finds a little relief sometimes in a good hearty sneeze ; as an old writer observes, "two or three neses be holsom ;" but some persons are so often taken with such violent fits of sneezing that they find it necessary to go out in the street to do it, in order to give full scope to their feelings. A writer in the " Schoole of Slovenrie" recommends his readers to perform the act in a very impolite manner :—

" When you would sneeze, strait turne yourself into your neibour's face :
As for my part, wherein to sneeze, I know no fitter place ;
It is an order, when you sneeze good men will pray for you ;
Marke him that doth so, for I thinke he is your friend most true.
And that your friend may know who sneezes, and may for you pray,
Be sure you not forget to sneeze full in his face alway.
But when thou hear'st another sneeze, although he be thy father,
Say not God bless him, but Choak up, or some such matter rather."

Howel says (1659), " He that hath sneezed thrice turn him out of the hospital." Bishop Hall alludes to the custom when speaking of a superstitious person :—"When he neeseth, thinks them not his friends that uncover not."—*Notes and Queries.*

LOVE-TOKENS.

BETWEEN two and three centuries ago, it was the custom, as stated in the old chronicles, for "enamoured maydes and gentilwomen" to give to their favourite swains, as tokens of their love, little handkerchiefs, about three or four inches square, wrought round about often in embroidery, with a button or tassel at each corner, and a little one in the centre. The finest of these favours were edged with gold lace, or twist ; and then, being folded in four cross folds, so that the middle might be seen, they were worn by the accepted lovers in their hats, or on their breast. Tokens were also given by the gentlemen and accepted by their fair mistresses. They are thus described in one of Beaumont and Fletcher's plays :—

" Given earrings we will wear,
Bracelets of our lovers' hair,
Which they on our arms shall twist,
(With our names carved) on our wrist."

THE LADYBIRD.

THE goddess Holda is only another form of Freyja or Fria, the wife of Adin and sister of Freyr or Fro, the god of the sun and of love, in whose attributes she participates. The Ladybird has many names, all of them mythic, and it is sacred to both goddesses. Its home is in heaven or in the sun, and German children tell it in rhyme to fly up thither, mount the chair (Freyja's throne), and bring back sunshine and fine weather. They believe that were they to kill the insect the sun would not shine the next day. The English rhyme—

> " Ladybird, ladybird, fly away home,
> Your house is on fire, your children will burn,"

seems to have some reference to the insect's ministrations with fire, the more so as the ladybird is very commonly addressed in Germany to the same purpose, and the children in Westphalia have a rhyme which plainly implies that the burning house is in heaven, for it states that the *angels* are crying about it. Lastly, this important little creature is appealed to in the same country as a child-bringer, and asked to fly up to heaven, and bring down a golden dish and in it a golden bantling.

The ladybird, which is so intimate with the goddess of love and with Frau Holda, must know a great many things. Its services in affairs of love were known to Gay—

> " This ladyfly I take from off the grass,
> Whose spotted back might scarlet red surpass.
> Fly, ladybird, north, south, or east, or west,—
> Fly where the man is found that I love best."

Little girls in Westphalia set the ladybird on the point of their fore-finger, and invoke it in rhyme to say when they will be married : in one year? two years? three years? etc. ; and they grow very impatient if the insect lets them count too high before it flies away. Sometimes it is asked, as it sits on the finger, how the questioner will fare in the next world. If it fly upwards, the questioner will go to heaven ; if downwards, to the opposite place ; if horizontally, to purgatory. In Sweden, if the black spots on the wing-covers of the ladybird exceed seven, the usual number, it is thought to be a sign that corn will be dear ; if they are fewer, a plentiful harvest is expected.—*Kelly's Indo-European Tradition and Folk-Lore.*

CHARMS FOR THE CURE OF AILMENTS.

DOCTORS are said to be at best but the assistants of nature, and if this be so even in these pre-eminently scientific days, assuredly Dame Nature must have been both doctor and nurse in those days when the practice of surgery and medicine had not yet developed into a science ; when ignorance, with its concomitant superstition and credulity, enabled blundering "leeches" to kill where nature could not cure. Perhaps the least harmful of the useless and (as they now seem to us) ridiculous practices employed in former times for the cure of disease was that of mumbling a certain formula of words, believed to constitute an all-powerful charm to remove certain physical ailments. Mr. Pepys has preserved, in his curious and interesting Diary, a few specimens of these "charms." It must not, of course, be supposed that the garrulous old diarist was himself a believer in their efficacy,—although even in the time of the second Charles medical practice was characterized by some very odd usages. For instance, Mr. Pepys records, in speaking of the queen's severe illness, that "she had to be shaved and *pigeons put to her feet.*"

The first "charme" is in Latin, and is "for the stenching of blood":—

> "Sanguis mane in te,
> Sicut Christus fuit in se ;
> Sanguis mane in tuâ venâ,
> Sicut Christus in suâ pœnâ ;
> Sanguis mane fixus,
> Sicut Christus quando fuit crucifixus."

Which may be thus translated :—

> "Blood, remain in thee,
> As Christ was in Himself ;
> Blood, remain in thy vein,
> As Christ in His own sufferings ;
> Blood, remain fixed,
> As Christ when He was crucified."

The next is "for a thorn": —

> "Jesus that was of a Virgin borne,
> Was prickèd both with nail and thorne ;
> It neither wealed, nor belled, rankled nor boned ;
> In the name of Jesus, no more shall this."

And here is another and somewhat improved version for the same complaint :—

> "Christ was of a Virgin borne,
> And He was prickèd with a thorne ;
> And it did neither bell nor swell,
> And I trust in Jesus this never will."

For the cure of a cramp :—

> "Cramp, be thou faintless,
> As our Lady was stainless,
> When she bore Jesus."

The following is a charm for a "burn," or "burning":—

> "There came three Angels out of the East ;
> The one brought fire, the other brought frost :—
> Out, fire ; in, frost ;
> In the name of Father, and Son, and Holy Ghost."

This last is, to say the least, obscure. Is it possible that the "three angels out of the East" could have any reference to the "wise men from the East" who brought costly presents to the infant Saviour at Bethlehem ? In mediæval times there were many legends concerning these mysterious personages, and although different accounts give different names, they all agree in the number of the " wise *kings* " as they are called, which was *three*. The allusion to *fire* having been brought from the East may perhaps be a relic of some olden tradition connecting these Magi (for such is the term in the Greek original, which in our version is translated " wise men from the East ") with the ancient fire-worshippers. But that *frost* should be brought from the East is utterly incomprehensible; and indeed but little sense is to be expected in these silly rhymes. It is curious to note that the fact of *three* angels having been mentioned is quite ignored in the second line —" *the one* brought fire, *the other* brought frost." But even in such apparently meaningless rhymes a clue has often been found leading to interesting discoveries in folk-lore. Whether the " charms " employed by our superstitious ancestors ever produced any effect or not—and it is well known that imagination plays a very important part in physical as well as mental ailments—they certainly were preferable to many of the nostrums of self-constituted doctors, ignorant of even the rudiments of the art of healing, inasmuch as nature was thus allowed full sway, and probably the " charm " was oft credited with having effected a cure which was due entirely to " the kind nurse of men."—*W. A. Clouston.*

THE CHILDHOOD OF ABRAHAM : A RABBINICAL APOLOGUE.

1. IN those days Nimrod the king persecuted Tharah, and sought after his life.

2. And Tharah fled into the caves of the rocks ; and Abram his son was born and reared within the darkness of the cave.

3. Yet even in the dark cave the law of God was in the heart of the boy ; and continually within himself he said, Who is my Creator ?

4. At length it came to pass that Abram walked abroad from the cave, and was in freedom to behold the heavens and the earth. Then did he earnestly survey all things, still meditating within himself, and saying, Who is He that made the heavens and the earth, and is the God of all things that be ?

5. Then Abram beheld the sun ascending in his glory, and he fell upon his knees, and said, Kingly, kingly art thou, O sun : Thou art the God of heaven.

6. And in this faith remained he all that day.

7. But when the evening was come, and the sun was gone down into the sea, then saw Abram the moon shining clearly in the east.

8. Then Abram said, The light that hath descended and been cast down into the sea, how can he be the God of heaven ? Behold, this lesser light is the king of heaven, and these stars that shine round about him are his nobles that do him homage, and his captains and his host.

9. But yet a little while, and the moon and the stars were clean

gone out of the firmament, and Abram was left alone in the wilderness.

10. Then ran he unto Tharah his father, and said unto him, I pray thee, O father, reveal unto me who verily is the God of the heavens and of the earth.

11. And Tharah took him by the hand, and led him into the inner chamber, where his idols stood ; and Tharah said unto Abram, These be the gods of the heavens and the earth : my son, bow down before them and worship them. And as his father commanded him even so did he.

12. Now after three days it came to pass that the mother of Abram gave unto him a certain sweet cake ; and Abram said unto himself, I will not eat of this cake, but make thereof an acceptable offering unto the gods of heaven and earth, whom my father showed unto me in his inner chamber.

13. And the boy went into the inner chamber and laid the cake upon the table before the carved images, saying, O ye gods of the heavens and the earth, let mine offering be well pleasing and find favour in your sight ; stretch forth your hands and take this cake.

14. But the images moved not, neither did they stretch forth their hands to take his offering.

15. And when Abram went in on the morrow, behold the cake was yet lying on the table, and none of the carved images had touched it nor tasted thereof.

16. Then Abram mused within himself, and said, Of a surety the gods of my father be not the true gods.

17. And Abram took a hammer, and he broke all the images, save one which stood in the midst of them ; and that image he left standing.

18. And he ran unto Tharah, and cried unto him with a loud voice, saying, My father, behold, the god that standeth in the middle of the table hath slain, in his anger, all the other gods, and broken them into pieces in the fury of his indignation, and utterly destroyed them.

19. Then Tharah waxed angry with Abram, saying, Verily it is thou that hast done all this evil.

20. As for the god thou speakest of, is he not the work of mine own hands ? Did I not carve him out of the timber of the tree which I cut down in the wilderness ? How then could he lift up his hand, being a piece of carved wood, or do violence upon his fellows ?

21. My son, thou hast deceived me. Thy hand hath broken my gods.

22. Then said Abram unto Tharah, May it please thee, my father, to consider what manner of thing this is that thou sayest. Behold, I am but a little child, and yet thou sayest unto me, that the thing which the god thou worshippest cannot do, that I, even I thy son, can do easily with these hands.

23. And Tharah wondered, but he wist not what to answer.

24. And not many days thereafter God showed himself unto Abram, and called him out of the land of the Chaldeans.

GERTRUDE'S BIRD : A NORSE TALE.

IN Norway the black red-crested woodpecker is called Gertrude's bird ; and the following tale, in which the names alone are Christian and all the rest purely heathen, makes the bird a transformed baker.

" In those days when our Lord and St. Peter wandered upon earth, they came once to an old wife's house who sat baking. Her name was Gertrude, and she had a red mutch on her head. They had walked a long way and were both hungry, and our Lord begged hard for a bannock to stay their hunger. Yes ; they should have it. So she took a little tiny piece of dough and rolled it out ; but as she rolled it, it grew till it covered the whole griddle. Nay, that was too big : they couldn't have that. So she took a tinier bit still ; but when that was rolled out, it covered the whole griddle just the same, and that bannock was too big, she said : they couldn't have that either. The third time she took a still tinier bit—so tiny you could scarce see it ; but it was the same story over again—the bannock was too big. ' Well,' said Gertrude, ' I can't give you anything ; you must just go without, for all these bannocks are too big.' Then our Lord waxed wroth and said, 'Since you love me so little as to grudge me a morsel of food, you shall have this punishment,—you shall become a bird, and seek your food between bark and bole, and never get a drop to drink save when it rains.' He had scarce said the last word before she was turned into a great black woodpecker, or Gertrude's bird, and flew from her kneading-trough right up the chimney ; and till this very day you may see her flying about, with her red mutch on her head, and her body all black, because of the soot in the chimney ; and so she hacks and taps away at the trees for her food, and whistles when rain is coming, for she is ever athirst, and then she looks for a drop to cool her tongue."—*Dr. Dasent's Popular Tales from the Norse.*

FROM THE KORAN OF MOHAMMED.

[THE origin of Parnell's celebrated poem of the " Hermit " has been traced as far back as the writings of Sir Percy Herbert, published in the year 1652, but it is probably to be found in the Talmud or other Rabbinical works. Mohammed has embodied the same interesting fable in the eighteenth chapter of the Koran, entitled " The Cave," which relates, as follows, the circumstances to have occurred between Moses and Elias ; and it is well known that the best parts of the Koran are corruptions of Biblical narratives and Talmudic traditions.]

" MOSES said unto him (Khedr), Shall I follow thee, that thou mayest teach me part of that thou hast been taught, for a direction unto me ? He answered, Verily, thou canst not bear with me ; for how canst thou patiently suffer those things the knowledge of which thou dost not comprehend ? Moses replied, Thou shalt find me patient if God please ; neither will I be disobedient to thee in anything. He said, If thou follow me, therefore, ask not concerning anything, until I shall declare the meaning thereof unto thee. So they both went on by the

seaside, until they went up into a ship ; and he made a hole therein :
Moses said unto him, Hast thou made a hole therein, that thou
mightest drown those who are on board? Now hast thou done a
strange thing. He answered, Did I not tell thee that thou couldst not
bear with me? Moses said, Rebuke me not, because I did forget, and
impose not on me a difficulty in what I am commanded. Wherefore
they left the ship, and proceeded until they met a youth, and he slew
him. Moses said, Hast thou killed an innocent person, without his
having killed another? Now hast thou committed an unjust action.
He answered, Did I not tell thee that thou couldst not bear with me?
Moses said, If I ask thee concerning anything hereafter, suffer me not
to accompany thee ; now hast thou received an excuse from me. They
went forward, therefore, until they came to the inhabitants of a certain
city, and they asked food of the inhabitants thereof ; but they refused
to receive them ; and they found therein a wall which was ready to fall,
and he set it upright. Whereupon Moses said unto him, If thou
wouldst, thou mightest doubtless have received a reward for it. He
answered, This shall be a separation between me and thee ; but I will
first declare unto thee the signification of that which thou couldst not
bear with patience. The vessel belonged to certain poor men who did
their business in the sea ; and I was minded to render it unservice-
able, because there was a thing behind them who took every sound
ship by force. As to the youth, his parents were true believers ; and
we feared lest he, being an unbeliever, should oblige them to suffer by
his perverseness and ingratitude ; wherefore we desired them that
their Lord might give them a more righteous child in exchange for
him, and one more affectionate towards them. And the wall belonged
to two orphans in the city, and under it was a treasure hidden which
belonged to them ; and their father was a righteous man ; and the
Lord was pleased that they should attain their full age, and take forth
their treasure, through the mercy of thy Lord. And I did not what
thou hast seen of mine own will, but by God's direction. This is the
interpretation of that which thou couldst not bear with patience."—
Sale's Translation of the Koran.

[This subject was formed into a Persian poem, by the celebrated
Moulavy-Jullal-addeen-Roumy, who died in the year 1262, which has
full as many admirers as the English "Hermit." Extracts of this
author's works are to be found in the writings of Sir William Jones,
from which a judgment may be formed of his style. Somewhat similar incidents are related by Voltaire, in his "Zadig ; or, the Book of
Fate."]

SCANDINAVIAN MYTHOLOGY.

THE mythology of the northern nations, that is, of the Norwegians,
Danes, Swedes, and Icelanders, is uncommonly curious and entertaining. The *Edda* and *Voluspa* contain a complete collection of fables
which have not the smallest affinity with those of the Greeks and
Romans. They are wholly of an Oriental complexion, and seem

almost congenial with the Persian fables. The Edda was compiled in Iceland in the thirteenth century. It is a kind of system of the Scandinavian mythology; and it has been reckoned, and we believe justly, a commentary on the Voluspa, which was the Bible of the northern nations. Odin or Othin, Woden or Waden, was the supreme divinity of these people. His exploits or adventures furnish the far greater part of their mythological creed. That hero is supposed to have come from the East, but from what country or at what period is not certainly known. His achievements are magnified beyond all credibility. He is represented as the god of battles, and slaughtering thousands at a blow. His palace is called Valhalla ; it is situated in the city of Midgard, where, according to the fable, the souls of heroes, who had bravely fallen in battle, enjoy supreme felicity. They spend the day in mimic hunting-matches or imaginary combats. At night they assemble in the palace of Valhalla, where they feast on the most delicious viands, dressed and served up by the Valkyriæ, virgins adorned with celestial charms, and flushed with drinking mead out of the skulls of enemies whom they had killed in their nature. Mead, it seems, was the nectar of the Scandinavian heroes.

Sleepner, Odin's horse, is celebrated along with his master. Hela, the hell of the Scandinavians, affords a variety of fables equally shocking and heterogeneous. Loke, the evil genius or devil of the northern people, nearly resembles the Typhon of the Egyptians. Signa, or Sinna, is the consort of Loke ; and from this name the English word *sin* is derived. The giants Weymur, Ferbanter, Belupher, and Hellunda, perform a variety of exploits, and are exhibited in the most frightful attitudes. One would be tempted to imagine that they perform the exact counterpart of the giants of the Greek and Roman mythologists.

The word Voluspa imports "the prophecy of Fola or Vola." This was, perhaps, a general name for the prophetic ladies of the North, as Sybil was appropriated to women endowed with the like faculty in the South. Certain it is that the ancients generally connected madness with the prophetic faculty. Of this we have two celebrated examples : the one in Lycophoron's Cassandra, and the other in the Sybil of the Roman poet. The word *vola* signifies "mad or foolish"; whence the English words, *fool, foolish, folly. Spa,* the latter part of the composition, signifies "to prophesy," and is still current among the common people of Scotland, in the word *spae,* which has nearly the same signification.

The Voluspa consists of between two and three hundred lines. The prophetess having imposed silence on all intelligent beings, declares that she is about to reveal the works of the Father of nature, the actions and operations of the gods, which no mortal ever knew before herself. She then begins with a description of the chaos ; and proceeds to the formation of the world, and the creation of the different species of its inhabitants, giants, men, and dwarfs. She then explains the employments of the fairies or destinies, whom the northern people call nornies ; the functions of the deities, their most memorable adventures, their disputes with Loke, and the vengeance which ensued. She at last concludes with a long and indeed animated description of the final state of the universe, and its dissolution by a general conflagration. In this catastrophe, Odin, and all the rabble of the pagan divinities, are to be confounded in the general ruin, no more to appear on the stage of the universe, and out of the ruins of the former world, a new one shall spring up, arrayed in all the bloom of celestial beauty.—*Encyclopædia Britannica.*

THE WREN: A MANX LEGEND.

IN the Isle of Man the wren is believed to be a transformed fairy. The ceremony of hunting the wren (says Brand, in his " Popular Antiquities ") is founded on this ancient tradition. A fairy of uncommon beauty once exerted such undue influence over the male population, that she seduced numbers at various times to follow her footsteps, till by degrees she led them into the sea, where they perished. This barbarous exercise of power had continued so long that it was feared the island would be exhausted of its defenders. A knight errant sprang up who discovered some means of countervailing the charms used by the siren, and even laid a plot for her destruction, which she only escaped at the moment of extreme hazard by assuming the form of a wren. But though she evaded punishment at that time, a spell was cast upon her, by which she was condemned to reanimate the same form on every succeeding New Year's-day, until she should perish by a human hand. In consequence of this legend, every man and boy in the island devotes the hours from the rising to the setting of the sun, on each returning anniversary, to the hope of extirpating the fairy. Woe to the wrens which show themselves on that fatal day : they are pursued, pelted, fired at, and destroyed without mercy. Their feathers are preserved with religious care ; for it is believed that every one of the relics gathered in the pursuit is an effectual preservative from shipwreck for the ensuing year, and the fisherman who should venture on his occupation without such a safeguard would by many of the natives be considered extremely foolhardy.

ABRAHAM AND THE STRANGER.

I HAVE heard that for one whole week no wayfarer
Came to open the tent of the " friend of God."
With no happy heart would he take his morning meal,
Unless some forlorn wanderer came in from the desert.
Forth he fared from his tent, and looked on every side,
To the skirts of the valley did he direct his gaze.
There saw he an old man, like a willow, alone in the desert,
His head and hair were white with the snows of age.
With affectionate kindness he bade him welcome ;
After the manner of the munificent he made his salutation :

" Oh thou," he said, " who art dear as the apple of mine eye,
Deign to honour me by partaking of my bread and salt !"
With a glad assent the old man leaped up and set forth,
For well knew he the saint's character—on whom be peace.
The servants in charge of Abraham's tent
Placed in the seat of honour that poor old man ;
And the master bade them make ready to eat,
And they all sate in order round the table.
But when they commenced their solemn grace in the name of God,
They heard no response from the old man's lips.
Abraham said unto him, " Oh, old man of ancient days,
I see not in thee the religion and devotion of age ;
Is it not thy custom, when thou eatest bread,
To name the name of the Lord, who giveth that daily meed ?"
He answered, " I never practise customs
Which I have not learned from the old priest of the fire-worshippers !"
Then knew the saint of blessèd omen
That the old man was a lost unbeliever ;
And he drove him ignominiously from his tent,
When he saw the stranger in his foulness in the presence of the pure.
Then came there an angel from the glorious Creator,
And with awful majesty rebuked the saint :
" For a hundred years, O Abraham, have I given him daily food and
   life ;
And canst thou not bear his presence for a single hour ? "   —*Sadi.*

HOCUS-POCUS.

THE papistical sacrament was called by the vulgar (at the dawn of
the Reformation) " Jack-in-the-Box," " Worm's-meat," " Hocus-pocus."
The latter epithet had its origin from the manner in which the priest
mumbled the words, *"Hoc est Corpus"—i.e.,* " This is My body," etc.
—*Disraeli.*

THE TALMUD.

THE Jewish Rabbis were wont to teach respecting the two divisions
of the Talmud, viz. : *Mishna* (the text) and *Gemara* (the commentary),
as follows :—" He that is learned in the Scriptures and not in the
Mishna is a blockhead. The Bible is like water ; the Mishna is like
wine ; the Gemara, spiced wine ; the law, salt ; the Mishna, pepper ;
the Gemara, balmy spice." Nevertheless, the Talmud contains admirable maxims, acute and excellent proverbs, gentle and instructive
tales, and much information in various branches of knowledge.
   In the Talmudic treatise, entitled, *Sepher Hachayim,* we have the
following similitude thus recorded :—

   " A certain man had three friends, two of whom he loved ; but the
third he did not highly esteem. Once on a time, the king commanded

him to be called before him, and, being alarmed, he sought to find an advocate. He went to the friend whom he loved most ; but he utterly refused to go with him. The second offered to go with him as far as the door of the king's palace, but refused to speak a word in his behalf. The third, whom he loved least, not only went with him, but pleaded his cause so well before the king, that he was cleared from all blame. In like manner every man has three friends, when he is cited by death to appear before God. The first friend, whom he loves most, viz. : his *money*, cannot accompany him at all. His second, viz. : his *relations* and *neighbours*, accompany him only to the grave, and then return ; but cannot deliver him from the Judge. The third friend, whom he holds in little esteem, viz. : the *law* and his *good works*, goes with him to the King, and delivers him from judgment."

In another treatise of the Talmud, entitled, *Sepher Haggadah,* will be found in the form of an allegory a legend which has a striking resemblance to one of the most popular of our nursery tales, viz., the one so familiarly known as, "This is the house that Jack built," the summary of which reads as follows :—

" Then came the Holy One,
Blessed be He,
And killed the angel of death,
That killed the butcher,
That killed the ox,
That drank the water,
That quenched the fire,

That burned the staff,
That beat the dog,
That bit the cat,
That ate the kid,
Which my Father bought
For two pieces of money."

The Talmud gives the following explanation of the above allegory. The *kid*, a clean animal, signifies the Jewish people ; the *Father*, who purchased it, Jehovah ; the *two pieces of money*, Moses and Aaron ; the *cat*, the Assyrians who carried the ten tribes into captivity ; the *dog*, the Babylonians, who destroyed the Assyrians ; the *staff*, the Persians, who conquered the Babylonians ; the *fire*, the Greeks, under Alexander, who overthrew the Persian monarchy ; the *water*, the Roman power, which vanquished the Grecians ; the *ox*, the Saracens, who ejected the Romans from the Holy Land ; the *butcher*, the Crusaders, who did the same for the Saracens ; the *angel of death*, the Turkish power, to which the Holy Land is subject. The commencement, " Then came the Holy One, blessed be He," is designed to show that *God will some day take signal vengeance on the Turks*, immediately after whose overthrow the Jews are to be restored to their own land, and to live under the government of their long-expected Messiah.— *The Quiver.*

CURIOSITIES OF PUBLIC AMUSEMENT

THE FIRST ENGLISH THEATRES.

IN the time of Queen Elizabeth, when our great dramatist donned the sock and buskin, the theatres were mere wooden erections, open to the weather, with the exception of the part over the stage, which was thatched. The pit was without seats, and court ladies and gallants sat in the boxes beneath the gallery, and were sometimes accommodated with stools on the stage, which was covered with rushes, and᷑ on which young gallants frequently reclined, smoking tobacco—then a novelty and a fashionable indulgence—while the play was being performed. Scenery was then unknown, unless rude imitations of trees, etc., may be termed so ; the names of the places of action (such as " Forest of Arden,"), being painted on boards, which were hung up in some conspicuous place during the performance. Movable scenery was introduced by Sir W. Davenant, soon after the Restoration. At one period of Queen Elizabeth's reign the theatres, as well as bear gardens, etc., were open on Sundays. During the time of the Commonwealth, public amusements were to a great extent prohibited, but noblemen were wont to have occasional theatrical entertainments at their mansions. (It has been wittily observed that the Puritans suppressed the sport of bear-baiting, not because it gave pain to the bear, but because it afforded pleasure to the people !) We find in the public records of the time of the Protectorate, that the play of "Midsummer's Night's Dream" having been enacted on a Sunday at the Bishop of Lincoln's palace, to the pious horror of the Puritans, the unlucky wight who played the part of Bottom, being the ringleader of this Sabbath-breaking, was condemned as a punishment to sit for twelve hours in the stocks, " attired with an ass's head and a bottle of hay before him bearing the following inscription on his breast :—

> " Good people, I have played the beast,
> And brought ill things to pass :
> I was a man, but thus have made
> Myself a silly ass."

After the Restoration, when play-going came once more into fashion, affairs theatrical were considerably improved ; but it would appear that the theatres still continued to be partially unroofed ; for, says Pepys, " Before the play was done, it fell such a storm of hayle, that we in the middle of the pit were fain to rise, and all the house in disorder."

Performances at theatres and other places of amusement began at a much earlier hour than is the case at the present day, viz., two or three o'clock ; the streets being so badly paved and lighted (if, indeed, they can be said to have been paved or lighted at all), and the general insecurity after dark on account of footpads and other evil-doers, rendering it necessary for all honest people to be in their homes and out of harm's way soon after sunset. It was customary after seeing the play to walk in the park or make purchases ; and accordingly we find our diarist frequently going "to the exchange to buy things for my wife." "To the king's house—where to Covent Garden to buy a maske for my wife," etc. However appropriate it may have been to term the actors in Shakspeare's time "poor players," it would appear that with the Restoration came their halcyon days ; for, quoth Mr. Pepys, "The gallants do begin to be tyred with the vanity and pride of the theatre actors, who are indeed grown very proud and rich."

W. A. Clouston.

FIRST APPEARANCE OF WOMEN ON THE STAGE.

IT is significant that it was during the reign of the second Charles that women first made their appearance on the stage. Previous to the Restoration, female characters were enacted by boys or effeminate-looking young men ; and perhaps this circumstance may palliate much of the coarse language with which most of the earlier plays abound. Colley Cibber relates an amusing story of the time when men enacted the parts of women on the stage. On one occasion, when the king had arrived, the play was not begun, which annoyed his majesty, and he sent for the manager to inquire the cause of the delay. The poor man lost no time in presenting himself at the royal box, and thinking it safest to tell the truth, he respectfully informed his majesty that "the queen was not yet *shaved !*" which so tickled the king as to furnish him with subject for jest during the rest of the evening. Under date, January 3, 1661, Mr. Pepys chronicles : "In the theatre, where was acted 'Beggar's Bush,' it being very well done, and here, for the first time, I saw women come upon the stage." This, however, was not the first venture of ladies upon the boards. It is said that in December, 1660, the part of Desdemona was acted by a lady for the first time. But actresses appear to have become soon familiarised to their calling,—soon became, as it were, "native and to the manner born," as our diarist remarks of a play entitled the "Parson's Wedding," that "it is a loose play that is acted by nothing but women at the King's house."—*Ibid.*

ITINERANT PLAYERS.

IN shabby state they strut, in tattered robe,
The scene a blanket, and a barn the globe :
No high conceits their moderate wishes raise ;
Content with humble profit, humble praise.
Let dowdies simper, and let bumpkins stare,
The strolling pageant hero treads in air :
Pleased for his hour, he to mankind gives law,
And snores the next out on a truss of straw.

Churchill.

HARLEQUIN AND COLUMBINE.

THE term harlequin is derived from the Scandinavian word *helle-quin*. At an early period the Scandinavians, especially the residents of Norway, rushed in great swarms into Normandy and other parts of France. They were pagans, and had many superstitious notions, among which was that of the *hellequina*, or "hell-queen." She was the famous Hela, or Hel, the death goddess, whence our word "hell," still used in the Creed, and obtained from our Anglo-Saxon or West Scandinavian forefathers. The Scandinavian belief in the wild hunt of the hellequina (the death goddess, and *meynie*) corresponded to that of the French *la mort*, or the "death goddess," who, in that superstitious age, was believed to have power over the spirits of the departed, and the terms came to be used synonymously. These superstitions led the country into the grotesque mummeries of *notre famille d'arlequin* (our harlequin family), meaning the spirits of the departed.

The word columbine is derived from the Italian, in which language *Columbina* would mean "pretty little dove," and in old Italian comedy it was used for the name of a coquettish girl. This is not quite the character which columbine takes on the English stage, but no doubt the name was thought pretty by the old writers who adopted it, and their successors have retained it.

NELL GWYNNE.

CONSPICUOUS among the rare beauties whose pictures adorn the walls of Hampton Court, is the full-length portrait of Nell Gwynne, a woman of origin as humble as her personal attractions were superb. "Pretty witty Nelly," as the gallant Pepys calls this famous courtesan, was among the first females that ventured on the bold experiment of appearing on the stage ; but to judge by our gossip's remarks, her *forte* seems to have been comedy rather than tragedy, and probably Nelly's gay spirits and madcap humour rendered her but ill-suited for a follower of Melpomene. Several other actresses are frequently mentioned by Mr. Pepys ; the two Marshalls, for instance, who, as Nelly sneeringly observed to one of them, were "the daughters of a praying presbyter." Extremes sometimes meet, they say, and here was an instance—the daughters of Stephen Marshall, the Puritan, mere players and "light-skirts." It may be that the loose state of the morals of the first female actors has done much to attach a stigma upon actresses in general, from the "gay" days of the second Charles down almost to our own time—at least among the common people.

When Nell was not engaged on the stage she would seat herself in the boxes, among the other "fine ladies" and gallants ; and it would seem that even the virtuous Mrs. Pepys did not blush to recognise her ; for at the King's Theatre one evening we read,—" In came Nelly, and I kissed her, and so did my wife ; and a mighty pretty soul she is !" Again, " We sat in an upper box," quoth Pepys, " and the jade Nell came and sat in the next box—a bold, merry slut, who lay laughing there upon the people."

The last words of the "Merry Monarch," when he was dying, after requesting his brother, the Duke of York, to be kind to his mistresses, were, "Don't let poor Nelly starve." And Nelly did not starve, but became "hopefully pious" in her later years. After James II. professed himself a Catholic, Nelly betook herself to the consolations of the Church—a not unusual procedure on the part of ladies who have "slipped" in their giddy youth. "I hear," writes Evelyn, "that John Dryden, the laureate, and his eldest son, and Nell Gwynne, the late King's mistress, now go to the Catholic chapel."—*W. A. Clouston.*

A STAGE "SCENE" IN THE MIDDLE AGES.

IT is well known that dramatic poetry in this and most other nations of Europe, owes its origin, or at least its revival, to those religious shows which, in the dark ages, were usually exhibited on the more solemn festivals. At those times they were wont to represent in the churches the lives and miracles of the saints, or some of the more important stories of Scripture. And as the most mysterious subjects were frequently chosen, such as the Incarnation, Passion, and Resurrection of Christ, etc., these exhibitions acquired the general name of Mysteries. At first they were probably a kind of dumb-shows, intermingled, it may be, with a few short speeches; at length they grew into a regular series of connected dialogues, formally divided into acts and scenes. How they were exhibited in their most simple form, we may learn from an ancient novel, often quoted by our old dramatic poets, entitled "A Merye Jest of a Man that was called Howleglas," etc., being a translation from the Dutch language in which he is named Ulenspiegle. Howleglas, whose waggish tricks are the subject of this book, after many adventures comes to live with a priest, who makes him his parish clerk. This priest is described as keeping a leman, or concubine, who had but one eye, to whom Howleglas owed a grudge for revealing his rogueries to his master. The story thus proceeds :—

"And than in the meane season, while Howleglas was parysh clarke, at Easter they should play the Resurrection of our Lorde : and for because than the men were not learned, nor could not read, the priest toke his leman, and put her in the grave for an Aungell : and this seeing, Howleglas toke to him three of the symplest persons that were in the towne, that played the three Maries ; and the person (*i.e.*, parson or rector) played Christe with a baner in his hand. Then said Howleglas to the symple persons : Whan the Aungell asketh you, whome you seke, you may saye, The parson's leman with one eye. And than the prieste might heare that he was mocked. Than it fortuned that the tyme was come that they must playe, and the Aungell asked them whome they sought, and than sayd they as Howleglas had shewed and learned them afore, We seke the prieste's leman with the one eye. And when the prieste's leman herd that, she arose out of the grave,

and would have smyten with her fist Howleglas upon the cheke, but she missed him and smote one of the symple persons that played one of the three Maries ; and he gave her another ; and then toke she him by the heare (hair) ; and that seeing, his wyfe came running hastily to smyte the prieste's leaman, and than the prieste seeing this, caste downe his baner and went to help his woman ; so that the one gave the other sore strokes, and made great noyse in the churche. And than Howleglas, seyn them lyinge together by the eares in the bodi of the churche, went his way out of the village, and came no more there."
—*Percy's Reliques of Ancient Poetry.*

HISTORICAL AND TRADITIONAL CURIOSITIES.

ASSASSINATION OF KING JAMES I. OF SCOTLAND.

ABOUT the year 1434, King James had ordered Sir Robert Graham, a powerful chieftain, to prison. The knight was subsequently liberated, but disgraced, on which he proposed a meeting of the chief men to represent their grievances to the king ; and in the next parliament Graham with great emotion approached the royal seat, and laid his hand on the king, and said, " I arrest you in the name of all the three estates of your realm ; for as your people have sworn to obey you, so you are constrained by an equal oath to govern by law, and not wrong your subjects, but in justice to maintain and defend them." Then, turning round to the assembly, he exclaimed, " Is it not thus as I say?" The members, probably from awe of James's presence, remained silent ; and the energetic sovereign ordered Graham to prison. Graham, who inveighed bitterly against those who were pledged to support him, was soon after banished, and his estates forfeited. From the farthest islands he defied the king, and threatened that he would with his own hand end the life of a tyrant, and give the crown to Sir Robert Stewart, Atholl's grandson. James offered a reward for Graham, alive or dead. Atholl, and Robert his grandson, were at the court of Perth, in the convent of Black Friars, in the evening of the 20th February, 1437. The company kept it up till a late hour, drank the parting cup, and had dispersed, when Graham, with about three hundred men, entered the garden. The king was in his bedchamber, standing before the fire in his nightgown, conversing gaily with the queen and her ladies, when he heard the noise as of armed men, and perceived the blaze of torches. The queen and her ladies, suspecting treason, ran to the chamber door, but found that the locks had been spoiled. The king, attempting to escape by the windows, found them barred with iron. With the fire-tongs he pulled up a board in the floor, and, dropping into an apartment destined to a far different purpose, had the board replaced. The only window in this retreat had by his own order been blocked up with stone three days before, to prevent the entrance of the tennis balls. Here, however, he might perhaps have remained safe had not his impatience betrayed him. Thinking that the search had ceased, he called to the ladies to bring sheets to draw him up out of his uncomfortable durance. In the attempt Elizabeth Douglas fell through the trap ; which being discovered, one of the assassins descended with a torch, and saw the king and the lady ; and,—in allusion to the ostensible reason of the search, a *match* for Sir Robert Stewart,—exclaimed, " Sir, the bride is found for whom we have sought and carolled all night." One of his associates then leaped down with a dagger, but was seized and trodden under foot by the king. Another followed, and was similarly received. James, however, had in vain endeavoured to wrest a dagger from either of them, and was wounded in his hands, so as to be incapable of further defence. Graham now also descended ; and on the king's imploring mercy, vociferated, " Thou cruel tyrant ! thou hadst never mercy upon thy noble kindred nor others ; so look for none." James besought him, for his soul's salvation, to let him have a confessor. Graham retorted, " Thou shalt have no confessor but this sword," and stabbed him. Seeing the king prostrate, he in some degree relented, and was about to withdraw; but his comrades insisted on his completing his intention, and James's body was pierced with a number of stabs. They now sought the queen's life, but she had escaped. Graham made good his retreat to the highlands ; but he and many of his associates in less than a month were captured, and imprisoned in Stirling Castle, where they were tortured and afterwards put to death.—*Mackie's Castles, Palaces, and Prisons of Mary of Scotland.*

LUXURY IN THE OLDEN TIME.

IN former times, there was much eating, with little variety ; at present, on the contrary, there is great variety, with more abstemiousness. Barbarous nations are fond of large joints of meat. A wild boar was roasted whole, as a supper-dish of Antony and Cleopatra ; and was stuffed with poultry and wild fowl. The hospitality of the Anglo-Saxons was sometimes displayed, for instance, by roasting an entire ox. This practice prevailed even among the Romans; for it is related that it was a favourite dish at Rome, and was termed a Trojan boar, in allusion to the Trojan horse.

William of Malmesbury, who wrote in the time of Henry II., says that " the English were universally addicted to drunkenness ; continuing over their cups day and night ; keeping open house, and spending the income of their estates in riotous feasts ; where eating and drinking were carried to excess, without any elegance." Hollinshed, writing of Henry VIII.'s time, says : "Heretofore, there hath been much more time spent in eating and drinking than commonly is in these days ; for whereas of old we had breakfasts in the forenoon, beverages or muncheons after dinner, and thereto rear-suppers, when it was time to get rest ; now these odd repasts, thanked be God, are very well left, and each one contenteth himself with dinner and supper only." He remarks that " claret and other French wines were despised, and only strong wines in request. The best were to be found in the monasteries ; for the merchant would have thought his soul would go straightway to the devil if he should serve monks with other than the best."

In early times, the people were very plain in their household furniture. At the beginning of the sixteenth century, substantial farmers slept on a straw pallet, with a log of wood to rest their head on—a pillow being only thought fit for a woman in child-bed ! Indeed, if a man, in the course of seven years after marriage, could purchase a flock bed, and a sack of chaff, as a substitute for a bolster, he thought himself as well lodged as the lord of the town. Wooden trenchers and wooden spoons were generally used about the same period, pewter vessels being accounted great luxuries, and prohibited from being hired, except on Christmas, Easter, St. George's Day, and Whitsunday.

By an act of parliament in Scotland, passed in the year 1429, none were permitted to wear silks, or costly furs, but knights and lords of two hundred merks yearly rent. But by another act, of 1457, the same dress was permitted to aldermen, bailies, and other good worthy men within burgh ; and, by a third act, it was granted to gentlemen of £100 yearly rent. As strongly illustrating the singular manners of the time, the following anecdote is related : — James I., British monarch, was during his infancy committed to the Dowager Countess of Mar, who had been educated in France. On one occasion, the king being seized with a colic during the night time, his household servants flew to his bed-chamber ; but the women as well as men were in a complete state of nudity ; nay, even the countess herself wore nothing but her chemise !

Hollinshed exclaims against the luxury and effeminacy that prevailed in his time. " In time past," he says, " men were contented to dwell in houses builded of sallow, willow, plumb-tree, or elm ; so that the use of oak was dedicated to churches, religious houses, princes' palaces, noblemen's lodgings, and navigation. But now these are rejected, and nothing but oak any whit regarded. And yet see the change ; for when our houses were builded of willow, then had we oaken men ; but now that our houses are made of oak, our men are not only become willow, but many, through Persian delicacy crept in among us, altogether of straw, which is a sore alteration."—*Jenoway's Antiquarian and Historical Notes.*

CORONATION FEASTS.

THE quantity of provisions consumed at the coronation feasts given by some of our early kings was extraordinarily great. For that of

King Edward I., February 10th, 1274, the different sheriffs were ordered to furnish butcher meat at Windsor, in the following proportions :—

	Oxen.	Swine.	Sheep.	Fowls.
Sheriff of Gloucester	60	101	60	3000
,, Bucks and Bedford	40	66	40	2100
,, Oxford	40	67	40	2100
,, Kent	40	67	40	2100
,, Surrey and Sussex	40	67	40	2600
,, Warwick and Leicester	60	98	40	3000
,, Somerset and Dorset	100	176	110	5000
,, Essex	60	101	60	3160
Total, twelve counties	440	743	430	23,060

In the year 1307, King Edward II. issued an order to the seneschal of Gascony and constable of Bordeaux, to provide a thousand pipes of good wine, and send them to London, to be used at the approaching coronation. The purchase and freight were to be paid by a company of Florentine merchants, who farmed the revenues of Gascony. The coronation oath was first taken by Ethelred II., A.D. 979 ; that now used, in 1377. It was amended in 1689. The first coronation sermon was preached in 1041.—*R. O. Jenoway.*

THE UNLUCKY DIAMOND NECKLACE.

JEANNE, Countess de Lamotte-Valois, the "princess of intrigue," as she has been aptly called, was born of poor parents, in 1757. Taken into service by the lady of the manor where her parents resided, the lady frequently heard the girl speak of valuable papers which were in the possession of her father. Those papers were examined, and proved to relate to the royal family of Valois, and Jeanne was discovered to be a descendant of that family, and entitled to the rank of countess. She married a private in the Guards, and was subsequently introduced to Queen Marie Antoinette ; and whilst in her service the countess resorted to an extraordinary trick to enrich herself. Cardinal Rohan had a passion for the queen, and Lamotte persuaded him to purchase for her majesty a diamond necklace of extraordinary beauty, which she said the queen longed to have (and which she said her majesty would arrange to pay for), and that by this means he would ingratiate himself in her favour, he having offended her. This necklace had been made by order of Louis XV. for his mistress, Madame du Barry. But Louis died before it was completed, and it remained on the jewellers' hands. The countess undertook herself to deliver the necklace to the queen, and to procure an interview between her majesty and the cardinal. The latter fell into the snare. He bought the necklace for 1,800,000 francs (£72,000), Lamotte having forged the queen's name to an order on the jewellers for the treasure to be paid for by instalments. The cardinal handed the necklace to the countess, and she told him she had given it to the queen, who would meet the cardinal in a garden to thank him. A friend of the countess's personated her majesty, met the cardinal for a few moments, thanked him, and promised him her protection. The countess, meanwhile had sent her husband to London with the necklace, where it was broken up in small pieces and sold. The first instalment falling due, the plot was discovered; the cardinal, the countess, and the woman who had personated the queen were arrested, but the countess alone was punished. She was condemned to ask the queen's pardon with a rope round her neck, to be whipped and branded on each shoulder with the letter V (probably for Valois, or for *voleuse*, thief), and imprisoned in La Salpêtrière. She, however, afterwards escaped to England, and died in London. The cardinal was declared innocent of all fraud, but was much ridiculed for his extreme credulity ; and was ordered into exile by the king, and compelled to resign all his posts.

A MONARCH'S LAST WORDS.

THE last words of Charles V. of France, surnamed "The Wise," are memorable for the noble moral for kings which they contain—and indeed, they are applicable to all, as every man has the power to do good or evil. " I have aimed at justice," said he to those around him ; " but what king can be certain that he has always followed it ? Perhaps I have done much evil of which I am ignorant. Frenchmen, who now hear me, I address myself to the Supreme Being and to you. *I find that kings are happy but in this—that they have the power of doing good."*

BUCCANEERS OF THE SPANISH MAIN.

THE successes of the English in the predatory incursions upon Spanish America, during the reign of Elizabeth, had never been forgotten ; and from that period downwards the exploits of Drake and Raleigh were imitated, upon a smaller scale indeed, but with equally desperate valour, by small bands of pirates, gathered from all nations, but chiefly French and English. The engrossing policy of the Spaniards tended greatly to increase the number of these freebooters, from whom their commerce and colonies suffered, in the issue, dreadful calamity. The Windward Islands, which the Spaniards did not deem worthy their own occupation, had been gradually settled by adventurers of the French and English nations. But Frederic of Toledo, who was despatched in 1630, with a powerful fleet against the Dutch, had orders from the court of Madrid to destroy these colonies, whose vicinity at once offended the pride and excited the jealous suspicions of their Spanish neighbours. This order the Spanish admiral executed with sufficient rigour ; but the only consequence was, that the planters, being rendered desperate by persecution, began, under the well-known name of buccaneers, a retaliation so horridly savage that the perusal makes the reader shudder. When they carried on their depredations at sea, they boarded, without respect to disparity

of number, every Spanish vessel that came in their way ; and de-
meaning themselves, both in the battle and after the conquest, more
like demons than human beings, they succeeded in impressing their
enemies with a sort of superstitious terror, which rendered them
incapable of offering effectual resistance.   From piracy at sea, they
advanced to making predatory descents on the Spanish territories, in
which they displayed the same furious and irresistible valour, the
same thirst of spoil, and the same brutal inhumanity to their captives.
The large treasures which they acquired in their adventures, they
dissipated by the most unbounded licentiousness in gaming, women,
wine, and debauchery of every species.   When their spoils were thus
wasted, they entered into some new association, and undertook new
adventures.—*Scott.*

ORIGIN OF STARCHING.

IN the year 1564, Mistress Dinghan Van den Plasse, born at
Haerlem, in Flanders, daughter to a worshipful knight of that province,
with her husband came to London for their better safeties, and there
professed herself a starcher, wherein she excelled ; unto whom her own
nation presently repaired, and paid her very liberally for her own work.
Some very few damsels, and most curious wives of that time, observing
the neatness of the Dutch, for whiteness and fine wearing of linen,
made their cambric ruffs and sent them to Mistress Dinghan to starch,
and then they began to send their daughters and nearest kinswomen
to Mistress Dinghan, to learn how to make starch.—*Stowe, the Antiquary.*

FAIRS.

ABOUT the beginning of the eleventh century, and perhaps even
earlier, trade was principally carried on by means of Fairs.   Many
marts of this sort were established by William the Conqueror and his
successors.   The merchants, who frequented them in numerous com-
panies, used every art to draw the people together ; hence the custom
of jugglers, buffoons, etc., assembling at these places.

TRIAL BY JURY.

AT what period trial by jury was first introduced into the English
laws cannot now be exactly ascertained, although it is certainly re-
ferable to the Saxon era.   Its origin may be traced to a principle in
use at a very early date.   When a man was accused of any crime, it
was a judicial custom of the Saxons, that he might clear himself, if he
could procure a certain number of persons to swear that they believed
him guiltless of the allegation.   These persons so produced were
called *compurgators*, and the *veredictum* sworn to by them so far
determined the case as to acquit the prisoner.   That trial by jury
existed at the time of the Conquest is not disputed.—*Jenoway.*

OUTLAWS OF SHERWOOD FOREST.

THE severity of those tyrannical forest laws that were introduced by our Norman kings, and the great temptation of breaking them by such as lived near the royal forests, at a time when the yeomanry of this kingdom were everywhere trained up to the long-bow, and excelled all other nations in the art of shooting, must constantly have occasioned great numbers of outlaws, and especially of such as were the best marksmen. These naturally fled to the woods for shelter, and forming into troops, endeavoured by their numbers to protect themselves from the dreadful penalties of their delinquency. The ancient punishment for killing the king's deer, was loss of eyes and castration, a punishment far worse than death. This will easily account for the troops of banditti which formerly lurked in the royal forests, and, from their superior skill in archery, and knowledge of all the recesses of those unfrequented solitudes, found it no difficult matter to resist or elude the civil power. Among all those, none was ever more famous than Robin Hood, whose chief residence was in Sherwood Forest, in Nottinghamshire ; and the heads of whose story, as collected by Stowe, are briefly these :—

" In this time (about the year 1190, in the reign of Richard I.) were many robbers and outlawes, among the which Robin Hood and Little John, renowned thieves, continued in woods, despoyling and robbing goods of the rich. They killed none but such as would invade them ; or by resistance for their own defence. The said Robert entertained an hundred tall men and good archers with such spoyles and thefts as he got, upon whom four hundred (were they ever so strong) durst not give the onset. He suffered no woman to be oppressed, violated, or otherwise molested ; poore men's goods he spared, abundantlie relieving them with that which by theft he had got from abbeys and the houses of rich earles : whom Maior (the historian) blameth for his rapine and theft, but of all thieves he affirmeth him to be the prince and the most gentle thiefe."

The personal courage of this celebrated outlaw, his skill in archery, his humanity, his levelling principle of taking from the rich and giving to the poor, have in all ages rendered him the favourite of the common people.—*Percy's Reliques.*

THE BUCENTAUR.

THE Bucentaur was a large galley, belonging to the State of Venice, which was finely adorned with pillars, splendidly gilt, and furnished with a covering of purple silk. In this vessel the doge received the great lords and persons of quality who visited Venice, accompanied by the ambassadors, councillors of state, and senators ; and the same vessel was employed on Ascension Day, in the magnificent ceremony of espousing the sea, by throwing a ring into it, as a symbolical expression of the dominion of the Venetians over the Gulf.

EXTRAORDINARY BIRTH OF TRIPLETS.

" IN the year 1666, in the county of Sussex, Mrs. Palmer, wife of

Edward Palmer, was delivered of three sons, after being fourteen days in labour : John was born on Whit-Sunday ; on Trinity Sunday came Henry ; and on the Sunday following, Thomas.   They all lived to be very brave men, and were knighted for their exploits."

The foregoing extraordinary statement appears in the *European Magazine*, vol. 66, 1814 ; and although no authority is cited, it is found to agree in all important points, with the exception of the date, with the following circumstantial account, by Horsefield, in his "History of Sussex," vol. ii., pp. 141, 142, 4to, 1835 :—

"Sir Edward Palmer, Knight, married Alice, one of the sisters and co-heirs of Sir Richard Clement, of the Moat, in Ightham, in Kent, and by her had *three sons, born on three Sundays successively, who all lived to be eminent in their generation.   All three were knighted for their bravery by Henry VIII* Sir John, the eldest, had the paternal seat at Angmering, and was twice sheriff of Surrey and Sussex.   Sir Thomas, the youngest of the trine brothers, made his fortune at the courts of Henry VIII. and Edward VI. ; but taking part with John Dudley, duke of Northumberland, in favour of Lady Jane's title to the crown, he was, on the accession of the lawless Mary, beheaded with the Duke upon Tower Hill.   Upon the scaffold he boldly avowed his religion to be Protestant.   The second of the three brothers, Sir Henry Palmer, settled at Wingham, in Kent, where his family long continued to flourish. He followed the profession of arms, and much distinguished himself at Guisnes, in Picardy, as also at the taking of Boulogne, where he had his arm broken.   In the defence of Guisnes he lost his life, when more than seventy years of age."

The date given in the first quotation, that of 1666, is evidently erroneous, but the fact of this remarkable freak of nature seems unquestionable.

CLOCKS AND WATCHES.

THE first pendulum clock made in England was constructed in the year 1622, by Fromantel, a Dutchman. Repeating clocks and watches were invented about 1676.   Until about 1631 neither clocks nor watches were very general.

MONKS AND FRIARS.

THERE was a distinction between the monks and friars, which caused the latter to become the object of hatred and envy.   Both the monastic, or regular, and parochial clergy encouraged the attacks made upon them.   The monks were, by most of their rules, absolutely forbidden to go out of their monasteries, and therefore could receive only such donations as were left to them.   On the contrary, the friars, who were professed mendicants, on receiving notice of the sickness of any rich person, constantly detached some of their members to persuade the sick man to bequeath alms to their convent ; thus often not only anticipating the monks, but likewise the parochial clergy.   Besides, as most of them were professed preachers, their sermons were frequently compared with those of the clergy, and, in general, not to the advantage of the latter. In these sermons, the poverty and distress of their order were topics that, of course, were neither omitted nor slightly passed over. Considering the power of the Church before the Reformation, it is not to be supposed that any of the poets, as Chaucer, etc., would have ventured to tell those ridiculous stories of the friars, with which their works abound, had they not been privately protected by the superior clergy.—*Jenoway.*

MAJESTY.

THIS title was first given to Louis XI. of France. Before his time, the sovereigns of Europe had been merely styled "Highness" or "Grace." In England, Henry IV. received the title of "Grace;" Henry VI. that of "Excellent Grace"; Edward IV. that of "High and Mighty Prince"; Henry VII. was styled "Highness"; Henry VIII., "Majesty"; and was the first and last who was styled "Dread Sovereign"; James I. was called "Sacred," or "Most Excellent Majesty."

INTRODUCTION OF THE RAPIER INTO ENGLAND.

THE use of defensive armour, and particularly of the buckler or target, was general in Queen Elizabeth's time, although that of the single rapier seems to have been occasionally practised much earlier. Rowland Yorke, however, who betrayed the port of Zutphen to the Spaniards, for which good service he was afterwards poisoned by them, is said to have been the first who brought the rapier-fight into general use. Fuller, speaking of the swash-bucklers, or bullies, of Queen Elizabeth's time, says, "West Smithfield was formerly called Ruffian's Hall, where such men usually met, casually or otherwise, to try *masteries* with sword and buckler. More were frightened than hurt, more hurt than killed therewith, it being accounted unmanly to strike beneath the knee. But since that desperate traitor, Rowland Yorke, first introduced thrusting with rapiers, sword and buckler are disused." In the "Two Angry Women of Abingdon," a comedy printed in 1599, we have a pathetic complaint:—"Sword and buckler fight begins to grow out of use. I am sorry for it; I shall never see good manhood again. If it be once gone, this poking fight of rapier and dagger will come up : then a tall man, and a good sword-and-buckler man, will be spitted like a cat or a rabbit." But the rapier had upon the Continent long superseded, in private duel, the use of sword and shield. The masters of the noble science of defence were chiefly Italians. They made great mystery of their art and mode of instruction, never suffered any person to be present but the scholar who was to be taught, and even examined closets, beds, and other places of possible concealment. Their lessons often gave the most treacherous advantages ; for the challenger, having the right to choose his weapons, frequently selected some strange, unusual, and inconvenient kind of arms, and thus killed at ease his antagonist, to whom it was presented for the first time on the field of battle. The Highlanders continued to use the broad sword and target until disarmed after the affair of 1745-6.—*Scott.*

CATTLE REIVERS.

WHAT manner of cattle-stealers they are that inhabit those valleys in the marches of both kingdoms, John Lesley, a Scotchman himself, and Bishop of Ross, will inform you. They sally out of their own borders in the night in troops, through unfrequented bye-ways and many intricate windings. All the daytime they refresh themselves and their horses in lurking holes they had pitched upon before, till they arrive in the dark in those places they have a design upon. As soon as they have seized upon the booty, they in like manner return home in the night, through blind ways, and fetching many a compass. The more skilful any captain is to pass through those wild deserts, crooked turnings, and deep precipices in the thickest mists, his reputation is the greater, and he is looked upon as a man of an excellent head. And they are so very cunning that they seldom have their booty taken from them, unless sometimes, when, by the help of bloodhounds following them exactly upon the track, they may chance to fall into the hands of their adversaries. When being taken, they have so much persuasive eloquence, and so many smooth insinuating words at command, that if they do not move their judges, nay, and even their adversaries (notwithstanding the severity of their natures), to have mercy, yet they incite them to admiration and compassion.—*Camden's Britannia.*

THE ROMAN CALENDAR.

THE word is derived from *calend* or *kalend,* which in the Roman chronology denoted the first day of every month ; and this word is taken from the Greek, signifying to call or proclaim, because the chief priest, whose duty it was daily to watch the appearance of the new moon, summoned the people to the Capitol, and with a loud voice proclaimed the number of kalends, or the day on which the nones would happen, or, according to another account, proclaimed the severa feasts or holidays in the month.

The kalends were reckoned backwards, thus : the first day of May was called the kalends of May, the 30th, or last day of April, the day before the kalends, *pridie kalendarum,* or second of the kalends of May ; the 29th of April, the third of the kalends of May ; and so on to the 13th of April, when the *ides* commence, which also are reckoned backwards to the 5th of April, when the *nones* commence, and are numbered backwards to the first, which takes the name of the kalends of April.

To find the day of the kalends corresponding to any day of the month, according to the modern computation of time, the following is the rule :—To the number of days yet remaining of the month, add two, and this number will denote the day of the kalends of the succeeding month ; thus : suppose it is required to convert the 22nd of April to the corresponding day in the old Roman kalendar, eight days are wanting to complete the month, or to bring it to the first of May, the day on which the kalends of May commence ; two being added to eight, the remaining number of ten marks the tenth of the kalends of May, because the last day of April is called the second day of the kalends, the last but one is the third day, and so on.— *Encyc. Edinensis.*

A PRINCELY LORD MAYOR.

FROISSART, a historian who wrote in the time of Edward III., gives the following interesting account of a great civic feast given by a wealthy Lord Mayor of London to the king and other royal and noble personages. The King of Cyprus, it may be mentioned, had then (1357) newly arrived in England. He was a very accomplished prince for that age, who could speak several languages, and had made the tour of Europe, as we now express it, in order to form a crusade against the Saracens in the Holy Land.

" Henry Picard, Vintner, Mayor of London, in one day did sumptuously feast Edward, King of England ; John, King of France ; the King of Cyprus ; David, King of Scots ; Edward, Prince of Wales ; with many noblemen and others ; and after, the said Henry Picard kept his hall against all comers whosoever, that were willing to play at dice and hazard. In like manner, the Lady Margaret, his wife, did also keep her chamber, to the same intent.

" The King of Cyprus, playing with the mayor in his hall, did win 50 marks ; but the mayor being very skilful in that art, altering his hand, did after win of the said king the same 50 marks, and 50 marks more ; which, when the said king began to take in ill part, although he dissembled the same, Henry Picard said unto him, ' My lord and king, be not aggrieved ; I covet not your gold, but your play ; for I have not bid you hither that I might grieve you but that, amongst other things, I might try your play ;' and gave him his money again, plentifully bestowing his own amongst the retinue. Besides, he gave many rich gifts to the King and other Nobles and Knights, who dined with him, to the great glory of the citizens of London in those days."

SIR HENRY LEE AND HIS DOG.

AT Ditchley, a former seat of the Lees, Earls of Lichfield, collatera descendants of Queen Elizabeth's knight, Sir Henry Lee, there was a curious painting of Sir Henry and his dog, with the motto, " More Faithful than Favoured." The traditional account of this picture is, that Sir Henry, on retiring to rest one night, was followed to his bed-room by the dog. The animal, being deemed an intruder, was at once turned out of the room ; but howled and scratched at the door so piteously that Sir Henry, for the sake of peace, gave it readmission, when it crept underneath the bed. After midnight, a treacherous servant, making his way into the room, was seized and pinned to the ground by the watchful dog. An alarm being given, and lights brought, the terrified wretch confessed that his object was to kill Sir Henry and rob the house. In commemoration of the event, Sir Henry had the portrait painted, as a monument of the gratitude of the master, the ingratitude of the servant, and the fidelity of the dog. It is very possible that this anecdote and picture may have given rise to the well-known story of a gentleman rescued from murder, at a lonely inn, by the fidelity and intelligence of his dog, who, by preventing him from getting into bed, induced him to suspect some treacherous design on the part of his landlord, who at midnight, with his accomplices, ascended through a trapdoor in the floor of the apartment, but were discomfited and slain by the gentleman, with the aid of the faithful animal.— *Chambers' Book of Days.*

COACHES.

COACHES were introduced into England, from France, in 1589, by the Earl of Arundel. Till this period, saddle-horses and carts were the only method of conveyance for all sorts of people. Even the queen herself rode behind her Master of the Horse, when she went in state to St. Paul's, attended by the nobility of both sexes on horseback. In 1601, an act of parliament was passed to prevent men from riding in coaches, as being considered an effeminate practice. Hackney coaches were first licensed in 1683.

A GRAVE COMPLAINT AGAINST STAGE COACHES.

IN the year 1672, when throughout the kingdom only six stage coaches were constantly going, a pamphlet was written by one John Cresset, of the Charter-house, for their suppression, and among the many grave reasons given against their continuance is the following : " These stage coaches make gentlemen come to London upon every small occasion, which otherwise they would not do but upon urgent necessity ; nay, the conveniency of the passage makes their wives often come up, who, rather than come such long journeys on horseback, would stay at home. Here, when they come to town, they must presently be in the mode, get fine clothes, go to plays and treats ; and by these means get such a habit of idleness, and love of pleasure, that they are uneasy ever after."

CURIOUS TREASONABLE LETTER.

THE writer of the following ingenious composition, having been long suspected of furnishing treasonable intelligence to the enemy, the government placed a spy over him, who succeeded in intercepting the letter, which was directed to a house in Paris. At first it was thought they had alighted on the wrong person ; but a few days afterwards, a second letter, addressed in the same handwriting to the same person, containing only the figures, was brought by the informant to the government. After careful examination, it was discovered that the figures were the key to the treasonable information contained in the letter, and the writer was accordingly arrested and kept in close confinement, until at the earnest intercession of his friends, he was permitted to leave this country under a promise not to return during the war.

LONDON, *April 6th*, 1798.

DEAR FRIEND,—

As I find there is an opportunity, I write to say how we are. My daughter Mary, who was seventeen last week, has an offer ; the man is a sail maker, honest and industrious ; he is very sober and of respectable family ; as to the trade, we do not object, since workmen in that line are sure of employment. My wife has been almost ready to go distracted with pain at her stomach ; after suffering for some days, she spit up some sharp matter, which greatly relieved her head ; then became again afflicted, and how long her illness may continue, Heaven knows. Any commands you may have to execute will be carefully attended to by, Yours truly.

The contents of the second letter were simply the following figures :

4	1	8	5	5	9
7	2	7	6	5	10
3	3	7	7	3	11
3	4	4	8	3	12
3	5				

The figures in the first column denote the *words* which, put together form the real purport of the letter, and the figures in the second column, the *lines*. By this means it was intended to convey to the French authorities the information that, " There are seventeen sail of the line at Spithead, Howe commands."

THE ROYAL WRESTLERS.

AT the celebrated interview which took place between Henry VIII. and Francis I., near Ardres, in France, in 1520, where they and their attendants displayed the greatest magnificence during eighteen days, which were passed in feats of chivalry, exercises, and pastimes, the following singular circumstance is described by the Marshal Fleuranges —who was present—to have taken place : "After the tournament, the French and English wrestlers made their appearance, and wrestled in the presence of the kings, and the ladies ; and as there were many stout wrestlers there, it afforded excellent pastime ; but as the king of France had neglected to bring any wrestlers out of Bretagne, the English gained the prize. After this, the kings of France and England retired to a tent, where they drank together, and the king of England seizing the king of France by the collar, said, ' My brother, I must wrestle with you ;' and endeavoured once or twice to trip up his heels ; but the king of France, who is a dexterous wrestler, twisted him round, and threw him on the earth with prodigious violence. The king of England wanted to renew the combat, but was prevented."

A GIGANTIC BOWL OF PUNCH.

ON the 25th October, 1694, Admiral Edward Russell, then commanding the Mediterranean fleet, gave a grand entertainment at Alicant. The tables were laid under the shade of orange trees in four garden walks meeting in a common centre, at a marble fountain, which last was for the occasion converted into a Titantic punchbowl. Four hogsheads of brandy, one pipe of Malaga wine, twenty gallons of limejuice, twenty-five hundred lemons, thirteen hundredweight of fine white sugar, five pounds weight of grated nutmegs, three hundred toasted biscuits, and eight hogsheads of water, formed the ingredients of this monster brewage. An elegant canopy placed over the potent liquor prevented much evaporation or dilution by rain ; while, in a boat built expressly for the purpose, a ship-boy rowed round the fountain to assist in filling cups for the six thousand persons who partook of it.

ORIGIN OF THE CUSTOM OF WATCHING THE DEAD.

IF a corpse were left in a house with the door ajar, it was supposed to be at the hazard of its being carried off by malevolent spirits. The spiritual parts being separated from the corporeal, and the latter no longer hallowed by the blessing pronounced at baptism, it was supposed to be incapable of invoking the aid of higher powers, and was therefore exposed to the machinations of the imps of darkness, unless carefully watched and guarded by the living. The custom, once established, continues, though people are no longer under the influence of the superstition from which it originated.

THE PEDAGOGUE AND THE PEDANTIC MONARCH.

LINLITHGOW exhibited its loyalty in a very remarkable manner in the year 1617, when King James touched at his mother's birthplace in the course of a progress through his kingdom of Scotland. James Wiseman, the schoolmaster of the town, was inclosed in a large plaster figure representing a lion, and placed at the extremity of the town in order to address his majesty as he entered. However ridiculous this exhibition may now appear, it no doubt pleased the grotesque fancy of the king, especially as the speech was highly laudatory, and composed in that peculiar style of poetry suited to the pedantic taste of the monarch. It was as follows :—

> " Thrice royal sir, here do I you beseech,
> Who art a lion, to hear a lion's speech—
> A miracle ! for since the days of Æsop
> No lion till these days a voice dared raise up
> To such a majesty ! Then, king of men,
> The king of beasts speaks to thee from his den :
> Who, though he now enclosèd be in plaster,
> When he was free was Lithgow's wise schoolmaster."
>
> *Mackie's Castles, etc., of Mary of Scotland.*

CURIOUS LETTER OF INTRODUCTION.

THE following is the translation of a letter said to be from Cardinal Mazarin to the French ambassador at Rome. Read across the line, the letter, it will be observed, speaks of the bearer in terms of high eulogy. The real purport of the letter will be found by reading only what is on the left side of the line :—

"SIR,—Mr. Campy, a Savoyard Friar is at present to be the bringer to you of this letter. He is one of the most vicious persons that ever I yet knew. He has earnestly desired me to give him a letter to you of recommendation, which I have granted to his importunity: for believe me, Sir, I should be very sorry if you should be mistaken in not knowing him well: as a great many other persons have been who are of my very best friends here. I am very desirous to advertise you to take particular notice of him, and to say nothing in his presence in any sort. For with truth I do assure you there cannot be a more unworthy person in the whole world. I am certain that as soon as you have occasion of knowing him, you will thank me for this advice. Civility will not permit me to say any more on this subject.

of the order of Saint Benedict, of particular news from me and wise, discreet, and least wicked or amongst all I have conversed with, to write to you in his favour, and credence on his own behalf, and my his merit, I do assure you, more than to he is one that deserves the best esteem. wanting to oblige him by your being I should be much afflicted if you were, on that account, who now esteem him, and Sir, for this, and for no other motive, that you are most particularly obliged and to give him all imaginable respect; that may offend or displease him say, I love him as I love myself, and strong or convincing argument of an than to be willing to do him an injury. cease to be a stranger to his virtue and will love him as much as I do, and The assurance I have of your great write any further of him to you, or to I am, etc.,
MAZARIN.

TRADITIONS OF MICHAEL SCOTT THE WIZARD.

HE was chosen, it is said, to go upon an embassy, to obtain from the King of France satisfaction for certain piracies committed by his subjects upon those of Scotland. Instead of preparing a new equipage and splendid retinue, the ambassador retreated to his study, opened his book, and evoked a fiend in the shape of a huge black horse, mounted upon his back, and forced him to fly through the air towards France. As they crossed the sea, the devil insidiously asked his rider, What it was that the old women of Scotland muttered at bedtime? A less experienced wizard might have answered, that it was the Paternoster, which would have licensed the devil to precipitate him from his back. But Michael sternly replied, " What is that to thee ? Mount, Diabolus, and fly ! " When he arrived at Paris, he tied his horse to the gate of the palace, entered, and boldly delivered his message. An ambassador, with so little of the pomp and circumstance of diplomacy, was not received with much respect ; and the king was about to return a contemptuous refusal to his demand, when Michael besought him to suspend his resolution till he had seen his horse stamp three times. The first stamp shook every steeple in Paris, and caused all the bells to ring; the second threw down three of the towers of the palace ; and the infernal steed had lifted his hoof to give the third stamp, when the king rather chose to dismiss Michael with the most ample concessions, than to stand the probable consequences.

Upon another occasion, the magician having studied so long in the mountains that he became faint from want of food, sent his servant to procure some from the nearest farm-house. The attendant received a churlish denial from the farmer. Michael commanded him to return to the rustic Nabal and lay before him his cap, or bonnet, repeating these words :—

"Master Michael Scott's man
Sought meat and gat nane."

When this was done and said, the enchanted bonnet became suddenly inflated, and began to run round the house with great speed, pursued by the farmer, his wife, his servants, and the reapers who were on the neighbouring *har'st rigg*. No one had the power to resist the fascination, or refrain from joining in pursuit of the bonnet, until they were totally exhausted with their ludicrous exercise.

Michael, like his predecessor Merlin, fell at last a victim to female art. His wife, or concubine, elicited out of him the secret that his art could ward off any danger except the poisonous qualities of broth made of the flesh of a *breme* sow. Such a mess she accordingly administered to the wizard, who died in consequence of eating it ; surviving, however, long enough to put to death his treacherous confidante.—*Sir Walter Scott.*

TOKENS.

In the year 1653 private persons had the liberty of coining pennies, halfpennies, and farthings, with their own device upon them, for the convenience of trade. Tokens issued by cities or villages generally expressed the name of the place and value of the piece on one side, and on the other, the arms of the city or town, or some other device. When, however, they were coined by private individuals, they expressed the town or street where the proprietors lived, together with their sign or trade. They were of different sizes or forms; and in general shamefully light. They continued current till the year 1672, when the king's copper halfpence and farthings took place of them. Copper money was first used in Scotland and Ireland in 1340 ; in France in 1581 ; and in England in 1609.—*Jenoway.*

A DESPERATE ENCOUNTER.

The celebrated Sir Ewan of Lochiel, chief of the clan Cameron, called, from his sable complexion, "Ewan Dhu," was the last man in Scotland who maintained the royal cause during the great civil war ; and his constant incursions rendered him a very unpleasant neighbour to the republican garrison at Inverlochy, now Fort William. The governor of the fort detached a party of three hundred men to lay waste Lochiel's possessions, and cut down his trees ; but in a sudden and desperate attack made upon them by the chieftain, with very inferior numbers, they were almost all cut to pieces. The skirmish is detailed in a curious memoir of Sir Ewan's life, printed in the appendix of Pennant's "Scottish Tour :"—

" In this engagement Lochiel himself had several wonderful escapes. In the retreat of the English, one of the strongest and bravest of the officers retired behind a bush, when he observed Lochiel pursuing, and seeing him unaccompanied with any, he leaped out, and thought him his prey. They met one another with equal fury. The combat was long and doubtful. The English gentleman had by far the advantage in strength and size, but Lochiel, exceeding him in nimbleness and agility, in the end tripped the sword out of his hand. They closed and wrestled till both fell to the ground in each other's arms. The English officer got above Lochiel, and pressed him hard, but stretching forth his neck by attempting to disengage himself, Lochiel, who by this time had his hands at liberty, with his left hand seized him by the collar, and jumping at his extended throat he bit it with his teeth quite through, and kept such a hold of his grasp that he brought away his mouthful, This, he said, was *the sweetest bite he ever had in his lifetime!"—* *Scott.*

TOUCHING FOR THE KING'S EVIL.

JULY 6, 1660. His Majestie [Charles II.] began first to *touch for the evil,* according to costome, thus : his Majestie sitting under his State in the Banquetting House, the chirurgeons cause the sick to be brought or led up to the throne, when, they kneeling, the King strokes their faces or cheeks with both hands at once, at which instant a chaplaine in his formalities says, ' He put his hands upon them and healed them.' This is sayed to every one in particular. When they have been all touched they come up again in the same order, and the other chaplaine kneeling, and having Angel* gold strung on white ribbon on his arme, delivers them one by one to his Majestie, who puts them about the necks of the touched as they passe, whilst the first chaplaine repeats, ' That is the true light that came into the world.' Then follows an epistle (as at first a gospel) with the liturgy, prayers for the sick, with some alteration, lastly a blessing ; and the Ld. Chamberlaine and Comptroller of the Household bring a basin, ewer, and towell, for his Majestie to wash.—*Evelyn's Diary.*

THE FLITCH OF DUNMOW.

DUNMOW is a manor in Essex, remarkable for the custom of delivering a gammon, or flitch, of bacon to any married couple who would take a prescribed oath. The custom is supposed by some writers to have originated in the Saxon or Norman times. However this may be, the earliest delivery of bacon on record was in the twenty-third year of Henry VI., when Richard Wright, of Bradbourg, in Norfolk, having been duly sworn before the prior and convent, had a flitch of bacon delivered to him agreeably to the tenure. The ceremonial established

---

* Angels were pieces of money, so called from having the figure of an angel on them. Queen Anne seems to have been the last of the English sovereigns who actually performed the ceremony of touching for the evil. Dr. Johnson, in Lent 1712, when he was three years of age, was amongst the persons touched by the queen.

11

for these occasions consisted in the claimants' kneeling on two sharp-
pointed stones in the churchyard, and there, after solemn chanting and
other rites performed by the convent, taking the following oath :—

> " You shall swear by custom of confession,
> That you ne'er made nuptial transgression ;
> Nor, since you were married man and wife,
> By household brawls or contentious strife,
> Or otherwise, at bed or board,
> Offended each other in deed or in word ;
> Or since the parish clerk said ' Amen !'
> Wished yourselves unmarried again ;
> Or in a twelvemonth and a day
> Repented in thought any way ;
> But continued true in thought and desire,
> As when you joined hands in holy choir.
> If to these conditions, without all fear,
> Of your own accord you will freely swear,
> A whole gammon of bacon you shall receive,
> And bear it hence with love and good leave ;
> For this is our custom at Dunmow, well known,
> Though the pleasure be ours, the bacon's your own."

This curious custom was originated by Robert Fitz-Walter, in the
year 1244, and the earliest recorded claim for the " Flitch of Bacon "
was, according to *Haydn's Dictionary of Dates*, in 1445, since when
to 1855 it had only been demanded five times. The last claimants
previous to 1855 were John Shakeshanks and his wife, 20 June, 1751,
who made a large sum by selling slices of the flitch to witnesses of
the ceremony (5000 persons). Flitches were awarded to Mr. and
Mrs. Barlow, of Chipping-Ongar, and the Chevalier Chatelaine and
his lady, 19 July, 1855. The lord of the manor opposed the revival,
but Mr. Harrison Ainsworth, the celebrated novelist, and some friends
defrayed the expense, and superintended the ceremonials. A flitch
was awarded in the year 1860.

THE ORIGINAL BLUEBEARD.

THE original Bluebeard of the popular nursery tale was the famous
Gilles, Marquis de Laval, Marshal of France, and a general of great
intrepidity. He greatly distinguished himself in the reigns of Charles
VI. and VII., but tarnished his glory by the most cruel murders and
licentiousness of every kind. His revenues were princely, but his
prodigalities were sufficient to render an emperor a bankrupt.
Wherever he went, he had in his suite a seraglio, a company of players,
a band of musicians, a society of sorcerers, packs of dogs of various
kinds, and above two hundred horses. Mezery, an author of high
repute, says that he encouraged and maintained men, who called
themselves sorcerers, to discover hidden treasure ; and corrupted
young persons of both sexes to attach themselves to him, and after-

wards killed them, for the sake of their blood, which was requisite to form his charms and incantations. He was, at length, for a state crime to the Duke of Brittany, sentenced to be burned alive in a field in Nantes, in the year 1440, but the Duke of Brittany, who was present at his execution, so far mitigated the sentence, that he was first strangled, and then burned, and his ashes buried.

TAVERN SIGNS.

THE "Bull and Gate" and "Bull and Mouth" are well-known corruptions of "Boulogne-gate" and "Boulogne-mouth;" but that of the "Bag of Nails," at Chelsea, is still more curious, being derived from "Bacchanals." The "Bell Savage Inn" was once the property of Arabella Savage, and familiarly called, "Bell Savage's Inn," probably represented by a bell and a savage, which was a rebus for her name. On any extraordinary occasion, the tavern keepers have not been backward to commemorate it on their signposts. At the Union with Scotland, the Crown with the Rose and Thistle adorned our taverns ; and, on the accession of our present royal family, the White Horse of Hanover prevailed.

The "Boar's Head" tavern in Eastcheap, London, makes a conspicuous figure in Shakspeare's plays ; and was standing in the latter part of last century. Under the sign was written, "THIS IS THE OLDEST TAVERN IN LONDON." There are extant among the small pieces called tradesmen's tokens, some used for change in this tavern, which are probably of the date of Elizabeth, antecedent to the copper coinage.

WASSAIL.

THIS was a liquor made of roasted apples, sugar, and ale, with bowls of which our forefathers were used to welcome in the New Year :—

> "Wassail ! wassail ! all o'er the town ;
> Our toast it is white, our ale it is brown ;
> Our bowl it is made of a maplin tree ;
> We be good fellows all : I drink to thee ! "

THE VICAR OF BRAY.

FULLER, in his Church History, gives the following account of this remarkable personage :—

The vivacious Vicar of Bray, living under King Henry VIII., Edward VI., Queen Mary, and Queen Elizabeth, was first a papist, then a protestant, then a papist, and then a protestant again. He had seen some martyrs burned (some two miles off) at Windsor, and found this fire too hot for his tender temper. The vicar, being taxed by one for being a turncoat and an inconsistent changeling,—" Not so (said he), for I always kept my principle, which is this,—to live and die the Vicar of Bray."

THE GLEE-MAIDEN.

THE jongeleurs, or jugglers, as we learn from the elaborate work of the late Mr. Strutt on the sports and pastimes of the people of England, used to call in the aid of various assistants to render these performances as captivating as possible. The glee-maiden was a necessary attendant. Her duty was tumbling and dancing ; and therefore the Anglo-Saxon version of Saint Mark's gospel states that the daughter of Herodias vaulted or tumbled before King Herod. In Scotland, these poor creatures seem, even at a late period, to have been bondswomen to their masters ; as appears from a case reported by Fountainhall :—" Reid, the mountebank, pursues Scott of Harden and his lady, for stealing away from him a little girl, called the tumbling lassie, that danced upon his stage ; and he claimed damages, and produced a contract, whereby he bought her from her mother for £30 Scots. But we have no slaves in Scotland, and mothers cannot sell their bairns, and physicians attested the employment of tumbling would kill her ; and her joints were now grown stiff, and she declined to return ; though she was at least a 'prentice, and so could not run away from her master, yet some cited Moses' law, that if a servant shelter himself with thee against the master's cruelty, thou shalt surely not deliver him up. The lords, *renitente cancellario*, assoilzied Harden on the 27th January, 1687."

The facetious qualities of the ape soon rendered him an acceptable addition to the strolling band of the jongleur. Ben Jonson, in his splenetic introduction to the comedy of " Bartholomew Fair," is at pains to inform the audience, " that he has ne'er a sword and buckler man in his fair, nor a juggler, with a well-educated ape, to come over the chain for the King of England, and back again for the prince, and sit still on his haunches for the pope and the King of Spain."—*Scott.*

A CURIOUS OLD LONDON CUSTOM.

IN the year 1705, Robert Dowe by his will gave an annual sum of £1 6s. 8d. to the sexton of St. Sepulchre, upon condition that a bell should be tolled, and the following words said to the prisoners in Newgate on the night preceding their execution :—

" All you that in the condemned hole do lie,
Prepare you, for to-morrow you shall die.
Watch all, and pray, the hour is drawing near
That you before the Almighty must appear ;
Examine well yourselves ; in time repent,
That you may not to eternal flames be sent ;
And when St. Sepulchre's bell to-morrow tolls,
The Lord alone have mercy on your souls."

On the night before executions take place, a person presents himself at the prison door, on the part of the sexton, and offers to perform the prescribed service, but is refused admission, and told that his services are not required. The sum, £1 6s. 8d., is derived from property in Smithfield, and is still continued to be paid to the sexton.

THE BEDAWIN, ROMANTIC AND REALISTIC.

" EASTERN life " has become with us in Europe almost synonymous with a life of romance, poetry, houris, and flowers, of gorgeous raiment and matchless steeds, of jewels and luxury. What can be more ro-mantic—in print—than the tameless son of the desert, free as air, chivalrous as Bayard, mounted on his priceless mare, returning from a successful onslaught on his foes, to lay the spoils of shawls from Khorassan and Kashmir, silks from Damascus, and gold filigree work from Cairo, at the feet of the dark-browed maiden whose gazelle-like eyes have caused more havoc in the desert than ever did the arrows of Abu Zayd the invincible? Are not the pearls of the harem said to be peerless in beauty and grace, and their wondrous loveliness to over-power the senses like the air heavy with scent of orange flowers and jessamine beneath their own sunny sky? Have not the "Arabian Nights" taught us that rubies as big as pigeon's eggs, and pearls the size of raspberries, are common ; while gold is dross to be scattered broadcast to gaping crowds by the princes of Islam? Alas ! that truth, with one stroke of a realistic pen, should destroy this dream of poetry ! Let us see the Bedawin as he is. Living under hair tents, in squalor, filth; and ignorance, his chivalry degenerates into simple freebooting ; his priceless mare is—*exceptis excipiendis*—a scraggy, thin-chested, drooping-flanked beast, capable, by some peculiar pro-vision of nature unknown to the horse of civilization, of going long wearisome journeys, with little water and less food ; her pace, however, is little more than three miles and a half per hour, and if pressed, she soon fails. The Bedawin's dark-eyed love is perhaps not ugly at twelve years old, but at twenty she is perfectly hideous, and looks forty. From earliest girlhood she is brought up as a hewer of wood and drawer of water. For the first seven or eight years of their lives, all the childre play about the ragged tents in happy community of ideas with the kids and lambs, puppies, chickens, calves, and camelets. After that they tend the flocks ; at ten or twelve the girls marry, and the boys, so soon as they are grown up, leave all toil to the women and children, as unworthy of their manly dignity. A successful foray raises them in the social scale, as a grand *coup* on the bourse or stock exchange does in more civilized lands. Though wealth be power everywhere, it is nowhere more potent than in the East, where competitive examina-tions and compulsory education are equally unknown. Still, a good word may be said for the Bedawin in districts where contact with Europeans has not spoilt them. They are then hospitable after their fashion, always offering a meal to the passing traveller, and though they will do their best to overreach and cheat in making a bargain, yet once the affair settled and their word given, a breach of faith is seldom

I may say never, known. As to the veiled beauties of the harem, we must trust to the perhaps somewhat *ex parte* descriptions of European ladies, and such stray glimpses as chance may show. Neither of them carry out the ideas of loveliness implanted by the "Arabian Nights," and one who has lived in the native quarters of Eastern towns will be well aware that the fair sex is cursed with a most vile shrewish tongue, and makes use of undiluted Billingsgate on the slightest provocation, in tones which force themselves to be heard by all the neighbours.—*Tyrwhitt Drake's Reports, Palestine Exploration Fund.*

SIR DAVID LINDSAY, THE POET, DESIRING THE OFFICE OF TAILOR TO THE KING.

ALIKE celebrated for his courage and his wit, Lindsay was no stickler at ceremony when in his mood. On one occasion, when the king was surrounded by a numerous train of nobility and prelates, Lindsay approached the monarch with due reverence and solemnity, and began to prefer a humble petition to be installed in an office which was then vacant. "I have," said the knight, "servit your grace long, and look to be rewarded as others are ; and now your maister taylor, at the pleasure of God, is departit ; wherefore I would desire your grace to bestowe this little benefit upon me." The king replied, that he was amazed at such a request from a man who could neither shape nor sew. "Sir King," rejoined the poet, "that makes nae matter, for you have given bishopricks and benefices to mony ane standin heir about you, and yet they can nouther teach nor preach ; and why may not I be as weil your taylor, though I can nouther shape nor sew? seein teachinge and preachinge are nae less requisite to their vocation than shapinge and sewinge to ane taylor."—*Mackie's Castles, etc., of Mary of Scotland.*

LACONIC AND SENTIMENTAL CURIOSITIES.

OF GOOD MEN.

THE parts and signs of goodness are many. If a man be gracious and courteous to strangers, it shows he is a citizen of the world, and that his heart is no island cut off from other lands, but a continent that joins to them. If he be compassionate towards the afflictions of others, it shows that his heart is like the noble tree that is wounded itself when it gives balm. If he easily pardons and remits offences, it shows that his mind is planted above injuries, so that he cannot be shot. If he be thankful for small benefits, it shows that he weighs men's minds, and not their trash.—*Bacon's Essays*

DIVINE TRUTH.

BEFORE thy mystic altar, heavenly Truth,
I kneel in manhood, as I knelt in youth :
Thus let me kneel, till this dull form decay,
And life's last shade be brightened by thy ray ;—
Then shall my soul, now lost in clouds below,
Soar without bound, without consuming glow.

Sir Wm. Jones.

OUR FOREFATHERS.

WHEN we look back upon our forefathers, we seem to look back upon the people of another nation, almost upon creatures of another species. Their vast rambling mansions, spacious halls, and painted casements, the Gothic porch, smothered with honeysuckles, their little gardens and high walls, their box edges, balls of holly, and yew-tree statues, are become so entirely unfashionable now, that we can hardly believe it possible that a people who resemble us so little in their taste should resemble us in anything else. But in everything else, I suppose they were our counterparts exactly, and time, that has sewed up the slashed sleeve, and reduced the large trunk hose to a neat pair of silk stockings, has left human nature just where it found it. The inside of the man has undergone no change. His passions, appetites, and aims, are just what they ever were. They wear, perhaps, a handsomer guise than they did in the days of yore, for philosophy and literature will have their effect upon the exterior, but in every other respect, a modern is only an ancient in a different dress.— *Cowper's Letters.*

"GIVE ME NEITHER POVERTY NOR RICHES."

ENOUGH for me this cloak, though homely spun ;
Fed on the flowers of song, your feasts I shun :
I hate your wealthy fool—the flatterer's god—
Nor hang I trembling on his awful nod :
Calm and contented, I have learned to feel
The blessèd freedom of a humble meal.—*Parmenio.*

I care not for those wide and fertile fields,
Nor all the wealth that Gyges held in fee :
What joy a self-sufficing fortune yields,
Such modest livelihood is dear to me.
The wise old maxim, "Not too much,"—
Too much has power my heart to touch.

Alpheus of Mitylene.

"THE GOLDEN MEAN."

ENJOY your goods as if your death were near ;
Save them as if 'twere distant many a year :

Sparing or spending, be thy wisdom seen
In keeping ever to the golden mean.—*Lucian.*

THE MISER.

ALL say that you are rich : I say, Not so :
You're poor.   Wealth only by its use we know.
What you enjoy is yours ; what for your heirs
You hoard, already is not yours but theirs.—*Anon.*

Yours is a pauper's soul, a rich man's pelf :
Rich to your heirs, a pauper to yourself.—*Lucillius.*

OUR ATTACHMENT TO LIFE.

THE young man, till thirty, never feels practically that he is mortal.
He knows it indeed, and if need were he could preach a homily on the
fragility of life ; but he brings it not home to himself any more than in
a hot June we can appropriate to our imagination the freezing days of
December.   But now—shall I confess a truth?—I feel these audits
but too powerfully.   I begin to count the probabilities of my duration,
and to grudge at the expenditure of moments and shortest periods like
misers' farthings.   In proportion as the years both lessen and shorten,
I set more count upon their periods, and would fain lay my ineffectual
finger upon the spoke of the great wheel.   I am not content to pass
away "like a weaver's shuttle."   Those metaphors solace me not, nor
sweeten the unpalatable draught of mortality.   I care not to be
carried with the tide that smoothly bears human life to eternity, and
reluct at the inevitable course of destiny.   I am in love with this green
earth, the face of town and country, the unspeakable rural solitudes,
and the sweet security of streets.   I would set up my tabernacle here.
I am content to stand still at the age to which I am arrived—to be no
younger, no richer, no handsomer.   I do not want to be weaned by
age, or drop, like mellow fruit, as they say, into the grave!   Any
alteration on this earth of mine, in diet or in lodging, puzzles and dis-
composes me.   My household gods plant a terribly fixed foot, and are
not rooted up without blood.   They do not willingly seek Lavinian
shores.   A new state of being staggers me.   Sun and sky, and breezes
and solitary walks, and summer holidays, and the greenness of fields,
and the juices of meats and fishes, and society, and the cheerful glass,
and candle-light, and fireside conversations, and jests and irony,—do
not these things go out with life?   Can a ghost laugh, or shake his
gaunt sides, when you are pleasant with him?—*Charles Lamb.*

FLEETING LIFE.

ALL human things are subject to decay :
And well the man of Chios tuned his lay—

" Like leaves on trees the race of man is found ; " *
Yet few receive the melancholy sound,
Or in their breasts imprint the solemn truth,
For hope is near to all, but most to youth.
Hope's vernal season leads the laughing hours,
And strews o'er every path the fairest flowers.
To cloud the scene, no distant mists appear ;
Age moves no thought, and death awakes no fear.
Ah ! how unmindful is the giddy crowd
Of this small span to youth and life allowed !
Ye who reflect, the short-lived good employ ;
And while the power remains indulge your joy.

Simonides, Translated by Merivale.

SUCCESS IN LIFE.

IT is success that colours all in life :
Success makes fools admired, makes villains honest :
All the proud virtue of this vaunting world
Fawns on success and power, howe'er acquired.—*Thomson*

CROSSES IN LIFE.

MANY, many are the ups and downs in life. Fortune must be uncommonly gracious to that mortal who does not experience a great
variety of them ; though, perhaps, to these may be owing as much of
our pleasures as our pains. There are scenes of delight in the vale as
well as in the mountain ; and the inequalities of nature may not be
less necessary to please the eye, than the varieties of life to improve
the heart. At best we are but a short-sighted race of beings, with
just light enough to discern our way. To do that is our duty, and
should be our care ; when a man has done this, he is safe, the rest is
of little consequence—

" Cover his head with a turf or a stone,
It is all one, it is all one ! "—*Sterne's Letters.*

CONTRASTS IN LIFE.

THINGS are carried on in this world, sometimes so contrary to all
our reasonings, and the seeming probability of success, that even the

---

* The words between inverted commas in the above are the first line of a well-
known passage in Pope's translation of Homer :—

" Like leaves on trees the race of man is found,
Now green in youth, now withering on the ground ;
Another race the following spring supplies,
They fall successive, and successive rise :
So generations in their course decay ;
So flourish these, when those have passed away."

race is not to the swift, nor the battle to the strong; nay, what is
stranger still, nor yet bread to the wise, who should least stand in need
of it,—nor yet riches to the men of understanding, whom you would
think best qualified to acquire them,—nor yet favour to men of skill,
whose merit and pretences bid the fairest for it ; but that there are
some secret and unseen workings in human affairs, which baffle all
our endeavours, and turn aside the course of things in such a manner,
that the most likely causes disappoint and fail of producing for us the
effects which we wish, and naturally expected from them.—*Sterne.*

LIFE TO BE ENJOYED.

DRINK and be glad: to-morrow what may be,
Or what hereafter, none of us can see.
Haste not nor fret: but now as well's you may,
Feast and be merry ; freely give away.
Remember joys can last but with the breath,
And think how short a space parts life and death :
An instant ; seize what good may now befall;
Dead, thou hast nothing, and another all.
                    From the Greek (Anon.).

To die is due by all: no mortal knows
Whether to-morrow's dawn his life may close.
Knowing this well, O man, let cheering wine,
That sweet forgetfulness of death, be thine.
Give way to love too: live from day to day,
And yield to fate o'er all things else the sway.
                    Palladas.

VICISSITUDES OF LIFE.

THERE is no condition in life so fixed and permanent as to be out
of danger, or the reach of change ; and we all may depend upon it,
that we shall take our turns of wanting and desiring. By how many
unforeseen causes may riches take wing ! The crowns of princes may
be shaken, and the greatest that ever awed the world have experienced
what the turn of the wheel can do. That which hath happened to one
man may befall another. Time and chance happen to all; and the
most affluent may be stripped of all, and find his worldly comforts, like
so many withered leaves, dropping from him.—*Sterne.*

EQUANIMITY.

TOSSED on a sea of troubles, Soul, my Soul,
    Thyself do thou control;
And to the weapons of advancing foes
    A stubborn breast oppose ;
Undaunted 'mid the might
Of squadrons burning for the fight

Thine be no boasting when the victor's crown
Wins thee deserved renown ;
Thine no dejected sorrow, when defeat
Would urge a base retreat :
Rejoice in joyous things—not overmuch
Let grief thy bosom touch
'Midst evil ; and still bear in mind,
How changeful are the ways of womankind.
Archilochus, B.C. 687.

To look on life with placid eye,
And neither fear nor wish to die.—*Martial.*

THE RIVULET.

[THIS fine passage from Shelley's "Alastor ; or, the Spirit of Soli-
tude," has been much admired. The alliteration in the first four lines
is peculiarly happy and appropriate.]
The rivulet,
Wanton and wild, through many a green ravine
Beneath the forest flowed. Sometimes it fell
Among the moss with hollow harmony,
Dark and profound. Now on the polished stones
It danced, like childhood, laughing as it went ;
Then through the plain in tranquil wanderings crept,
Reflecting every herb and drooping bud
That overhung its quietness.

TIME.

TIME travels in divers paces with divers persons. I'll tell you who
Time ambles withal, who Time trots withal, who Time gallops withal,
and who he stands still withal. Marry, he trots hard with a young
maid between the contract of her marriage and the day it is solemnized :
if the interim be but a se'nnight, Time's pace is so hard that it seems
the length of seven years. He ambles withal with a priest that lacks
Latin, and the rich man that hath not the gout : for the one sleeps
easily, because he cannot study ; and the other lives merrily, because
he feels no pain. The one lacking the burden of lean and wasteful
learning ; the other knowing no burden of heavy tedious penury : these
Time ambles withal. He gallops withal with a thief to the gallows ;
for though he go as softly as foot can fall, he thinks himself too soon
there. He stays withal, with lawyers in the vacation : for they sleep
between term and term, and then they perceive not how time moves.—
Shakspeare.

Time wastes too fast : every letter I trace tells me with what rapidity
life follows my pen. The days and hours of it,—-more precious, my dear
Jenny, than the rubies about thy neck,—are flying over our heads like
light clouds of a windy day, never to return more. Everything presses
on. While thou art twisting that lock, see ! it grows grey ; and every

time I kiss thy hand to bid adieu, and every absence which follows it, are preludes to that eternal separation which we are shortly to make. *—Sterne.*

Time is painted with a lock before, and bald behind; signifying thereby that we must take time (as we say) by the forelock, for when it is once passed there is no recalling it.*—Swift.*

MAN.

That heavenly ray
He Reason calls, and uses so that he
Grows the most brutish of the brutes to be ;
And—by your grace's leave—appears to me
Like to those long-legged grasshoppers that pass
A short-lived flight upon the wing,
But quickly fall again to sing
The same old song amid the grass !*—Goethe's Faust.*

Beautiful !
How beautiful is all this visible world !
How glorious in its action and itself !
But we, who deem ourselves its sovereigns,—we,
Half-dust, half-deity, alike unfit
To sink or soar,—with our mixed essence make
A conflict of its elements, and breathe
The breath of degradation and of pride,
Contending with low wants and lofty will,
Till our mortality predominates,
And men are—what they name not to themselves,
And trust not to each other.*—Byron's Manfred.*

O God, what is man?—Even a thing of naught ; a poor, infirm, miserable, short-lived creature, that passes away like a shadow, and is hastening off the stage where the theatrical titles and distinctions, and the whole mask of pride which he has worn for a day will fall off, and leave him naked as a neglected slave.*—Sterne.*

MEMORY AND FORGETFULNESS.

[Themistocles, when Simonides proposed to teach him mnemonics, or the art of memory, observed that he would rather learn the art of forgetfulness.]

Memory, and thou, Forgetfulness, all hail !
Each in her province greatly may avail.
Memory, of all things good remind us still :
Forgetfulness, obliterate all that's ill.*—Macedonius.*

EDUCATION.

I CONSIDER the human soul without education like marble in the quarry, which shows none of its inherent beauties till the skill of the polisher fetches out the colours, makes the surface shine, and discovers every ornamental cloud, spot, and vein that runs through the body of it. Education, after the same manner, when it works upon a noble mind, draws out to view every latent virtue and perfection, which without such help are never able to make their appearance.— *Addison.*

MAXIMS FROM "POOR RICHARD'S ALMANACK."

LET honesty and industry be thy constant companions, and spend one penny less than thy clear gains. Then shall thy hide-bound pocket soon begin to thrive, and will never again cry with the empty bellyache; neither will creditors insult thee, nor nakedness freeze thee. The whole hemisphere will shine brighter, and pleasure spring up in every corner of thy heart. Now, therefore, embrace these rules and be happy. Banish the bleak winds of sorrow from thy mind, and live independent. Then shalt thou be a man, and not hide thy face at the approach of the rich, nor suffer the pain of feeling little when the sons of fortune walk at thy right hand; for independency, whether with little or much, is good fortune, and places thee on even ground with the proudest of the golden fleece. Oh, then, be wise, and let industry walk with thee in the morning, and attend thee until thou reachest the evening hour for rest. Let honesty be as the breath of thy soul, and never forget to have a penny whenever thy expenses are enumerated and paid: then shalt thou reach the point of happiness, and independence shall be thy shield and buckler, thy helmet and crown; then shall thy soul walk upright, nor stoop to the silken wretch because he hath riches, nor pocket an abuse because the hand which offers it wears a ring set with diamonds.

Remember that money is of a prolific generating nature. Money can beget money, and its offspring can beget more, and so on. Five shillings turned is six; turned again it is seven and three pence; and so on till it becomes a hundred pounds. The more there is of it, the more it produces every turning, so that the profits rise quicker and quicker. He that kills a breeding sow, destroys all her offspring to the thousandth generation. He that murders a crown, destroys all that it might have produced, even scores of pounds.

Three removes are as bad as a fire; and keep thy shop, and thy shop will keep thee; and again, if you would have your business done, go; if not, send. Again,—

" He that by the plough would thrive,
Himself must either hold or drive."

And again, the eye of the master will do more work than both his hands; and again, want of care does us more damage than want of knowledge; and again, not to oversee workmen is to leave them your purse open.

Pride is as loud a beggar as want, and a great deal more saucy. When you have bought one fine thing, you must buy ten more, that your appearance may be all of a piece; but it is easier to suppress the first desire than to satisfy all that follow it.

He that hath a trade, hath an estate, and he that hath a calling, hath an office of profit and honour; but then the trade must be worked at, and the calling well followed, or neither the estate nor the office will enable us to pay our taxes.

A little neglect may breed great mischief. For want of a nail the shoe was lost; for want of shoe the horse was lost; and for want of a horse the rider was lost, being overtaken and slain by the enemy—all for want of care about a horse-shoe nail.

Remember that time is money. He that can earn ten shillings a day by his labour, and goes abroad or sits idle one half of that day, though he spends but sixpence during his diversion and idleness, ought not to reckon that the only expense, he has really spent, or rather thrown away, five shillings besides.

Leisure is time for doing something useful; this leisure the diligent man will obtain, but the lazy man never; so that, as Poor Richard says, a life of leisure and a life of laziness are two things.—*Franklin.*

LACONICS FROM GOETHE.

THE hope of bringing back old happy days burns up again in us, as if it never could be extinguished.

There are but few men who care to occupy themselves with the immediate past. Either we are forcibly bound up in the present, or we lose ourselves in the long gone by, and seek back for what is utterly lost; as if it were possible to summon it up again and rehabilitate it.

As the emerald refreshes the sight with its beautiful hues, and exerts, it is said, a beneficent influence on that noble sense, so does human beauty work with far larger potency on the outward than on the inward sense; whoever looks upon it is charmed against the breath of evil, and feels in harmony with himself and the world.

Sweet sleep, like pure joy, thou comest most readily unasked, un-prayed for! Thou loosest the knot of troubled thoughts, and from before thee flee all the images of woe and sadness. The circle of inward harmonies rolls on undisturbed, and, hidden in pleasing delusion, we lose ourselves, and cease to be.

We may imagine ourselves in what situation we please, we always conceive ourselves seeing. I believe men only dream that they may not cease to see. Some day, perhaps, the inner light may come out from within us, and we shall not any more require another.

The year dies away, the wind sweeps over the stubble, and there is nothing left to stir it under its touch. But the red berries on yonder tall tree seem as if they would still remind us of brighter things; and the stroke of the thrasher's flail awakes the thought, how much of nourishment and life lies buried in the sickled ear.

Observe a young lady as a lover, as a bride, as a housewife, as a mother. She always stands isolated. She is always alone. Even the most empty-headed woman is in the same case. Each one of them excludes all the others. It is her nature to do so, because of each one of them is required what the entire sex have to do. With a man it is altogether different. But a woman might live to an eternity, without even so much as producing a duplicate of herself.

FROM THE PERSIAN FABLES.

A LITTLE boy went one day into a river, and not having learned to swim, had like to have been drowned. Seeing, however, a man at a distance, he called out to him for help. The man, as soon as he saw the lad's distress, began to expostulate with him on the folly of going into a river before he had learned to swim. The boy, instead of answering him, cried out, " Save me, save me, then chide as long as you will."—*Lokman.*

The goose and the swallow entered into a league of friendship, and resolved to live together. In the course of their wanderings, they came unluckily to a place where the fowlers were watching. The swallow, as soon as she saw them, flew away ; but the poor goose, not being able to make use of her wings, was taken and killed."—*Ibid.*

One day as I was in the bath, a friend of mine put into my hand a piece of scented clay. I took it, and said to it, " Art thou musk or ambergris, for I am charmed with thy perfume !" It answered, " I was a despicable piece of clay, but I was some time in the company of the rose ; the sweet quality of my companion was communicated to me, otherwise I should only be a bit of clay, as I appear to be."—*Sadi.*

PLEASURES OF OBSERVATION AND STUDY.

WHAT a large volume of adventures may be grasped within the little span of life, by him who interests his heart in everything ; and who, having eyes to see what time and chance are perpetually holding out to him as he journeyeth on his way, misses nothing he can fairly lay his hands on ! If this won't turn out something, another will. No matter ; 'tis an essay upon human nature ; I get my labours for my pains,—'tis enough ; the pleasure of the experiment has kept my senses and the best part of my blood awake, and laid the gross to sleep. I pity the man who can travel from Dan to Beersheba, and cry, 'Tis all barren ! And so it is ; and so is all the world to him who will not cultivate the fruit it offers. I declare, that were I in a desert, I would find out wherewith in it to call forth my affections. If I could do no better, I would fasten them upon some sweet myrtle, or seek some melancholy cypress to connect myself to ; I would court their shade, and greet them kindly for their protection. I would cut my name upon them, and swear they were the loveliest trees throughout the desert. If their leaves withered, I would teach myself to mourn ; and when they rejoiced, I would rejoice with them.—*Sterne's Sentimental Journey.*

SANCHO'S IDEAS OF SLEEP.

I ONLY know that while I'm asleep I have neither fear nor hope, nor trouble nor glory. Blessings light on him who first invented sleep ! It covers a man all over, body and soul, like a cloak ; it is meat to the hungry, drink to the thirsty, heat to the cold, and cold to the hot. It is the coin that can purchase all things, the balance that makes the shepherd equal with the king, the fool with the wise man. It has only one fault, as I have heard say,—which is that it looks very like death ; for between the sleeper and the corpse there is but little to choose.— *Don Quixote.*

BOOKS.

IT is chiefly through books that we enjoy intercourse with superior minds ; and these invaluable means of communication are in the reach of all. In the best books great men talk to us, give us their most precious thoughts, and pour their souls into ours. God be thanked for books ! They are the voices of the distant and the dead, and make us heirs of the spiritual life of past ages. Books are the true levellers. They give to all, who will faithfully use them, the society, the spiritual presence, of the best and greatest of our race.—*W. E. Channing.*

He who loves not books before he comes to thirty years of age, will hardly love them enough afterwards to understand them.—*Clarendon.*

A good book is the precious life-blood of a master-spirit, embalmed and treasured up to a life beyond life.—*Milton.*

To divert at any time a troublesome fancy, run to thy books ; they presently fix thee to them, and drive the other out of thy thoughts. They always receive thee with the same kindness.—*Fuller.*

> Books are yours,
> Within whose silent chambers treasure lies,
> Preserved from age to age, more precious far
> Than that accumulated store of gold
> And orient gems, which, for a day of need,
> The sultan hides in his ancestral tombs.
> These hoards of sweets you can unlock at will
> And music waits upon your skilful touch.—*Wordsworth.*

> How differently do mental pleasures
>   Lead us from book to book to roam
> And ever, with these ancient treasures,
>   How cheerful winter nights become !

A happy life grows warm in every limb;
And if a precious parchment you unroll,
Your senses in delight appear to swim,
And heaven itself descends upon your soul.
Goethe's Faust.

Books are faithful repositories, which may be awhile neglected or forgotten ; but when they are opened again, will again impart their instruction.—*Johnson.*

Books are a part of man's prerogative:
In formal ink, they thought and voices hold;
Then we to them our solitude may give,
And make time travel as of old.
Our life, Fame pieceth longer at the end,
And books it farther backward do extend.
Sir T Overbury.

Books give
New views to life, and teach us how to live ;
They soothe the grieved, the stubborn they chastise,
Fools they admonish, and confirm the wise.—*Crabbe.*

THE CONSOLATIONS OF LITERATURE.

I FIND my joy and solace in literature. There is no gladness that this cannot increase ; no sorrow that it cannot lessen. Troubled as I am by the ill health of my wife, by the dangerous condition—sometimes, alas ! by the death—of my friends, I fly to my studies as the one alleviation of my fears. They do me this service—they make me understand my troubles better, and bear them more patiently. Certainly there is a pleasure in these pursuits, but they themselves prosper best when the mind is light.—*Pliny.*

Experience enables me to depone to the comfort and blessing that literature can prove in seasons of sickness and sorrow ; how powerfully intellectual pursuits can help in keeping the head from crazing and the heart from breaking.—*Thomas Hood.*

PURSUITS OF LITERATURE.

SUCH a superiority do the pursuits of literature possess above every other occupation, that even he who attains but a mediocrity in them, merits the pre-eminence above those that excel most in the common and vulgar professions.—*Hume.*

GIVING ADVICE.

No part of conduct asks for skill more nice,
Though none more common, than to give advice ;
Misers themselves in this will not be saving,
Unless their knowledge makes it worth the having :
And where's the wonder ? When we will obtrude
A useless gift, it meets ingratitude.—*Stillingfleet.*

I

The most difficult province in friendship is the letting a man see his faults and errors; which should, if possible, be so contrived that he may perceive our advice is given him, not so much to please ourselves, as for his own advantage. The reproaches, therefore, of a friend should always be strictly just and not too frequent.—*Budgell.*

THE GENERAL SUBJUGATOR.

A PAIR of bright eyes, with a dozen glances, suffice to subdue a man, to enslave him, and to inflame him, to make him even forget. They dazzle him so that the past becomes straightway dim to him, and he so prizes them that he would give all his life to possess 'em. What is the fond love of the dearest friends compared to this treasure? Is memory as strong as expectancy? fruition as hunger? gratitude as desire? I have looked at royal diamonds in the jewel rooms in Europe, and thought how wars have been made about 'em; Mogul sovereigns deposed and strangled for them, or ransomed with them; and daring lives lost in digging out the little shiny toys, that I value no more than the button in my hat. And so there are other glittering baubles (of rare water, too) for which men have been set to kill and quarrel ever since mankind began, and which last for a score of years, when their sparkle is over. Where are those jewels now that beamed under Cleopatra's forehead, or shone in the sockets of Helen?— *Thackeray's Esmond.*

MUTABILITY.

THE flower that smiles to-day
    To-morrow dies;
All that we wish to stay
    Tempts, and then flies.
What is this world's delight?
Lightning, that mocks the night,
Brief, even as bright!

Virtue, how frail it is!
    Friendship, too rare!
Love, how it sells poor bliss
    For proud despair!
But we, though soon they fall,
Survive their joy, and all
Which ours we call.

Whilst skies are blue and bright,
    Whilst flowers are gay,
Whilst eyes that change ere night
    Make glad the day;
Whilst yet the calm hours creep,
Dream thou,—and from thy sleep
Then wake to weep.—*Shelley.*

PRECEPT AND EXAMPLE.

THOUGH "the words of the wise be as nayles fastened by the masters of the assemblies," yet sure their examples are the hammer to drive them in to take the deeper hold. A father that whipt his son for swearing, and swore himself while he whipt him, did more harm by his example than good by his correction.—*Fuller.*

NEW ACQUAINTANCES.

IF a man does not make new acquaintances as he advances in life, he will soon find himself alone. A man should keep his friendship in constant repair.—*Johnson.*

LAUGHTER.

NO man who has once heartily and wholly laughed can be altogether irreclaimably bad. How much lies in laughter—the cipher key wherewith we decipher the whole man ! Some men wear an everlasting barren simper ; in the smile of others lies a cold glitter as of ice ; the fewest are able to laugh what can be called laughing, but only sniff, and titter, and snigger, and titter, from the throat outwards, or at best produce some whiffling husky cachinnation, as if they were laughing through wool ; of none such comes good. The man who cannot laugh is not only fit for treasons, stratagems, and spoils, but his whole life is already a treason and a stratagem.—*Carlyle.*

OCCUPATIONS IN RETIREMENT.

LET our station be as retired as it may, there is no want of playthings, and associations, nor much need to seek them in this world of ours. Business, or what presents itself to us under that imposing character, will find us out, even in the stillest retreat, as a just demand upon our attention. It is wonderful how, by means of such real or seeming necessities, my time is stolen away. I have just time to observe that time is short, and by the time I have made the observation, time is gone.—*Cowper's Letters.*

DREAMS.

DREAMS are but interludes which Fancy makes :
When monarch Reason sleeps, this mimic wakes ;
Compounds a medley of disjointed things,
A court of cobblers, and a mob of kings.
Light fumes are merry, grosser fumes are sad :
Both are the unreasonable soul run mad ;
And many monstrous forms in sleep we see,
That neither were, nor are, nor e'er can be.
Sometimes forgotten things, long cast behind,
Rush forward in the brain, and come to mind.

The nurse's legends are for truth received,
And the man dreams but what the boy believed ;
Sometimes we but rehearse a former play,
The night restores our actions done by day ;
As hounds in sleep will open for their prey.
In short, the farce of dreams is of a piece
In chimeras all, and more absurd or less.

Dryden : Chaucer.

HUMAN FRAILTY.

THE best of men appear sometimes to be strange compounds of contradictory qualities ; and were the accidental oversights and folly of
the wisest man,—the failings and imperfections of a religious man,—
the hasty acts and passionate words of a meek man,—were they to rise
up in judgment against them, and an ill-natured judge to be suffered
to mark in this manner what has been done amiss, what character so
unexceptionable as to be able to stand before him ?—*Sterne.*

POOR SCHOLARS.

IT is but too often the fate of scholars to be servile and poor.   Many
of them are driven to hard shifts, and turn from grasshoppers into
humble bees, from humble bees into wasps, and from wasps into parasites, making the Muses their mules to satisfy their hunger-starved
paunches, and get a meal's meat ; their abilities and knowledge only
serving them to curse their fooleries with better grace.   They have
store of gold, without knowing how to turn it to advantage ; and, like
the innocent Indians, are drained of their riches without receiving a
suitable reward.—*Burton.*

MARRIED LIFE.

THE treasures of the deep are not so precious
As are the concealed comforts of a man
Locked up in woman's love.   I scent the air
Of blessings when I come but near the house.
What a delicious breath marriage sends forth !
The violet bed's not sweeter.   Honest wedlock
Is like a banqueting house built in a garden,
On which the spring's chaste flowers take delight
To cast their modest odours ; when base lust,
With all her powders, paintings, and best pride,
Is but a fair house built by a ditch side.—*Thos. Middleton.*

Have you ever seen pure rose-water kept in a crystal glass ?   How fine
it looks, how sweet it smells, while the beautiful urn imprisons it !
Break the glass, and let the water take its own course : doth it not
embrace dust, and lose all its former sweetness and fairness ?   Truly

so are we, if we have not the stay rather than the restraint of marriage.—*Sir P. Sidney.*

> Though fools spurn Hymen's gentle powers,
> We, who improve its golden hours,
> By sweet experience know
> That marriage, rightly understood,
> Gives to the tender and the good
> A paradise below.—*Cotton.*

> Yet wedlock's a very awful thing !
> 'Tis something like that feat in the ring,
> Which requires good nerve to do it—
> When one of a " Grand Equestrian Troupe "
> Makes a jump at a gilded hoop,
> Not certain at all
> What may befall
> After his getting through it !—*Hood.*

> Wha weds for siller, weds for care ;
> Wha weds for beauty, weds nae mair ;
> But he that weds them baith thegither,
> Content wi' ane, enjoys the ither.

> Though wedlock by most men be reckoned a curse,
> Three wives did I marry, for better for worse :
> The first for her person, the next for her purse,
> The third for a warming-pan, doctor, and nurse.

THE BRIDE.

I KNOW no sight more charming and touching than that of a young and timid bride, in her robes of virgin white, led up trembling to the altar. When I thus behold a lovely girl, in the tenderness of her years, forsaking the house of her fathers and the home of her childhood, and, with implicit confidence and the sweet self-abandonment which belong to woman, giving up all the world for the man of her choice,— when I hear her, in the good old language of the ritual, yielding herself to him " for better for worse, for richer for poorer, in sickness and in health, to love, honour, and obey, till death us do part,"—it brings to mind the beautiful and affecting devotion of Ruth : " Whither thou goest I will go, and where thou lodgest I will lodge ; thy people shall be my people, and thy God my God."—*Washington Irving.*

LOVE.

> LOVE was made to soothe and share
> The ills that wait our mortal birth ;
> Love was made to teach us where
> One trace of Eden haunts our earth.

Timid as the tale of woe ;
 Tender as the wood-dove's sigh ;
 Lovely as the flowers below ;
 Changeless as the stars on high.—*L. E. Landon.*

A MOTHER'S LOVE.

IF there be one thing pure,
 When all beside is sullied ;
That can endure
 When all else pass away ;
 If there be aught
Surpassing human deed, or word, or thought,—
 It is a mother's love !

MEMORY.

O MEMORY ! thou fond deceiver!
 Still importunate and vain ;
To former joys recurring ever,
 And turning all the past to pain ;
Thou, like the world, the oppressed oppressing,
 Thy smiles increase the wretch's woe ;
And he who wants each other blessing,
 In thee must ever find a foe.—*Goldsmith.*

BRITISH FREEDOM.

IT is not to be thought that the flood
Of British Freedom, which to the open sea
Of the world's praise from dark antiquity
Hath flowed, " with pomp of water unwithstood,"
Roused though it be full often to a mood
Which spurns the check of salutary bands,
That this most furious stream in bogs and sands
Should perish, and to evil and to good
Be lost for ever.   In our halls is hung
Armoury of the invincible knights of old ;
We must be free or die, who speak the tongue
That Shakspeare spake, the faith and morals hold
Which Milton held.   In everything we are sprung
Of earth's first blood, have titles manifold.—*Wordsworth.*

THE HUMAN SEASONS.

FOUR seasons fill the measure of the year ;
There are four seasons in the mind of man :
He has his lusty Spring, when fancy clear
Takes in all beauty with an easy span ;

He has his Summer, when luxuriously
Spring's honied cud of youthful thought he loves
To ruminate, and by such dreaming high
Is nearest unto heaven ; quiet coves
His soul has in its Autumn, when his wings
He furleth close ; contented so to look
On mists in idleness—to let fair things
Pass by unheeded as a threshold brook.
He has his Winter too, of pale misfeature,
Or else he would forego his mortal nature.—*Keats.*

GREEK EPIGRAMS.

FATHER of flatterers, GOLD, of pain and care begot,
A fear it is to have thee, and a pain to have thee not—*Palladus*

Grey hairs are wisdom—if you hold your tongue :
Speak, and they are but hairs, as in the young.—*Philo.*

The *happy* think a lifetime a short stage :
One night to the *unhappy* seems an age.—*Lucian.*

Slow-footed *Counsel* is most sure to gain ;
Rashness still brings repentance in her train.—*Ibid.*

FROM THE PERSIAN.

ON parent knees, a naked new-born child,
Weeping thou sat'st, when all around thee smiled ;
So live that, sinking in thy last long sleep,
Calm thou may'st smile, while all around thee weep.

What boots it to repeat
How time is slipping underneath our feet ?
Un-born To-morrow, and dead Yesterday,
Why fret about them if To-day be sweet?

HEALTH.

THE surest road to health, say what they will
Is never to suppose we shall be ill.
Most of those evils we poor mortals know,
From doctors and imagination flow.—*Churchill.*

OLD AGE AND DEATH.

THE seas are quiet when the winds give o'er ;
So calm are we when passions are no more :
For then we know how vain it was to boast
Of fleeting things too certain to be lost.

Clouds of affection from our younger eyes
Conceal that emptiness which age descries.
The soul's dark cottage, battered and decayed,
Lets in new light through chinks that time has made ;
Stronger by weakness, wiser men become,
As they draw near to their eternal home.
Leaving the old, both worlds at once they view,
That stand upon the threshold of the new.—*Waller.*

OF TREASON.

TREASON doth never prosper ; what's the reason?
For if it prosper, none dare call it treason.—*Sir J. Harrington.*

OF FORTUNE.

FORTUNE, men say, doth give too much to many,
But yet she never gave enough to any.—*Ibid.*

THE WORLD'S HUZZA.

I HAVE seen too much of success in life to take off my hat and huzza
to it as it passes by in its gilt coach, and would do my little part with
my neighbours on foot that they should not gape with too much
wonder, nor applaud too loudly. Is it the Lord Mayor going in state
to mince pies and the Mansion House ? Is it poor Jack of Newgate's
procession, with the sheriff and javelin-men conducting him on his
last journey to Tyburn ? I look into my heart, and think I am as good
as my Lord Mayor, and as bad as Tyburn Jack. Give me a chain
and red gown and a pudding before me, and I could play the part of
alderman very well, and sentence Jack after dinner. Starve me, keep
me from books and honest people,—educate me to love dice, gin, and
pleasure, and put me on Hounslow Heath, with a purse before me, and
I will take it. "And I shall be deservedly hanged," say you, wishing
to put an end to this prosing. I don't say no ; I can't but accept
the world as I find it, including a rope as long as it is in fashion.—
Thackeray.

THE TRUE CONSOLER.

HE who doth not smoke hath either known no great griefs, or re-
fuseth himself the softest consolation next to that which comes from
heaven. "What, softer than woman?" whispers the young reader.
Young reader, woman teases as well as consoles. Woman makes half
the sorrows which she boasts the privilege to soothe. Woman consoles us, it is true, while we are young and handsome ; when we are
old and ugly, woman snubs and scolds us. On the whole, then, woman
in this scale, the weed in that,—Jupiter. hang out thy balance, and weigh

them both ; and if thou give the preference to woman, all I can say is, the next time Juno ruffles thee,—O Jupiter! try the weed.—*Lord Lytton's " What will he do with it ? "*

INSPIRATION FROM TOBACCO.

THE pungent, nose-refreshing weed,
Which, whether, pulverised, it gain
A speedy passage to the brain,
Or whether, touched with fire, it rise
In circling eddies to the skies,
Doth thought more quicken and refine
Than all the breath of all the Nine.—*Cowper.*

TOBACCO.

THE fact is, squire, the moment a man takes to a pipe, he becomes a philosopher ;—it's the poor man's friend ; it calms the mind, soothes the temper, and makes a man patient under difficulties. It has made more good men, good husbands, kind masters, indulgent fathers, than any other blessed thing on this universal earth.—*Sam Slick: The Clock-maker.*

ONE MAN'S LOSS, ANOTHER MAN'S GAIN.

DENADES, the Athenian, condemned a fellow-citizen who furnished out funerals, for demanding too great a price for his goods ; and if he got an estate, it must be by the death of a great many people : but I think it a sentence ill-grounded, forasmuch as no profit can be made but at the expense of some other person, and that every kind of gain is by that rule to be condemned. The tradesman thrives by the de-bauchery of youth, and the farmer by the dearness of corn ; the archi-tect by the ruin of buildings ; the officers of justice by quarrels and law-suits,—nay, even the honour and function of divines is owing to our mortality and vices. No physician takes pleasure in the health of even his best friends, said the ancient Greek comedian, nor soldier in the peace of his country, and so of the rest. And what is yet worse, let every one but examine his own heart, and he will find that his private wishes spring and grow up at the expense of some other person. Nature does not hereby deviate from her general policy, for the naturalist holds the birth, nourishment, and increase of any one thing, is the decay and corruption of another.—*Montaigne's Essays.*

MINUTE PHILOSOPHY: AN APOLOGUE.

ONE fine summer's evening an adventurous Bee was giving the history of his day's excursion to the assembled multitude before the door of the hive. " I soared so high," said he, " that I lost sight of the earth beneath me ; the flowers upon its surface were no longer visible." " Not that your flight was so extensive, but your sight is so narrow," interposed the Swallow ; " I saw you all the time, just above the furze on the common. Luckily for you I was not hungry."

Thus many things are pronounced *impossible* which are only *incomprehensive* to the speaker. Many subjects are said to be above human reason, which are only above the reason of the reasoner.

READING.

IDLENESS is a disease that must be combated, but I would not advise a rigid adherence to a particular plan of study. I myself have never persisted in any plan for two days together. A man ought to read just as inclination leads him ; for what he reads as a task will do him little good. A young man should read five hours in the day, and so may acquire a great deal of knowledge.—*Johnson.*

THE BEST WAY OF LIFE.

SILENUS was said to have taught, It is better either to have never been born, or immediately to die. This sentiment is embodied in the following verses which have been ascribed to Posidippus :—

> Which the best way of life ? The forum rings
> With bickering brawls; home, too, vexation brings ;
> Toil in the country, terror reigns at sea ;
> Abroad wealth trembles lest its goods may flee;
> And want is woe ; trouble, thy name is wife;
> A single is a solitary life :
> Children are cares; cheerless a childless state;
> Youth is but folly; weak a hoary pate.
> Since thus it is, a wise man still should cry,
> Ne'er to be born, or being born, to die.

The other side of the argument is maintained by Metrodorus :—

> Good all the ways of life : the forum rings
> With deeds of glorious enterprise ; home brings
> Sweet rest; the charms of nature clothe the fields;
> The sea brings gain ; abroad wealth honour yields;
> Want may be hid; comfort, thy name is wife ;
> A single is a free and easy life.
> Children are joys ; care shuns the childless bed ;
> Strength attends youth ; reverence the hoary head.
> Since thus it is, a wise man's choice should be,
> Both to be born, and born such good to see.

The above translations are both by Mr. Hay.

THE BEST AGE FOR MARRIAGE.

THE best time for marriage will be towards thirty, for as the younger times are unfit, either to choose or to govern a wife and family, so, if thou stay long, thou shalt hardly see the education of thy family, who being left to strangers, are in effect lost. And better were it to be unborn than ill-bred; for thereby thy posterity shall either perish, or remain a shame to thy name and family.—*Sir W Raleigh to his Son.*

> Let not passion's force so powerful be
> Over thy reason, soul, and liberty,
> As to ensnare thee to a wedded life
> Ere thou art able to maintain a wife.

CHEERFULNESS.

> WHO told man that he must be cursed on earth ?
>   The God of Nature ?   No such thing !
> Heaven whispered him the moment of his birth,
>   Don't cry, my lad, but dance and sing ;
> Don't be too wise, and be an ape ;
> In colours let the soul be dressed, not crape.
>
> Roses shall smoothe life's journey, and adorn ;
> Yet, mind me, if through want of grace,
> Thou mean'st to fling my blessing in my face,
> Thou hast full leave to tread upon a thorn.
>
> Yet some there are, of men I think the worst,
> Poor imps ! unhappy if they can't be curst ;
> For ever brooding over misery's eggs,
>   As though life's pleasures were a deadly sin,
>   Mousing for ever for a gin,
> To catch their happiness by the legs.
>   *Peter Pindar (Dr. Wolcot).*

HUMAN EVENTS.

HOW quick is the succession of human events !   The cares of to-day are seldom the cares of to-morrow ; and when we lie down at night, we may safely say to the most of our troubles, "Ye have done your worst, and we shall meet no more."—*Cowper's Letters.*

APOPHTHEGMS FROM BEN JONSON.

THERE are many that with more ease will find fault with what is spoken foolishly, than can give allowance to that wherein you are wise silently.

If we will look with our understanding, and not our senses, we may behold virtue and beauty (though covered with rags) in their brightness ; and vice and deformity so much the fouler, in having all the splendour of riches to gild them, or the false light of honour and power to help them.

No man is so foolish but may give another good counsel sometimes ; and no man is so wise but may easily err, if he will take no other's counsel but his own.

A man cannot imagine that thing so foolish, or rude, but will find or enjoy an admirer.

Ill-fortune never crushed that man whom good-fortune deceived not.

I am glad when I see any man above the infamy of a vice ; but to shun the vice itself were better.

Wisdom without honesty is mere craft and cozenage.

He knows not his own strength that hath not met adversity.

Be not ashamed of thy virtues ; honour's a good brooch to wear in a man's hat at all times.

LACONICS.

HASTE and rashness are storms and tempests, breaking and wrecking business ; but nimbleness is a full, fair wind, blowing it with speed to the haven.—*Fuller.*

Friendship is the only thing in the world concerning the usefulness of which all mankind are agreed.—*Cicero.*

He that cannot forgive others, breaks the bridge over which he must pass himself ; for every man had need to be forgiven.—*Lord Herbert.*

He that is a good man is three quarters of his way towards being a good Christian, wheresoever he lives, and whatsoever he is called.—*South.*

As thrashing separates the corn from the chaff, so does affliction purify virtue.—*Burton.*

The more honesty a man has, the less he affects the air of a saint ; the affectation of sanctity is a blotch on the face of piety.—*Lavater.*

The person whose clothes are extremely fine I am too apt to consider as not being possessed of any superiority of fortune, but resembling those Indians who are found to wear all the gold they have in the world in a bob at the nose.—*Goldsmith.*

False friendship, like the ivy, decays and ruins the walls it embraces ; but true friendship gives new life and animation to the object it supports.—*Burton.*

Affections, like the conscience, are rather to be led than drawn ; and 'tis to be feared, they that marry where they do not love, will love where they do not marry.—*Fuller.*

As amber attracts a straw, so does beauty admiration, which only lasts while the warmth continues ; but virtue, wisdom, goodness, and real worth, like the loadstone, never lose their power. These are the true graces, which, as Homer feigns, are linked and tied hand and hand, because it is by their influence that human hearts are so firmly united to each other.—*Burton.*

Remember that if thou marry for beauty, thou bindest thyself all thy life for that which perchance will neither last nor please thee one year ; and when thou hast it, it will be to thee of no price at all, for the desire dieth when it is attained, and the affection perisheth when it is satisfied.—*Sir W Raleigh to his Son.*

Marriage is a desperate thing. The frogs in Æsop were extremely wise : they had a great mind to some water, but they would not leap into the well because they could not get out again.—*Selden.*

There is not so poor a book in the world that would not be a prodigious effort, were it wrought out entirely by a single mind, without the aid of prior investigation.—*Johnson.*

Prudent men lock up their motives, letting familiars have a key to their heart, as to their garden.—*Shenstone.*

He is rich whose income is more than his expenses ; and he is poor whose expenses exceed his income.—*Bruyère.*

No man is the wiser for his learning : it may administer matter to work in, or objects to work upon ; but wit and wisdom are born with a man.—*Selden.*

Fools are often united in the strictest intimacies, as lighter kinds of wood are the most closely glued together.—*Shenstone.*

He who seldom speaks, and with one calm, well-timed word can strike dumb the loquacious, is a genius or a hero.—*Lavater.*

As I approve of a youth that has something of the old man in him, so I am no less pleased with an old man that has something of the youth. He that follows this rule may be old in body, but can never be so in mind.—*Cicero.*

There is nothing so bad which will not admit of something to be said in its defence.—*Sterne.*

Such is the encouragement given to flattery in the present times, that it is made to sit in the parlour, while honesty is turned out of doors. Flattery is never so agreeable as to our blind side ; commend a fool for his wit, or a knave for his honesty, and they will receive you into their bosom.—*Fielding.*

There appears to exist a greater desire to live long than to live well. Measure by man's desires, he cannot live long enough ; measure by his good deeds, and he has not lived long enough ; measure by his evil deeds, and he has lived too long.—*Zimmerman.*

A man's genius is always, in the beginning of life, as much unknown to himself as to others ; and it is only after frequent trials, attended with success, that he dares think himself equal to those undertakings in which those who have succeeded have fixed the admiration of mankind.—*Hume.*

Pride may be allowed to this or that degree, else a man cannot keep up his dignity. In gluttony there must be eating, in drunkenness there must be drinking ; 'tis not the eating, nor 'tis not the drinking, that must be blamed, but the excess. So in pride.—*Selden.*

The premeditation of death is the premeditation of liberty ; he who has learned to die has forgot to serve.—*Montaigne.*

Long and curious speeches are as fit for despatch as a robe or mantle with a long train is for a race. Prefaces, and passages, and excusations, and other speeches of reference to the person, are great wastes of time ; and though they seem to proceed of modesty they are bravery.—*Lord Bacon.*

Base is their nature who will not have their branches lopped till their bodies be felled ; and will let go none of their goods, as if it presaged their speedy death ; whereas it does not follow that he that puts off his cloak must presently go to bed.—*Fuller.*

Worldly wealth is a devil's bait ; and those whose minds feed upon riches, recede, in general, from real happiness in proportion as their stores increase ; as the moon when she is fullest of light is farthest from the sun.—*Burton.*

There are but three classes of men : the retrograde, the stationary, and the progressive.—*Lavater.*

So far is it from being true that men are naturally equal, that no two people can be half an hour together but one shall acquire an evident superiority over the other.—*Johnson.*

Good counsels observed are chains to grace, which, neglected, prove halters to strange undutiful children.—*Fuller.*

Mankind have a great aversion to intellectual labour, but even supposing knowledge to be easily attainable, more people would be content to be ignorant than would take even a little trouble to acquire it.—*Johnson.*

There are four good mothers, of whom are often born four unhappy daughters ; truth begets hatred, happiness pride, security danger, and familiarity contempt.—*Steele.*

You may depend upon it that he is a good man whose intimate friends are all good, and whose enemies are characters decidedly bad. —*Lavater.*

There is scarce any lot so low, but there is something in it to satisfy the man whom it has befallen ; Providence having so ordered things, that in every man's cup, how bitter soever, there are some cordial drops—some good circumstances, which, if wisely extracted, are sufficient for the purpose he wants them,—that is to make him contented, and if not happy, at least resigned.—*Sterne.*

The superiority of some men is merely local. They are great, because their associates are little.—*Johnson.*

The greatest part of mankind employ their first years to make their last miserable.—*Bruyère.*

A joker is near akin to a buffoon ; and neither of them is the least akin to a wit.—*Chesterfield.*

When all is done, human life is, at the greatest and the best, but like a forward child, that must be played with and humoured a little to keep it quiet, till it falls asleep, and then the care is over.—*Sir W Temple.*

A man who has taken his ideas of mankind from study alone, generally comes into the world with a heart melting at every fictitious distress. Thus he is induced by misplaced liberality to put himself into the indigent circumstances of the person he relieves.—*Goldsmith.*

We are a restless set of beings ; and, as we are likely to continue so to the end of the world, the best we can do in it is to make the same use of this part of our character which wise men do of other bad propensities : when they find they cannot conquer them, they endeavour, at least, to divert them into good channels.—*Sterne.*

Those who in consequence of superior capacities and attainments, disregard the common maxims of life, ought to be reminded that nothing will supply the want of prudence ; and that negligence and irregularity, long continued, will make knowledge useless, wit ridiculous, and genius contemptible.—*Johnson.*

A man cannot possess anything that is better than a good woman, nor anything that is worse than a bad one.—*Simonides.*

Some men are more beholden to their bitterest enemies than to friends who appear to be sweetness itself. The former frequently tell the truth, but the latter never.—*Cato.*

Those beings only are fit for solitude who like nobody, are like nobody, and are liked by nobody.—*Zimmerman.*

Old friends are best. King James used to call for his old shoes ; they were easiest for his feet.—*Selden.*

To be happy, the passion must be cheerful and gay, not gloomy and melancholy. A propensity to hope and joy is real riches ; one to fear and sorrow, real poverty. — *Hume.*

As a man's salutation, so is the total of his character ; in nothing do we lay ourselves so open, as in our manner of meeting and salutation.—*Lavater.*

A contented mind is the greatest blessing a man can enjoy in this world ; and if in the present life his happiness arises from the subduing of his desires, it will arise in the next from the gratification of them.—*Addison.*

It is sweet to feel by what fine-spun threads our affections are drawn together.—*Sterne.*

I asked a poor man how he did ? He said he was like a washball, always in decay.—*Swift.*

Love covers a multitude of sins. It is like the painter, who, being to draw the picture of a friend having a blemish in one eye, would picture only the other side of his face.—*South.*

He is happy whose circumstances suit his temper ; but he is more excellent whose temper suits his circumstances.—*Hume.*

The roses of pleasure seldom last long enough to adorn the brow of him who plucks them, and they are the only roses which do not retain their sweetness after they have lost their beauty.—*Blair.*

Look not mournfully into the past. It comes not back again. Wisely improve the present. It is thine. Go forth to meet the shadowy future, without fear, and with a manly heart.—*Longfellow.*

Good breeding is the result of much good sense, some good nature, and a little self-denial for the sake of others, and with a view to obtain the same indulgence from them.—*Chesterfield.*

When a man writes from his own mind, he writes very rapidly : the greatest part of a writer's time is spent in reading, in order to write ; a man will turn over half a library to make one book.—*Johnson.*

I look upon indolence as a sort of suicide ; for the man is efficiently destroyed, though the appetite of the brute may survive.—*Chesterfield.*

The first ingredient in conversation is truth, the next good sense, the third good humour, and the fourth wit.—*Sir W Temple.*

A man who hath no virtue in himself ever envieth virtue in others ; for men's minds will either feed upon their own good, or upon other's evil ; and who wanteth the one, will prey upon the other.—*Bacon.*

All other knowledge is hurtful to him who has not the science of honesty and good-nature.—*Montaigne.*

One principal point of good-breeding is to suit our behaviour to the three several degrees of men ; our superiors, our equals, and our inferiors.—*Swift.*

Hypocrisy is a sort of homage that vice pays to virtue.—*Fuller.*

Time, with all its celerity, moves slowly on to him whose whole employment is to watch its flight.—*Johnson.*

"A fool and his words are soon parted," for so should the proverb run.—*Shenstone.*

All affectation is the vain and ridiculous attempt of poverty to appear rich.—*Lavater.*

What is birth to a man, if it shall be a stain to his dead ancestors to have left such offspring ?—*Sir P. Sidney.*

Philosophers that are poor praise poverty because they are gainers by its effects ; and the opulent Seneca himself has written a treatise on its benefits, though he was known to give nothing away.—*Goldsmith.*

The creditor whose appearance gladdens the heart of a debtor, may hold his head in sunbeams, and his foot on storms.—*Lavater.*

Reading maketh a full man ; conference, a ready man ; and writing, an exact man ; and, therefore, if a man write little, he had need have a great memory ; if he confer little, he had need have a present wit ; and if he read little, he had need have much cunning, to seem to know that he doth not.—*Lord Bacon.*

The only disadvantage of an honest heart is credulity.—*Sir P. Sidney.*

Frugality is founded on the principle that all riches have limits.— *Burke.*

A man's wisdom is his best friend ; folly his worst enemy.—*Sir W Temple.*

The sight of a drunkard is a better sermon against that vice, than the best that was ever preached upon that subject.—*Saville.*

He travels safe, and not unpleasantly, who is guarded by poverty and guided by love.—*Sir P. Sidney.*

> Weariness
> Can snore upon the flint, when restive sloth
> Finds the downy pillow hard.—*Shakspeare.*

Poetry is music in words ; and music is poetry in sound : both excellent sauce, but they have lived and died poor that made them their meat.—*Fuller.*

The web of life is of a mingled yarn, good and ill together : our virtues would be proud if our faults whipped them not ; and our crimes would despair, if they were not cherished by our virtues.—*Shakspeare.*

If a fool knows a secret, he tells it because he is a fool ; if a knave knows one, he tells it whenever it is his interest to tell it. But women and young men are very apt to tell what secrets they know, from the vanity of having been trusted. Trust none of these whenever you can help it.—*Chesterfield.*

K

A man should never be ashamed to own he has been in the wrong, which is but saying in other words, that he is wiser to-day than he was yesterday.—*Pope.*

The end of learning is to know God, and out of that knowledge to love Him, and to imitate Him, as we may the nearest, by possessing our souls of true virtue.—*Milton.*

Sleep is death's younger brother, and so like him, that I never dare trust him without my prayers.—*Sir T Browne.*

The most manifest sign of wisdom is continued cheerfulness : her estate is like that of things in the regions above the moon, always clear and serene.—*Montaigne.*

The heart never grows better by age : I fear rather worse ; always harder. A young liar will be an old one ; and a young knave will only be a greater knave as he grows older.—*Chesterfield.*

There is only one quarter of an hour in human life passed ill, and that is between the calling for the reckoning and paying it.—*Rabelais.*

Wit, like every other power, has its boundaries. Its success depends on the aptitude of others to receive impressions ; and as some bodies, indissoluble by heat, can set the furnace and the crucible at defiance, there are minds upon which the rays of fancy may be pointed without effect, and which no fire of sentiment can agitate, or exalt.—*Johnson.*

Exile is no evil : mathematicians tell us that the whole earth is but a point compared to the heavens. To change one's country then is little more than to remove from one street to another. Man is not a plant, rooted to a certain spot of earth : all soils and all climates are suited to him alike.—*Plutarch.*

None was ever a great poet that applied himself to anything else. —*Sir W. Temple.*

Our greatest glory is not in never falling, but in rising every time we fall.—*Confucius.*

He who gives himself airs of importance, exhibits the credentials of impotence.—*Lavater.*

Want of prudence is too frequently the want of virtue ; nor is there on earth a more powerful advocate for vice than poverty.—*Goldsmith.*

A miser grows rich by seeming poor ; an extravagant man grows poor by seeming rich.—*Shenstone.*

As a walled town is worthier than a village, so is the forehead of a married man more honourable than the bare brow of a bachelor.— *Shakspeare.*

Love is exactly like war, in this ; that a soldier, though he has escaped three weeks o' Saturday night—may nevertheless be shot through his heart on Sunday morning.—*Sterne.*

Trust him little who praises all, him less who censures all, and him least who is indifferent to all.—*Lavater.*

Human happiness has always its abatements; the brightest sunshine of success is not without a cloud.—*Johnson.*

People seldom improve, when they have no other model but themselves to copy after.—*Goldsmith.*

Human nature is not so depraved as to hinder us from respecting goodness in others, though we ourselves want it.—*Steele.*

The setting of a great hope is like the setting of the sun. The brightness of our life is gone. Shadows of evening fall around us, and the world seems but a dim reflection—itself a broader shadow. We look forward into the coming lonely night. The soul withdraws into itself. Then stars arise, and the night is lonely.—*Longfellow.*

In the bottle, discontent seeks for comfort, cowardice for courage, and bashfulness for confidence.—*Johnson.*

No man can possibly improve in company for which he has not respect enough to be under some degree of restraint.—*Chesterfield.*

Let a man be never so ungrateful or inhuman, he shall never destroy the satisfaction of my having done a good office.—*Seneca.*

No cord or cable can draw so forcibly, or bind so fast, as love can do with only a single thread.—*Burton.*

A good schoolmaster minces his precepts for children to swallow, hanging clogs on the nimbleness of his own soul, that his scholars may go along with him.—*Fuller.*

It is a point out of doubt with me, that the ladies are most properly the judges of men's dress, and the men of that of the ladies.—*Shenstone.*

O blessed health! thou art above all gold and treasure; 'tis thou who enlargest the soul, and openest all its powers to receive instruction, and to relish virtue. He that has thee has little more to wish for; and he that is so wretched as to want thee, wants everything with thee.—*Sterne.*

Good manners is the art of making those people easy with whom we converse. Whoever makes the fewest persons uneasy, is the best bred in the company.—*Swift.*

Rabelais and all other wits are nothing compared with Johnson. You may be diverted by them; but Johnson gives you a forcible hug, and shakes laughter out of you whether you will or no.—*Garrick.*

He who freely praises what he means to purchase, and he who enumerates the faults of what he means to sell, may set up a partnership with honesty.—*Lavater.*

A man of wit is not incapable of business, but above it. A sprightly generous horse is able to carry a pack-saddle as well as an ass ; but he is too good to be put to the drudgery.—*Pope.*

What is the life of man ? Is it not to shift from side to side— from sorrow to sorrow ? To button up one cause of vexation and un- button another ?—*Sterne.*

Education begins the gentleman, but reading, good company, and reflection must finish him.—*Locke.*

The man who threatens the world is always ridiculous; for the world can easily go on without him, and, in a short time, will cease to miss him.—*Johnson.*

The world produces for every pint of honey, a gallon of gall ; for every dram of pleasure, a pound of pain ; for every inch of mirth, an ell of moan ; and as the ivy twines around the oak, so do misery and misfortune encompass the happiness of man. Felicity, pure and unalloyed felicity, is not a plant of earthly growth ; her gardens are the skies.—*Burton.*

Humility is a virtue all preach, none practise, and yet everybody is content to hear. The master thinks it good doctrine for his servant, the laity for the clergy, and the clergy for the laity.—*Selden.*

The lightsome countenance of a friend giveth such an inward deck- ing to the house where it lodgeth as proudest palaces have cause to envy the gilding.—*Sir P Sidney.*

Men are not judged by their looks, habits, and appearance ; but by the character of their lives and conversation, and by their works. 'Tis better that a man's own works, than another man's words, should praise him.—*Sir R. L'Estrange.*

Obscurity in writing is commonly an argument of darkness in the mind : the greatest learning is to be seen in the greatest plainness.— *Bishop Wilkins.*

The best rules to form a young man are, to talk little, to hear much, to reflect alone upon what has passed in company, to distrust one's own opinions, and value others that deserve it.—*Sir W Temple.*

Kings most commonly, though strong in legions, are but weak at arguments ; as they are ever accustomed from the cradle to use their will only as their right hand, their reason always as their left.—*Milton.*

A more glorious victory cannot be gained over another man than this, that when the injury began on his part, the kindness should begin on ours.—*Tillotson.*

I am living fast to see the time when a book that misses its tide shall be neglected, as the moon by day, or like mackerel a week after the season.—*Swift.*

A sentence well couched takes both the sense and the understanding. I love not those cart-rope speeches that are longer than the memory of man can fathom.—*Feltham.*

As a man when he is once imprisoned for debt finds that every creditor immediately brings his action against him, and joins to keep him in ruinous captivity; so when any discontent seriously seizes on the human mind, all other perturbations instantly set upon it; and then, like a lame dog or a broken-winged goose, the unhappy patient droops and pines away, and is brought at last to the ill habit or malady of melancholy itself.—*Burton.*

In answering a book, 'tis best to be short, otherwise he that I write against will suspect that I intend to weary him, not to satisfy him. Besides, in being long, I shall give my adversary a huge advantage ; somewhere or other he will pick a hole.—*Selden.*

Deference is the most complicate, the most indirect, and the most elegant of all compliments.—*Shenstone.*

The truly valiant dare everything but doing any other body an injury.—*Sir P. Sidney.*

Speaking much is a sign of vanity; for he that is lavish in words is a niggard in deed.—*Sir W Raleigh.*

Men are never so ridiculous for the qualities they have as for those they affect to have.—*Charron.*

Deference often shrinks and withers upon the approach of intimacy, as the sensitive plant does upon the touch of one's finger.—*Shenstone.*

I know no friends more faithful, more inseparable, than hard heartedness and pride, humility and love, lies and impudence.—*Lavater.*

To be deprived of the person we love is a happiness in comparison of living with one we hate.—*Bruyère.*

A brave captain is as a root, out of which (as in branches) the courage of his soldiers doth spring.—*Sir P Sidney.*

The man who has not anything to boast of but his illustrious ancestors is like a potato—the only good belonging to him is under ground.—*Sir T. Overbury.*

Hail, ye sweet courtesies of life ! for smooth do ye make the road of it ; like grace and beauty, which beget inclinations to love at first sight, 'tis ye who open the door, and let the stranger in.—*Sterne.*

The jealous is possessed of a " fine mad devil" and a dull spirit at once.—*Lavater.*

As the sword of the best tempered metal is most flexible, so the truly generous are most pliant and courteous in their behaviour to their inferiors. —*Fuller.*

The difference between a rich man and a poor man is this,—the former eats when he pleases, and the latter when he can get it.—*Raleigh.*

What real good does an addition to a fortune already sufficient procure? Not any. Could the great man, by having his fortune increased, increase also his appetites, then precedence might be attended with real amusement.—*Goldsmith.*

Show me the man who knows what life is, who dreads death, and I'll show thee a prisoner who dreads his liberty.—*Sterne.*

When a person is once heartily in love, the little faults and caprices of his mistress, the jealousies and quarrels to which that commerce is so subject, however unpleasant they be, and rather connected with anger and hatred, are yet to be found, in many instances, to give additional force to the prevailing passion.—*Hume.*

Love sees what no eye sees; love hears what no ear hears; and what never rose in the heart of man love prepares for its object.—*Lavater.*

Let grace and goodness be the principal loadstone of thy affections. For love which hath ends will have an end; whereas that which is founded on true virtue will always continue.—*Dryden.*

As love without esteem is languid and capricious, esteem without love is languid and cold.—*Hawkesworth.*

Most females will forgive a liberty rather than a slight; and if any woman were to hang a man for stealing her picture, although it were set in gold, it would be a new case in law; but if he carried off the setting and left the portrait, I would not answer for his safety.—*Colton.*

Read not to contradict and confute, nor to believe and take for granted, nor to find talk and discourse, but to weigh and consider.—*Bacon.*

The pleasantest part of a man's life is generally that which passes in courtship, provided his passion be sincere, and the party beloved kind with discretion. Love, desire, hope, all the pleasing motions of the soul rise in pursuit.—*Addison.*

If the devil ever laughs it must be at hypocrites: they are the greatest dupes he has; they serve him better than any others, and receive no wages; nay, what is still more extraordinary, they submit to greater mortifications to go to hell than the sincerest Christian to go to heaven.—*Colton.*

Where men are the most sure and arrogant they are commonly the most mistaken, and have there given reins to passion without that proper deliberation and suspense which can alone secure them from the grossest absurdities.—*Hume.*

As riches forsake a man, we discover him to be a fool, but nobody could find it out in his prosperity.—*La Bruyère.*

A good word is an easy obligation; but not to speak ill requires only our silence, which costs us nothing.—*Tillotson.*

The reason why so few marriages are happy is because young ladies spend their time in making nets, not in making cages.—*Swift.*

Marriage is a feast where the grace is sometimes better than the dinner.—*Colton.*

Open your mouth and purse cautiously, and your stock of wealth and reputation shall, at least in repute, be great.—*Zimmerman.*

The reason why great men meet with so little pity or attachment in adversity would seem to be this,—the friends of a great man were made by his fortunes, his enemies by himself, and revenge is a much more punctual paymaster than gratitude.—*Colton.*

Make not a bosom friend of a melancholy soul : he'll be sure to aggravate thy adversity and lessen thy prosperity.   He goes always heavy loaded, and thou must bear half.   He's never in good humour, and may easily get into a bad one, and fall out with thee.—*Fuller.*

No man possesses a genius so commanding that he can obtain eminence unless a subject suited to his talents should present itself, and an opportunity occur for their development.—*Pliny.*

Consolation indiscreetly pressed upon us when we are suffering under affliction, only serves to increase our pain, and to render grief more poignant.—*Rousseau.*

In private conversation with intimate friends, the wisest men very often talk like the weakest; for indeed the talking with a friend is nothing else but thinking aloud.—*Addison.*

The portable quality of good humour seasons all the parts and occurrences we meet with, in such a manner that there are no moments lost : but they all pass with so much satisfaction that the heaviest of loads (when it is a load), that of time, is never felt by us.—*Steele.*

Real friendship is a slow flower, and never thrives unless engrafted upon a stock of known and reciprocal merit.—*Chesterfield.*

Friendship is compounded of all those soft ingredients which can insinuate themselves and slide insensibly into the nature and temper of men of the most different constitutions, as well as of those strong and active spirits which can make their way into perverse and obstinate dispositions ; and because discretion is always predominant in it, it works and prevails least upon fools.   Wicked men are often reformed by it, weak men seldom.—*Clarendon.*

The first glass for myself, the second for my friends, the third for good humour, and the fourth for mine enemies.—*Sir W. Temple.*

To endeavour to work upon the vulgar with fine sense is like attempting to hew blocks with a razor.—*Pope.*

There is no defence against reproach but obscurity; it is a kind of concomitant to greatness, as satires and invectives were an essential part of a Roman triumph.—*Addison.*

Wishes run over in loquacious impotence; *will* presses on with laconic energy.—*Lavater.*

Alas! the flame of friendship shines but in the weights of life; for the sun of prosperity overpowers its rays.—*Ernest Schultz.*

Let humility be the virtue of the wise man, that he may appear like the fruit-burthened bough, pressed down by the weight of his own worth.—*Sadi.*

Joy makes us grieve for the brevity of life; sorrow causes us to be weary of its length; trouble and industry can alone render it supportable.—*Morritz.*

The test of an enjoyment is the remembrance which it leaves behind it.—*J. Paul.*

The throb of the heart is the voice of fate.—*Schiller.*

Serenity of mind is nothing worth unless it has been earned; a man should be at once susceptible of passions and able to subdue them.—*J. Paul.*

True virtue is like precious odours—sweeter the more incensed and crushed.—*Bacon.*

If idleness be the root of all evil, then matrimony's good for something, for it sets many a poor woman to work.—*Vanbrugh.*

Some people take more care to hide their wisdom than their folly.—*Swift.*

The scholar, without good breeding, is a pedant; the philosopher, a cynic; the soldier, a brute; and every man, disagreeable.—*Chesterfield.*

The polite of every country seem to have but one character. A gentleman of Sweden differs but little, except in trifles, from one of any other country. It is among the vulgar we are to find those distinctions which characterize a people.—*Goldsmith.*

There is never wanting some good-natured person to send a man an account of what he has no mind to hear.—*Tatler.*

Sorrow is a kind of rust of the soul, which every new idea contributes in its passage to scour away. It is the putrefaction of stagnant life, and is remedied by exercise and motion.—*Johnson.*

To endeavour all one's days to fortify our minds with learning and philosophy, is to spend so much in armour that one has nothing left to defend.—*Shenstone.*

What a luxurious man in poverty would want for horses and foot-men, a good-natured man wants for his friend or the poor.—*Pope.*

Mental pleasures never cloy; unlike those of the body, they are increased by repetition, approved of by reflection, and strengthened by enjoyment.—*Colton.*

Poetry is in itself strength and joy, whether it be crowned by all mankind, or left alone in its own magic language.—*Sterling.*

He who loves not books before he comes to thirty years of age will hardly love them enough afterwards to understand them.—*Clarendon.*

To divert at any time a troublesome fancy, run to thy books : they presently fix thee to them, and drive the other out of thy thoughts. They always receive thee with the same kindness.—*Fuller.*

To be always intending to live a new life, but never to find time to set about it ; this is as if a man should put off eating and drinking and sleeping from one day and night to another, till he is starved and destroyed.—*Tillotson.*

If a man be sincerely wedded to Truth, he must make up his mind to find her a portionless virgin, and he must take her for herself alone. The contract, too, must be to love, cherish, and obey her, not only until death, but beyond it ; for this is a union that must survive not only Death, but Time, the conqueror of Death.—*Colton.*

Every man has just as much vanity as he wants understanding. —*Pope.*

Perfection is attained by slow degrees ; she requires the hand of time.—*Voltaire.*

When thou makest presents, let them be of such sort as will last long ; to the end that they may be in some sort immortal, and may frequently refresh the memory of the receiver.—*Fuller.*

In conversation, humour is more than wit, easiness more than knowledge ; few desire to learn, or to think they need it ; all desire to be pleased, or if not, to be easy.—*Sir W. Temple.*

A healthy old fellow, that is not a fool, is the happiest creature living. It is at that time of life only men enjoy their faculties with pleasure and satisfaction. It is then we have nothing to manage, as the phrase is ; we speak the downright truth, and whether the rest of the world give us the privilege or not, we have so little to ask of them, that we can take it.—*Steele.*

Before dinner, men meet with great inequality of understanding ; and those who are conscious of their inferiority have the modesty not to talk ; when they have drunk wine, every man feels himself happy, and loses that modesty, and grows impudent and vociferous ; but he is not improved ; he is only not sensible of his defects.—*Johnson.*

Money and time are the heaviest burdens of life, and the unhappiest of all mortals are those who have more of either than they know how to use.—*Johnson.*

Let not the enjoyment of pleasures now within your grasp be carried to such excess as to incapacitate you from future repetition.—*Seneca.*

Choose such pleasures as recreate much, and cost little.—*Fuller.*

"NEXT MORNING."

WE are apt to connect the voice of conscience with the stillness of midnight. But I think we wrong that innocent hour. It is that terrible "NEXT MORNING," when reason is wide awake, upon which remorse fastens its fangs. Has a man gambled away his all, or shot his friend in a duel—has he committed a crime, or incurred a laugh—it is the *next morning*, when the irretrievable Past rises before him like a spectre ; then doth the churchyard of memory yield up its grisly dead ; then is the witching hour when the foul fiend within us can least tempt perhaps, but most torment. At night we have one thing to hope for, one refuge to fly to—oblivion and sleep ! But at morning, sleep is over, and we are called upon coldly to review, and react, and live again the waking bitterness of self-reproach.—*Lord Lytton's "Ernest Maltravers."*

TROUBLED THOUGHTS.

OH, wretched man, whose too busy thoughts
Ride swifter than the galloping heavens round,
With an eternal hurry of the soul :
Nay, there's a time when e'en the rolling year
Seems to stand still ; dead calms are on the ocean,
When not a breath disturbs the drowsy waves :
But man, the very monster of the world,
Is ne'er at rest : the soul for ever wakes.—*Lee's Œdipus.*

Restless thoughts, that like a deadly swarm
Of hornets armed in throngs come rushing on me.
                                        Milton.

            Thus my thoughts are tired·
With tedious journeys up and down my mind :
Sometimes they lose their way ; sometimes as slow
As beast o'erladen, heavily they move,
Pressed by the weight of sorrow or of love.
                        Howe's "Vestal Virgin."

Turn not to thought, my brain, but let me find
Some unfrequented shade ; then lay me down,
And let forgetful dulness steal upon me,
To soften and assuage the pain of thinking.
                        Rowe's " Fair Penitent."

CURIOUS NOTES ON NATURE AND ART

SUMMER IN THE ORKNEYS.

FROM the absence of woodland scenery in Orkney, there is never the same delightful feeling of the presence of spring, such as the dwellers in the "sweet south" experience when the multitudinous leaves are trembling in the soft airs, and choirs of singing birds make the outgoings of the evening and the morning to rejoice. Indeed, the vernal season has only a transitory and troubled existence, and abdicates, ere seed-time is passed, in favour of summer. In occasional moods of relenting tenderness, winter graciously grants to impatient spring the morning hours of some special day at the beginning of April ; but the mood is of short continuance, and no sooner have Orcadian farmers begun to congratulate themselves on the return of oat-sowing weather than the "ruler of the inverted year," reclaims his boon ere the sun has reached the meridian, blots out with blustering blasts the genial beauty of the day, and, with a wrathful frown glooming on his brow, drives off the flower-crowned spring weeping from his footstool. But with tears and smiles the pleading spring returns, leading summer by the hand ; and we know that the sister seasons, mingling into one, have prevailed at last when the thick clouds fine away into fleecy flakes that melt in the blue depths of heaven, and the verdure of the pasture lands is wooed forth by the warmer sunshine.

Signs on sea and shore, new sights and sounds, make known the presence of the Orcadian summer-time, in which lives and moves the transmigrated spirit of spring. You awake from sleep when dawn is breaking, and instead of the pitiless, pelting storm, you hear delicious music warbled by a thrush, from some bush or solitary tree nigh your chamber window. It may excite surprise that a bird with voice so beautiful, and whose favourite haunt in the south is the wooded dell, should take up his abode in these remote groveless islands. Nevertheless, you are grateful for the song of the morning, pulsing abroad on the still air in liquid warbling gushes, and instinctively you bless the bird that revives old memories of bygone springs and summers with his melodious notes. In the summer mornings of these northern regions there is a delightful freshness. The breeze brings health and a benison from far-off leagues of sea, and in the calm translucent air the island hills and coasts lie clearly and beautifully defined.

May-time in Orkney resembles April in the Scottish Lowlands, and the fine freshness of the season kindles an irresistible longing to wander forth among the fields and moors, to climb the brown slopes of heathy hills, or to saunter aimlessly along the sea-shore. As we walk abroad the eye is gladdened by the tender green of the grass, the ploughman following his team, the sower with measured tread and swinging arm scattering the seed abroad, and all those familiar accompaniments of rural labour which leave so many pleasant pictures and impressions on the mind. Not less charming and gladsome are the sounds that salute the ear. Like Miriam and her maidens, summer has come with timbrels and with dances, and overhead the blue vault of heaven rings with the rich running raptures of countless larks. The islands at this season can almost afford to want the woodlands with their vocal verdure when the sky seems to dissolve in drops of liquid melody. The shower of enraptured song falls over the green and furrowed fields, mingles with the murmur of the sea on the shelly shore, and comes wafted to the ear in trembling notes from the far-off heathy slopes of the hills. The skylark—beautifully addressed by the Ettrick Shepherd as the "bird of the wilderness, blithesome, and cumberless"—is the chief songster of Orkney, and he fears no rivals as he sings and soars. Mingling with the minstrelsy of the lark, the mellow note of the cuckoo, soft and low as a dream-voice, may be heard issuing from some sheltered patch of stunted copse-wood.—*Gorrie.*

AMBER.

OF all the gem-like substances used for personal adornment, amber is of the highest antiquity. It is mentioned by Homer, and is found introduced in the most ancient specimens of Etruscan jewellery. In the collection of the Prince Canino was a necklace of very choice Etruscan workmanship, having pendants in the form of scarabei of alternate sardonyx and amber. The Greeks termed amber, *electron*, from Elector, one of the names of the sun-god. Amongst the Romans also the substance was greatly prized. Pliny tells us that a small figure carved in amber had been known to sell at a higher price than a living slave in vigorous health. In the time of Nero, one of the equestrian order was sent to Germany by Julianus, the manager of the gladiatorial exhibitions, in order to procure a supply of this gem. He succeeded so well, and brought back such vast quantities, that the very nets that protected the podium against the wild beasts, the litters upon which the slain gladiators were carried away, and all other articles used were studded with amber. Sir Thomas Browne, also, in his "Urn Burial," mentions among the contents of a Roman urn in the possession of Cardinal Farnese, not only jewels, but an ape in agate, and a grasshopper and an elephant carved in amber.

Wherever beds of lignite occur, amber is found : so that it is generally diffused over the world. But the shores of the Baltic, between Memel and Konigsberg, is the only district that supplies it in quantities. As much as four thousand pounds weight of amber yearly is said to be the product of that country. It is mostly found on the seashore, but in Prussia there are also mines. They are thus described : "First, at the surface of the earth, is found a stratum of sand. Immediately under this sand is a bed of clay filled with small flints. Under this clay is a stratum of black earth or turf, filled with fossil wood, half decomposed and bituminous ; this stratum is extended upon minerals containing little metal except iron, which are consequently pyrites. Lastly, under this bed, the amber is found scattered about in pieces and sometimes accumulated in heaps." It is accounted for in the following manner : " The oils in the woody stratum have been impregnated by the acid contained in the clay of the upper stratum, which has descended by the filtration of water. This mixture of oil and acid has become bituminous : the most pure and liquid parts of this bitumen have descended on the mineral stratum and in traversing it have become charged with particles of iron ; and the result of this last combination is the formation of the amber which is found below."

In Shakspeare's time, amber would seem to have been fashionable as an ornament, as he more than once alludes to it. When Petruchio promises to take Katherine on a visit to her father, he mentions " amber bracelets " among the "bravery" with which she is to be adorned. Amongst the artists of the Renaissance period it was chiefly used in the formation of jewel caskets and such-like elegant objects. It is still much valued in the East ; but the chief market at present is China, where it is crushed into powder and burned as incense. Mouth-pieces for cigars, beads, and other ornaments in this material are, however, extensively manufactured in the workshops of Dantzig, Hamburg, and elsewhere.—*The Argosy.*

WARBLERS.

AT first the lark, when she means to rejoice, to cheer herself and those that hear her, she then quits the earth and sings as she ascends higher into the air ; and having ended her heavenly employment, grows then mute and sad to think she must descend to the dull earth, which she would not touch but for necessity.

How do the black-bird and throssel [song-thrush], with their melodious voices, bid welcome to the cheerful spring, and in their fixed months warble forth such ditties as no art or instrument can reach to! Nay, the smaller birds also do the like in their particular seasons, as, namely, the laverock [sky-lark], the tit-lark, the little linnet, and the honest robin, that loves mankind both alive and dead.

But the nightingale, another of my airy creatures, breathes such sweet loud music out of her little instrumental throat, that it might make mankind to think miracles are not ceased. He that at midnight, when the very labourer sleeps securely, should hear, as I have very often, the clear airs, the sweet descants, the natural rising and falling, the doubling and redoubling of her voice, might well be lifted above earth, and say, " Lord, what music hast Thou provided for the saints in heaven, when Thou affordest bad men such music on earth !"—*Izaak Walton.*

VOICES OF SEA BIRDS.

I HAVE noted that the voices of birds have ever something in common with the loneliness or loveliness of their haunts and homes. Sea-birds utter a wild, dreary wail that blends harmoniously with the mournful monotone of the deep ; the cry of the bittern rises like a natural exhalation from the desolate pool ; the plaint of the lapwing accords with the wild brown waste of the moors ; and the blackbird's song seems the mellow voice of the luxuriant summer woods.—*Gorrie.*

ANCIENT GLASS.

THE manufacture of glass was known very early ; but glass, in a perfectly transparent condition, was reckoned so valuable, that Nero is said to have given £50,000 for two cups with handles.   When the excavations were made in the ancient city of Pompeii, which was buried by an eruption of Vesuvius, A.D. 79, the windows of some of the houses were found glazed with a thick kind of glass, which, however, was not transparent.   In others, talc was substituted, split into thin plates. Glass windows were first introduced into England, from France, about the year 1180.   In the beginning of the fourteenth century, from the Fabric-roll of Exeter Cathedral, it appears that both plain and co-loured glass was brought from Rouen in Normandy, at the charge of eightpence per foot for the stained, and fourpence for the white glass. Bottles of glass were first made in England about 1557 ; and the first plate-glass manufactory in England was established at Lambeth, in the year 1674.

STATISTICS OF HUMAN LIFE.

THE total number of human beings on earth is now computed, in round numbers, at 1,000,000,000.   They speak 3064 tongues, in which upwards of 1100 religions are preached.   The average duration of life is 33½ years.   One-fourth of those born die before the seventh, and one-half before the seventeenth year.   Out of 100 persons, only six reach the age of 60 and upwards.   Out of the 1,000,000,000 living persons 33,000,000 die annually, 91,000 daily, 3730 every hour, 60 every minute, and, consequently, one every second.   The loss is, how-ever, balanced by the gain in new births.   Marriages are in proportion to single life (bachelors and spinsters) as 100 : 75.   Both births and deaths are more frequent in the night than in the day.   One-fourth of men are capable of bearing arms, but not one in a thousand is by nature inclined for the profession.

BASKET-MAKING IN CHINA.

THE art of basket-making is one of the most ancient practised by man, and it dates from a period more remote than the records of authentic history.   There is no nation in the world that excels, per-haps there is none that equals, the Chinese in this branch of industry. It is one of those crafts that seem peculiarly their own; and in it, as in the carving of ivory and the making of porcelain, they stand un-rivalled.   The Chinese baskets are a marvel to European craftsmen in the same art, and they never dream of imitating them.   The pa-tience, the industry, and the manual skill of the Chinese workman have raised the craft of the basket-maker almost to one of the fine arts. He makes not only baskets, but numberless beautiful articles and appliances for the work-table or toilet-table, manufactured either of osiers, of split bamboo, of the plaited bark of trees, of the coloured straw of the rice-plant, or of any pliant material that comes to hand. These materials he plaits and interlaces in a variety of beautiful patterns and elegant designs, quite inimitable by western workmen. It is true that, in making baskets and panniers for common use, he lays the twigs much on the same plan as the European, but with how much more firmness and regularity may be guessed from the fact that the common Chinese basket will hold water without leaking—that it will serve, and indeed does serve, for a pail or bucket as well as a basket. China produces the willow and osier in immense variety and abundance. On the high lands grows a willow of a peculiar kind ; it is a creeping plant, of the thickness of the finger, which gives out very long shoots resembling cords. This plant is exceedingly pliant and tough, and is twisted into cables and other cordage. There is another kind of willow, the wood of which yields an agreeable odour, and from which a fragrant perfume is distilled. The Chinese basket-maker has therefore an extensive assortment of material on which to exercise his ingenuity.—*Leisure Hour.*

NIGHT AND MORNING SONGS OF THE FOREST.

THE gold of the sunset had gilded up the dark pine-tops and disappeared, like a ring taken slowly from an Ethiop's finger ; the whip-poor-will had chanted the first stave of his lament ; the bat was abroad ; and the screech-owl, like all bad singers, commenced without waiting to be importuned, though we were listening for the nightingale. The air had been all day breathless, but, as the first chill of evening displaced the warm atmosphere of the departed sun, a slight breeze crisped the mirrored bosom of the canal, and then commenced the night anthem of the forest, audible, I would fain believe, in its soothing changes, by the dead tribes whose bones whiten amid the perishing leaves.

First, whisperingly yet articulately, the suspended and wavering foliage of the birch was touched by the many-fingered wind, and, like a faint prelude, the silver-lined leaves rustled in the low branches ; and with a moment's pause, when you could hear the moving of the vulture's claws upon the bark, as he turned to get his breast to the wind, the increasing breeze swept into the pine-tops, and drew forth from their fringe-like and myriad tassels a low monotone, like the refrain of a far-off dirge ; and still, as it murmured (seemingly to you sometimes like the cathedral floor), the blast strengthened and filled, and the rigid leaves of the oak, and the swaying fans and chalices of the magnolia, and the rich cups of the tulip-trees, stirred and answered with their different voices like many-toned harps ; and when the wind was fully abroad, and every moving thing on the breast of the earth was roused from its daylight repose, the irregular and capricious blast, like a player on an organ of a thousand stops, lulled and strengthened by turns ; and from the hiss of the rank grass, low as the whisper of the fairies, to the thunder of the impinging and groaning branches of the larch and fir, the anthem went ceaselessly through its changes, and the harmony (though the owl broke in with its scream, and though the over-blown monarch of the wood came crashing to the earth) was still perfect and without a jar. It is strange that there is no sound of nature out of tune. The roar of the waterfall comes into this anthem of the forest like an accompaniment of bassoons, and the occasional bark of the wolf, or the scream of the night-bird, or even the deep-throated croak of the frog, is no more discordant than the outburst of an octave flute above the even melody of an orchestra ; and it is surprising how the large rain-drops, pattering on the leaves, and the small voice of the nightingale (singing, like nothing but himself, best in the darkness), seems an intensitive and a low burden to the general anthem of the earth—as it were a single voice among instruments.

I had what Wordsworth calls a " couchant ear " in my youth, and I must tell of another harmony that I learned to love in the wilderness.

There will sometimes come in the spring—say in May, or whenever the sulphur-butterflies are tempted out by the first timorous sunshine—there will come, I say, in that yearning and youth-renewing season, a warm shower at noon. Our tents shall be pitched on the skirts of a forest of young pines, and the evergreen-foliage, if it may be so called, shall be a daily refreshment to our eye while watching, with the west wind upon our cheeks, the unclothed branches of the elm. The rain descends softly and warm ; but with the sunset, the clouds break away, and it grows suddenly cold enough to freeze. The next morning you shall come out with me to a hill-side looking upon the south, and lie down with your ear to the earth. The pine-tassels hold, in every four of their fine fingers, a drop of rain frozen like a pearl in a long ear-ring, sustained in their loose grasp by the rigidity of the cold. The sun grows warm at ten, and the slight green fingers begin to relax and yield, and by eleven they are all dropping their icy pearls upon the dead leaves, with a murmur through the forest like the swarming of the bees of Hybla. There is not much variety in the music, but it is a pleasant monotone for thought ; and if you have a restless fever in your bosom (as I had when I learned to love—it soothed and satisfied then), you may lie down with a crooked root under your head in the skirts of the forest, and thank Heaven for an anodyne to care. And it is better than the voice of your friend or the song of your lady-love ; for it exacts no gratitude, and will not desert you ere the echo dies upon the wind.

Oh, how many of these harmonies there are ! how many that we hear, how many that are "too constant to be heard " ! I could go back to my boyhood now, with this thread of recollections, and unsepulture a hoard of simple and long-buried joys, that would bring the blush upon my cheek to think how many senses are dulled since such things could give me pleasure ! Is there no " well of Kanathos " for renewing the youth of the soul? no St. Hillary's cradle? no elixir to cast the slough of heart-sickening and heart-tarnishing custom? Find me an alchymy for *that*, with your alembic and crucible, and you may resolve into dross again your philosopher's stone.—*N. P. Willis' "Life Here and There."*

THE LOVE OF NATURE.

IT is strange to observe the callousness of some men, before whom all the glories of heaven and earth pass in daily succession without touching their hearts, elevating their fancy, or leaving any durable remembrance. Even of those who pretend to sensibility, how many are there to whom the lustre of the rising or setting sun, the sparkling concave of the midnight sky, the mountain forest tossing and rearing to the storm, or warbling with all the melodies of a summer evening ; the sweet interchange of hill and dale, shade and sunshine, grove, lawn, and water, which an extensive landscape offers to the view ; the scenery of the ocean, so lovely, so majestic, and so tremendous, and the many pleasing varieties of the animal and vegetable kingdoms, could never afford such real satisfaction as the steams and noise of a ball-room, the insipid fiddling and squeaking of an opera, or the vexatious wranglings of a card-table !

But some minds there are of a different make, who, even in the early part of life, receive from the contemplation of nature a species of delight which they would hardly exchange for any other ; and who, as avarice and ambition are not the infirmities of that period, would with equal sincerity and rapture exclaim—

> " I care not, Fortune, what you me deny ;
> You cannot rob me of free Nature's grace ;
> You cannot shut the windows of the sky,
> Through which Aurora shows her brightening face ;
> You cannot bar my constant feet to trace
> The woods and lawns by living stream at eve."

Such minds have always in them the seeds of true taste, and frequently o imitative genius. At least, though their enthusiastic or visionary tone of mind, as the man of the world would call it, should not always incline them to practise poetry or painting, we need not scruple to affirm that, without some portion of this enthusiasm, no person ever became a true poet or painter. For he who would imitate the works of nature, must first accurately observe them ; and accurate observation is to be expected from those only who take great pleasure in it.—*Beattie's Essays.*

A PARADISE OF SEA-FOWL.

WENDING our way from the fields to the shore, the strange cries and calls of sea-fowl of every wing blend not unmusically with the land voices of summer. The wailing screams that mingled with the wintry tempest have lost much of their harshness in the joyance of the new season ; and even in the plaintive cry of the gull there is a jubilant tone, like the far-heard trumpeting of the wild swan winging its flight to lonely meres. Flocks of sea-birds are congregated about the sands, flitting uneasily to and fro, or calling in chorus as they lightly dip in the long shore-wave that melts away in music and a sparkle of foam. Farther out in the bickering gleam of the dimpling sea, families of teisties are luxuriating in the water like Roman senators in their marble baths. Down they dive, one by one, into the green domains of the finny tribes, and their bills emit a chuckling gurgle of delight when they reappear at intervals upon the water. Truly Orkney is the paradise of sea-fowl, beloved by teisties and terns, scarffs and kittiwakes, divers, oyster-catchers, and stormy petrels; and now, when the summer sunshine is sparkling on the waters, their many-voiced calls and shrill pipings may be heard around the coasts from the Altars of Linay to the Brough of South Ronaldshay.—*Gorrie's Summers and Winters in the Orkneys.*

OLD PORCELAIN TEAPOTS.

No specimen of the ceramic art possesses greater variety of orm than the teapot. On none has the ingenuity of the potter been more fully exercised; and it is worthy of remark, that the first successful production of Bottcher in hard porcelain, was a teapot. The so-called Elizabethan teapots must be of a later date, for tea was not known in England until the time of Charles II.; but it is interesting to trace the gradual increase in the size of the teapot, from the diminutive productions of Elers, in the time of Queen Anne and George I., when tea was sold in apothecaries' shops, to the capacious vessel which supplied Dr. Johnson with "the cup that cheers but not inebriates." Mr. Croker, in his edition of Boswell's Life, mentions a teapot that belonged to Dr. Johnson, which held two quarts; but this sinks into insignificance compared with the superior magnitude of that in the possession of Mrs. Marryat, of Wimbledon, who purchased it at the sale of Mrs. Piozzi's effects, at Streatham. This teapot, which was the one generally used by Dr. Johnson, holds more than three quarts. It is of old oriental porcelain, painted and gilded, and, from its capacity, was well suited to the taste of one "whose tea-kettle had no time to cool—who with tea solaced the midnight hour, and with tea welcomed the morn." George IV. had a large assemblage of teapots piled in pyramids, in the Pavilion at Brighton. Mrs. Elizabeth Carter was also a collector of teapots, each of which possessed some traditionary interest, independently of its intrinsic merit; but the most diligent collector of teapots was the late Mrs. Hawes. She bequeathed no less than three hundred specimens to her daughter, Mrs. Donkin, who has arranged them in a room appropriated for the purpose. Among them are several formerly belonging to Queen Charlotte. Many are of the old Japan; one with two divisions and two spouts, for holding both black and green tea; and another of curious device, with a small aperture at the bottom to admit the water, there being no opening at the top, atmospheric pressure preventing the water from running out. This singular Chinese toy has been copied in the Rockingham ware.—*Joseph Marryat.*

THE TRAVELLING OF LIGHT.

THE rays of light travel one hundred and fifty thousand miles in a second, and are seven minutes in completing their passage from the great luminary to our earth—a distance of about seventy millions of miles. The velocity with which they travel from the sun is so astonishing, that a ball discharged from the mouth of a cannon would be several weeks in accomplishing the task. It has been ascertained that a ray of light is one continued stream of small particles, so minute that a lighted candle, in a second of time, diffuses hundreds of millions more particles of light than there are grains in the whole earth.

SPEED OF OCEAN WAVES.

THE largest waves proceed at the rate of from thirty to forty miles an hour ; yet it is a vulgar belief that the water itself advances with the speed of the wave. The *form* of the wave only advances, while the substance, excepting a little spray above, remains rising and falling in the same place.

CURIOUS MODE OF DISCOVERING A CRIMINAL.

THE secretion of the saliva seems to be under the influence of the same mental emotions as affect the functions of the stomach. Fear, anxiety, and various other depressing passions, diminish digestion, and most probably produce this effect by stopping the secretion of the gastric juice. Observation shows us that they have a decided influence in lessening, or even in entirely arresting, the secretion of saliva —a circumstance not unknown to the observant nations of the East. In illustration of this, it may be mentioned that the conjurors in India often found upon this circumstance a mode of detecting theft among servants. When a robbery has been committed in a family, a conjuror is sent for, and great preparations are made. A few days are allowed to elapse before he commences his operations, for the purpose of allowing time for the restitution of the stolen property. If, however, it be not restored by the time fixed, he proceeds with his operations, one of which is as follows. He causes a quantity of boiled rice to be produced, of which all those suspected must eat ; and after masticating it for some time, he desires them all to spit it upon certain leaves, for the purposes of inspection and comparison. He now examines this masticated rice very knowingly, and immediately points out the culprit, from observing that the rice which he has been masticating is perfectly dry, while that which was masticated by the others is moistened by the saliva.—*Dr. Hayden.*

THE SENSES.

THE ivory palace of the skull, which is the central abode of the soul, although it dwells in the whole body, opens to the outer world four gateways, by which its influences may enter ; and a fifth, whose alleys are innumerable, unfolds its thousand doors on the surface of every limb. These gateways, which we otherwise name the Organs of the Senses, and call in our mother-speech, the Eye, the Ear, the Nose, the Mouth, and the Skin, are instruments by which we see, and hear, and smell, and taste, and touch; at once loop-holes through which the spirit gazes out upon the world, and the world gazes in upon the spirit: porches which the longing, unsatisfied soul would often gladly make wider, that beautiful material nature might come into it more freely and fully; and fenced doors, which the sated and dissatisfied spirit would, if it had the power, often shut and bar altogether. The soul and its servants were not intended to be at war with each other, and the better the wise king is served the more kingly will he appear. We have a strange fear of our bodies, and are ever speaking as if we could right the spirit by only wronging the flesh, and could best sharpen our intellects by blunting our senses. But our souls would only be gainers by the perfection of our bodies, were they wisely dealt with; and for every human being we should aim at securing, so far as they can be attained, an eye as keen and piercing as that of an eagle; an ear as sensible to the faintest sound as that of the hare; a nostril as far-scenting as that of the wild deer; a tongue as delicate as that of the butterfly; and a touch as acute as that of the spider. No man ever was so endowed, and no one ever will be; but all come infinitely short of what they should achieve were they to make their senses what they might be made. The old have outlived their opportunity, and the diseased never had it; but the young, who have still an undimmed eye, an undulled ear, and a soft hand, an unabated nostril, and a tongue which tastes with relish the plainest fare, can so cultivate their senses as to make the narrow ring which for the old and the infirm encircles things sensible, widen for them into an almost limitless horizon.--*Wilson's " Five Gateways of Knowledge."*

THE HALCYON, OR KINGFISHER.

THE kingfisher is the halcyon of the ancient poets, who placed it on a floating nest, and endowed it with power to calm the adverse winds and waves. Nay, Aristotle and Pliny gravely relate that it sat only a few days in the depth of winter, when the mariner might prosecute his voyage in full security; and hence the *halcyon days*—an expression which has descended to our own times. The ancients, moreover, believed that it rendered the fisherman's labour prosperous, dispelled lightning, imparted personal grace and beauty to individuals, and diffused peace and harmony among families. Even at the present day the Tartars and Ostiacs apply the feathers of this bird to many superstitious uses. The former pluck them, cast them in the water, and carefully preserve such as float; and they pretend that if with one of them they touch a woman, or even her clothes, she must fall in love with them. The Ostiacs enclose the skin, the bill, and the claws in a purse, and as long as they preserve this sort of amulet, they believe that they have nothing to fear. An idea long prevailed in the most enlightened portions of Europe, that if the body of a kingfisher was suspended by a thread the breast always pointed to the north. The flesh, too, was believed to be incorruptible, and to guard wardrobes and the stores of the woollen draper from the depredations of moths. —*Encyc. Edinensis.*

THE HAND.

IF the hand munificently serves the body, not less amply does it give expression to the genius and the art, the courage and the affection, the will and the power of man. Put a sword into it, and it will fight for him ; put a plough into it, and it will till for him ; put a harp into it, and it will play for him ; put a pencil into it, and it will paint for him ; put a pen into it, and it will speak for him, plead for him, pray for him. What will it not do? What has it not done? A steam-engine is but a larger hand, made to extend its powers by the little hand of man ! An electric telegraph is but a long pen for that little hand to write with ! All our huge cannons and other weapons of war, with which we effectually slay our brethren, are only Cain's hand made bigger and stronger and bloodier ! What, moreover, is a ship, a rail-way, a lighthouse, or a palace—what indeed is a whole city, all the cities of the globe, nay the very globe itself, in so far as man has changed it, but the work of that giant hand with which the human race, acting as one mighty man, has executed its will! When I think of all that man and woman's hand has wrought, from the day when Eve put forth her erring hand to pluck the fruit of the forbidden tree, to that dark hour when the pierced hands of the Saviour of the world were nailed to the predicted tree of shame, and of all that human hands have done of good and evil since, I lift up my hand, and gaze upon it with wonder and awe. What an intrument for good it is ! What an instrument for evil ! and all the day long it is never idle. There is no implement which it cannot wield, and it should never in working hours be without one. We unwisely restrict the term handi-craftsmen, or hand-worker, to the more laborious callings ; but it belongs to all honest, earnest men and women, and is a title which each should covet. For the queen's hand there is the sceptre, and for the soldier's hand the sword ; for the carpenter's hand the saw ; for the smith's hand the hammer ; for the farmer's hand the plough ; for the miner's hand the spade ; for the sailor's hand the oar ; for the painter's hand the brush ; for the sculptor's hand the chisel ; for the poet's hand the pen ; and for the woman's hand the needle. If none of these or the like will fit us, the felon's chain should be on our wrist, and our hand on the prisoner's crank. But for each willing man and woman there is a tool they may learn to handle ; for all there is the command : " Whatsoever thy hand findeth to do, do it with all thy might."—*Wilson's " Five Gateways of Knowledge."*

OLD VIOLINS.

PERHAPS it never occurred to our readers that there was much difference between one fiddle-head and another ; yet a Stradiuarius is known from a Stainer, for instance, by his head, as surely as you can tell a Greek from a Jewish face. Take up your Stradiuarius, hold it straight against the light with its belly towards you, and take in the commanding outline of the head, full front. The two sides of the scroll seem to be almost in motion, like curling wood thrown off by a revolving centre-bit or a plane in action. The two points seem a little lifted up with incomparable energy and strength, and lightly balanced with each other. The dip of the head, relieved by the fine fluting, is powerful but not heavy ; and in the finest Stradiuarius and Joseph Guarnerius patterns, reminds one of a lion's face in repose, only the Stradiuarius is invariably more graceful and beautiful in its majesty, where the Guarnerius is strong, with a sort of rough and massive grandeur. But turn from either of these full-fronted heads to lesser magnates, and what a falling off is there—some are what we may call potbellied heads ; others brutal, snub, bull-dog heads ; others lean and poor ; others simply coarse and stupid ; others cut mechanically, without character, or top-heavy, poor and thin flanked near the neck ; others without any sense of proportion, the two sides of the scroll uneven, one dipping down lop-eared, and the other turning up like a *nez retroussé*, and so on, until the eye comes back and rests upon the perfect and dignified charms of the Stradiuarius head. It will bear inspection—look at it sideways, mark the throw of the scroll; was there any carving of Gibbons or the Belgians, any trailing vine-stem, any circling ivy cut in rich oak, more finely felt in its sensitive edges, its harmonious sweep, its delicate tendril-curves, than the Stradiuarius maple scroll, with its smooth flesh-like flutings, its soft clean edge and circular bends, which, like the convolvulus or jessamine coil, is never any part of a true circle ?

And then look at the varnish lying like a sheet of thin jasper on the back and belly, at once shielding these from decay, whilst revealing century after century the transparent filaments of the mottled maple or sycamore, and the symmetrical deal crossed between the fibres with millions of tiny rays which show where lie the desiccated cells now hollow and fit for perfect resonance through which the sap once flowed. The rich, almost orange-coloured varnish, is as good as a magnifying glass ; through it we can at this day judge of the loving selection made of the choicest timber, and the infinite care bestowed upon its preparation, the tempering as well as the carving of it.

And this same varnish, how was it made ? And can it not be made now ? The ingredients of it are pretty well known, but how were they put together and applied ? That is not known, and it seems now, after infinite controversy and analysis, that it never will be known. There was gum-dragon, or dragon's blood, from Africa, which the ships brought into Venice ; there was fine oil ; there was rare spirit ; and above all, there was plenty of time, a beautiful climate, and a life of such absorbed devotion and cumulative experience as, in these days of hurry and demand, can scarcely be looked for over again. We seek in vain for the conditions under which the great violins were produced. Even if we had the love, the patience, and the inspiration for the work, the work itself would never pay—it would never fetch the price of the labour and time bestowed upon it. The instrument itself, simple as it looks, is to be composed of no less than seventy-one pieces. Sycamore or maple must be got for the back, sides, neck, and circle. Soft deal for the belly, bass bar, sound post, and six internal blocks ; ebony for the finger-board and tail-piece ; white and ebony for the purfling. The wood must be cut only in December and Janu- ary, and only that part must be used which has been exposed to the sun. You may cut up planks and planks before you find a piece suitable for a really fine back or belly. Witness the grain of a Stradi- uarius or Amati violin ; mark the almost pictorially beautiful health and evenness of its wavy lines, free from all knots and irregularity of growth, studded with symmetrical and billowy veins, where the rich sap once flowed. And when the wood is cut, it must be tempered and dried, not with artificial warmth, but with the slow and penetrating influence of a dry warm Cremona climate. For no customer, for no market, can the process be hurried. And the application of the varnish required cor- responding care. It was to be perfectly wedded to the rare wood ; a companionship destined to last for ages, to outlast so many genera- tions of men and women, was not to be enterprised or undertaken lightly.

In the spring, when the air got clear and bright, and the storms were past, the subtle gums and oils were mixed slowly and deliberately ; hours to stand, hours to settle, hours for perfect fusion and amalgama- tion of parts ; clear white light gleaming from roads strewn with the dazzling marble dust of Lombardy ; clear blue sky, warm dry air, and the skill of an alchemist,—these were the conditions for mixing the in- comparable Cremona varnish. So deliberately was it prepared and laid on, just when the wood was fit to receive it—laid on in three coats in such a manner as to sink into the desiccated pores and be- come a part of the wood, as the aromatic herbs and juices become a part of the flesh that is embalmed for a thousand years. All through the summer did that matchless varnish, which some say contained ground amber, and which, at any rate, was charged with subtle secrets, sink and soak into the sycamore and deal plates, until now, when age has rubbed away its clear and agate crust in many places, the violin is found no longer to need that protection ; for the wood itself seems to have become petrified into clear agate, and is capable, throughout its myriad pores and fibres, of resisting the worm, and even damp, and the other ravaging influences of ordinary decay.

The old varnishes have been closely imitated by M. Vuillaume and other clever makers, but a good judge can tell the genuine from the false. It has often been maintained that the dryness of the wood gave the fine quality of tone desired ; and the French makers have accord- ingly baked the wood of their new violins ; but although the tone has been thus, to some extent, prematurely mellowed, there is every reason to fear that the baked fiddles, like some old fiddles made of too slight wood, and cut too thin, have a tendency to get " played out "—that is, after attaining tone they lose tone. Age, no doubt, improves wood ;

and the constant vibration of playing tends, it is said, to shake into hollows the pores of the wood, and expel the particles of dried sap in dust. But the grand secret, after all, lay in the manufacture of the original instrument,—in the shape, in the preparation of the wood before the parts were fixed together, in the varnish and general adjustments of the interior. The violin, as it came from the hands of the great makers, was always fine. Age and playing cannot make a good fiddle out of a bad one ; although age and playing doubtless improve good fiddles. There are hosts of instruments a hundred years old which are, and always will be, bad to the last degree.—*H. R. Haweis in the Contemporary Review.*

LITERARY GEMS, OLD AND NEW

OF WIT.

IT may be demanded, what the thing we speak of is ?   Or what this facetiousness doth import ?   To which questions I might reply, as Democritus did to him that asked the definition of a man : " 'Tis that which we all see and know."   Any one better apprehends what it is by acquaintance than I can inform him by description.   It is, indeed, a thing so versatile and multiform, appearing in so many shapes, so many postures, so many garbs, so variously apprehended by several eyes and judgments, that it seemed no less hard to settle a clear and certain notion thereof than to make a portrait of Proteus, or to define the figure of the fleeting air.   Sometimes it lieth in pat allusion to a known story, or in seasonable application of a trivial saying, or in forging an apposite tale ; sometimes it playeth in words and phrases, taking advantage from the ambiguity of their sense, or the affinity of their sound ; sometimes it is wrapped in a dress of humorous expression ; sometimes it lurketh under an odd similitude ; sometimes it is lodged in a sly question, in a smart answer, in a quirkish reason, in a shrewd intimation, in cunningly diverting or cleverly retorting an objection ; sometimes it is couched in a bold scheme of speech, in a tart irony, in a lusty hyperbole, in a startling metaphor, in a plausible reconciling of contradictions, or in acute nonsense ; sometimes a scenical representation of persons or things, a counterfeit speech, a mimical look or gesture, passeth for it ; sometimes an affected simplicity, sometimes a presumptuous bluntness, giveth it being ; sometimes it riseth only from a lucky hitting upon what is strange ; sometimes from a crafty wresting obvious matter to the purpose.   Often it consisteth in one knows not what, and springeth up one can hardly tell how.   Its ways are unaccountable and inexplicable ; being answerable to the numberless rovings of fancy and windings of language.   It is, in short, a manner of speaking out of the simple and plain way (such as reason teacheth and proveth things by), which by a pretty surprising uncouthness in conceit or expression, doth affect and amuse the fancy, stirring in it some wonder, and breeding some delight thereto. It raiseth admiration, as signifying a nimble sagacity of apprehension, a special felicity of invention, a vivacity of spirit, and reach of wit more than vulgar ; it seeming to argue a rare quickness of parts, that one can fetch in remote conceits applicable ; a notable skill, that he can dexterously accommodate them to the purpose before him ; together with a lively briskness of humour, not apt to damp those sportful flashes of imagination. It also procureth delight, by gratifying curiosity with its rareness, as semblance of difficulty (as monsters, not for their beauty, but their rarity ; as juggling tricks, not for their use, but their abstruseness, are beheld with pleasure) ; by diverting the mind from its road of serious thoughts ; by instilling gaiety and airiness of spirit ; by provoking to such dispositions of spirit in way of emulation or complaisance ; and by seasoning matters, otherwise distasteful or insipid, with an unusual and thence graceful tang.—*Dr. Isaac Barrow.*

[This is considered to be the finest definition of the nature of wit in the language.]

GATHER YE ROSE-BUDS.

TO THE VIRGINS, TO MAKE MUCH USE OF THEIR TIME.

GATHER ye rose-buds while ye may;
  Old time is still a flying,
And this same flower that smiles to-day,
  To-morrow will be dying.

The glorious lamp of heaven, the sun,
  The higher he's a getting,
The sooner will his race be run,
  And nearer he's to setting.

That age is best which is the first,
  When youth and blood are warmer ;
But being spent, the worse and worst
  Time shall succeed the former.

Then be not coy, but use your time,
  And, while ye may, go marry ;
For having lost but once your prime,
  You may for ever tarry.
                              Robert Herrick, 1591–1674.

THE SOUL'S ERRAND.

[This impressive poem has been attributed to various writers, but Sir Walter Raleigh is now generally credited with the authorship.]

Go, soul, the body's guest,
  Upon a thankless errand !

Fear not to touch the best,
  The truth shall be thy warrant.
  Go, since I needs must die,
  And give the world the lie.

Go, tell the Court it glows
  And shines like rotten wood ;
Go, tell the Church it shows
  What's good, and doth no good :
  If Church and Court reply,
  Then give them both the lie.

Tell potentates they live
  Acting by others' actions ;
Not loved unless they give,
  Not strong but by their factions.
  If potentates reply,
  Give potentates the lie.

Tell men of high condition
  That rule affairs of state,
Their purpose is ambition,
  Their practice only hate.
  And if they once reply,
  Then give them all the lie.

Tell them that have it most,
  They beg for more by spending,
Who in their greatest cost,
  Seek nothing but commending.
  And if they make reply,
  Then give them all the lie.

Tell zeal it lacks devotion ;
  Tell love it is but lust ;
Tell time it is but motion ;
  Tell flesh it is but dust ;
  And wish them not reply,
  For thou must give the lie.

Tell age it daily wasteth ;
  Tell honour how it alters ;
Tell beauty how she blasteth ;
  Tell favour how she falters.
  And as they shall reply,
  Give every one the lie.

Tell wit how much it wrangles
  In tickle points of niceness ;
Tell wisdom she entangles
  Herself in over-wiseness.
  And when they do reply,
  Straight give them both the lie.

Tell physic of her boldness ;
Tell skill it is pretension ;
Tell charity of coldness ;
Tell law it is contention.
And as they do reply,
So give them still the lie.

Tell fortune of her blindness ;
Tell nature of decay ;
Tell friendship of unkindness ;
Tell justice of delay.
And if they will reply,
Then give them all the lie.

Tell arts they have no soundness,
But vary by esteeming ;
Tell schools they want profoundness,
And stand too much on seeming.
If arts and schools reply,
Give arts and schools the lie.

Tell faith it's fled the city ;
Tell how the country erreth ;
Tell manhood shakes of pity ;
Tell virtue least preferreth.
And if they do reply,
Spare not to give the lie.

So when thou hast, as I
Commanded thee, done blabbing ;
Although to give the lie,
Deserves no less than stabbing :
Yet stab at thee who will,
No stab the soul can kill.

TO ALTHEA, FROM PRISON.

WHEN love, with unconfinèd wings,
Hovers within my gates,
And my divine Althea brings
To whisper at my grates ;
When I lie tangled in her hair,
And fettered with her eye,
The birds that wanton in the air,
Know no such liberty.

When flowing cups run swiftly round,
With no allaying Thames,
Our careless heads with roses crowned,
Our hearts with loyal flames ;

When thirsty grief in wine we steep,
    When healths and draughts go free,
Fishes that tipple in the deep
    Know no such liberty.

When, linnet-like confinèd, I
    With shriller notes shall sing
The mercy, sweetness, majesty,
    And glories of my king ;
When I shall voice aloud how good
    He is, how great should be,
Th' enlargèd winds, that curl the flood,
    Know no such liberty.

Stone walls do not a prison make,
    Nor iron bars a cage ;
Minds innocent and quiet take
    These for a hermitage ;
If I have freedom in my love,
    And in my soul am free,
Angels alone, that soar above,
    Enjoy such liberty.

Richard Lovelace, 1618–1658.

LONDON AT SUNRISE.

A SONNET COMPOSED ON WESTMINSTER BRIDGE.

EARTH has not anything to show more fair ;
Dull would he be of soul who could pass by
A sight so touching in its majesty :
The city now doth like a garment wear
The beauty of the morning ; silent, bare,
Ships, towers, domes, theatres, temples, lie
Open unto the fields and to the sky,
All bright and glittering in the smokeless air.
Never did sun more beautifully steep,
In his first splendour, valley, rock, and hill ;
Ne'er saw I, never felt, a calm so deep !
The river glideth at his own sweet will :
Dear God ! the very houses seem asleep ;
And all that mighty heart is lying still !—*Wordsworth.*

TITANIA'S PICTURE OF SHAKSPEARE.

NAY, by the golden lustre of thine eye,
And by thy brow's most fair and ample span,
Thought's glorious palace, famed for fancies high,
And by thy cheek thus passionately wan,

I know the signs of an immortal man,—
Nature's chief darling and illustrious mate,
Destined to foil old death's oblivious plan,
And shine untainted by the fogs of Fate,
Time's famous rival till the final date!
Hood's " Plea of the Midsummer Fairies."

LAST POEM OF CHARLES THE FIRST.

[This poem is given by Nahum Tate, in his *"Miscellanea Sacra,"* 1698.]

CLOSE thine eyes and sleep secure,
Thy soul is safe, thy body sure ;
He that guards thee, He that keeps,
Never slumbers, never sleeps.
A quiet conscience in a quiet breast,
Has only peace, has only rest ;
The music and the mirth of kings
Are out of tune unless she sings.
Then close thine eyes in peace, and rest secure,
No sleep so sweet as thine, no rest so sure.

ON NOTHING.

[This poem, by the witty Earl of Rochester (*temp.* Charles II.), is termed by Dr. Johnson " the strongest effort of his Muse."]

NOTHING ! thou elder brother even to shade,
Thou hadst a being ere the world was made,
And, well-fixed, art of ending not afraid.

Ere Time and Place were, Time and Place were not,
When primitive Nothing Something straight begot,
Then all proceeded from the great united—what ?

Something, the general attribute of all,
Severed from thee, its sole original,
Into thy boundless self must undistinguished fall.

Yet Something did thy mighty power command,
And from thy fruitful emptiness's hand
Snatched men, beasts, birds, fire, air, and land.

Matter, the wicked'st offspring of thy race,
By form assisted, flew from thy embrace ;
And rebel light obscured thy reverend dusky face.

With Form and Matter, Time and Place did join ;
Body, thy foe, with thee did leagues combine,
To spoil thy peaceful realm and ruin all thy line.

But turn-coat Time assists the foe in vain,
And, bribed by thee, assists thy short-lived reign,
And to thy hungry womb drives back thy slave again.

Though mysteries are barred from laic eyes,
And the divine alone, with warrant, pries
Into thy bosom, where the truth in private lies ;

Yet this of thee the wise may freely say,
Thou from the virtuous nothing tak'st away,
And to be part with thee the wicked wisely pray.

Great Negative ! how vainly would the wise
Inquire, define, distinguish, teach, devise,
Didst thou not stand to point their dull philosophies ?

Is or *is not*, the two great ends of Fate,
And true or false the subject of debate,
That perfect or destroy the vast designs of Fate,

When they have racked the politician's breast,
Within thy bosom most securely rest,
And when reduced to thee are least unsafe and best.

But, Nothing, why does Something still permit
That sacred monarchs should at council sit
With persons highly thought at best for nothing fit,

While weighty Something modestly abstains
From princes' coffers, and from statesmen's brains,
And nothing there like stately Nothing reigns ?

Nothing, who dwells with fools in grave disguise,
For whom they reverend shapes and forms devise,
Lawn sleeves, and furs, and gowns, when they, like thee, look wise.

French truth, Dutch prowess, British policy,
Hibernian learning, Scotch civility,
Spaniards' despatch, Danes' wit, are mainly seen in thee.

The great man's gratitude to his best friend,
King's promises, false vows, towards thee they bend,
Flow swiftly into thee, and in thee ever end.

LIFE DELUSIVE.

Albeit the flesh to death be thrall,
God hath the soul made immortal,
And so of his benignity,
Hath mixt his justice with mercy ;
Therefore call to remembrànce,
Of this false world the variànce:
How we like pilgrims, even and morrow,
Are travelling through this vale of sorrow;
Sometime in vain prosperity,
And sometime in great misery;
Sometime in bliss, sometime in bail,
Sometime right sick, and sometime hale;

Sometime full rich, and sometime poor :
Wherefore, my son, take little cure,
Neither of great prosperity,
Nor yet of greater misery,
But pleasant life, and hard mischance,—
Ponder them both in one balànce, ͵
Considering none other authority,—
Richcs, wisdom, nor dignity,
Empire of realms, beauty, nor strength,
May not one day our livès length :
Since we are sure that we must die,
Farewell all vain felicity.—*Sir David Lindsay.*

GO, LOVELY ROSE.

Go, lovely rose !
Tell hcr that wastes her time and mc,
    That now she knows
When I resemble her to thec,
How sweet and fair she seems to be.

    Tell her that's young,
And shuns to have her graces spied,
    That hadst thou sprung
In deserts where no men abide,
Thou must have uncommended died.

    Small is the worth
Of beauty from the light retired ;
    Bid her come forth,
Suffer herself to be desircd,
And not blush to be admired.

    Then die ! that shc
The common fate of all things rarc
    May read in thec,
How small a part of timc they share
That are so wondrous sweet and fair.
                Edmund Waller, 1605–1687.

THE UNKNOWN WORLD.

VERSES OCCASIONED BY HEARING A PASS-BELL.

[" The following piccc of original poetry, by Sterne, has been
handed down in succession from the composcr to the rev. gentlemen
who have succeeded him in thc living of Coxwold, and through the
kindness of the Rev. Gcorge Scott is now presented to the public."—
Gill's " Vallis Eboracencis."]

HARK, my gay friend, that solemn toll,
Spcaks the departure of a soul ;
'Tis gone, that's all we know—not where,
Or how the unbodied soul does fare.

In that mysterious world none knows
But He alone to whom it goes ;
To whom departed souls return
To take their doom, to smile or mourn.
Oh ! by what glimmering light we view
The unknown world we're hast'ning to !
God has locked up the mystic page,
And curtained darkness round the stage !
Wise Heaven, to render search perplext,
Has drawn 'twixt this world and the next
A dark impenetrable screen,
All behind which is yet unseen !

We talk of heaven, we talk of hell ;
But what they mean, no tongue can tell !
Heaven is the realm where angels are,
And hell the chaos of despair.

But what these awful truths imply,
None of us know before we die !
Whether we will or no, we must
Take the succeeding world on trust.

This hour perhaps our friend is well,
Death-struck the next, he cries, " Farewell !
I die !"—and yet for aught we see,
Ceases at once to breathe and be.

Thus launched from life's ambiguous shore,
Ingulfed in death, appears no more ;
Then, undirected, to repair
To distant worlds, we know not where.

Swift flies the soul ; perhaps 'tis gone
A thousand leagues beyond the sun,
Or twice ten thousand more thrice told,
Ere the forsaken clay is cold !

And yet, who knows, if friends we loved,
Though dead, may be so far removed ?
Only the veil of flesh between,
Perhaps they watch us though unseen.

Whilst we, their loss lamenting, say
They're out of hearing far away ;
Guardians to us, perhaps they're near,
Concealed in vehicles of air.

And yet no notices they give,
Nor tell us where, nor how they live ;
Though conscious whilst with us below,
How much themselves desired to know.

As if bound up by solemn fate
To keep the secret of their state,
To tell their joys or pains to none,
That man might live by faith alone.

Well, let my Sovereign, if He please,
Lock up His marvellous decrees ;
Why should I wish Him to reveal
What He thinks proper to conceal?
  It is enough that I believe
Heaven's brighter than I can conceive :
And he that makes it all his care
To serve God here shall see Him there !
  But oh ! what worlds shall I survey
The moment that I leave this clay?
How sudden the surprise, how new !
Let it, my God, be happy too.—*Laurence Sterne.*

"LIKE AS THE DAMASK ROSE YOU SEE."

[This fine poem has been attributed to Wastell, Quarles, Drake, and other seventeenth century authors. A correspondent of *Notes ana Queries* has recently claimed it for Richard Wates, as it is found in a manuscript book dated 1663, by that author. The authorship of the poem is, however, still unsettled.]

LIKE as the damask rose you see,
Or like the blossom on a tree,
Or like the dainty flower in May,
Or like the morning to the day,
Or like the sun, or like the shade,
Or like the gourd which Jonas had ;
Even such is man, whose thread is spun,
Drawn out and cut, and so is done.
  The rose withers, the blossom blasteth,
  The flower fades, the morning hasteth,
  The sun sets, the shadow flies,
  The gourd consumes, and man he dies.

Like to the grass that's newly sprung,
Or like a tale that's new begun,
Or like the bird that's here to-day,
Or like the pearlèd dew of May,
Or like an hour, or like a span,
Or like the singing of a swan;
Even such is man, who lives by breath,
Is here, now there, in life and death.
  The grass withers, the tale is ended,
  The bird is flown, the dew's ascended,
  The hour is short, the span not long,
  The swan's near death, man's life is done.

Like to the bubble in the brook,
Or in a glass much like a look,

M

Or like the shuttle in weaver's hand,
Or like the writing on the sand,
Or like a thought, or like a dream,
Or like the gliding of the stream ;
Even such is man, who lives by breath,
Is here, now there, in life and death.
　　The bubble's out, the look's forgot,
　　The shuttle's flung, the writing's blot,
　　The thought is past, the dream is gone,
　　The waters glide, man's life is done.

Like to an arrow from the bow,
Or like swift course of water-flow,
Or like that time 'twixt flood and ebb,
Or like the spider's tender web ;
Or like a race, or like a goal,
Or like the dealing of a dole ;
Even such is man, whose brittle state
Is always subject unto fate.
　　The arrow's shot, the flood soon spent,
　　The time no time, the web soon rent,
　　The race soon run, the goal soon won,
　　The dole soon dealt, man's life soon done.

Like to the lightning from the sky,
Or like a post that quick doth hie,
Or like a quaver in a song,
Or like a journey three days long,
Or like the snow when summer's come,
Or like the pear, or like the plum ;
Even such is man, who heaps up sorrow,
Lives but this day, and dies to-morrow.
　　The lightning's past, the post must go,
　　The song is short, the journey so,
　　The pear doth rot, the plum doth fall,
　　The snow dissolves, and so must all.

THE OLD FAMILIAR FACES.

I LOVED a love once, fairest among women :
Closed all her doors on me, I must not see her—
All, all are gone, the old familiar faces.

I have a friend, a kinder friend has no man ;
Like an ingrate, I left my friend abruptly,
Left him to muse on old familiar faces.

I have had playmates, I have had companions,
In my days of childhood, in my joyful school days,—
All, all are gone, the old familiar faces.

I have been laughing, I have been carousing;
Drinking late, sitting late, with my bosom cronies,—
All, all are gone, the old familiar faces.

Ghost-like I paced round the haunts of my childhood,
Earth seemed a desert I was bound to traverse,
Seeking to find the old familiar faces.

Friend of my bosom, thou more than a brother,
Why wert thou not born in my father's dwelling?
So might we talk of the old familiar faces.

How some they have died, and some they have left me,
And some are taken from me ; all are departed,—
All, all are gone, the old familiar faces.—*Charles Lamb.*

GEMS FROM THE OLD FRENCH POETS.

BALLAD.

OH ! fool of fools, and mortal fools,
    Who prize so much what Fortune gives ;
Say, is there aught man owns or rules
    In this same earth whereon he lives ?
What do his proper rights embrace,
Save the fair gifts of Nature's grace ?
    If from you then, by Fortune's spite,
    The goods you deem your own be torn,
    No wrong is done the while, but right ;
    For you had nought when you were born.

Then pass the dark brown hours of night
    No more in dreaming how you may
Best load your chests with golden freight ;
    Crave nought beneath the moon, I pray,
From Paris even to Pampelune,
Saving alone such simple boon
    As needful is for life below.
    Enough if fame your name adorn,
    And you to earth with honour go ;
    For you had nought when you were born.

When all things were for common use—
    Apples, all blithesome fruit of trees,
Nuts, honey, and each gum and juice,
    Both man, and woman too, could please.
Strife never vexed these meals of old :
Be patient then of heat and cold ;
    Esteem not Fortune's favours sure ;
    And of her gifts when you are shorn,
    With moderate grief your loss endure ;
    For you had nought when you were born.

Envoy.

If Fortune does you any spite—
Should even the coat be from you torn—
Pray, blame her not—it is her right ;
For you had nought when you were born.

Alain Chartier, 1386-1447.

THE BEREAVED LOVER.

IN sorrow's dark and lonesome grove
    I chance to find me on a day,
And meet the deity of Love,
    And hear her ask me of my way ;
I answer, that to make me flee
    To these dark woods, Fate long since chose,
And that she well might title me
A wandering man who knows not where he goes.

With sweet and condescending smile,
    Replies she, " Friend, if I but knew
Wherefore thou sufferest this while,
    I would give willing aid to you.
I set thee once in pleasure's way,
    Nor know how thou that way didst lose ;
It grieves me now to see thee stray,
A wandering man who knows not where he goes."

" Alas ! " said I, " most sovereign queen,
    The truth that thou must know why tell ?
By death's rude doings have I been
    Deprived of her I loved so well.
She was my only hope, my guide
    Through life and all its dreary woes ;
Now am I, since she left my side,
A wandering man who knows not where he goes."

SPRING.

THE season now hath cast away
    Its garb of cold and wind and rain,
And dons its bright and fair array
    Of smiling sunshine once again.
Once more do beast and bird assay
    To wake the unforgotten strain,
Because the season casts away
    Its garb of cold and wind and rain.

Charles D'Orleans, b. 1391.

DRINKING SONG.

WITH my back to the fire and my face to the board,
And flagons around me with jolly wine stored,

It shall not be my fate here below
Like a chick with the pip to dwindle away,
When the rosy wine ought to boast of a violet ray,
And my face beat the crimson in glow.
When my nose takes a hue, half of red half of blue,
I shall than bear the colours my love likes to view ;
Oh, your wine gives the loveliest glows !
There sure is more taste in a bright touch of red,
With rubies enriched, than in tints pale and dead,
Like those which your drink-water shows.
A swill at the spring is forbidden by all,
Lest a dropsical fate should my worship befall ;
And I die if I swallow a drop.
Wanting savour or smack, could I take to a drink ?
No, surely ; nor will any neighbour, I think,
With a grain of good sense in his top.
'Tis the love of good wine shows a good-natured soul,
And since the defunct never trowl the brown bowl,
Let us drink, as unsure of the morrow.
Here's a health then, all round, to this company,
Let each one who loves me my follower be,
And away with all moping and sorrow!

Oliver Basselin, 1440–1508.

NURSING MELANCHOLY

MOST pleasant it is, at first, to such as are melancholy given, to lie in bed whole days, and keep their chambers ; to walk alone in some solitary grove, betwixt wood and water, by a brook side, to meditate upon some delightsome and pleasant subject which shall affect them most ; *amabilis insania,* and *mentis gratissimus error;* a most incomparable delight it is so to melancholise and build castles in the air, to go smiling to themselves, acting an infinite variety of parts, which they suppose and strongly imagine they represent, or that they see acted or done. So delightsome these toys are at first, they could spend whole days and nights without sleep, even whole years alone in such contemplations and fantastical meditations, which are like unto dreams and they will hardly be drawn from them or willingly interrupted ; so pleasant their vain conceits are that they hinder their ordinary tasks and necessary business, they cannot address themselves to them or almost to any study or employment. These fantastical and bewitching thoughts so covertly, so feelingly, so continually set upon, creep in, insinuate, possess, overcome, distract, and detain them ; they cannot, I say, go about their more necessary business, stave off or extricate themselves, but are ever musing, melancholising, and carried along, as he (they say) that is led round about a heath with a *Puck* in the night ; they run earnestly on in this labyrinth of anxious and solicitous melancholy meditations, and cannot well or willingly refrain, or easily move off, winding and unwinding themselves as so many clocks, and still pleasing their humours, until at last the scene is turned upon a sudden by some bad object, and they being now habituated to such vain meditations and solitary places can endure no company, can ruminate on nothing but harsh and distasteful subjects. Fear, sorrow, suspicion, *subrusticus pudor,* discontent, cares, and weariness of life, surprise them in a moment, and they can think of nothing else, continually suspecting. No sooner are their eyes open but this infernal plague or melancholy seizeth on them, and terrifies their souls, representing some dismal object to their minds, which now by no means, no labour, no persuasion, they can avoid: " *hæret lateri lethalis arundo.*" —*Burton's Anatomy of Melancholy.*

FROM "A BALLAD UPON A WEDDING."

HER finger was so small, the ring
Would not stay on, which they did bring ;
　・ It was too wide a peck :
And to say truth (for out it must),
It looked like the great collar just
　About our young colt's neck

Her feet beneath her petticoat
Like little mice stole in and out
　As if they feared the light ;
And oh! she dances such a way
No sun upon an Easter-day
　Is half so fine a sight !

Her cheeks so rare a white was on,
No daisy makes comparison,
　(Who sees them is undone !)
For streaks of red were mingled there
Such as are on a Kath'rine pear,
　(The side that's next the sun.)

Her lips were red, and one was thin,
Compared to that was next the chin
　(Some bee had stung it newly) ;
But, Dick, her eyes so guard her face,
I durst no more upon her gaze
　Than on the sun in July.

Her mouth so small, when she does speak,
Thoud'st swear her teeth her words did break,
　That they might passage get ;
But she so handled still the matter,
They came as good as ours, or better,
　And are not spent a whit.—*Sir John Suckling.*

CHOOSING A WIFE AND TRAINING CHILDREN.

WHEN it shall please God to bring thee to man's estate, use great providence and circumspection in choosing thy wife ; for from thence will spring all thy future good or evil ; and it is an action of life, like unto a stratagem of war, wherein a man can err but once. If thy state be good, match near home, and at leisure ; if weak, far off and quickly. Inquire diligently of her disposition, and how her parents have been inclined in her youth. Let her not be poor, how generous, well-born soever ; for a man can buy nothing in the market with gentility, nor choose a base and uncomely creature altogether for wealth ; for it will cause contempt in others, and loathing in thee. Neither make choice of a dwarf, or a fool ; for by one thou shalt beget a race of pigmies ; the other will be thy continual disgrace, and it will irk thee to hear her talk ; for thou shalt find it to thy grief, that there is nothing more fulsome than a she-fool.

Bring thy children up in learning and obedience, yet without outward austerity. Praise them openly, reprehend them secretly, give them good countenance and convenient maintenance according to thy ability ; otherwise thy life will seem their bondage, and what portion thou shalt leave them at thy death, they will thank death for it, and not thee. And I am persuaded that the foolish cockering of some parents, and the overstern carriage of others, cause more men and women to take ill courses than their own vicious inclination. Marry thy daughters in time, lest they marry themselves. And suffer not thy sons to pass the Alps ; for they shall learn nothing there but pride, blasphemy, and atheism. And if by travel they get a few broken languages, that shall profit them nothing more than to have meat served in diverse dishes. Neither by my consent shalt thou train them up in wars ; for he that sets up his rest to live by that profession, can hardly be an honest man or a good Christian. Besides, it is a science no longer in request than use. For soldiers in peace are like chimneys in summer.—*Lord Burleigh to his Son.*

THE MARRIED MAN'S BEST PORTION.

[This quaint but excellent ballad appears to be very old, possibly of the time of Queen Elizabeth. It was re-printed as an " Old Ballad " in a popular magazine half a century ago.]

AMONGST those worldly joys of which
  Men equally may have their share,
Whereof the poor as well as rich
  Most commonly possessors are,
The greatest happiness I find
Is that which comes from women-kind :
  There is no comfort in this life
  Like to a constant loving wife.

A virtuous woman doth excel
   The richest treasure of the earth ;
Who can describe her parallel,
   Or fully set her praises forth ?
She is a Phœnix very rare,
She is a jewel past compare.
   There is no comfort in this life
   Like to a constant loving wife.

That man is happy in his choice,
   Who unto such a one is wed,
He may with cheerfulness rejoice
   Because that he so well hath sped ;
He hath his portion with the best
That with a virtuous wife is blest.
   There is no comfort in this life
   Like to a constant loving wife.

How sweet a sight it is to see
   A married pair so truly joined
In perfect love, that though there be
   Two persons, yet there's but one mind.
Such couples do enjoy content,
And in true peace their lives are spent.
   There is no comfort in this life
   Like to a constant loving wife.

A virtuous woman evermore
   Her husband's pleasure doth fulfil,
She treasures up his love in store,
   And always strives to do his will ;
She gives consent to what he says,
When he commands then she obeys.
   There is no comfort in this life
   Like to a constant loving wife.

She useth not abroad to roam
   Amongst the gossips' idle crew,
But careful is and stays at home
   With diligence her work to do :
Her family she will direct,
And give her husband due respect.
   There is no comfort in this life
   Like to a constant loving wife.

She's wary and she's provident,
   And often saves what others lose,
By right forecasting the event,
   She well doth know which way to choose.
Accordingly her course she steers,
And daily orders her affairs.

There is no comfort in this life
Like to a constant loving wife.

If that her husband fault doth find
  With anything that is amiss,
As soon as e'er she knows his mind
  She rests not till it mended is :
His love doth all her pains requite,
And in the same she takes delight.
  There is no comfort in this life
  Like to a constant loving wife.

When he with sickness is oppressed,
  Or any ways cast down with grief,
She suffers not her heart to rest,
  Till she hath gained him some relief ;
When he doth mourn, then she is sad,
When he rejoices she is glad.
  There is no comfort in this life
  Like to a constant loving wife.

If sometimes for a little space
  His business calls him forth from home,
She greatly longs to see his face,
  And often wishes he would come.
His presence gives her full content,
His absence she doth much lament.
  There is no comfort in this life
  Like to a constant loving wife.

She will not vary in the least
  From what at first she seemed to be ;
Her constancy shall be increased,
  But not disminished one degree ;
Her husband she hath vowed to love,
And she to him will faithful prove.
  There is no comfort in this life
  Like to a constant loving wife.

Thus having set before your eyes,
  In characters right plain to read,
A virtuous woman's qualities,
  I wish you now even well to speed :
Choose a good wife, and you shall see
My words will all fulfillèd be.
  There is no comfort in this life
  Like to a constant loving wife.

THE GOOD WIFE.

THE good wife is none of our dainty dames, who loves to appear in
a variety of suits every day new ; as if a good gown, like a stratagem

in war, were to be used but once. But our good wife sets up a sail according to the keel of her husband's estate ; and if of high parentage, she doth not so remember what she was by birth, that she forgets what she is by match. The good wife commandeth her husband, in any equal matter, by constantly obeying him. It was always observed that what the English gained of the French in battle by valour, the French regained of the English in cunning by treaties. So if the husband should chance by his power in his passion to prejudice his wife's right, she wisely knoweth by compounding and complying to recover and rectify it again.—*Fuller.*

A GOOD AND VIRTUOUS WIFE.

WHO doth desire that chaste his wife should be,
  First be he true, for truth doth truth deserve ;
Then be he such as she his worth may see,
  And, always one, credit with her preserve ;
Not toying kind, nor causelessly unkind,
Not stirring thoughts, nor yet denying right,
Not spying faults, nor in plain errors blind,
  Never hard hand, nor ever reins too tight ;
As far from want, as far from vain expense,
  Th' one doth enforce, the other doth entice ;
Allow good company, but drive from thence
  All filthy mouths that glory in their vice :
This done thou hast no more but leave the rest
To nature, fortune, time, and woman's breast.
                                        Sir Philip Sidney.

DEATH'S FINAL CONQUEST.

THE glories of our birth and state
  Are shadows, not substantial things ;
There is no armour against fate ;
  Death lays his icy hand on kings :
      Sceptre and crown
      Must tumble down,
And in the dust be equal made
With the poor crookèd scythe and spade.

Some men with swords may reap the field,
  And plant fresh laurels where they kill;
But their strong nerves at last must yield :
  They tame but one another still :
      Early or late
      They stoop to fate,
And must give up their murmuring breath,
When they, pale captives, creep to death.

The garlands wither on your brow,
Then boast no more your mighty deeds ;
Upon death's purple altar now
See where the victor victim bleeds :
All heads must come
To the cold tomb,—
Only the actions of the just
Smell sweet, and blossom in the dust.—*Shirley.*

[This poem is said to have been a favourite with Charles I.]

ON A GIRDLE.

THAT which her slender waist confined
Shall now my joyful temples bind :
It was my heaven's extremest sphere,
The pale which held that lovely deer ;
My joy, my grief, my hope, my love,
Did all within this circle move !
A narrow compass ! and yet there
Dwelt all that's good and all that's fair,—
Give me but what this ribbon bound,
Take all the rest the sun goes round.— *Waller.*

SICKNESS AND CONVALESCENCE.

SICKNESS.

FAREWELL, Life ! my senses swim,
And the world is growing dim :
Thronging shadows crowd the light,
Like the advent of the night.
Colder, colder, colder still,
Upwards steals a vapour chill ;
Strong the earthly odour grows—
I smell the mould above the rose !

RETURNING HEALTH.

Welcome, Life ! the spirit strives !
Strength returns, and hope revives ;
Cloudy fears and shapes forlorn
Fly like shadows at the morn :
O'er the earth there comes a bloom ;
Sunny light for sullen gloom,
Warm perfume for vapour cold—
I smell the rose above the mould !—*Thomas Hood.*

THE DEAD IN THE SEA.

UNDER the sea-waves bright and clear,
  Deep on the pearly, gravelly sands,
Sleeps many a brave his slumbers drear,
  Who joined the gay and festive bands
That pushed from forth their land and home,
Companions of the wild sea-foam,
When blasts arose and tossed their bark,
Till, whelmed beneath the waters dark,
The Storm King claimed them for his own,
That late in life and beauty shone !

Under the sea-waves green and bright,
  Deep on the pearly, gravelly sands,
Sleeps many a one in slumbers light,
  But not by the Storm King's ruthless hands ;
For there, within his narrow berth,
Lies the cold corpse of clammy earth !
Never to hail a harbour more,
Never to reach the friendly shore ;
To a rude plank his form they lash,
Heave overboard--waves sullen plash !
        *   *   *   *
There might be seen the stately mast,
  Bearing its freight of corpses lashed,
Clasped by the sea-rock, where the blast,
  Shattering it fiercely, wildly dashed ;
Gnawed by the worms, unconscious sleeper,
Rooted to rock-cliff all the deeper ;
Dreams perchance of the granite tower,
Beetling above his home's sweet bower ;
For under the sea-waves bright and green,
Among pure pearls of the silvery sheen,
Many a rustic companion sleeps,
Who sank in the wave-worn ocean deeps.

Slumber they far from home and hall ;
  Flowers there are none to deck their bier ;
Friends are not nigh to spread the pall,
  O'er their pale forms to shed the tear.
Balmy rosemary there is none ;
Rose-tree never shall breathe upon
Graves where, sweet, they sleep 'neath the billow,
Waving around no weeping willow.

Matters it not ! Though fall no tear
O'er the corpse in his briny bier,
Troubles it not the " dead in the sea "—
Salt tears around them flow ceaselessly.—*Freiligrath.*

ON THE TOMBS IN WESTMINSTER.

MORTALITY, behold and fear
What a charge of flesh is here !
Think how many royal bones
Sleep within these heaps of stones :
Here they lie, had realms and lands,
Who now want strength to stir their hands ;
Where from their pulpits, sealed with dust,
They preach—in greatness is no trust.
Here's an acre sown indeed
With the richest, royal'st seed
That the earth did e'er suck in,
Since the first man died for sin :
Here the bones of birth have cried,
Though gods they were, as men they died :
Here are wands, ignoble things,
Dropt from the ruined sides of kings.
Here's a world of pomp and state,
Buried in dust, once dead by fate.

Francis Beaumont, 1585-1616.

TO THE GRASSHOPPER.

HAPPY insect, what can be
In happiness compared to thee ?
Fed with nourishment divine,
The dewy morning's gentle wine !
Nature waits upon thee still,
And thy verdant cup doth fill ;
'Tis filled wherever thou dost tread,
Nature's self thy Ganymede ;
Thou dost drink and dance and sing,
Happier than the happiest king !
All the fields which thou dost see,
All the plants belong to thee ;
All that summer hours produce,
Fertile made with early juice.
Man for thee does sow and plough,
Farmer he, and landlord thou !
Thou dost innocently joy,
Nor does thy luxury destroy ;
The shepherd gladly heareth thee,
More harmonious than he.
Thee country hinds with gladness hear,
Prophet of the ripened year ;
Thee Phœbus loves and does inspire,
Phœbus is himself thy sire.

To thee, of all things upon earth,
Life is no longer than thy mirth.
Happy insect, happy thou!
Dost neither age nor winter know ;
But when thou'st drunk and danced and sung
Thy fill, the flowery leaves among,
(Voluptuous and wise withal,
Epicurean animal !)
Sated with thy summer's feast
Thou retir'st to endless rest !—*Cowley's Anacreontics.*

POETASTERS.

THESE equal syllables alone require,
Tho' oft the ear the open vowels tire ;
While expletives their feeble aid do join,
And ten low words oft creep in one dull line ;
While they ring round the same unvaried chimes,
With sure returns of still expected rhymes :
Where'er you find the cooling western breeze,
In the next line it " whispers through the trees ;"
If crystal streams " with pleasing murmurs creep,"
The reader's threatened (not in vain) with "sleep ;"
Then at the last, and only couplet, fraught
With some unmeaning thing they call a thought ;
A needless Alexandrine ends the song,
That, like a wounded snake, drags its slow length along.—*Pope.*

MODERATION.

THINGS which are in themselves fair and good, are liable to be spoiled by our handling, as if there was something infectious in our very touch. Virtue itself will become vice, if we clasp it with a desire too eager and violent. As for saying that there is never any excess of virtue, because it is no longer virtue if there be excess in it, it is mere playing upon words.

The wise for mad, the just for unjust pass,
If more than need, e'en virtue they embrace.—*Horace.*

This is a subtle consideration in philosophy. A man may both be too much in love with virtue, and carry himself to excess in a just action. Holy Writ agrees with this way of thinking. St. Paul says, " No man should think of himself more highly than he ought, but think soberly." I knew a great man who blemished his reputation for religion by making a show of greater devotion than all men of his condition. I love natures that are temperate and between the extremes.

An immoderate zeal, even for that which is good, though it does not offend me, astonishes me ; and I really am at a loss what name to give it. Neither the mother of Pausanias, who first pointed out the way, and laid the first stone for the destruction of her son ; nor the dictator Posthumius, who put his son to death, whom the heat of youthful blood had pushed with success upon the enemy a little before the other soldiers of his rank : neither of these instances, I say, seem to me so just as they are strange, and I should not like either to advise or imitate a virtue so savage and so expensive. The archer that shoots beyond the mark, misses it as much as he that comes short of it. And it offends my sight as much to lift up my eyes on a sudden to a great light, as to cast them down to a dark cavern. Callicles, in Plato, says that, "the extremity of philosophy is hurtful," and advises "not to dive deeper into it than what may turn to good account ; taken with moderation, it is pleasant and profitable, but in the extreme it renders a man brutish and vicious, a contemner of religion and the common laws, an enemy to civil conversation and all human pleasures, incapable of all political administration, and of assisting others, or even himself, and a fit object to be buffeted with impunity." And he says true, for in its excess it enslaves our natural liberty, and, by an impertinent curiosity, leads us out of the fair and smooth path which has been planned out for us by nature.—*Montaigne's Essays.*

WITHOUT GLADNESS AVAILS NO TREASURE.

BE merry, man, and tak not sair in mind
 The wavering of this wretched warld of sorrow ;
To God be humble, to thy friend be kind,
 And, with thy neighbours, gladly lend and borrow ;
 His chance to-night, it may be thine to-morrow ;
Be blythe in heart for my aventure,
 For oft with wise men it hath been said aforrow,
With Gladness avails no Trèasure.

Make thee gude cheer of all that God thee sends,
 For warld's wrak but welfare nought avails ;
Na gude is thine save only that thou spends,
 Remainent all thou bruikis but with bails ;
 Seek to solace when sadness thee assails ;
In dolour lang thy life may not endure,
 Wherefore of comfort set up all thy sails :
Without Gladness avails no Trèasure.

Follow on pity, flee trouble and debate,
 With famous folkès hold thy company ;
Be charitable and hum'le in thy estate,
 For warldly honour lashes but a cry,
 For trouble in earth tak no melancholy ;
Be rich in patience, if thou in gudes be poor ;
 Who lives merrily he lives mightily :
Without Gladness avails no Trèasure.

Dunbar, Ob. 1520.

THE HOUSE OF SLEEP.

HE making speedy way through spersèd air,
And through the world of waters wide and deep,
To Morpheus' house doth hastily repair.
Amid the bowels of the earth full steep,
And lo ! where dawning day doth never peep
His dwelling is ; there Tethys his wet bed
Doth ever wash, and Cynthia still doth steep
In silver dew his ever-drooping head,
While sad Night over him her mantle black doth spread.

Whose double gates he findeth lockèd fast,
The one fair framed of burnisht ivory,
The other all with silver overcast ;
And wakeful dogs before them far do lie,
Watching to banish Care, their enemy,
Who oft is wont to trouble gentle Sleep.
By them the sprite doth pass in quietly,
And unto Morpheus comes, whom drownèd deep
In drowsy fit he finds ; of nothing he takes keep [heed].

And more to lull him in his slumber soft,
A trickling stream from high rock tumbling down,
And ever-drizzling rain upon the loft,
Mixt with a murmuring wind, much like to sounc
Of swarming bees, did cast him in a swoune.
No other noise, nor people's troublous cries,
As still are wont t' annoy the wallèd town,
Might there be heard ; but careless Quiet lies
Wrapt in eternal silence far from her enemies.

Spenser, 1553-1599.

ON A CONTENTED MIND.

WHEN all is done and said,
 In the end thus shall you find,
He most of all doth bathe in bliss,
 That hath a quiet mind :
And, clear from worldly cares,
 To deem can be content
The sweetest time in all his life
 In thinking to be spent.

The body subject is
 To fickle Fortune's power,
And to a million of mishaps
 Is casual every hour :
And Death in time doth change
 It to a clod of clay ;
Whenas the mind, which is divine,
 Runs never to decay.

Companion none is like
Unto the mind alone :
For many have been harmed by speech ;
Through thinking, few, or none.
Fear oftentimes restraineth words,
But makes not thought to cease ;
And he speaks best that hath the skill
When for to hold his peace.

Our wealth leaves us at death,
Our kinsmen at the grave ;
But virtue of the mind unto
The heavens with us we have.
Wherefore, for virtue's sake,
I can be well content,
The sweetest time of all my life
To deem in thinking spent.

By Lord Vaux, from " The Paradise of Dainty Devices," 1576.

YOUTH AND AGE.

VERSE, a breeze 'mid blossoms straying,
Where Hope clung feeding, like a bee—
Both were mine ! Life went a Maying
With Nature, Hope, and Poesy,
When I was young !
When I was young ? Ah, woeful When !
Ah ! for the change 'twixt Now and Then !
This breathing house not built with hands,
This body that does me grievous wrong,
O'er airy cliffs and glittering sands,
How lightly then it flashed along :—
Like those trim skiffs, unknown of yore,
On winding lakes and rivers wide,
That ask no aid of sail or oar,
That fear no spite of wind or tide !
Nought eared this body for wind or weather
When Youth and I lived in't together.

Flowers are lovely ; Love is flower-like,
Friendship is a sheltering tree ;
Oh, the joys, that came down shower-like,
Of Friendship, Love, and Liberty,
Ere I was old !
Ere I was old ? Ah, woeful Ere,
Which tells me, Youth's no longer here !
O Youth ! for years so many and sweet,
'Tis known that thou and I were one,
I'll think it but a fond conceit—
It cannot be, that thou art gone !

N

Thy vesper-bell hath not yet tolled :—
And thou wert aye a masker bold !
What strange disguise hast now put on,
To make believe that thou art gone ?
I see these locks in silvery slips,
This drooping gait, this altered size ;
But springtide blossoms on thy lips,
And tears take sunshine from thine eyes !
Life is but thought : so think I will
That Youth and I are house-mates still.

Dewdrops are the gems of morning,
But the tears of mournful eve !
Where no hope is, life's a warning
That only serves to make us grieve
        When we are old :
That only serves to make us grieve,
With oft and tedious taking-leave ;
Like some poor nigh-related guest,
That may not rudely be dismist,
Yet hath outstayed his welcome while,
And tells the jest without the smile.—*Coleridge.*

THE CHARACTER OF A HAPPY LIFE.

[This little moral poem was written by Sir Henry Wotton, who died Provost of Eton, in 1639. Ben Jonson, when he visited Drummond at Hawthornden, had these verses " by heart."]

HOW happy is he born or taught
    That serveth not another's will ;
Whose armour is his honest thought,
    And simple truth his highest skill :

Whose passions not his masters are ;
    Whose soul is still prepared for death ;
Not tied unto the world with care
    Of prince's ear or vulgar breath :

Who hath his life from rumours freed ;
    Whose conscience is his strong retreat :
Whose state can neither flatterers feed,
    Nor ruin make oppressors great :

Who envies none whom chance doth raise,
    Or vice : who never understood
How deepest wounds are given with praise ;
    Nor rules of state, but rules of good :

Who God doth late and early pray,
    More of His grace than gifts to lend ;
And entertains the harmless day
    With a well-chosen book or friend ;—

This man is freed from servile bands
Of hope to rise or fear to fall ;
Lord of himself, though not of lands,
And having nothing, yet hath all.

PRUDENT HOUSEKEEPING.

TOUCHING the guiding of thy house, let thy hospitality be
moderate ; and according to the means of thy estate, rather
plentiful than sparing, but not costly ; for I never knew any
man grow poor by keeping an orderly table. But some consume
themselves by secret vices, and their hospitality bears the
blame. But banish swinish drunkards out of thine house, which is
a vice impairing health, consuming much, and makes no show. I
never heard praise ascribed to the drunkard, but for the well-bearing
of his drink, which is a better commendation for a brewer's horse or a
drayman, than for either a gentleman or a serving man. Beware thou
spend not above three of four parts of thy revenues, nor above a third
of that in thy house; for the other two parts will do more than defray thy
extraordinaries, which always surmount the ordinary by much ; otherwise thou shalt live like a rich beggar, in continual want. And the
needy man can never live happily or contentedly. For every disaster
makes him ready to mortgage or sell. And that gentleman who sells
an acre of land sells an ounce of credit. For gentility is nothing else
but ancient riches, so that if the foundation shall at any time sink, the
building must needs follow. Let thy kindred and allies be welcome
to thy house and table ; grace them with thy countenance, and further
them in all honest actions. For by this means thou shalt double the
band of nature, as thou shalt find them so many advocates to plead
an apology for thee behind thy back. But shake off those glow-
worms, I mean parasites and sycophants, who will feed and fawn upon
thee in the summer of thy prosperity ; but in an adverse storm they
will shelter thee no more than an arbour in winter.—*Lord Burleigh to
his Son.*

MORNING.

WAKE now, my love, awake ; for it is time ;
The rosy morn long since left Tithon's bed,
All ready to her silver coach to climb ;
And Phœbus 'gins to show his glorious head.
Hark ! how the cheerful birds do chant their lays.
And carol of Love's praise.
The merry lark her matins sings aloft ;
The thrush replies ; the mavis descant plays ;
The ousel shrills ; the ruddock warbles soft ;
So goodly all agree, with sweet consent,
To this day's merriment.
Ah ! my dear love, why do you sleep thus long,
When meeter were that you should now awake.

T' await the coming of your joyous make, [mate]
And hearken to the birds' love-learnèd song,
The dewy leaves among !
For of their joy and pleasance to you sing,
That all the woods them answer and their echo ring.
Spenser.

NIGHT.

MYSTERIOUS night ! when our first parent knew
Thee from report divine, and heard thy name,
Did he not tremble for this lovely frame,
This glorious canopy of light and blue ?
Yet 'neath a curtain of translucent dew,
Bathed in the rays of the great setting flame,
Hesperus with the host of heaven came ;
And lo ! Creation widened in man's view.
Who could have thought such darkness lay concealed
Within thy beams, O Sun ! or who could find,
Whilst fly and leaf and insect stood revealed,
That to such countless orbs thou mad'st us blind !
Why do we then shun death with anxious strife ?
If Light can thus deceive, wherefore not Life ?
Blanco White

HUMAN LIFE.

LIKE to the falling of a star,
Or as the flights of eagles are ;
Or like the fresh spring's gaudy hue,
Or silver drops of morning dew ;
Or like a wind that chases the flood,
Or bubbles which on waters stood,—
Even such is man, whose borrowed light
Is straight called in, and paid to-night.
The wind blows out ; the bubble dies ;
The spring entombed in autumn lies ;
The dew dries up ; the star is shot ;
The flight is past, and man forgot.
Dr. Henry King, 1591–1669.

FADE, flowers ! fade ; nature will have it so ;
'Tis what we must in our autumn do !
And as your leaves lie quiet on the ground,
The loss alone by those that loved them found ;
So in the grave shall we as quiet lie,
Missed by some few that loved our company ;
But some so like to thorns and nettles live,
That none for them can, when they perish, grieve.
Waller (from the French)

SLEEP.

CARE-CHARMER, Sleep, son of the sable Night,
  Brother to Death, in silent darkness born,
Relieve my anguish, and restore the light,
  With dark forgetting of my care return :
And let the day be time enough to mourn
  The shipwreck of my ill-advisèd youth ;
Let waking eyes suffice to wail their scorn,
  Without he torments of the night's untruth.
Cease, dreams, the images of day's desires,
  To model forth the passions of to-morrow ;
Never let the rising sun prove you liars,
  To add more grief to aggravate my sorrow.
    Still let me sleep, embracing clouds in vain,
    And never wake to feel the day's disdain.

Samuel Daniel, 1562–1619.

FAIR AND FICKLE.

HAST thou seen the down in the air
  When wanton blasts have tossed it
Or the ship on the sea,
  When ruder winds have crossed it ?
Hast thou marked the crocodiles weeping,
  Or the foxes sleeping ?
Or hast thou viewed the peacock in his pride,
  Or the dove by his bride ?
Oh, so fickle ; oh, so vain ; oh, so false, so false is she !

Sir John Suckling.

SONNET TO SLEEP.

COME, Sleep, O Sleep, the certain knot of peace,
  The baiting-place of wit, the balm of woe ;
The poor man's wealth, the prisoner's release,
  The indifferent judge between the high and low !
With shield of proof shield me from out the press [crowd]
  Of those fierce darts despair doth at me throw ;
Oh make in me those civil wars to cease :
  I will good tribute pay, if thou do so.
Take thou of me smooth pillows, sweetest bed ;
  A chamber deaf to noise and blind to light ;
A rosy garland and a weary head.
  And if these things, as being thine by right,
Move not thy heavy grace, thou shalt in me
Livelier than elsewhere Stella's image see.

Sir Philip Sidney.

ODE TO A FLY.

[Song, made extempore, by a gentleman, occasioned by a fly drinking out of his cup of ale.]

Busy, curious, thirsty fly,
Drink with me, and drink as I ;
Freely welcome to my cup,
Couldst thou sip and sip it up.
Make the most of life you may ;
Life is short, and wears away.

Both alike are mine and thine
Hastening quick to their decline :
Thine's a summer, mine no more,
Though repeated to threescore ;
Threescore summers when they're gone,
Will appear as short as one.

W. Oldys (Antiquary).

THE SWEET NEGLECT.

Still to be neat, still to be drest
As you were going to a feast ;
Still to be powdered, still perfumed,
Lady, it is to be presumed,
Though art's hid causes are not found,
All is not sweet, all is not sound.
Give me a look, give me a face,
That makes simplicity a grace ;
Robes loosely flowing, hair as free ;
Such sweet neglect more taketh me
Than all th' adulteries of art :
They strike mine eyes, but not my heart.

Ben Jonson.

SHAKSPEARE'S WIFE.

[The following poem is said to have been addressed by Shakspeare to Ann Hathaway, a Warwickshire beauty, whom he afterwards married. Although the authorship is, to say the least, doubtful, the lines exhibit an amusing and clever play upon the lady's surname.]

TO THE IDOL OF MY EYE, AND DELIGHT OF MY HEART,
ANN HATHAWAY.

Would ye be taught, ye feathered throng,
With love's sweet notes to grace your song,
To pierce the heart with thrilling lay,
Listen to mine Ann Hathaway !
She hath a way to sing so clear,
Phœbus might wondering stop to hear.

To melt the sad, make blithe the gay,
And Nature charm, Ann hath a way ;
    She hath a way,
    Ann Hathaway ;
To breathe delight, Ann hath a way.

When Envy's breath and rancorous tooth
Do soil and bite fair worth and truth,
And merit to distress betray,
To soothe the heart Ann hath a way.
She hath a way to chase despair,
To heal all grief, to cure all care,
From foulest night to fairest day.
Thou know'st, fond heart, Ann hath a way ;
    She hath a way,
    Ann Hathaway ;
To make grief bliss, Ann hath a way.

Talk not of gems,—the orient list,
The diamond, topaz, amethyst,
The emerald mild, the ruby gay ;
Talk of my gem, Ann Hathaway !
She hath a way, with her bright eye,
Their various lustre to defy,—
The jewels she, and the foil they,
So sweet to look Ann hath a way ;
    She hath a way,
    Ann Hathaway ;
To shame bright gems, Ann hath a way.

But were it to my fancy given
To rate her charms, I'd call them heaven ;
For though a mortal made of clay,
Angels must love Ann Hathaway ;
She hath a way so to control,
To rapture, the imprisoned soul,
And sweetest heaven on earth display,
That to be heaven Ann hath a way ;
    She hath a way,
    Ann Hathaway ;
To be heaven's self, Ann hath a way !

MARSTON MOOR.

To horse ! to horse ! Sir Nicholas ; the clarion's note is high !
To horse ! to horse ! Sir Nicholas, the big drum makes reply ;
Ere this hath Lucas marched, with his gallant cavaliers,
And the bray of Rupert's trumpets grows fainter in our ears.
To horse ! to horse ! Sir Nicholas ; white Guy is at the door,
And the Raven whets his beak o'er the field of Marston Moor.

Up rose the lady Alice from her brief and broken prayer,
And she brought a silken banner down the narrow turret stair ;
Oh, many were the tears that those radiant eyes had shed,
As she traced the bright word " Glory," in the gay and glancing
    thread ;
And mournful was the smile which o'er those lovely features ran,
As she said, " It is your lady's gift ; unfurl it in the van ! "

" It shall flutter, noble wench, where the best and boldest ride,
Midst the steel-clad files of Skippon, the black dragoons of Pride ;
The recreant heart of Fairfax shall feel a sicklier qualm,
And the rebel lips of Oliver give out a louder psalm,
When they see my lady's gewgaw flaunt proudly on the wing,
And hear the loyal soldiers shout, ' For God, and for the king ! '"

'Tis noon ; the ranks are broken along the Royal line.
They fly, the braggarts of the court ! the bullies of the Rhine !
Stout Langdale's cheer is heard no more, and Astley's helm is down,
And Rupert sheaths his rapier with a curse and with a frown ;
And cold Newcastle mutters, as he follows in their flight,
" The German boar had better far have supped in York to-night ! "

The knight is left alone, his steel-cap cleft in twain,
His good buff jerkin crimsoned o'er with many a gory stain :
Yet still he waves his banner, and cries amidst the rout,
" For Church and King, fair gentlemen ! spur on, and fight it out ! "
And now he wards a Roundhead's pike, and now he hums a stave,
And now he quotes a stage-play, and now he fells a knave.

God aid thee now, Sir Nicholas ! thou hast no thought of fear ;
God aid thee now, Sir Nicholas ! for fearful odds are here !
The rebels hem thee in, and at every cut and thrust,
" Down, down," they cry, " with Belial ! down with him to the dust ! "
" I would," quoth grim old Oliver, " that Belial's trusty sword
This day were doing battle for the saints and for the Lord ! "
                        W. M. Praed.

REMONSTRANCE AGAINST CRUELTY.

Why should man's high aspiring mind
    Burn in him with so proud a breath,
When all his haughty views can find
    In this world yields to Death ?
The fair, the brave, the vain, the wise,
    The rich, the poor, and great and small,
Are each but worms' anatomies
    To strew his quiet hall.

Power may make many earthly gods,
    Where gold and bribery's guilt prevails,
But Death's unwelcome honest odds
    Kicks o'er the unequal scales.

The flattered great may clamours raise
　Of power, and their own weakness hide,
But Death shall find unlooked-for ways
　To end the farce of pride.

An arrow, hurteled e'er so high,
　From e'en a giant's sinewy strength,
In time's untraced eternity
　Goes but a pigmy length.
Nay, whirring from the tortured string,
　With all its pomp of hurried flight,
'Tis by the skylark's little wing
　Outmeasured in its height.

Just so man's boasted strength and power
　Shall fade before Death's lightest stroke
Laid lower than the meanest flower
　Whose pride o'ertopt the oak.
And he who, like a blighting blast,
　Dispeopled worlds with war's alarms,
Shall be himself destroyed at last
　By poor despisèd worms.

Tyrants in vain their powers secure,
　And awe slaves' murmurs with a frown ;
But unawed Death at last is sure
　To sap the Babels down.
A stone thrown upward to the sky
　Will quickly meet the ground again ;
So men-gods of earth's vanity
　Shall drop at last to men ;

And power and pomp their all resign,
　Blood purchased thrones and banquet-halls
Fate waits to sack Ambition's shrine
　As bare as prison walls,
Where the poor suffering wretch bows down
　To laws a lawless power hath past ;
And pride, and power, and king, and clown,
　Shall be Death's slaves at last.

Time, the prime minister of Death,
　There's nought can bribe his honest will ;
He stops the richest tyrant's breath,
　And lays his mischief still :
Each wicked scheme for power all stops,
　With grandeurs false and mock display,
As eve's shades from high mountain-tops
　Fade with the rest away.

Death levels all things in his march,
　Naught can resist his mighty strength ;

The palace proud, triumphal arch,
  Shall mete their shadows' length ;
The rich, the poor, one common bed
  Shall find in the unhonoured grave,
Where weeds shall crown alike the head
  Of tyrant and of slave.—*Andrew Marvel.*

THE SHEPHERD'S RESOLUTION.

SHALL I, wasting in despair,
Die because a woman's fair?
Or make pale my cheeks with care,
'Cause another's rosy are ?
Be she fairer than the day,
Or the flowery meads in May,
    If she be not so to me,
    What care I how fair she be ?

Shall my foolish heart be pined,
'Cause I see a woman kind ?
Or a well-disposèd nature
Joinèd with a lovely feature ?
Be she meeker, kinder than
The turtle-dove or pelican,
    If she be not so to me,
    What care I how kind she be ?

Shall a woman's virtues move
Me to perish for her love ?
Or, her well-deservings known,
Make me quite forget mine own ?
Be she with that goodness blest
Which may merit name of Best,
    If she be not such to me,
    What care I how good she be ?

'Cause her fortune seems too high,
Shall I play the fool, and die?
Those that bear a noble mind,
Where they want of riches find,
Think what with them they would do
That without them dare to woo ;
    And unless that mind I see,
    What care I how great she be ?

Great or good, or kind or fair,
I will ne'er the more despair ;
If she love me, this believe,
I will die ere she will grieve.

If she slight me when I woo,
I ean scorn and let her go ;
If she be not fit for me,
What eare I for whom she be ?
George Wither, 1588-1667.

THE GARLAND.

THE pride of every grove I chose,
The violet sweet and lily fair,
The dappled pink and blushing rose,
To deck my darling Chloe's hair.

At morn the nymph vouchsafed to plaee
Upon her brow the various wreath ;
The flowers less blooming than her faee,
The scent less fragrant than her breath.

The flowers she wore along the day,
And every nymph and shepherd said,
That in her hair they looked more gay
Than growing in their native bed.

Undressed at evening, when she found
Their odours lost, their colours past,
She changed her look, and on the ground
Her garland and her eyes she east.

The eye dropped sense distinet and elear
As any Muse's tongue could speak,
When from its lid a pearly tear
Ran trickling down her beauteous eheek.

Dissembling what I knew too well,
My love, my life, said I, explain
This change of humour ; prithee tell,
That falling tear,—what does it mean ?

She sighed, she smiled, and to the flowers
Pointing, the lovely moral'st said,
See, friend, in some few fleeting hours,
See, yonder, what a change is made !

Ah, me ! the blooming pride of May
And that of beauty are but one :
At noon both flourish bright and gay,
Both fade at evening, pale and gone.
Matthew Prior, 1664-1721.

TO LUCASTA, ON GOING TO THE WARS.

TELL me not, sweet, I am unkind,
That from the nunnery
Of thy chaste breast and quiet mind,
To war and arms I fly.

True, a new mistress now I chase,
  The first foe in the field ;
And with a stronger faith embrace
  A sword, a horse, a shield.

Yet this inconstancy is such,
  As you, too, shall adore ;
I could not love thee, dear, so much,
  Loved I not honour more.—*Richard Lovelace.*

CONSTANCY.

OUT upon it ! I have loved
  Three whole days together ;
And am like to love three more,
  If it prove fine weather.

Time shall moult away his wings,
  Ere he shall discover
In the whole wide world again
  Such a constant lover.

But the spite on't is, no praise
  Is due at all to me ;
Love with me had made no stays
  Had it any been but she.

Had it any been but she,
  And that very face,
There had been at least ere this,
  A dozen in her place.
                    Sir John Suckling, 1608–1641.

RETROSPECTION.

THERE are moments in life that are never forgot,
  Which brighten and brighten as time steals away ;
They give a new charm to the happiest lot,
  And they shine on the gloom of the loneliest day !
These moments are hallowed by smiles and by tears,—
  The first look of love, and the last parting given,—
As the sun in the dawn of his glory appears,
  And the cloud weeps and glows with the rainbow in heaven.

There are hours, there are minutes, which memory brings,
  Like blossoms of Eden to twine round the heart ;
And as Time rushes by on the might of his wings,
  They may darken awhile, but they never depart :
Oh, these hallowed remembrances cannot decay ;
  But they come on the soul with a magical thrill,
And in days that are darkest, they kindly will stay,
  And the heart in its last throb will beat with them still.

They come like the dawn in its loveliness now,
  The same look of beauty that shot to my soul ;
The snows of the mountains are bleached on her brow,
  And her eyes in the blue of the firmament roll.
The roses are dimmed by the cheek's living bloom,
  And her coral lips part like the opening of flowers ;
She moves through the air in a cloud of perfume,
  Like the wind from the blossoms of jessamine bowers.

From the eyes' melting azure there sparkles a flame,
  That kindled my young blood to ecstacy's glow ;
She speaks—and the tones of her voice are the same
  As would once, like the wind-harp, in melody flow :
That touch, as her hand meets and mingles with mine,
  Shoots along to my heart with electrical thrill ;
'Twas a moment for earth too supremely divine,
  And while life lasts its sweetness shall cling to me still.

We met, and we drank from the crystalline well
  That flows from the fountain of science above ;
On the beauties of thought we would silently dwell,
  Till we looked, though we never were talking of love :
We parted—the tear glistened bright in her eye,
  And her melting hand shook as I dropped it for ever;
Oh, that moment will always be hovering by—
  Life may frown, but its light shall abandon me never !

Percival (American).

LABOUR.

O MORTAL man, who livest here by toil,
  Do not complain of this thy hard estate ;
That like an emmet thou must ever moil,
  Is the sad sentence of an ancient date.
And certes there is for it reason great;
  For though sometimes it makes thee weep and wail
And curse thy star, and early drudge and late,
  Withouten that would come a heavier bale,—
Loose life, unruly passions, and diseases pale.

Thomson's " Castle of Indolence."

THE AGE OF WISDOM.

Ho, pretty page, with dimpled chin,
  That never has known the barber's shear,
All your wish is woman to win,
This is the way that boys begin,—
  Wait till you come to Forty Year.

Curly gold-locks cover foolish brains,
  Billing and cooing is all your cheer ;
Sighing and singing of midnight strains,
Under Bonny Bell's window-panes,—
  Wait till you come to Forty Year.

Forty times over let Michaelmas pass,
  Grizzling hair the brain doth clear,—
Then you know a boy is an ass,
Then you know the worth of a lass,
  Once you have come to Forty Year !

Pledge me round, I bid ye declare,
  All good fellows whose beards are grey ;
Did not the fairest of the fair,
Common grow and wearisome, ere
  Ever a month was passed away ?

The reddest lips that ever have kissed,
  The brightest eyes that ever have shone,
May pray and whisper, and we not list,
Or look away, and never be missed,
  Ere yet ever a month is gone.

Gillian is dead.   God rest her bier !
  How I loved her twenty years syne !
Marian is married, while I sit here,
Alive and merry at Forty Year,
  Dipping my nose in Gascon wine !—*Thackeray.*

FROM COLERIDGE'S "KHUBLA KHAN.'

THE shadow of the dome of pleasure
  Floated midway on the waves,
Where was heard the mingled measure
  From the fountain and the caves.
It was a miracle of rare device :
A sunny pleasure-dome with caves of ice !

A damsel with a dulcimer
  In a vision once I saw ;
It was an Abyssinian maid,
And on her dulcimer she played,
  Singing of mount Abora.
Could I revive within me,
  Her sympathy and song,
To such deep delight 'twould win me,
  That with music loud and long,
I would build that dome in air,
  That sunny dome ! those caves of ice !
And all who heard should see them there,
And all should cry, Beware ! Beware !

Her flashing eyes, her floating hair !
Weave a circle round him thrice,
And close your eyes with holy dread,
For he on honey-dew hath fed,
And drank the milk of Paradise.

SPRING.

As biting Winter flies, lo ! Spring with sunny skies,
   And balmy airs ; and barks long dry put out again from shore ;
Now the ox forsakes his byre, and the husbandman his fire,
   And daisy-dappled meadows bloom where winter frosts lay hoar.

By Cytheria led, while the moon shines overhead,
   The Nymphs and Graces hand in hand with alternating feet
Shake the ground, while swinking Vulcan strikes the sparkles fierce
   and red
   From the forges of the Cyclops, with reiterated beat.

'Tis the time with myrtle green to bind our glistening locks,
   Or with flowers, wherein the loosened earth herself hath newly dressed,
And to sacrifice to Faunus in some glade amidst the rocks
   A yearling lamb, or else a kid, if such delight him best.

Death comes alike to all—to the monarch's lordly hall,
   Or the hovel of the beggar, and his summons none shall stay.
O Sestius, happy Sestius ! use the moments as they pass ;
   Far-reaching hopes are not for us, the creatures of a day.

Thee soon shall night enshroud ; and the manes' phantom crowd
   And the starveling house unbeautiful of Pluto shut thee in ;
And thou shalt not banish care by the ruddy wine-cup there,
   Nor woo the gentle Lycidas, whom all are mad to win.
                     Horace (Trans. Theo. Martin).

THE DIRGE.

What is the existence of man's life,
But open war or slumbered strife ;
Where sickness to his sense presents
The combat of the elements ;
And never feels a perfect peace
Till death's cold hand signs his release.

It is a storm—where the hot blood
Outvies in rage the boiling flood ;
And each loose passion of the mind
Is like a furious gust of wind,
Which beats his bark with many a wave,
Till he casts anchor in the grave.

It is a flower—which buds and grows
And withers as the leaves disclose ;
Whose spring and fall faint seasons keep,
Like fits of waking before sleep ;
Then shrinks into the fatal mould
Where its first being was enrolled.

It is a dream—whose seeming truth
Is moralized in age and youth ;
Where all the comforts he can share
As wandering as his fancies are ;
Till in a mist of dark decay
The dreamer vanish quite away.

It is a dial—which points out
The sunset as it moves about ;
And shadows out in lines of night
The subtle stages of Time's flight ;
Till all-obscuring earth hath laid
His body in perpetual shade.

It is a weary interlude—
Which doth short joys, long woes include :
The world the stage, the prologue tears,
The acts vain hopes and varied fears ;
The scene shuts up with loss of breath,
And leaves no epilogue but death.

Dr. Henry King.

THE FOUNTAIN OF BANDUSIA.

Bandusia's fount, in clearness crystalline,
    O worthy of the wine, the flowers we vow !
To-morrow shall be thine
    A kid, whose crescent brow

Is sprouting, all for love and victory,
    In vain ; his warm red blood so early stirred,
Thy gelid stream shall dye,
    Child of the wanton herd.

Thee the fierce Sirian star, to madness fired,
    Forbears to touch ; sweet cool thy waters yield
To ox with ploughing tired,
    And flocks that range afield.

Thou too one day shall win proud eminence
    'Mid honoured founts, while I the ilex sing
Crowning the cavern, whence
    Thy babbling wavelets spring.

Horace (Trans. by Prof. Conington).

SWEET THINGS.

'TIS sweet to hear,
At midnight on the blue and moonlit deep,
The song and oar of Adria's gondolier,
By distance mellowed, o'er the waters sweep ;
'Tis sweet to see the evening star appear ;
'Tis sweet to listen as the night winds creep
From leaf to leaf ; 'tis sweet to view on high
The rainbow, based on ocean, span the sky.

'Tis sweet to hear the watch-dog's honest bark
Bay deep-mouthed welcome as we draw near home ;
'Tis sweet to know there is an eye will mark
Our coming, and look brighter when we come ;
'Tis sweet to be awakened by the lark,
Or lulled by falling waters ; sweet the hum
Of bees, the voice of girls, the song of birds,
The lisp of children, and their earliest words.

Sweet is the vintage, when the showering grapes
In Bacchanal profusion reel to earth,
Purple and gushing ; sweet are our escapes
From civic revelry to rural mirth ;
Sweet to the miser are his glittering heaps ;
Sweet to the father is his first-born's birth ;
Sweet is revenge—especially to women,
Pillage to soldiers, prize-money to seamen.

Sweet is a legacy, and passing sweet
The unexpected death of some old lady
Or gentleman of seventy years complete,
Who've made " us youth " wait too, too long already
For an estate, or cash, or country-seat,—
Still breaking, but with stamina so steady,
That all the Israelites are fit to mob its
Next owner for their double-damned post-obits.

'Tis sweet to win, no matter how, one's laurels,
By blood or ink ; 'tis sweet to put an end
To strife ; 'tis sometimes sweet to have our quarrels,
Particularly with a tiresome friend ;
Sweet is old wine in bottles, ale in barrels ;
Dear is the helpless creature we defend
Against the world ; and dear the schoolboy spot
We ne'er forget, though there we are forgot.

Byron.

BROKEN FRIENDSHIP.

ALAS ! they had been friends in youth ;
But whispering tongues can poison truth ;

O

But constancy lives in realms above ;
   And life is thorny and youth is vain ;
And to be wroth with one we love
   Doth work like madness in the brain.
And thus it chanced, as I divine,
With Roland and Sir Leoline.
Each spake words of high disdain,
   And insult to his heart's best brother ;
They parted—ne'er to meet again !
   But never either found another
To free the hollow heart from paining ;
They stood aloof, the scars remaining
Like cliffs which had been rent asunder :
   A dreary sea now floats between—
But neither heat, nor frost, nor thunder,
   Shall wholly do away, I ween,
   The marks of that which once hath been.

Coleridge.

ODE TO THE NIGHTINGALE.

OH for a draught of vintage that hath been
   Cooled a long age in the deep-delvèd earth,
Tasting of Flora and the country green,
   Dance, and Provençal song, and sun-burnt mirth.
Oh for a beaker full of the warm South,
   Full of the blue, the blushful Hippocrene,
With beaded bubbles winking at the brim,
   And purple-stainèd mouth ;
That I might drink, and leave the world unseen,
And with thee fade away into the forest dim.

Fade far away, dissolve, and quite forget
   What thou amongst the leaves hast never known,
The weariness, the fever, and the fret,
   Here, where men sit, and hear each other groan ;
Where palsy shakes a few sad, last grey hairs,
   Where youth grows pale and spectre-thin, and dies,
Where but to think is to be full of sorrow
   And leaden-eyed despairs,
Where beauty cannot keep her lustrous eyes,
   Or new love pine again before to-morrow.

Away ! away ! for I will fly to thee,
   Not charioted by Bacchus and his pards,
But on the viewless wings of Poesy,
   Though the dull brain perplexes and retards :
Already with thee ! tender is the night,
   And happy the Queen Moon is on her throne,

Clustered around by all her starry fays ;
But here there is no light,
Save what from heaven is by the breezes blown
Through verdurous glooms and winding mossy ways

I cannot see what flowers are at my feet,
Nor what soft incense hangs upon the boughs,
But in embalmèd darkness guess each sweet,
Wherewith the seasonable month endows
The grass, the thicket, and the fruit-tree wild ;
White hawthorn and the pastoral eglantine ;
Fast-fading violets covered up in leaves,
And Mid-May's eldest child,
The coming musk-rose full of dewy wine,
The murmurous haunt of flies on summer eves.

Darkling I listen, and for many a time
I have been half in love with easeful Death,
Called him soft names in many a musèd rhyme,
To take into the air my quiet breath.
Now more than ever seems it sweet to die,
To cease upon the midnight with no pain,
While thou art pouring forth thy soul on high
In such an ecstasy !
Still wouldst thou sing, and I have ears in vain,
To thy high requiem become a sod.

Thou wast not born for death, immortal bird !
No hungry generations tread thee down ;
The voice I hear this passing night was heard
In ancient days by emperor and clown :
Perhaps the self-same song that found a path|
Through the sad heart of Ruth, when, sick for home,
She stood in tears amid the alien corn,
The same that oft times hath
Charmed magic casements opening on the foam
Of perilous seas, in faëry lands forlorn.

Forlorn !—the very sound is like a bell
To toll me back from thee to my sole self:
Adieu !—the fancy cannot cheat so well
As she is famed to do, deceiving elf.
Adieu !—adieu ! Thy plaintive anthem fades—
Past the near meadows—over the still stream—
Up the hill-side ; and now 'tis buried deep
In the next valley's glades :
Was it a vision, or a waking dream ?
Fled is that music ! Do I wake or sleep ?—*Keats.*

CARPE DIEM.

LET not the frowns of fate
   Disquiet thee, my friend;
Nor, when she smiles on thee, do thou, elate,
   With vaunting thoughts ascend
Beyond the limits of becoming mirth ;
For, Dellius, thou must die, become a clod of earth !

Whether thy days go down
   In gloom and dull regrets,
Or shunning life's vain struggle for renown,
   Its fever and its frets,
Stretched on the grass, with old Falernian wine,
Thou giv'st the thoughtless hours a rapture all divine.

Where the tall spreading pine
   And white-leaved poplar grow,
And, mingling their broad boughs in leafy twine,
   A grateful shadow throw,
Where down its broken bed the wimpling stream
Writhes on its sinuous way with many a quivering gleam,

There wine, there perfumes bring,
   Bring garlands of the rose,
Fair and too short-lived daughter of the spring,
   While youth's bright current flows
Within thy veins,—ere yet hath come the hour
When the dread Sisters Three shall clutch thee in their power.

Thy woods, thy treasured pride,
   Thy mansion's pleasant seat,
Thy lawns washed by the Tiber's yellow tide,
   Each favourite retreat,
Thou must leave all—all, and thine heir shall run
In riot through the wealth thy years of toil have won.

It recks not whether thou
   Be opulent and trace
Thy birth from kings, or bear upon thy brow
   Stamp of a beggar's race ;
In rags or splendour, death at thee alike,
That no compassion hath for aught of earth, will strike.

One road, and to one bourne
   We all are goaded.   Late
Or soon will issue from the urn
   Of unrelenting Fate
The lot, that in yon bark exiles us all
To undiscovered shores, from which is no recall.

                   Horace (trans. Theo. Martin).

FROM COLERIDGE'S "CHRISTABEL."

THE night is chill, the forest bare ;
Is it the wind that moaneth bleak ?
There is not wind enough in the air
To move away the ringlet curl
From the lovely lady's cheek ;
There is not wind enough to twirl
The one red leaf, the last of its clan,
That dances as often as dance it can,
Hanging so light and hanging so high,
On the topmost twig that looks up at the sky.

Hush ! beating heart of Christabel !
Jesu Maria shield her well !
She foldeth her arms beneath her cloak,
And stole to the other side of the oak.
          What sees she there ?
There she sees a damsel bright,
Dressed in a silken robe of white,
That shadowy in the moonlight shone :
The neck that made that white robe wan,
Her stately neck and arms were bare ;
Her blue-veined feet unsandalled were ;
And wildly glittered here and there
The gems entangled in her hair.
I guess 'twas frightful there to see
A lady so richly clad as she—
Beautiful exceedingly !

WASTED YOUTH.

BUT now at thirty years my hair is gray—
    (I wonder what it would be like at forty !
I thought of a peruke the other day)—
    My heart is not much greener ; and, in short, I
Have squandered my whole summer while 'twas May,
    And feel no more the spirit to retort ; I
Have spent my life, both interest and principal,
And deem not, what I deemed, my soul invincible.

No more—no more—Oh never more on me
    The freshness of the heart can fall like dew,
Which out of all the lovely things we see
    Extracts emotions beautiful and new,
Hived in our bosoms like the bag o' the bee,
    Think'st thou the honey with these objects grew ?
Alas ! 'twas not in them, but in thy power
To double even the sweetness of a flower.

No more—no more—oh never more, my heart,
  Canst thou be my sole world, my universe ;
Once all in all, but now a thing apart,
  Thou canst not be my blessing or my curse ;
The illusion's gone for ever, and thou art
  Insensible, I trust, but none the worse ;
And in thy stead, I've got a deal of judgment,
Though heaven knows how it ever found a lodgment.

My days of love are over ; me no more
  The charms of maid, wife, and still less of widow,
Can make the fool of which they made before,—
  In short, I must not lead the life I did do ;
The credulous hope of mutual minds is o'er ;
  The copious use of claret is forbid, too ;
So for a good old-gentlemanly vice,
I think I must take up with avarice.

Ambition was my idol, which was broken
  Before the shrines of Sorrow and of Pleasure ;
And the two last have left me many a token,
  O'er which reflection may be made at leisure ;
Now, like Friar Bacon's brazen head, I've spoken,
  "Time is, Time was, Time's past ;"—a chymic treasure
Is glittering youth, which I spent betimes—
My heart in passion, and my head in rhymes.—*Byron.*

DEATH THE COMMON LEVELLER.

WHATE'ER our rank may be,
We all partake one common destiny !
  In fair expanse of soil,
Teeming with rich return of wine and oil,
  His neighbour one outvies ;
  Another claims to rise
  To civic dignities,
Because of ancestry and noble birth,
Or fame, or proud pre-eminence of worth,
Or troops of clients, clamorous in his cause ;
  Still Fate doth grimly stand,
  And with impartial hand
The lots of lofty and of lowly draws
  From that capacious urn,
Whence every name that lives is shaken in its turn.

To him, above whose guilty head,
  Suspended by a thread,
The naked sword is hung for evermore,

Not feasts Sicilian shall
With all their cates recall
That zest the simplest fare could once inspire ;
Nor song of birds, nor music of the lyre
Shall his lost sleep restore :
But gentle sleep shuns not
The rustic's lowly cot,
Nor mossy bank o'ercanopied with trees,
Nor Tempe's leafy vale stirred by the western breeze.

The man who lives content with whatsoe'er
Sufficeth for his needs,
The storm-tossed ocean vexeth not with care,
Nor the fierce tempest which Arcturus breeds
When in the sky he sets,
Nor that which Hœdus, at his rise, begets ;
Nor will he grieve although
His vines be all laid low
Beneath the driving hail ;
Nor though, by reason of the drenching rain,
Or heat, that shrivels up his fields like fire,
Or fierce extremities of winter's ire,
Blight shall o'erwhelm his fruit-trees and his grain,
And all his farms delusive promise fail.

The fish are conscious that a narrower bound
Is drawn the seas around
By masses huge hurled down into the deep.
There, at the bidding of a lord, for whom
Not all the land he owns is ample room,
Do the contractor and his labourers heap
Vast piles of stone, the ocean back to sweep.
But let him climb in pride,
That lord of halls unblest,
Up to their topmost crest,
Yet ever by his side
Clim Terror and Unrest ;
Within the brazen galley's sides,
Care, ever wakeful, flits,
And at his back, when forth in state he rides,
Her withering shadow sits.

If thus it fare with all,
If neither marbles from the Phrygian mine,
Nor star-bright robes of purple and of pall,
Nor the Falernian wine,
Nor costliest balsams fetched from farthest Ind,
Can soothe the restless mind,
Why should I choose
To rear on high, as modern spendthrifts use,

A lofty hall, might be the home for kings,
With portals vast, for Malice to abuse,
Or Envy make her theme to point a tale ;
Or why for wealth, which new-born trouble brings,
Exchange my Sabine vale?

Horace (trans. Theo. Martin).

A PERSIAN SONG.

SWEET maid, if thou wouldst charm my sight,
And bid these arms thy neck enfold ;
That rosy cheek, that lily hand,
Would give the poet more delight
Than all Bokhara's vaunted gold,
Than all the gems of Samarcand.

Boy, let yon liquid ruby flow,
And bid thy pensive heart be glad,
Whate'er the frowning zealots say :
Tell them their Eden cannot show
A stream so clear as Rocnabad,
A bower so sweet as Mosellay.

Oh, when these fair perfidious maids,
Whose eyes our secret haunts infest,
Their dear destructive charms display,
Each glance my tender breast invades,
And robs my wounded soul of rest,
As Tartars seize their destined prey.

In vain with love our bosoms glow :
Can all our tears, can all our sighs,
New lustre to those charms impart?
Can cheeks, whose living roses blow
Where nature spreads her richest dyes,
Require the borrowed gloss of art ?

Speak not of fate : ah ! change the theme,
And talk of odours, talk of wine,
Talk of the flowers that round us bloom :
'Tis all a cloud, 'tis all a dream ;
To love and joy thy thoughts confine,
Nor hope to pierce the sacred gloom.

Beauty has such resistless power,
That even the chaste Egyptian dame
Sighed for the blooming Hebrew boy ;
For her, how fatal was the hour
When to the banks of Nilus came
A youth so lovely and so coy !

But ah ! sweet maid, my counsel hear—
Youth should attend when those advise
Whom long experience renders sage—
While music charms the ravished ear,
While sparkling cups delight our eyes,
Be gay, and scorn the frowns of age.

What cruel answer have I heard ?
And yet, by Heaven, I love thee still.
Can ought be cruel from thy lip ?
Yet say, how fell that bitter word
From lips which streams of sweetness fill,
Which nought but drops of honey sip ?

Go boldly forth, my simple lay,
Whose accents flow with artless ease,
Like orient pearls at random strung
Thy notes are sweet, the damsels say,
But oh ! far sweeter, if they please
The nymph for whom these notes are sung !—*Hafiz.*

TIMES GO BY TURNS.

THE loppèd tree in time may grow again,
    Most naked plants renew both fruit and flower ;
The sorriest wight may find release of pain,
    The driest soil suck in some moistening shower.
Times go by turns, and chances change by course,
From foul to fair, from better hap to worse.

The sea of fortune doth not ever flow ;
    She draws her favours to the lowest ebb :
Her tides have equal times to come and go ;
    Her loom doth weave the fine and coarsest web.
No joy so great but runneth to an end,
No hap so hard but may in fine amend.

Not always fall of leaf, nor ever spring,
    Not endless night, nor yet eternal day ;
The saddest birds a season find to sing,
    The roughest storm a calm may soon allay.
Thus with succeeding turns God tempers all,
That man may hope to rise, yet fear to fall.

A chance may win that by mischance was lost ;
    That net that holds no great, takes little fish ;
In some things all, in all things none are crost ;
    Few all they need, but none have all they wish.
Unmingled joys here to no man befall ;
Who least, hath some, who most hath never all.
                    Robert Southwell, 1560-1592.

THE JOURNEY OF LIFE.

WE rise in the morning of youth, full of vigour and full of expectation ; we set forward with spirit and hope, with gaiety and with diligence, and travel on a while in a straight road of piety towards the mansions of rest. In a short time we remit our fervour, and endeavour to find some mitigation of our duty, and some more easy means of obtaining the same end. We then relax our vigour, and resolve no longer to be terrified with crimes at a distance, but rely upon our own constancy, and venture to approach what we resolve never to touch. We thus enter the bowers of ease, and repose in the shades of security. Here the heart softens, and vigilance subsides ; we are then willing to inquire whether another advance cannot be made, and whether we may not, at least, turn our eyes upon the gardens of pleasure. We approach them with scruple and hesitation ; we enter them, but enter timorous and trembling, and always hope to pass through them without losing the road of virtue, which we, for a while, keep in our sight, and to which we propose to return. But temptation succeeds temptation, and one compliance prepares us for another ; we in time lose the happiness of innocence, and solace our disquiet with sensual gratifications. By degrees we let fall the remembrance of our original intention, and quit the only adequate object of rational desire. We entangle ourselves in business, immerge ourselves in luxury, and rove through the labyrinths of inconstancy, till the darkness of old age begins to invade us, and disease and anxiety obstruct our way. We then look back upon our lives with horror, with sorrow, with repentance ; and wish, but too often vainly wish, that we had not forsaken the ways of virtue. Happy are they who shall remember, that though the day is past and their strength wasted, there yet remains one effort to be made ; that reformation is never hopeless, nor sincere endeavours ever unassisted ; that the wanderer may at length return after all his errors ; and that he who implores strength and courage from above, shall find danger and difficulty give way before him.—*Johnson's "Rambler."*

CORPORAL TRIM ON THE FIFTH COMMANDMENT.

" I WILL enter into obligations this moment," said my father, " to lay out all my Aunt Dinah's legacy in charitable uses (of which, by the bye, my father had no high opinion), if the corporal has any one determinate idea annexed to any one word he has repeated." " Prithee, Trim," quoth my father, turning round to him, " what dost thou mean by ' honouring thy father and thy mother' ? " " Allowing them, an' please your honour, three-halfpence a day out of my pay when they grew old." " And didst thou do that, Trim ? " said Yorick. " He did, indeed," replied my Uncle Toby. " Then, Trim," said Yorick, springing out of his chair, and taking the corporal by the hand, " thou art the best commentator upon that part of the Decalogue ; and I honour thee more for it, Corporal Trim, than if thou hadst had a hand in the Talmud itself."—*Tristram Shandy.*

CURIOUS AND WITTY QUIPS AND CRANKS.

ACROSTIC ON NAPOLEON.

THE following acrostic on Napoleon was composed by a professor at Dijon, as soon as the entrance of the allies into that town had enabled its loyal population to declare in favour of its legitimate sovereign :—

N ihil fuit;
A ugustus evenit ;
P opulos reduxit ;
O rbem disturbavit ;
L ibertatem oppressit ;
E cclesiam distraxit ;
O mnia esse voluit ;
N ihil erit.

It would be difficult to give a more concise and more faithful history of Napoleon's whole career. Subjoined is a translation of this acrostic. It is impossible, of course, in a translation to preserve the order of letters which characterize this species of composition.

He was nothing ;
He became emperor ;
He conquered nations ;
He disturbed the world ;
He oppressed liberty ;
He distracted the church ;
He wished to be everything ;
He shall be nothing.

THE SEVEN WISE MEN OF GREECE.

I'LL tell the names and sayings, and the places of their birth,
Of the seven great ancient sages so renowned on Grecian earth :
The Lindian CLEOBULUS said, " The mean was still the best ;"
The Spartan CHILO, "Know thyself," a heav'n-born phrase confessed ;
Corinthian PERIANDER taught " Our anger to command :"
" Too much of nothing," PITTACUS, from Mitylene's strand ;
Athenian SOLON thus advised, " Look to the end of life,"
And BIAS from Prienè showed, " Bad men are the most rife ;"
Milesian THALES urged that " None should e'er a surety be :"
Few were their words, but if you look, you'll much in little see."
The Greek Anthology.—Anon.

THE TWELVE LABOURS OF HERCULES.

THE Nemean monster and the Hydra dire
I quelled ; the Bull, the Boar I saw expire

Under my hands.   I seized the queenly Zone,
And Diomede's fierce steeds I made my own.
I plucked the golden Apples ; Geryon slew,
And what I could achieve Augèas knew.
The Hind I caught, the vile Birds ceased their flight,
Cerberus I upwards dragged, and gained Olympus' height.

Philippus.

SIMILES.

As wet as a fish—as dry as a bone ;
As live as a bird—as dead as a stone ;
As plump as a partridge—as poor as a rat ;
As strong as a horse—as weak as a cat ;
As hard as a flint—as soft as a mole ;
As white as a lily—as black as a coal ;
As plain as a pike-staff—as rough as a bear ;
As tight as a drum—as free as the air ;
As steady as time—uncertain as weather ;
As heavy as lead—as light as a feather ;
As hot as an oven—as cold as a frog;
As gay as a lark—as sick as a dog ;
As slow as the tortoise—as swift as the wind ;
As true as the gospel—as false as mankind ;
As thin as a herring—as fat as a pig ;
As proud as a peacock—as blithe as a grig ;
As savage as tigers—as mild as a dove ;
As stiff as a poker—as limp as a glove ;
As blind as a bat—as deaf as a post ;
As cool as a cucumber—as warm as a toast ;
As flat as a flounder—as round as a ball ;
As blunt as a hammer—as sharp as an awl ;
As red as a ferret—as safe as the stocks ;
As bold as a thief—as shy as a fox ;
As straight as an arrow—as crook'd as a bow ;
As yellow as saffron—as black as a sloe ;
As brittle as glass—as tough as a gristle ;
As neat as my nail—as clean as a whistle ;
As good as a feast—as bad as a witch ;
As light as is day—as dark as is pitch ;
As wide as a river—as deep as a well ;
As still as a mouse—as loud as a bell ;
As sure as a gun—as true as the clock ;
As fair as a promise—as firm as a rock ;
As brisk as a bee—as dull as an ass ;
As full as a tick—as solid as brass ;
As lean as a greyhound—as rich as a Jew ;
And ten thousand similes equally new.

THE SOVEREIGNS OF ENGLAND.

FIRST, William the Norman, then William his son,
Henry, Stephen, and Henry, then Richard and John ;
Next, Henry the Third, Edwards one, two, and three,
And again, after Richard, three Henries we see ;
Two Edwards, third Richard, if rightly I guess,
Two Henries, sixth Edward, Queen Mary, Queen Bess,
Then Jamie the Scotchman, then Charles, whom they slew,
Yet received, after Cromwell, another Charles too ;
Next Jamie the Second ascended the throne,
Then William and Mary together came on ;
Till Anne, Georges four, and fourth William, all past,
God sent us VICTORIA,—may she long be the last.

MATRIMONY.

MATCHES are made for many reasons,—
  For love, convenience, money, fun, and spite ;
How many against common sense are treasons,
  How few the happy pairs that match aright !
In the fair breast of some bewitching dame,
  How many a youth will strive fond love to waken !
And when, at length, successful in his aim,
  Be first *mis*-led and afterwards *mis*-taken !
Then curse his fate, at matrimony swear,
  And, like poor Adam, have a *rib* to spare !
Old men young women wed—by way of nurses ;
  Young men old women—just to fill their purses :
Nor young men only,—for 'tis my belief
  (Nor do I think the metaphor a bold one),
When folks in life turn over a new leaf,
  Why, very few would grumble at a *gold* one !

CRITICS.

TILL critics blame and judges praise,
  The poet cannot claim his bays ;
On me when dunces are satiric,
  I take it for a panegyric ;
Hated by fools, and fools to hate,—
  Be that my motto, and my fate.—*Swift.*

THE TRIUMPH OF TOBACCO OVER SACK AND ALE.

NAY, soft ! by your leaves !
  Tobacco bereaves
You both of the garland ; forbear it :

You are two to one,
Yet tobacco alone
Is like both to win it and wear it.

Though many men crack,
Some of ale, some of sack,
And think they have reason to do it,
Tobacco hath more
That will never give o'er
The honour they do unto it.

Tobacco engages
Both sexes, all ages,
The poor as well as the wealthy ;
From the court to the cottage,
From childhood to dotage,
Both those that are sick and the healthy.

It plainly appears,
That in a few years
Tobacco more custom hath gained
Than sack or than ale,
Though they double the tale
Of the times wherein they have reigned.

And worthily too,
For what they undo
Tobacco doth help to regain ;
On fairer conditions
Than many physicians,
Puts an end to much grief and pain.

It helpeth digestion,
Of that there's no question ;
The gout and the toothache it easeth ;
Be it early or late,
'Tis never out of date,
He may safely take it that pleaseth.

Tobacco prevents
Infection by scents,
That hurt the brain and are heady.
An antidote is,
Before you're amiss,
As well as an after-remèdy.

The cold it doth heat,
Cools them that do sweat,
And them that are fat maketh lean ;
The hungry doth feed,
And, if there be need,
Spent spirits restoreth again.

The poets of old
Many fables have told,
Of the gods and their symposia ;
But tobacco alone,
Had they known it, had gone
For their nectar and ambrosia.

It is not the smack
Of ale or of sack,
That can with tobacco compare ;
For taste and for smell,
It bears off the bell
From them both, wherever they are.

For all their bravado,
It is Trinidado
That both their noses will wipe
Of the praises they desire,
Unless they conspire
To sing to the tune of his pipe.

Wit's Recreation, 1650.

THE ONE THING NEEDFUL.

WE may live without poetry, music, and art ;
We may live without conscience, and live without heart ;
We may live without friends, we may live without books,—
But civilized men cannot live without cooks.
He may live without books—what is knowledge but grieving ?
He may live without hope—what is hope but deceiving ?
He may live without love—what is passion but pining?
But where is the man that can live without dining ?

Owen Meredith.

RHYME AND REASON.

" GIVE," said Queen Elizabeth to Lord Burleigh, while Spenser knelt, poems in hand, "Give the youth one hundred pounds." " What," exclaimed Burleigh, " all this for a song ? " " Then give him what's reason," said the queen, thus leaving him in the hands of Burleigh, who ended in making him indeed Poet Laureate, but never bestowed the promised guerdon. Spenser's patience wearing out, he wrote these lines to the queen, which had the desired effect :—

" I was promised on a time,
To have Reason for my Rhyme ;
From that time until this season,
I've got neither Rhyme nor Reason."

ANAGRAMS.

AN anagram is the dissolution of any word or sentence into letters as its elements, and then making some other word or sentence from it, applicable to persons or things named in such original word or sentence.   The following is a selection of some of the best transpositions :—

Astronomers	Moonstarers.
Democratical	Comical trade.
Gallantries	All great sin.
Lawyers	Sly ware.
Misanthrope	Spare him not.
Masquerade	Queer as mad.
Monarch	March on.
Matrimony	Into my arm.
Melodrama	Made moral.
Midshipman	Mind his map.
Old England	Golden land.
Punishment	Nine thumps.
Penitentiary	Nay, I repent it.
Parishioners	I hire parsons.
Parliament	Partial men.
Radical reform	Rare mad frolic.
Revolution	To love ruin.
Sweetheart	There we sat.
Telegraph	Great help.

KISSES.

KISSES admit of a greater variety of character than, perhaps, even the ladies are aware, or than Johannes Secundus has recorded.   Eight basial diversities are mentioned in Scripture, viz. :—

Salutation	1 Sam. xx. 41 ; 1 Thess. v. 26.
Valediction	Ruth i. 9.
Reconciliation	2 Sam. xiv. 33.
Subjection	Ps. ii. 12.
Approbation	Prov. xxiv. 26.
Adoration	1 Kings xix. 18.
Treachery	Matt. xxvi. 49.
Affection	Gen. xlv. 15.

But the most honourable kiss, both to the giver and receiver, was that which Margaret, Queen of France, in the presence of the whole court, impressed upon the lips of the ugliest man in the kingdom, Alain Chartier, whom she one day found asleep, exclaiming to her astonished attendants, " I do not kiss the man, but the mouth that has uttered so many charming things."   Ah, it was worth while to be a poet in those days !—*Horace Smith's " Tin Trumpet."*

A QUARRELSOME FELLOW.

IT was said of John Lilburn, while living, by Judge Jenkins, that " if the world was emptied of all but himself, Lilburn would quarrel

with John, and John with Lilburn ;" which part of his character gave
occasion for the following lines at his death :—

> Is John departed, and is Lilburn gone ?
> Farewell to both, to Lilburn and to John.
> Yet, being dead, take this advice from me,
> Let them not both in one grave buried be :
> Lay John here, and Lilburn thereabout,
> For if they should both meet, they would fall out.

> > *Notes to Butler's "Hudibras."*

THE TIPPLING VICAR.

> An honest vicar, and a kind consort,
> That to the alehouse friendly would resort,
> To have a game at tables now and then,
> Or drink his pot as soon as any man ;
> As fair a gamester, and as free from brawl,
> As ever man should need to play withal ;
> Because his hostess pledged him not carouse,
> Rashly, in choler, did forswear her house :
> Taking the glass, this was the oath he swore,—
> " Now, by this drink, I'll ne'er come hither more."
> But mightily his hostess did repent,
> For all her guests to the next alehouse went,
> Following their vicar's steps in everything,
> He led the parish even by a string ;
> At length his ancient mistress did complain
> She was undone unless he came again ;
> Desiring certain friends of hers and his
> To use a policy which should be this :
> Because with coming, he should not forswear him,
> To save his oath they on their backs should bear him.
> Of this good course the vicar well did think,
> And so they always carried him to drink.—*Rowlands.*

THE SIEGE OF BELGRADE.

[This curious anonymous specimen of elaborate literary trifling
combines alliteration and acrostic].

> An Austrian army, awfully arrayed,
> Boldly by battery besieged Belgrade ;
> Cossacks commanding cannonading come,
> Dealing destruction's devasting doom ;
> Every endeavour engineers essay
> For fame, for fortune, forming furious fray.
> Gaunt gunners grapple, giving gashes good,
> Heaves high his head, heroic hardihood ;

Ibrahim, Islam, Ismail, imps in ill,
Jostle John Jarlovitz, Jem, Joe, Jack, Jill ;
Kicking kindling Kutuzoff, kings kingsmen kill,
Labour low levels loftiest longest lines ;
Men march 'mid moles, 'mid mounds, 'mid murderous mines.
Now nightfall's near, now needful nature nods,
Opposed, opposing, overcoming odds.
Poor peasants, partly purchased, partly pressed,
Quite quaking, " Quarter ! quarter !" quickly quest :
Reason returns, recalls redundant rage ;
Saves sinking soldiers, softens signiors sage.
Truce, Turkey, truce ! truce, treacherous Tartar train !
Vanish, vile vengeance ! vanish, victory vain !
Wisdom wails war—wails warring words. What were
Xerxes, Xantippe, Ximines, Xavier ?
Yet Yassy's youth, ye yield your youthful yest,
Zealously, Zanies, zealously, zeal's zest.

FIVE REASONS FOR DRINKING.

[These amusing lines were written by Aldrich (circ. 1690), author of " Hark ! the Bonny Christ Church Bells."]

IF on my theme I rightly think,
There are five reasons why men drink :
Good wine ; a friend ; because I'm dry ;
Or lest I should be by-and-by ;
Or any other reason why.

WOMAN'S WILL.

THE man's a fool who thinks by force of skill
To stem the torrent of a woman's will ;
For if she will, she *will*, you may depend on't,
And if she won't, she *won't*, and there's an end on't.

NUMBER NINE.

THERE are nine Muses to a poet ; nine tailors to a man ; nine points of the law to " one possessed ;" nine lives to a cat ; nine tails to a flogging ; nine points to an agony of whist ; nine diamonds to Pope Joan ; nine ninepins to a bowl ; nine cheers to a toast,—thrice to thine, and thrice to mine, and thrice again to make up nine !

EPIGRAMS.

ON SIR THOMAS MORE.

When *More* sometime had chancellor been,
No *More* suits did remain ;
The same shall never *More* be seen,
Till *More* be there again.

ON GARIBALDI.

When Garibaldi ceased his high command,
　And sheathed his sword—that sword a bright and keen one,
Nought in his pocket put he but his hand,
　A mighty hand, and nobler still, a *clean* one.

BAD MUSIC.

Men die when the night raven sings or cries,
But when Dick sings, e'en the night raven dies.
　　　　　　　　　　　　　　　Nicharchus.

The harper Simylus, the whole night through,
Harped till his music all the neighbours slew :
All but deaf Origen, for whose dull *ears*
Nature atoned by giving length of *years.—Leonidas.*

THE DECLARATION.

" Faith ! women are riddles !" I muttered one day,
　As I sat by my beautiful Bess ;
It seems very queer that whatever they say,
　Their meaning no mortal can guess.

I knew that she loved me by many a sign
　That served her affection to show ;
But when I suggested, Will Betty be mine ?
　Confound her !—she answered me, " No !"

'Tis the way with the sex—so I often had heard—
　And thus their assent they express ;
But I couldn't but think it extremely absurd
　That a " No" was the same as a " Yes."

So I asked her again, with my heart in a whirl,
　And said, " Do not answer me so !"
When twice in succession the mischievous girl
　Repeated that odious " No."

" There !" she said with a laugh, " that is certainly plain ;
　And your learning is not over-nice,
Or you wouldn't have forced me to say it again,
　For I think I have spoken it twice."

" I see," I exclaimed, as I clasped in my own
　The hand of my beautiful Bess ;
" I now recollect—what the grammar has shown—
　Two negatives equal a ' Yes.' "

　　　　　　　　　　　　John Godfrey Saxe.

DEAN SWIFT'S RECIPE FOR COURTSHIP.

Two or three dears, and two or three sweets,
Two or three balls, or two or three treats,
Two or three serenades, given as a lure,
Two or three oaths how much they endure,
Two or three messages sent in one day,
Two or three times led out from the play,
Two or three tickets for two or three times,
Two or three love-letters, writ all in rhymes ;
Two or three months' keeping strict to these rules
Can never fail making a couple of fools.

HOMER'S BIRTHPLACE.

Seven Grecian cities vied for Homer dead,
Through which the living Homer begged his bread.

Seven cities vied for Homer's birth, with emulation pious,—
Salamis, Samos, Colophon, Rhodes, Argos, Athens, Chios.

From the Greek.

A JACOBITE TOAST.

This clever *équivoque* is not generally accurately printed. The correct version is the following :—

" God bless the King, I mean the Faith's Defender,
God bless—no harm in blessing—the Pretender :
Who that Pretender is, and who is King,—
God bless us all, that's quite another thing."

These lines, " intended to allay the violence of party-spirit," were spoken extempore by John Byrom of Manchester, a man in his day renowned for his learning, his social qualities, and his sterling excellence of character, but better known as the inventor of a new system of shorthand.—*Notes and Queries.*

ALPHABET OF PROVERBS.

A grain of prudence is worth a pound of craft.
Boasters are cousins to liars.
Confession of a fault makes half amends.
Denying a fault doubles it.
Envy shooteth at others and woundeth herself.
Foolish fear doubles danger.
God reaches us good things by our own hands.
He has hard work who has nothing to do.
It costs more to revenge wrongs than to bear them.
Knavery is the worst trade.
Learning makes a man fit company for himself.
Modesty is a guard to virtue.

Not to hear conscience, is the way to silence it.
One hour to-day is worth two to-morrow.
Proud looks make foul work in fair faces.
Quiet conscience gives quiet sleep.
Richest is he that wants least.
Small faults indulged are little thieves that let in greater.
The boughs that bear most hang lowest.
Upright walking is sure walking.
Virtue and happiness are mother and daughter.
Wise men make more opportunities than they find.
You never lose by doing a good turn.
Zeal without knowledge is fire without light.

NOVEMBER.

No sun—no moon !
No morn—no noon—
No dawn—no dusk—no proper time of day—
No sky—no earthly view—
No distance looking blue—
No road—no street—no " t'other side the way--"
No end to any row—
No indications where the crescents go—
No top to any steeple—
No recognitions of familiar people—
No courtesies for showing 'em—
No knowing 'em !
No travelling at all—no locomotion—
No inkling of the way—no notion—
" No go—" by land or ocean—
No mail—no post—
No news from any foreign coast—
No park—no ring—no afternoon gentility—
No company—no nobility—
No warmth—no cheerfulness—no healthful ease—
No comfortable feel in any member—
No shade, no shine, no butterflies, no bees,
No fruits, no flowers, no leaves, no birds,—
November !—*Thomas Hood.*

ODE TO A GOOSE.

GOOSE, a bird, and word of reproach ; but I know not why. M. de Cotton, the French jurist, who came to this country to digest our laws and our dinners, and who pronounced our *cuisine* to be *fade et bornée,* records with an affectation of delicate disgust, that even at decent tables he had seen a goose—Gadso ! I can easily believe it, if he sat opposite a mirror. Why this calumniated fowl should be a byword for ridicule in our discourse, or an object of abomination at polite tables, is an enigma which it might puzzle Œdipus to solve. Every one knows that the Roman State was saved by the cackling of geese ;

a hint which has by no means been thrown away upon some of our short-witted and long-winded senators. Among the Romans the gander and his spouse were a favourite and a fashionable dish ; but learned commentators maintain that the particular bird to which the commonwealth was so much indebted was preserved, as well as all its immediate descendants, with the utmost care ; a circumstance which must have been much deplored by the epicures of that day, since it became impossible to have a Capitol goose for dinner.

Then, as now, the giblets were thought great delicacies, and good livers deemed their livers good, as appears by the following extract from Francis's Horace, B. II., Sat. 8 :—

> " And a white gander's liver,
> " Stuffed fat with figs, bespoke the curious giver."

Whence also we may see that epicurism extended even to colour. A modern white gander is a *rara avis.* Queen Elizabeth was cutting up a goose when she learned that the Spanish Armada had been cut up by a Drake ; why, then, should a bird, ennobled by so many historical, and endeared by so many culinary recommendations, be treated with scorn and contumely? If the reader sympathise with the writer in wishing to see some zealous, though tardy reparation made by a featherless biped to the biped who supplies us with feathers, he will peruse with a kindred complacency and indulgence the following,—

ODE TO A GOOSE.

(*Written after dinner on the Feast of Saint Michael.*)

Strophe I.

O bird most rare ! although thou art
    Uncommon common on a common,
        What man or woman
Can in one single term impart
A proper name for thee? An ancient Roman
Would answer, "Anser." Sure I am that no man,
Knowing thy various attributes, would choose
        To call thee Goose !

Antistrophe I

No, Goose ! thou art no Goose ! Well stuffed with sage,
    And titillating things both dead and living,
        For ever art thou giving
Solace to man in life's brief pilgrimage.

Epode I.

Jove's eagle wielding the avenging thunder,
Is but a folio-hawk, a bird of plunder,
        Minerva's owl,
        (Both are foul fowl !)

Shunning the light, should ne'er have been preferred
To rank as Wisdom's bird ;—
As for the young and stately swan,
A Scottish lawyer is the man
　　To sing its praises.
I am no writer to the cygnet—so
　　Avoiding further periphrasis,
For thee alone, O Goose ! my verse shall flow.

Strophe II.

O bird of Morpheus ! half our lives are sped,
Ay, and the happiest, too, upon a bed
Stuffed with thy feathers.　On thy breast
　　Thou hushest us to rest
　　As if we were thy goslings,
　　Till we forget life's hubble bubble,
　　　　Its toil and trouble,
　　　　Its crossings and its jostlings,
And borne in dreams to empyrean latitudes,
Revel in ecstasies and bright beatitudes.

Antistrophe II.

Churls that we are ! what snoozing hum
　　Ascends to thee ?—what pæans what adorings ?
Our mouths, perchance, are open, but they're dumb :
　　　　Our sole harangues
　　　　Are nasal twangs,
　　And all our gratitude consists of snorings.

Epode II.

Bird of Apollo ! worthy to pluck grass
　　On the Parnassian mountain,
　　Beside the classic fountain
Of Hippocrene, what Muse with thee can class
To whose inspiring wing we owe
　　All that the poets past have writ ;
From whose ungathered wings shall flow
　　All our whole store of future wit ?
　　　　Well may'st thou start,
　　　　Proud of thy pens uncut,
　　　　Which shall cut jokes,
　　　　In after times, for unborn folks,—
Well may'st thou plume thyself upon thy plumage—all
　　Is erudite and intellectual,
　　Each wing a cyclopædia, fraught
　　With genius multiform, a world of thought !
　　Ah ! when thou putt'st thy head
　　Beneath that wing to bed,

In future libraries thou tak'st a nap,
And dream'st of Paternoster Row, mayhap !
What are *they* dreaming of that they forget
   (The publishing and scribbling set)
   To apotheosize thee, O Goose !
   As the tenth Muse ?

Antistrophe III.

And then the darling driblets,
That constitute thy giblets,
   Whether in soup or stewed,
Oh ! what delectable and dainty food !
Full of my subject ('twas my dinner dish),
   No wonder that I feel all over goosy,
   Fired with what Braham calls " entusimusy,"
So much so, I could almost wish
   If fate were nothing loth,
   To be a Goose, instead of man.
" Be doubly happy in thy present plan "
   (Methinks the reader cries),
   " And thank the favouring destinies,
     " For now thou'rt *both!*"—*Horace Smith.*

SOPHOCLES' EPITAPH.

BY SIMMAIS OF THEBES.

CREEP, gently ivy, ever gently creep,
   Where Sophocles sleeps on in calm repose ;
Thy pale green tresses o'er the marble sweep,
   While all around shall bloom the purpling rose.
There let the vine with rich full clusters hang,
   Its fair young tendrils fling around the stone ;
Due meed for that sweet wisdom which he sang,
   By Music and by Graces called thine own.
          Translated by Professor Plumptre.

RIDDLE OF THE SPHYNX.

A BEING with four feet has two feet and three feet and only one voice ;
but its feet vary, and, when it has most, it is weakest.
   The answer of Œdipus :—
Hear thou against thy will, thou dark-winged Muse of the slaughtered ;
Hear from my lips the end bringing a close to thy crime :
Man is it thou hast described, who when on earth he appeareth,
First as a babe from the womb, four-footed creeps on his way ;
Then when old age cometh on, and the burden of years weighs full
   heavy,
Bending his shoulders and neck, as a third foot useth his staff.
     Sophocles' Œdipus. Translated by Prof. Plumptre.

A WISHING WELL.

ON a certain day in the year the young women of Abbotsbury used to go to the well near St. Catherine's Chapel, Milton Abbey, where they made use of the following prayer :—

"A husband, St. Catherine.
A handsome one, St. Catherine.
A rich one, St. Catherine.
A nice one, St. Catherine.
And soon, St. Catherine."

Notes and Queries.

NEWTON'S RIDDLE.

HORACE WALPOLE sends Lady Ossory "a very old riddle ; but if you never saw you will like it, and revere the riddle-maker, which was one Sir Isaac Newton, a great star-gazer and conjuror :"—

Four people sat down at a table to play,
They played all that night, and some part of next day ;
This one thing observed, that when all were seated,
Nobody played with them, and nobody betted ;
Yet when they got up, each was winner a guinea :
Who tells me this riddle I'm sure is no ninny.

The answer, "Musicians," is given in a subsequent letter. Lady Ossory had guessed it, though Walpole could not.

Notes and Queries.

FEMALE COURTSHIP.

TWO or three looks when your swain wants to kiss,
Two or three noes when he bids you say "yes,"
Two or three smiles when you utter the "no,"
Two or three frowns if he offers to go,
Two or three laughs when astray for small chat,
Two or three tears, though you can't tell for what,
Two or three letters when your vows are begun,
Two or three quarrels before you have done,
Two or three dances to make you jocose,
Two or three hours in a corner sit close,
Two or three starts when he bids you elope,
Two or three glances to intimate hope,
Two or three pauses before you are won,
Two or three swoonings to let him press on,
Two or three sighs when you've wasted your tears,
Two or three hums when the chaplain appears,
Two or three squeezes when the hand's given away,
Two or three coughs when you come to "*obey.*"
Two or three lasses may have by these rhymes,
Two or three little ones,—two or three times.

CURIOUS EPITAPH.

DEAD drunk here Elderton doth lie ;
Dead as he is, he still is dry :
So of him it may well be said,
Here he, but not his thirst, is laid.

This Elderton, who had been originally an attorney in the sheriff's court of London, and afterwards (according to Oldys) a comedian, was a facetious fuddling companion, whose tippling and rhymes rendered him famous among his contemporaries. He was the author of " The King of Scots and Andrew Browne," and of many other popular songs and ballads. He is believed to have fallen a victim to the bottle before the year 1592.—*Percy.*

CURIOUS ARITHMETICAL PROBLEM.

AN eminent Indian mathematician, named Seffa, is said to have invented the game of chess for the amusement of his royal master. The prince, in the usual style of Eastern ostentation, desired him to ask some reward adequate to his ingenuity, and worthy the munificence of a king. Seffa required only a quantity of wheat, equal to the number of grains arising from the successive doubling of a single grain for the first square of the chess-board, two for the second, and so on, doubling each product to the sixty-fourth square, and adding all the products together. When the quantity of wheat thus arising was computed, it was found to exceed all that Asia, or even the whole earth, could produce in one year. This question may be solved by multiplication and addition, but more expeditiously by geometrical progression. By this method it appears that the number of grains of wheat amounts to— 18,446,744,073,709,551,615. Allowing 9216 grains to an English pint, the quantity in bushels is easily calculated. For 9216 multiplied by 8 gives 73,728 grains in a gallon, and that by 8 gives 589,824 grains in a bushel. Dividing the original number by this last, we have 31,274,997,412,295 for the number of bushels. Now, if 30 bushels be the average product of an acre in a year, it requires 1,042,499,913,743 acres to produce so many bushels, or about eight times the surface of the globe.—*Encyc. Edinensis.*

SATIRICAL ADVERTISEMENT.

DURING the wars with France about the beginning of the present century, gold became very scarce in this country, Bank Notes being the common " circulating medium " instead of coin. The following amusing mock-advertisement regarding the scarcity of standard currency then prevalent, was published in the *European Magazine,* 1814 :—

A WHOLE FAMILY LOST ! ! !

If any of the relations, or next of kin, of one Mr. GUINEA, who about the year 1800 was much seen in England, and is supposed to be an

Englishman, will give information where he can *now* be met with, they will be handsomely rewarded on application to Mr. JOHN BULL, Growling Lane, opposite Threadneedle Street. A proportionate reward will be given for information relative to his son, Mr. HALF-GUINEA ; or his grandson, young SEVEN SHILLING PIECE. *Papers* innumerable have been issued in consequence of their disappearance, but all in vain ; and they are believed by many persons to have left the kingdom ; though others shrewdly suspect they lie hid somewhere in the country, waiting for more favourable times before they dare make their appearance ; as they have reason to suppose they would be instantly *taken up*, and put in *close confinement*. Their sudden disappearance is particularly to be regretted, as they were in great favour with the people, and enjoyed even the *King's countenance* to such a degree, that they actually bore the *Royal Arms*.

Notwithstanding they are persons of real worth, yet it must be confessed, that by getting occasionally into bad company, they have lost some little of their *weight* in society ; yet if they will return, all faults will be forgiven, no questions will be asked ; but they may depend upon being received with open arms by their disconsolate friends, who by this temporary separation have learnt how to appreciate their *sterling* worth.

They resemble each other very closely, and may very easily be known by their *round faces*, and by their complexion, which is of a *bright yellow ;* for though they, it is true, were born, and acquired their *polish* and insinuating manners in London, yet it is well ascertained that the family originally came, and derived their name, from the coast of *Guinea*, a place too well known in Liverpool to require any description.

GAFFER GRAY.

[This song is found in "Hugh Trevor," a novel, by Thomas Holcroft 1794.]

Ho ! why dost thou shiver and shake,
    Gaffer Gray ;
And why does thy nose look so blue ?
    " 'Tis the weather that's cold,
    'Tis I'm grown very old,
And my doublet is not very new,
    Well-a-day !"

Then line thy worn doublet with ale,
    Gaffer Gray ;
And warm thy old heart with a glass.
    " Nay, but credit I've none,
    And my money's all gone ;
Then say how may that come to pass ?
    Well-a-day ! "

Hie away to the house on the brow,
    Gaffer Gray ;
And knock at the jolly priest's door.

" The priest often preaches
Against worldly riches,
But ne'er gives a mite to the poor
Well-a-day ! "

The lawyer lives under the hill,
Gaffer Gray ;
Warmly fenced both in back and in front.
" He will fasten his locks,
He will threaten the stocks,
Should he ever more find me in want,
Well-a-day ! "

The squire has fat beeves and brown ale,
Gaffer Gray ;
And the season will welcome you there.
" His fat beeves and his beer,
And his merry new year
Are all for the flush and the fair,
Well-a-day ! "

My keg is but low, I confess,
Gaffer Gray ;
What then ?   While it lasts, man, we 'll live.
" The poor man alone,
When he hears the poor moan,
Of his morsel a morsel will give,
Well-a-day ! "

A SLIGHT OMISSION.

I HAPPENED to mention to my friend Simplex, that I knew an old man who, at the age of sixty, had cut a complete new set of teeth; and he immediately wrote an essay of fourteen sheets upon the subject, which he read with infinite applause at the Royal Society.   It was an erudite production, beginning with Marcus Curius Dentalus, and Cneius Papirius Carbo, who were born with all their teeth ; quoting the cases of Pyrrhus, king of Epirus, and Prussias, son of the king of Bithynia, who had only one continued tooth, reaching the whole length of the jaw; noticing the assertions of Mentzalius, a German physician, and our English Dr. Slare, who state instances of a new set of teeth being cut at the ages of 80 and 110 ; and embracing, in the progress of the discussion, all the opinions that had been expressed upon the subject, from Galen down to Peyer, Dr. Quincey, M. de la Harpe, Dr. Derham, Riolanus, and others.   I omitted at the time to mention one circumstance, which might have saved Simplex a deal of trouble, and the Society a deal of time.   The man to whom I alluded was—a *comb-cutter.—The Portfolio of a Punster.*

LYING EPITAPHS.

THE familiar maxim, "*De mortuis nil nisi bonum*," appears to be faithfully practised by epitaph writers. Dr. Johnson has said that the maxim should rather be, "After death, nothing but the *truth;*" but while sorrowing relatives may be excused from recording on the tombstone erected by affection the frailties of the "poor inhabitant below," it is certain they are not justified in crediting the deceased with having been distinguished by the noblest virtues when the reverse was the case. The following will serve as an example of the mendacious conventional epitaph :—

> "Here rests from labour and all worldly care,
> The *tender* father and the husband *dear*,
> Each fleeting day affection sweet did tend
> The *kind companion* and the *faithful friend ;*
> Mixed with its native dust the body lies,
> The *soul triumphant soars above the skies.*
> Stop, passenger, survey the hallowed spot,
> What now is here shall one day be thy lot."

Now, from the above one would naturally conclude that the person thus eulogized must have been an amiable and exemplary man,— "fondly loved" through life, and "deeply regretted" in death. It is asserted, however, that the deceased was "one of the worst of fathers, the most brutal of husbands, who spent most of his time in alehouses and brothels, and who finally fell a sacrifice to his own intemperance !" Dr. Donne thus ingeniously ridicules this practice of writing untruthful and verbose epitaphs,—

> "Friend, in your epitaphs I'm grieved,
> So very much is said ;
> One half will never be believed,
> The other never read."

THE HUSBAND'S PETITION.

> COME hither, my heart's darling,
> Come sit upon my knee,
> And listen while I whisper
> A boon I ask of thee.
>
> I feel a bitter craving,—
> A dark and deep desire
> That glows within my bosom
> Like coals of kindled fire.
>
> Nay, dearest, do not doubt me,
> Though madly thus I speak,—
> I feel thy arms about me,
> Thy tresses on my cheek ;

I know the sweet devotion
    That links thy heart with mine ;
I know my soul's emotion
    Is doubly felt by thine ;

And deem not that a shadow
    Has fallen across my love ;
No, sweet, my love is shadowless
    As yonder heaven above.

Oh, then, do not deny me
    My first and fond request :
I pray thee by the memory
    Of all we cherish best,—

By that great vow which bound thee
    For ever to my side,
And by the ring that made thee
    My darling and my bride !

Thou wilt not fail nor falter,
    But bind thee to the task,—
Put buttons on my shirt, love,
    That's all the boon I ask !

                    Bon Gaultier Ballads.

OLD SONG, IN PRAISE OF ALE.

[The sentiments contained in these verses, which were written in the reign of Charles II., will perhaps afford modern readers a pretty correct idea of what ale was in times past.]

WHEN the chill north-east wind blows,
    And winter tells a heavy tale,
When pyes and daws, and doobs and crows,
Do sit and curse the frosts and snows,
        Then give me Ale.

Ale, that the absent battle fights,
    And forms the march o' the Swedish drum,
Disputes the prince's laws and rights,
What's gone and past tells mortal wights,
        And what's to come.

Ale, that the ploughman's heart upleaps,
    And equals it to tyrant's thrones,
That wipes the eye that never weeps,
And lulls in soft and easy sleeps
        The tirèd bones.

Ale, that securely climbs the tops
Of cedars tall, and lofty towers,
When giddy grapes and creeping hops
Are holden up with poles and props,
For lack of powers.

When the Septentrion seas are froze
By Boreas his biting gale,
To keep unpinched the Russian's nose,
And save unrot the Vandal's toes,
Oh ! give them Ale.

Grandchild to Ceres, Barley's daughter,
Wine's emulous neighbour, if but stale,
Ennobling all the nymphs of water,
And filling each man's heart with laughter—
Ha ! give me Ale !

SHREWD DECISION OF ALI, CALIPH OF BAGDAD.

IN the preliminary dissertation of Richardson's "Arabic Dictionary," the following curious anecdote is recorded :—Two Arabians sat
down to dinner; one had five loaves, the other three. A stranger
passing by, desired permission to eat with them, which they agreed to.
The stranger dined, laid down eight pieces of money, and departed.
The proprietor of the five loaves took up five pieces, and left three for
the other, who objected, and insisted on having one half. The cause
came before Ali, who gave the following judgment :—"Let the owner of
the five loaves have seven pieces of money, and the owner of the three
loaves one ; for, if we divide the eight by three, they make twenty-
four parts ; of which he who laid down the five loaves had fifteen,
whilst he who laid down the three had only nine ; as all fared alike,
and eight shares was each man's portion, the stranger ate seven parts
of the first man's property, and only one belonging to the other ; the
money in justice must be divided accordingly."

OPPORTUNITY.

[The following is a translation (by Lord Neaves, in the Greek
Anthology) of an epigram composed by Posidippus on a statue of
Opportunity, executed by Lysippus the sculptor.]

" THE sculptor whence ?" " From Sicyon." " Who ?" " Lysippus is
    his name."
" And you ?" " I'm Opportunity, that all things rule and tame."
" On tiptoe why ?" " I always run." " Why winglets on your feet —
And double too ?" " Before the wind I fly with progress fleet."
" Why is a razor in your hand ?" " To teach men this to know,
That sharper than a razor's edge the times for action grow."

"Why this lock on your forehead?"   "That you all may seize me
   there."
"And why then is your occiput so very bald and bare ?"
"That none who once have let me pass may ever have the power
To pull me back, and bring again the once-neglected hour."
"Why did the artist fashion you ?"   "For your instruction, friend,
And placed me in this vestibule these lessons to commend."

REMOTE ANCESTRY.

SOME years before the French Revolution, one of the *Fermiers
Généraux*, who had raised himself from a low condition to great
opulence, being asked by a supercilious nobleman if his family were
very ancient, he replied, "My lord, there were three sons of Noah,
who came with him out of the ark ; I am descended from one of them,
but have not been able exactly to ascertain which."

A SERENADE.

THOUGH your drink were Tanais, the chillest of rivers,
   And your lot with some conjugal savage were cast,
You would pity, sweet Lycè, the poor soul that shivers
   Out here at your door in the merciless blast.

Only hark how the doorway goes straining and creaking,
   And the piercing wind pipes through the trees that surround
The court of your villa, while black frost is streaking
   With ice the crisp snow that lies thick on the ground.

In your pride—Venus hates it—no longer envelop ye,
   Or haply you'll find yourself laid on the shelf ;
You never were made for a cruel Penelope,
   'Tis not in the blood of your sires or yourself.

Though nor gifts nor entreaties can win a soft answer,
   Nor the violet pale of my love-ravaged cheek ;
To your husband's intrigue with a Greek ballet-dancer
   Though still you are blind and forgiving and meek,

Yet be not as cruel—forgive my upbraiding—
   As snakes, or as hard as the toughest of oak :
To stand out here, drenched to the skin, serenading
   All night, may in time prove too much of a joke !—*Horace.*

A BACHELOR'S SOLILOQUY.

To wed, or not to wed ? That is the question.
Whether it is advisable to bear
The dull privations of a single life,
Or marry, and in wedlock seek relief
From many woes ? To desperately woo
Some charming woman, decked with seraph lips,

And eyes that speak an ocean-stream of love ?
To marry her ? It is a consummation
Devoutly to be wished ; but where's the chance ?
To wed—to set up an establishment,
And have "a lot of bairns"?   Ay, there's the rub.
For it may be I shall not have the means
To do my duty to them all, and leave
My mortal reckoning ; bequeathing merit.
Hence reasoning makes me pause, and show respect
That dates celibacy a lengthy term ;
For how could I, chief party to a deed
In what is promised, faithfully and true,
A constant, generous, and a manly aid,
Fulfil my trust, unless I could afford it ?
I'd like to wed, for who would single be,
Or snore in solitude the live-long night.
But that the fear of curtain lectures, and
A yearly levy of "incumbrances"
(As heathen, churlish men their offspring call),
Perplexes me, and makes me rather bear
The ills I have, than fly to those unknown.

THE CUCKOO'S NOTE.

[These lines are attributed to Lawrence Sterne, the witty author of
·· Tristram Shandy."]

THE lark hath got a shrill, fantastic pipe,
  With no more music than a snipe ;
    Whereas the cuckoo's note
    Is measured and composed by rote :
    His method is distinct and clear,
        And dwells,
        Like bells,
      Upon the ear,
  Which is the sweetest music one can hear.

THE FRIEND OF HUMANITY AND THE NEEDY KNIFE-GRINDER.

[In this piece Canning ridicules the youthful Jacobin effusions of
Southey, in which, he says, it was sedulously inculcated that there was
a natural and eternal warfare between the poor and the rich.   The
Sapphic rhymes of Southey afforded a tempting subject for ludicrous
parody; and Canning quotes the following stanza lest he should be
suspected of painting from fancy, and not from life :—

  " Cold was the night-wind : drifting fast the snows fell ;
  Wide were the downs, and shelterless and naked ;
  When a poor wanderer struggled on her journey,
          Weary and foot-sore."
                          Chambers' Cyc. Eng. Lit.]
                          Q

FRIEND OF HUMANITY.

NEEDY Knife-Grinder ! whither are you going ?
Rough is the road, your wheel is out of order ;
Bleak blows the blast, your hat has got a hole in't,
    So have your breeches !

Weary Knife-Grinder ! little think the proud ones,
Who in their coaches roll along the turnpike-
Road, what hard work 'tis crying all day, " Knives and
    Scissors to grind, O !"

Tell me, Knife-Grinder, how came you to grind knives ?
Did some rich man tyrannically use you ?
Was it the squire, or parson of the parish,
    Or the attorney ?

Was it the squire, for killing of his game, or
Covetous parson, for his tithes distraining ?
Or roguish lawyer, made you lose your little
    All in a lawsuit ?

(Have you not read the " Rights of Man," by Tom Paine ?)
Drops of compassion tremble on my eyelids,
Ready to fall, as soon as you have told your
    Pitiful story.

KNIFE-GRINDER.

Story ! God bless you ! I have none to tell, sir.
Only last night, a-drinking at the Chequers,
This poor old hat and breeches, as you see, were
    Torn in a scuffle.

Constables came up for to take me into
Custody ; they took me before the justice ;
Justice Oldmixon put me in the parish-
    Stocks for a vagrant.

I should be glad to drink your honour's health in
A pot of beer, if you will give me sixpence ;
But for my own part I never love to meddle
    With politics, sir.

FRIEND OF HUMANITY.

I give thee sixpence ! I will see thee d——d first—
Wretch whom no sense of wrongs can rouse to vengeance—
Sordid, unfeeling, reprobate, degraded,
    Spiritless outcast !

(*Kicks Knife-Grinder, overturns his wheel, and exit in a transport
of republican enthusiasm and universal philanthropy.*)

JOLLY GOOD ALE AND OLD.

[This is a very old song. It is found in "Gammer Gurton's Needle," one of the earliest attempts in English comedy, supposed to have been written in 1565 by John Still, Master of Arts, and afterwards Bishop of Bath and Wells ; but the song is older than the play. Mr. Dyce, in his edition of Skelton, has printed an earlier copy of it from a MS.]

BACK and side go bare, go bare,
    Both foot and hand go cold ;
But, belly, God send thee good ale enough,
    Whether it be new or old.
I cannot eat but little meat,
    My stomach is not good,
But sure I think that I can drink
    With him that wears a hood :
Though I go bare, yet take no care,
    I am nothing a-cold ;
I stuff my skin so full within
    Of jolly good ale and old.
        Back and side go bare, etc.

I love no roast, but a nut-brown toast,
    And a crab laid in the fire ;
A little bread shall do me stead,
    Much bread I not desire.
No frost nor snow, no wind I trow,
    Can hurt me if I wolde,
I am so wrapt and thoroughly lapt
    Of jolly good ale and old.
        Back and side go bare, etc.

And Tib, my wife, that as her life,
    Loveth well good ale to seek,
Full oft drinks she, till ye may see
    The tears run down her cheek :
Then doth she troll to me the bowl,
    Even as a malt-worm sholde :
And saith, Sweetheart, I took my part
    Of this jolly good ale and old.
        Back and side go bare, go bare,
            Both foot and hand go cold ;
        But, belly, God send thee good ale enough,
            Whether it be new or old.

WOMAN'S REMONSTRANCE.

THEY'RE always abusing the women,
    As a terrible plague to men :
They say we're the root of all evil,
    And repeat it again and again ;

Of war and quarrels and bloodshed,
All mischief, be what it may :
And pray, then, why do you marry us,
If we're all the plagues you say ?

And why do you take such care of us,
And keep us so safe at home,
And are never easy a moment,
If ever we chance to roam ?

When you ought to be thanking Heaven
That your Plague is out of the way—
You all keep fussing and fretting—
" Where *is* my Plague to-day ? "

If a Plague peeps out of the window,
Up go the eyes of the men ;
If she hides, then all keep staring,
Until she looks out again.

Aristophanes. Trans. by Rev. W Lucas Collins, M.A.

DROLL QUESTIONS.

WE are tolerably familiar with the kind of out-door sports and pastimes of our ancestors in the olden time, but very little is known as to how they managed to get through the time when the inclemency of the weather precluded such exercises. It is true, the halls of the great were frequented by the ever-welcome wandering minstrels, or harpers, who entertained their noble and gentle patrons with recitations of metrical romances, and chanting " thrilling " tales of enchanted castles, fierce giants, doughty knights, and ladies of high degree, and who also related such items of news as they had gathered in the course of their travels throughout the country ; but how the humbler sort of people spent the long winter evenings, before the invention of printing placed books within their reach, has not been discovered. It is conjectured that the telling of stories, more or less legendary, and dealing largely with the supernatural, and asking each other what were thought to be difficult questions,—or *posers*, as we should call them,—probably formed their principal and favourite fireside amusements. Some notion of the kind of questions on which our ancestors were wont to exercise their wits is afforded by a sort of riddle-book, entitled " Demands Joyous," which was printed by Wynkyn de Worde, in 1511, and from which are selected the following " demands " and " responses " :—

Dem. What bore the best burden that was ever borne ?
Res. The ass that carried our Lady, when she fled with our Lord into Egypt.
Dem. What became of that ass ?
Res. Adam's mother ate her.

Dem. Who was Adam's mother?

Res. The earth.

Dem. How many calves' tails would it take to reach from the earth to the sky?

Res. No more than one, if it be long enough.

Dem. What is the distance from the surface of the earth to the deepest part thereof?

Res. Only a stone's throw.

Dem. What is it that never was and never will be?

Res. A mouse's nest in a cat's ear.

Dem. Why do men make an oven in a town?

Res. Because they cannot make a town in an oven.

Dem. How may a man discern a cow in a flock of sheep?

Res. By his eyesight.

Dem. Why doth a cow lie down?

Res. Because it cannot sit.

Dem. What is it that never freezeth?

Res. Boiling water.

Dem. How many straws go to a goose's nest?

Res. Not one; for straws not having feet, cannot go anywhere.

Dem. Who killed the fourth part of all the people in the world?

Res. Cain, when he killed Abel.

Dem. What man getteth his living backwards?

Res. A ropemaker.

Dem. Which are the most profitable saints of the church?

Res. Those painted on the glass windows, for they keep the wind from wasting the candles.

Dem. Who were the persons that made all, and sold all; that bought all, and lost all?

Res. A smith made an awl and sold it to a shoemaker, who lost it.

Dem. Why doth a dog turn round three times before he lieth down?

Res. Because he knoweth not his bed's head from the foot thereof.

Dem. What is the worst bestowed charity that one can give?

Res. Alms to a blind man; for he would be glad to see the person hanged that gave it to him.

WHOLESOME ADVICE.

I.

LIKE a fool, when near manhood, I got sick of home,
And, to better my state, was determined to roam;
As my father from evils was anxious to save me,
This wholesome advice, ere I left him, he gave me:
At first setting out, boy, be frugally bent,
For 'tis too late to spare, when, alas! all is spent;
And old age soon will come; so before youth declines,
You must strive to " make hay while the sun brightly shines."

II.

If you'd avoid troubles, and live without wrath,
Be sure " cut your coat as it best suits your cloth."
Ne'er be like to those men who themselves so enthral,
Nor like some, who "rob Peter to pay it to Paul."
Be not (if with good sense you'd always appear)
" Penny wise and pound foolish," as too many are ;
And take care not to say what you're told you should not,
For all will allow, " a fool's bolt is soon shot."

III.

If wisely you'd act, when ill-treated you are,
"Ne'er seek that by foul means which should be by fair :"
Nor insult any one, lest you meet with your match,
For " he who harm watches will often harm catch."
Think not all are friends though they seem you to prize,
For, " if daubed with honey, you ne'er will want flies :"
But should fortune frown, you'll be left e'en to chance,
For " 'tis no longer pipe, alas ! no longer dance."

IV.

If a man's kind to you, be to him a kind brother,
For surely " one good turn's deserving another;"
But if men are ungrateful with wine never treat 'em,
Nor " fool-like make feasts for wise men to eat 'em."
If employment you want, ne'er stand idle about,
You had best play a small game than stand wholly out ;
But if you prefer the pure gold to the dross,
Remember, " the rolling stone gathers no moss."

ON A DEAF HOUSEKEEPER.

[Paraphrased from the Greek. Anonymous.]

OF all the plagues I recommend to no man
To hire as a domestic a deaf woman.
I've got one who my orders does not hear,—
Mishears them rather, and keeps blundering near.
Thirsty and hot, I asked her for a *drink*,
She bustled out and brought me back some *ink*.
Eating a good rump steak, I called for *mustard*,
Away she went and whipped me up a *custard*.
I wanted with my chicken to have *ham*,
Blundering once more she brought a pot of *jam*.
I wished in season for a cut of *salmon*,
And what she brought me was a huge fat *gammon*.
I can't my voice raise higher and still higher,
As if I were a herald or town crier.
'Twould better be if she were deaf outright ;
But, anyhow, she quits my house this night.

CURIOUS EPITAPHS AND EPIGRAMS.

ON A MAN AND HIS WIFE.

HERE lies the man Richard,
And Mary his wife ;
Their surname was Prichard.
They lived without strife ;
And the reason was plain—
They abounded in riches,
Nor care had, nor pain,
And the wife *wore the breeches.—Anon.*

WHEN Elizabeth died, O Lord, prayed I,
Let me die too, and beside her lie.
The Lord was good, and heard my prayer,
And here we lie, a faithful pair.—*Anon.*

HE first deceased ; she for a little tried
To live without him, liked it not, and died,—*Wotton.*

ON A YOUNG LADY.

UNDERNEATH this stone doth lie
As much virtue as could die ;
Which, when alive, did vigour give
To as much beauty as could live.—*Ben Jonson.*

ON A SCOLDING WOMAN.

HERE lies, thank God, a woman who
Quarrelled and stormed her whole life through ;
Tread gently o'er her mouldering form,
Or else you'll rouse another storm.

ON A MISER.

HERE lies old father Gripe, who never cried " *Jam Satis,*"
'Twould wake him did he know you read his tomb-stone gratis.

AT CHELTENHAM.

HERE lie I and my three daughters,
Killed by drinking the Cheltenham waters ;
If we'd stuck to Epsom salts,
We shouldn't have been lying in these here vaults.

ON AN EASY-GOING COUPLE.

INTERRED beneath this marble stone,
Lie sauntering Jack and idle Joan ;
While rolling threescore years and one
Did round this globe their courses run.
If human things went ill or well,
If changing empires rose or fell,
The morning past, the evening came,
And found this couple still the same.
They walked and ate—good folks, what then?
Why then they walked and ate again !
They soundly slept the night away,
They did just nothing all the day.
Without love, hatred, joy, or fear,
They led a kind of—as it were :
Nor wished, nor cared, nor laughed, nor cried,—
And so they lived, and so they died.

ON AN EASY-GOING PERSON.

HERE lies one who was born, and cried,
Told three-score years, and then he died ;
His greatest actions that we find,
Were, that he washed his hands and dined.

THE FOLLOWING IS IN ONE OF THE LONDON CITY CHURCHES :

EARTH goes to ⎫
Earth treads on ⎪ ⎧ As mould to mould,
Earth as to ⎬ Earth, ⎨ Glittering in gold,
Earth shall be ⎪ ⎩ Return ne'er should,
⎭ Goe where he would.
Earth upon ⎫
Earth goes to ⎪ ⎧ Consider may,
Earth though on ⎬ Earth, ⎨ Naked away,
Earth shall on ⎪ ⎩ Be stout and gay,
⎭ Pass Poor away.

Be merciful and charitable,
Relieve the poor as thou art able ;
A shroud to thy grave
Is all that thou shalt have !

ANOTHER relic of this species of writing, on an old monument in St. Ann and St. Agnes, London, is equally ingenious, and much more laconic and excellent :

Qu   an   tris   di   c   vul   stra
   os   guis   ti   ro   um   nere   vit.
H   san   chris   mi   t   mu   la

In this distich the last syllable of each word in the upper line is the same as that of each corresponding word in the last line, and is to be found in the centre. It reads thus :

Quos anguis tristi diro cum vulnere stravit
Hos sanguis christi miro tum munere lavit.

Translated thus :

Those who have felt the serpent's venom'd wound
In Christ's miraculous blood have healing found.

ON THOMAS CROSSFIELD, M.D.

BENEATH this stone Tom Crossfield lies,
Who cares not now who laughs or cries ;
He laughed when sober, and when mellow,
Was a harum-scarum, harmless fellow :
He gave to none designed offence,
So—" *Honi soit qui mal y pense.*"

The subjoined is copied from an old churchyard at Llanfilantwthyl, Wales :

UNDER this stone lies Meredith Morgan,
Who blew the bellows of our church organ ;
Tobacco he hated, to smoke most unwilling,
Yet never so pleased as when pipes he was filling.
No reflection on him for rude speech could be cast,
Though he made our old organ give many a blast.
No puffer was he, though a capital blower,
He could fill double G and now lies a note lower.

IN the churchyard of St. Anne, Soho, London, is the following curious epitaph on Theodore, King of Corsica ; it is from the pen of Horace Walpole :—Near this place is interred Theodore, King of Corsica, who died in the parish, Dec. 11, 1756 ; immediately after leaving the King's Bench prison, by the benefits of the act of Insolvency ; in consequence he registered his kingdom of Corsica for the benefit of his creditors.

The Grave, great teacher, to a level brings
Heroes and beggars, galley-slaves and kings ;
But Theodore this moral learned, ere dead :
Fate poured its lessons on his living head,
Bestowed a kingdom, and denied him bread !

IRISH BULLS IN EPITAPHS.

HERE lies father and mother, sister and I,
We all died within the space of one short year ;
They all be buried at Wimble, except I,
And I be buried here.

HERE lies John Higley, whose father and mother were drowned in their passage from America. Had they both *lived, they would have been buried here !*

ON MARY HOPE.

ALL the rich qualities that poets framed
On those they most adored, *Hope* justly claimed,—
Wit, virtue, wisdom, all in *Hope* are gone,
Far from this world of weary trouble flown,
To that dread course oft travelled, yet unknown,
To meet a glorious resurrection.
Mourn wisely, then ; *Hope* does not truly die,
But change her being for eternity.

ON A MAN NAMED MILES.

THIS tombstone is a *Milestone* ; ha ! how so ?
Because, beneath lies *Miles,*—who's Miles below.

EPIGRAMS

WHAT ! rise again, with all my bones ?
  Quoth Giles, I hope you fib ;
I trusted, when I went to heaven,
  To go without my *rib !*

    The gravest Beast's an Ass ;
    The gravest Bird's an Owl ;
    The gravest Fish is an Oyster ;
    And the gravest Man's a Fool.

I never dine at home, said Harry Skinner ;
True ! when you dine not out, you get no dinner.

Thou addest daily to thy store thy gains,
Will a gold fleece give to a sheep more brains ?

Adam lay down and slept—and from his side
  A woman in her magic beauty rose ;
Dazzled and charmed he called that woman " bride,"
And his first sleep became his last repose.

A BISHOP'S BLESSING.

With covered head, a country boor
Stood, while the Bishop blessed the poor—
The mitred prelate lifted high
His voice—" Take off your hat "—" Not I.
Your blessing's little worth," he said,
" If through the hat 'twont reach the head."

Of all Job lost, his history tells us plain,
God gave him double portions back again ;
God did not take his plaguy wife—'tis true,
What could the patient man have done with *two?*

    Is it a wonder—with his pelf,
      That Tom his friends remembers not ?
    For friends are easily forgot
      By him who can forget himself.

ORIGIN OF PHRASES AND CUSTOMS.

"GOD TEMPERS THE WIND TO THE SHORN LAMB."

THE very beautiful sentiment, "God tempers the wind to the shorn lamb," has been so long a popular saying that it may almost rank as a proverb. It is well known that it occurs in Sterne's *Sentimental Journey*, published in 1768 ; but it is not very generally known that Herbert has the same idea in his "*Jacula Prudentum*," 1640 : "To the shorn sheep God gives wind by measure ;" and Herbert borrowed it from *Prémices*, by Henri Estienne, 1594, where it is thus expressed : "Dieu mesure le froid à la brebis tondue." There can be little doubt that Sterne borrowed from Herbert, who in his turn had it from the French author.

NATIONAL PROVERBS COMPARED.

SOMETIMES the proverb does not actually in so many words repeat itself in various tongues. We have indeed exactly the same thought ; but it takes an outward shape and embodiment, varying according to the various countries and periods in which it has been current. We have proverbs totally diverse from one another in their form and appearance, but which yet, when we look a little deeper into them, prove to be at heart one and the same ; all these differences being thus only, so to speak, variations of the same air. These are always an amusing, often an instructive study ; and to trace this likeness in difference has an interest lively enough. Thus the forms of the proverb, which brings out the absurdity of those reproving others for a defect or a sin, to whom the same cleaves in an equal or in a greater degree, have sometimes no visible connection at all, or the very slightest, with one another ; yet for all this the proverb is at heart and essentially but one. We say in English : "The kiln calls the oven, 'Burnt house ;'" the Italians : "The pan says to the pot, 'Keep off, or you'll smutch me ;'" the Spaniards : "The raven crieth to the crow, 'Avaunt, Blackamoor ;'" the Germans : "One ass nicknames another, 'Long-ears ;'" while it must be owned that there is a certain originality in the Catalan version of the proverb : "Death said to the man with his throat cut, 'How ugly you look.'" Under how rich a variety of forms does one and the same thought array itself here !

Let me quote another illustration of the same fact. We probably take for granted that "Coals to Newcastle" is a thoroughly English expression of the absurdity of sending to a place that which already abounds there,—water to the sea, faggots to the wood ; and English of course it is in the outward garment which it wears ; but in its innermost being it belongs to the whole world and to all times. Thus the Greeks said : "Owls to Athens," Attica abounding with these birds ;

the Rabbis : "Enchantments to Egypt," Egypt being of old esteemed the head-quarters of all magic ; the Orientals : "Pepper to Hindostan ;" and in the middle ages they had this proverb : "Indulgences to Rome," Rome being the centre and source of spiritual traffic ; and these by no means exhaust the list.

Let me adduce some other variations of the same description, though not running through quite so many languages. Thus compare the German : "Who lets one sit on his shoulders, shall have him presently sit on his head," with the Italian : "If thou suffer a calf to be laid on thee, within a little they'll clap on the cow ;" and again with the Spanish : "Give me where I may sit down, I will make where I may lie down." They all plainly contain one and the same hint, that undue liberties are best resisted at the outset, being otherwise liable to be followed up by other and greater ones ; but this under how rich and humorous a variety of forms. Not very different are these that follow. We say : "Daub yourself with honey, and you'll be covered with flies ;" the Danes : "Make yourself an ass, and you'll have every man's sack on your shoulders ;" while the French : "Who makes himself a sheep, the wolf devours him ;" and the Persians : "Be not all sugar, or the world will swallow thee up ;" to which they add, however, as its necessary complement, "nor yet all wormwood, or the world will spit thee out." Or again, we are content to say without a figure : "The receiver's as bad as the thief ;" but the French : "He sins as much who holds the sack, as he who puts into it ;" and the Germans ; "He who holds the ladder is as guilty as he who mounts the wall."—*Trench on the Lessons in Proverbs.*

"EXTREMES MEET."

CONSIDER such a proverb as the short but well-known one, "Extremes meet." Short as it is, it is yet a motto on which whole volumes might be written, which is finding its illustration every day,—in small and in great, in things trivial and in things most important, in the histories of single men, and in those of nations and of Churches. Consider some of its every-day fulfilments : old age ending in second childhood ; cold performing the effects of heat, and scorching as heat would have done ; the extremities alike of joy and of grief find utterance in tears ; the second singular "thou," instead of the plural "you," employed in so many languages to inferiors and to God—never to equals ; just as servants and children are alike called by the Christian name, but not those who stand in the midway of intimacy between them. Or, to take some further illustrations from the moral world of extremes meeting, observe how often those who begin their lives as spendthrifts end them as misers ; how often the flatterer and the calumniator meet in the same person ; out of a sense of which the Italians say well : "Who paints me before, blackens me behind ;" observe how those who yesterday would have sacrificed to Paul as a god, will to-day stone him as a malefactor ; even as Roman emperors would one day have blasphemous honours paid to them by the populace, and the next their bodies would be dragged by a hook through the streets of the city, to be flung into the common sewer. Or note again, in what close alliance, hardness and softness, cruelty and self-indulgence, are continually found ; or in law, how the *summum jus*, where unredressed by equity, becomes the *summa injuria*, as in the case of Shylock's pound of flesh, which was indeed no more than was in the bond. Or, once more, consider the exactly similar position in respect of Scripture, taken up by the Romanists on the one side, the Quakers and Familists on the other. Seeming, and in much being, so remote from one another, they yet have this fundamental in common : that Scripture, insufficient in itself, needs a supplement from without; those finding it in a Pope, and these in what they call the "inward light." With these examples before you, not to speak of the many others which may be adduced, you will own, I think, that the proverb, "Extremes meet," or its parallel, "Too far east is west," reaches very far into the heart of things.—*Trench.*

ORIGIN OF THE WORD "TARIFF."

ANOTHER word, of which I have never seen the true derivation in any English dictionary, although probably a good Spanish would supply it, is "Tariff;" nor is it unworthy to be traced. We all know the meaning of the word, that it signifies a fixed scale of duties levied upon imports. If you turn to a map of Spain, you will observe at its southern point, and running out into the Straits of Gibraltar, a promontory, which from its position is admirably adapted for commanding the entrance of the Mediterranean Sea, and watching the exit and entrance of all ships. A fortress stands upon this promontory, called now, as it was also called in the times of the Moorish domination in Spain, "Tarifa." The name, indeed, is of Moorish origin ; it was the custom of the Moors to watch from this point all merchant ships going into or coming out of the midland sea ; and issuing from this stronghold, to levy a certain fixed scale of duty on all merchandise passing in and out of the Straits, and this was called, from the place where it was levied, "Tarifa, or Tariff;" and in this way we have acquired the word. —*Trench on the Study of Words.*

THE BROOM AT A SHIP'S MAST-HEAD.

THE practice of hanging out a broom at the mast-heads of ships offered for sale, originated from that period of our history when the Dutch admiral, Van Tromp, with his fleet, appeared on our coasts, in hostility against England ; and to indicate that he would sweep the English navy from the seas, hoisted a broom at the masthead of his ship. To repel this insolence the English admiral hoisted a horse-whip, equally indicative of his intention to chastise the Dutchman. The pennant, which symbolised the horsewhip, has ever since been the distinguishing mark of ships of war.

HOB AND NOB.

THIS phrase, according to Grose the antiquary, arose as follows:
—When large chimneys were in fashion, there was at each corner of
the hearth a small elevated projection, called the hob.   In winter time
the beer was placed on the hob to warm, and the cold beer was set on
a small table called the *nob;* so the question " Will you hob or nob?"
meant, " Will you have warm or cold beer ?"   Another author says
that the phrase is a corruption of the old *hab-nab*, from the Saxon,
habban, to have, and *nabban*, not to have.

" THESE COSTERMONGER TIMES."

A COSTERMONGER, or costard-monger, is a dealer in apples, which
are so called because they are shaped like a costard, *i.e.* a man's
head.—*Stevens.*

Johnson explains the phrase eloquently :—" In these times when the
prevalence of trade has produced that meanness that rates the merit
of everything by money."

TORTURES OF TANTALUS.

A PHRASE applied to the placing of pleasures, benefits, etc., just
within one's reach, and snatching them away ere the hand can grasp
them.   *Origin :* Tantalus is represented by the poets as punished in
hell with insatiable thirst, and placed up to the chin in the midst of
a pool of water, which, however, flows away as soon as he attempts to
taste it.   There hangs also above his head a bough richly loaded with
delicious fruits ; which, as soon as he attempts to seize, is carried away
from his reach by a sudden blast of wind.   According to some mythologists, his punishment is to sit under a huge stone hung at some distance over his head, and as it seems every moment ready to fall, he is
kept under continual alarms and never-ceasing fears : and hence is
derived the word *Tantalizing.*

" MIND YOUR P'S & Q'S."

THE origin of the phrase, " Mind your P's and Q's," is not generally
known.   In ale-houses, where chalk scores were formerly marked upon
the wall or behind the door of the taproom, it was customary to put
these initial letters at the head of every man's account, to show the
number of *pints* and *quarts* for which he was in arrears; and one may
presume many a friendly rustic to have tapped his neighbour on the
shoulder when he was indulging too freely in his potations, and to have
pointed to the score, " Giles ! Giles ! mind your P's and Q's."
[This is the explanation generally accepted by antiquaries ; but it
seems more probable that the phrase has a typographical origin, and
is really a caution to the young printer to be careful in the operation
of " distribution," to distinguish between two letters of somewhat simi-

lar formation, which, as they are of course reversed in the type from which the impression is taken, might easily be mistaken by an unpractised hand. Several other familiar phrases which much puzzle some diligent seekers after recondite explanations, are derived from the phraseology of the printing office. For instance, a person not well or not in good spirits is described as " out of sorts," a phrase which every printer perfectly well understands, meaning that he is deficient of some particular " sorts" of letters required for his work.]

"BLUE STOCKING."

ABOUT this time it was much the fashion for several ladies to have evening assemblies where the fair sex might participate in conversation with literary and ingenious men, animated by a desire to please. These societies were denominated "Blue Stocking Clubs," the origin of which title being little known, it may be worth while to relate it. One of the most eminent members of these societies, when they first commenced, was Mr. Stillingfleet, whose dress was remarkably grave, and in particular it was observed that he wore blue stockings. Such was the excellence of his conversation that his absence was felt as so great a loss that it used to be said : " We can do nothing without the 'Blue Stockings,'" and thus by degrees the title was established. Miss Hannah More has admirably described a " Blue Stocking Club " in her *Bas Bleu*, a poem in which many of the persons who were most conspicuous there are mentioned.—*Boswell.*

"SCRAPING AN ACQUAINTANCE."

ALTOGETHER those Twelve Cæsars were men compounded of the most opposite qualities, with a small modicum of what is called wit among the whole of them. Out of all those who followed, one alone, Hadrian, made a standing and a sterling joke, a joke which has descended to us and added a slang phrase to our vulgar tongue. To "scrape an acquaintance" comes to us from Hadrian. He was at the public baths one day when he saw one of his veteran soldiers scraping his body with a tile. That was such a poor luxury that he ordered that his old comrade should be supplied with more suitable cleansing materials, and also with money. On a subsequent occasion, when the emperor again went to the bath, the spectacle before him was very amusing. A score of old soldiers who had fought under Hadrian were standing in the water, and each was currying himself with a tile, and wincing at the self-inflicted rubbing. The emperor perfectly well understood what he saw, and what was the purpose of the sight. "Ha! ha !" he exclaimed, "you had better scrape one another, my good fellows !" He added, " You certainly shall not scrape acquaintance with me !"

[The above, taken from a popular magazine, is another instance of looking back a long way for the origin of a phrase. The mode in which a very obsequious individual endeavours to introduce himself to the notice of some person of superior position, with a "a bow and a scrape" (that is, a backward movement or "scrape" on the floor of one foot, while making a dancing master's bow), offers a much more probable explanation of the phrase.]

THE FENIANS.

ACCORDING to tradition the Fenians, or Finians, were a national militia established in Ireland by Fin, or Fionn, the son of Cumhal, who "flourished" in the third century. Each member of the band swore never to receive a portion with a wife, but to choose her for her good manners and virtues ; never to offer violence to any woman ; never to refuse to relieve the poor to the utmost of his power ; and never to flee before nine champions. Other authorities regard the ancient Fenians as a distinct Celtic race who migrated at an early period from Germany into northern Scotland and Ireland ; and others conjecture that the word is a corruption of " Phœnicians."

CABAL.

THE celebrated name of the ministers of Charles II., the first letters of whose names, Clifford, Ashley, Buckingham, Arlington, and Lauderdale compose the word Cabal, which has since been applied to associations formed for the purpose of contriving or executing illegal measures.

A GARLAND OF CURIOUS SELECTIONS, IN PROSE AND VERSE.

"SUFFICIENT UNTO THE DAY," ETC.

A RULER of Damascus was once calling aloud upon his people in a mosque to thank the Most High that during his fortunate reign Allah had been pleased to take away the plague. But a certain Arab cried out to him, "Of a truth, Allah is too merciful to give us both thee and the plague at the same time ! "

A LIBEL ON HUSBANDS AND WIVES.

[The following profess to be certain rules to discover married couples in large societies or in public. We do not believe in them.]

1. IF you see a gentleman and lady disagree upon trifling occasions, or correcting each other in company, you may be assured they have tied the matrimonial noose.

2. If you see a silent pair in a coach, lolling carelessly one at each

window, without seeming to know they have a companion, the sign is infallible.

3. If you see a lady drop her glove, and a gentleman by the side of her kindly telling her to pick it up, you need not hesitate in forming an opinion ; or,—

4. If you see a lady presenting a gentleman with anything carelessly, her head inclined another way, and speaking to him with indifference ; or,—

5. If you meet a couple in the fields, the gentleman twenty yards in advance of the lady, who perhaps is getting over a stile with difficulty, or picking her way through a muddy path ; or,—

6. If you see a lady whose beauty and accomplishments attract the attention of every gentleman in the room but *one*, you can have no difficulty in determining their relationship to each other—the *one* is her husband.

7. If you see a gentleman particularly courteous, obliging, and good-natured, relaxing into smiles, saying smart things, and toying with every pretty woman in the room, except *one*, to whom he appears particularly reserved, cold, and formal, and is unreasonably cross,—who that *one* is, nobody can be at a loss to discover.

8. If you see a young or an old couple jarring, checking and thwarting each other, differing in opinion before the opinion is expressed ; eternally anticipating and breaking the thread of each other's discourse, yet using kind words, like honey bubbles floating on vinegar, which soon are overwhelmed by the preponderance of the fluid ; they are to all intents man and wife ; it is impossible to be mistaken.

The rules above quoted are laid down as infallible in just interpretation—they may be resorted to with confidence ; they are upon unerring principles, and deduced from every-day experience.

THE MONTHS.

JANUARY.

CAME old January, wrappèd well
In many weeds to keep the cold away ;
Yet did he quake and quiver like to quell,
And blowe his nayles to warm them if he may ;
For they were numbed with holding all the day
An hatchet keene, with which he fellèd wood,
And from the trees did lop the needlesse spray ;
Upon an huge Earth-pot Steane he stood,
From whose wide mouth there flowèd forth the Romane flood.

FEBRUARY.

Then came old February, sitting
In an old wagon, for he could not ride,
Drawn by two Fishes for the season fitting,
Which through the flood before did softly slide

R

And swim away ; yet had he by his side
His plough and harness fit to till the ground,
And tools to prune the trees, before the pride
Of hasting prime did make them bourgeon wide.

MARCH.

Sturdy March, with brows full sternly bent,
And armèd strongly, rode upon a Ram,
The same which over Hellespontus swam,
Yet in his hand a spade he also bent,
And in a bag all sorts of weeds, the same
Which on the earth he strewèd as he went,
And filled her womb with fruitful hope of nourishment.

APRIL.

Next came fresh April, full of lustyhed,
And wanton as a kid whose horne new buds ;
Upon a Bull he rode, the same which led
Europa floating through th' Argolick floods :
His horns were gilden all with golden studs,
And garnishèd with garlands goodly sight,
Of all the fairest flowers and freshest buds,
Which the earth brings forth ; and wet he seemed in sight
With waves through which he waded for his love's delight.

MAY.

Then came fair May, the fayrest mayd on ground,
Deckt all with dainties of her season's pryde,
And throwing flowres out of her lap around :
Upon two brethren's shoulders she did ride,
The Twinnes of Leda, which on either side
Supported her, like to their soveraine queene.
Lord ! how all creatures laught, when her they spide,
And leapt and daunced as they had ravisht beene !
And Cupid selfe about her fluttered all in greene.

JUNE.

—After her came jolly June, arrayed
All in green leaves, as he a player were ;
Yet in his time he wrought as well as played,
That by his plough-irons mote right well appear.
Upon a Crab he rode, that did him bear,
With crooked crawling steps, an uncouth pace,
And backward rode, as bargemen wont to fare,
Bending their force contràry to their face ;
Like that ungracious crew which feigns demurest grace.

JULY.

Then came hot July, boiling like to fire,
That all his garments he did cast away ;
Upon a Lion raging yet with ire
He boldly rode, and made him to obey
(It was the beast that whilom did foray
The Nemæan forest, till the Amphitrionide
Him slew, and with his hide did him array) :
Behind his back a scythe, and by his side,
Under his belt, he bore a sickle circling wide.

AUGUST.

The eighth was August, being rich arrayed
In garment all of gold, down to the ground :
Yet rode he not, but led a lovely maid
Forth by the lily hand, the which was crowned
With ears of corn, and full her hand was found.
That was the righteous Virgin, which of old
Lived here on earth, and plenty made abound ;
But after wrong was loved and justice sold,
She left the unrighteous world, and was to heaven extolled.

SEPTEMBER.

Next him September marchèd eke on foot,
Yet was he hoary, laden with the spoil
Of harvest riches, which he made his boot,
And him enriched with bounty of the soiL
In his one hand, as fit for harvest toil,
He held a knife-hook ; and in the other hand
A pair of Weights, with which he did assoil
Both more or less, where it in doubt did stand,
And equal gave to each, as justice duly scanned.

OCTOBER.

Then came October, full of merry glee ;
For yet his noule was totty of the must,
Which he was treading in the wine-fat's see,
And of the joyous oyle, whose gentle gust
Made him so frolic and so full of lust :
Upon a dreadful Scorpion he did ride,
The same which by Dianæ's doom unjust
Slew great Orion ; and eke by his side
He had his ploughing share and coulter ready tyde.

NOVEMBER.

Next was November ; he full grosse and fat
As fed with lard, and that right well might seeme ;
For he had been a fatting hogs of late,
That yet his browes with sweat did reck and steem.

And yet the season was full sharp and breem ;
In planting eke he took no small delight :
Whereon he rode, not easy was to deeme ;
For it a dreadful Centaure was in sight,
The seed of Saturne and fair Nais, Chiron hight.

DECEMBER.

And after him came next the chill December ;
Yet he through merry feasting which he made
And great bonfires, did not the cold remember ;
His Saviour's birth his mind so much did glad.
Upon a shaggy bearded Goat he rode.
The same wherewith Dan Jove in tender years,
They say, was nourisht by th' Idean mayd ;
And in his hand a broad deep bowle he beares,
Of which he freely drinks an health to all his peeres.

Spenser.

THE POET HAFIZ.

HAFIZ (which signifies one who knows the Koran and the Traditions by heart), or to give his full name, Mohammed Shems-ed-Din
Hafiz, was born at Shiraz, a port on the Caspian Sea, about the beginning of the fourteenth century, and early in life showed a great love
for the pursuit of learning.   He was appointed teacher in the royal
family of the reigning house of Muzaffer, and even a college was
founded for him.   Numerous tempting offers of place and power were
held out to Hafiz, but the poet was content to remain in the self-chosen
humble condition of a dervish.   Hafiz was married, and lived to a good
old age.   His death took place in the year 1388.   His tomb is situated
about two miles north-east of Shiraz, and even at the present day—
nearly five hundred years from the time of his death—the splendid
tomb of the gifted Persian is resorted to by flocks of pious pilgrims
from all parts of Persia.   Hafiz may be termed the Persian Anacreon,
for his poetry is chiefly in praise of love and wine, flowers and birds,
and other forms of sensuous beauty. He did not, however, confine
himself to the composition of love chansons and songs in praise of
wine ; he wrote several works on jurisprudence and theology, and
some of his poems abound in profound reflections on the mutability
of human life, and withering sarcasms on the cant and hypocrisy of
the professional devotees of his day.   Such was the bitter rancour
which his plain-speaking engendered in the breasts of the priests, that
they refused to read the usual prayers over his remains.   The name
Shems-ed-Din signifies Sun of Religion ; another of his cogno-
mens was Lishan-al-Ghaid—the Voice of Mystery ; and his verses
were so mellifluous that he was frequently termed *Tschegerleb*, or
Sugar-lip.

WOMAN.

[These lines, by Moore, were published for the first time, it is believed, in the *Athenæum*, Nov. 1872.]

WHEN life looks lone and dreary,
What light can dispel the gloom ?
When Time's swift wing is weary,
What charm can refresh his plume ?
'Tis Woman, whose sweetness beameth
On all that we feel or see :
And if man of heaven e'er dreameth,
'Tis when he thinks purely of thee,
Oh, Woman !

THE WISE MAN AND HIS FOOLISH WIFE.

AN old wise man, who had married twice and lived very happily with both wives, was over-persuaded by his friends to marry again. For his part, he thought it a mistake ; but as his friends spoke of a beautiful young girl, who, they said, had been nurtured and taught by a very careful and clever mother, he yielded to their advice, and married her.

Soon after their marriage the young girl went to her mother, saying she was sure her husband did not love her. So her mother told her what to do to prove her husband's love.

The old man had in his garden a favourite tree, under which he would sit every day; and for that reason he took great pains to trim and to train it. His wife cut it down, had it sawn into logs, and in the evening made an immense fire with them. The old man sat in silence before this fire with his wife, until all the logs were burnt to ashes. Then he asked why she had cut down this particular tree to make a fire.

She answered, "As you liked it best, I judged it would warm you most."

But, instead of losing his temper, he merely said, "I am no warmer from this tree than I should have been from any other tree."

Then the girl went to her mother, who asked, "Was he cross ?" "No," said the daughter. "Then you ought to be satisfied." But still the girl begged for another way to prove her husband's love. After awhile her mother told her one.

The old man had a dog of which he was very fond, always feeding and tending it with his own hand. So one night as the lady sat by her lord, arrayed in her richest robe of samite, and a pelisse of costly fur, she took the dog into her lap, and killed it with a knife from off the table ; and all her clothing was bedabbled with the blood, and quite spoiled.

The wise man was silent for a little space. Then he quietly remarked, "I think it is time to go to bed."

Yet still his wife was not content, but went again to her mother, saying her husband was not cross, and asking for another way to prove his love ; and this her mother told her. In a few days the wise man made a feast, and invited his friends. Spread upon the table were his choicest cups and flagons, filled with ale and mead, and the meats were served upon his costliest dishes. His wife carried at her girdle a bunch of keys, and having twisted these among the fringes of the table-cloth, she rose up suddenly, just before the feast began, as though to reach something from behind, and dragged the whole banquet to the floor.

Not a frown appeared upon the wise man's countenance. He merely said a grace, and helped to pick up the things.

But next morning, when the lady arose, she found a fire in her room, and a table covered with porringers and towels, and beside it a great chair, against which stood a barber talking to the wise man.

"Madam," said her husband in his kindest voice, "after two happy marriages, I know too well the native gentleness of womankind to attribute these strange freaks of yours to the fault of female nature. They arise, in my judgment, from three measures full of bad blood, which must be taken from your veins in order to make you complaisant like other women."

In spite of tears and cries, her husband placed her in the chair and bared her arms, while the barber bled her of three porringers full of blood. When she got well enough to go out again, she went and told her mother. But her mother said it served her right. And the wise man told her if such freaks broke out again, he never could lay the blame to her charming disposition, but to a porringer full of bad blood, of which he would promise to see her relieved for every freak. But there were no more porringers full of blood, since there were no more freaks ; and ever afterwards the wise man had a happy and contented wife.—*Beeton's Christmas Annual,* 1872.

PADDY O'RAFTER.

PADDY, in want of a dinner one day,
Credit all gone, and no money to pay,
Stole from the priest a fat pullet, they say,
    And went to confession just afther :
"Your riv'rence," says Paddy, "I stole this fat hen."
"What, what !" says the priest ; "at your ould tricks again?
"Faith, you'd rather be staaling, than saying *Amen,*
        Paddy O'Rafther !"

"Sure you wouldn't be angry," says Pat, "if you knew
That the best of intintions I had in my view ;
For I stole it, to make it a present to you,
    And you can absolve me afther."
"Do you think," says the priest, "I'd partake of your theft ?
Of your seven small senses you must be bereft—
You're the biggest blackguard that I know, right or left,
        Paddy O'Rafther !"

"Then what shall I do with the pullet," says Pat,
"If your riv'rence won't take it? By this and by that,
I don't know no more than a dog or a cat
    What your riv'rence would have me be afther."
"Why, then," says his riv'rence, "you sin-blinded owl,
Give back to the man that you stole from his fowl,
For if you do not, 'twill be worse for your sowl,
                                    Paddy O'Rafther."

Says Paddy, "I asked him to take it, 'tis thrue
As this minnit I'm talking, your riv'rence, to you;
But he wouldn't resaive it—so what can I do?"
    Says Paddy, nigh choking with laughter.
"By my throth," says the priest, "but the case is absthruse;
If he won't take his hen, why the man is a goose.
'Tis not the first time my advice was no use,
                                    Paddy O'Rafther!"

"But for sake of your sowl, I would sthrongly advise
To some one in want you would give your supplies:
Some widow, or orphan, with tears in their eyes;
    And *then* you may come to *me* afther."
So Paddy went off to the brisk Widow Hoy,
And the pullet, between them, was eaten with joy;
And says she, "'Pon my word, you're the cleverest boy,
                                    Paddy O'Rafther!"

Then Paddy went back to the priest the next day,
And told him the fowl he had given away
To a poor lonely widow, in want and dismay,
    The loss of her spouse weeping afther.
"Well, now," says the priest, "I'll absolve you, my lad,
For repintantly making the best of the bad,
In feeding the hungry, and cheering the sad,
                                    Paddy O'Rafther!"
                                    Samuel Lover.

LITERARY FAME.

I WAS out of spirits—read the papers—thought what *fame* was, on reading, in a case of murder, that "Mr. Wych, grocer, at Tunbridge, sold some bacon, flour, cheese, and, it is believed, some plums, to some gipsy woman accused." He had on his counter (I quote faithfully) a book, the "Life of Pamela," which he was tearing for wastepaper, etc. etc. In the cheese was found, etc., and a *leaf of " Pamela" wrapped round the bacon.* What would Richardson, the vainest and luckiest of living authors (*i.e.* while alive), he who, with Aaron Hill, used to prophesy and chuckle over the presumed fall of Fielding (the *prose* Homer of human nature), and of Pope (the most beautiful of poets),—what would he have said could he have traced his pages from

their place on the French prince's toilet (see *Boswell's Johnson*) to the grocer's counter and the gipsy murderer's bacon !
What would he have said ? What can anybody say, save what Solomon said long before us ? After all, it is but passing from one counter to another, from the bookseller's to the other tradesman's— grocer or pastry-cook. For my part, I have met with most poetry upon trunks ; so that I am apt to consider the trunk-maker as the sexton of authorship.—*Byron's Journals.*

POOR RELATIONS.

A POOR RELATION is the most irrelevant thing in nature ; a piece of impertinent correspondency ; an odious approximation ; a haunting conscience ; a preposterous shadow, lengthening in the noontide of your prosperity ; an unwelcome remembrancer; a perpetually recurring mortification ; a drain on your purse ; a more intolerable dun upon your pride ; a drawback upon success ; a rebuke upon your rising ; a stain in your blood ; a blot on your 'scutcheon ; a rent in your garment ; a death's head at your banquet ; Agathocles' pot ; a Mordecai in your gate ; a Lazarus at your door ; a lion in your path ; a frog in your chamber ; a fly in your ointment ; a mote in your eye ; a triumph to your enemy ; an apology to your friends ; the one thing not needful ; the hail in harvest ; the ounce of sour in the pound of sweet. His memory is unseasonable ; his compliments perverse ; his talk a trouble ; his stay pertinacious ;—and when he goeth away, you dismiss his chair into a corner as precipitately as possible, and feel fairly rid of two nuisances.—*Charles Lamb.*

MARRIAGE.

MAN is for woman made,
And woman made for man ;
As the spur is for the jade,
As the scabbard for the blade,
As for liquor is the can,
So man's for woman made,
And woman made for man.

As the sceptre to be swayed,
As to night the serenade,
As for pudding is the pan,
As to cool us is the fan,
So man's for woman made,
And woman made for man.

Be she widow, wife, or maid,
Be she wanton, be she staid,
Be she well or ill-arrayed,
So man's for woman made,
And woman made for man.

Motteaux.

PIOUS FRAUDS; OR, THE KNIGHT AND THE FRIAR.

A MONK was standing at a convent gate,
With sanctimonious phiz and shaven pate,
Promising, with solemn cant,
To all that listened to his rant,
A full and perfect absolution,
With half-a-dozen hallowed benedictions,
If they would give some contribution,
Some large donation supererogatory :
To ransom fifty murdered Christians,
And free their precious souls from purgatory :
When (he asserted) they would gain
A passport from the realms of pain,
And find a speedy passage to the skies.
A knight was riding by, and heard these lies ;
He stopped his horse, "*Salve*," the parson cried ;
And "*Benedicite,*" the youth replied.
" Most reverend father," quoth the knight,
    Who, it appears, was sharp and witty,
" These martyred Christians' wretched plight
    Believe me, I sincerely pity :
Nay, more—their sufferings to relieve,
I will these fifty ducats give."
This was no sooner said than done :
The priest pronounced his benison.
" Now, I presume," the soldier said,
" The spirits of these Christians dead
Have reached their final place of rest ? "
" Most true," replied the reverend friar,
(Unless Saint Francis is a liar) ;
And, to reward the pious action
Of this most Christian benefaction,
You will, no doubt, eternally be blest."
" Well, then," exclaimed the soldier-youth,
" If what you say indeed be truth,
And these same pieces that I've given,
Have snatched their souls from purgatory's pains,
And bought them a snug place in heaven,
No further use for them remains."
He said thus much to prove, at least,
He was as cunning as the priest :
Then put the ducats in his poke,
And rode off, laughing at the joke.

CHESHIRE CHEESE.

CHESHIRE retains its celebrity for cheese-making. The pride of its
people in the superiority of its cheese may be gathered from the follow-

ing provincial song, published, with music, in 1746, during the Spanish war, in the reign of George II.

> A Cheshire man sailed into Spain
> To trade for merchandise ;
> When he arrivèd from the main,
> A Spaniard he espies—

> Who said, " You English rogue, look here,
> What fruits and spices fine
> Our land produces twice a year ;
> Thou hast not such in thine."

> The Cheshire man ran to his hold,
> And fetched a Cheshire cheese ;
> And said, " Look here, you dog ; behold,
> We have such fruits as these !

> " Your fruits are ripe but twice a year,
> As you yourself do say ;
> But such as I present you here,
> Our land brings twice a day."

> The Spaniard in a passion flew,
> And his rapier took in hand ;
> The Cheshire man kicked up his heels,
> Saying, " Thou art at my command."

> So never let a Spaniard boast,
> While Cheshire men abound,
> Lest they should teach him, to his cost,
> To dance a Cheshire round.

KING CHARLES I. AND THE MARQUESS OF WORCESTER.

THE sphere of a poet's influence is far wider than that of his own age ; and however we may now deem of this grave and ancient poet [Gower], he still found understanding admirers so late as the reign of Charles the First. In the curious "conference" which took place when Charles the First visited the Marquess of Worcester at Raglan Castle, with his court, there is the following anecdote respecting the poet Gower.

The marquess was a shrewd though whimsical man, and a favourite of the king for his frankness and his love of the arts. His lordship entertained the royal guest with extraordinary magnificence. Among his rare curiosities was a sumptuous copy of Gower's volume.

Charles the First usually visited the marquess after dinner. Once he found his lordship with the book of John Gower lying open, which the king said he had never before seen. "Oh," exclaimed the marquess, "it is a book of books ! and if your Majesty had been well versed in it, it would have made you a king of kings." " Why so, my lord?" "Why, here is set down how Aristotle brought up and instructed Alexander the Great in all the rudiments and principles belonging to a prince." And under the persons of Aristotle and Alexander, the marquess read the king such a lesson that all the standers-by were amazed at his boldness.

The king asked whether he had his lesson by heart, or spake out of the book. "Sir, if you would read my heart, it may be that you might find it there; or if your Majesty pleased to get it by heart, I will lend you my book." The king accepted the offer.

Some of the new-made lords fretted and bit their thumbs at certain passages in the marquess's discourse; and some protested that no man was so much for the absolute power of a king as Aristotle. The marquess told the king that he would indeed show him one remarkable passage to that purpose; and turning to the place read:

"A king can kill, a king can save;
A king can make a lord a knave,
And of a knave a lord also."

On this several new-made lords shrank out of the room, which the king observing told the marquess, "My lord, at this rate you will drive away all my nobility."—*Disraeli's Amenities of Literature.*

GREAT MEN'S LOVE FOR CATS.

CHAMPFLEURY has one interesting chapter on the love of distinguished characters for cats. Tasso addressed the finest of his sonnets to his cat; Petrarch had his favourite cat embalmed in the Egyptian style; Cardinal Wolsey gave audience with his cat seated beside him. There is or was a statue in a niche of the ancient prison of Newgate, representing the famous Whittington, Lord Mayor of London, with his right hand resting on a cat. Mahomet on one occasion cut off the skirt of his robe, so that he might rise without disturbing his cat, which was sleeping on it. Cardinal Richelieu, the great prime minister of France, always kept a number of kittens in his cabinet, to amuse him with their pranks. Chateaubriand loved cats all his life; and his passion for them was so notorious, that when he was ambassador at Rome, the Pope made him a present of one. Michelet, the historian, and the essayist on Love and Women, is so fond of these animals that he will even pet a deformed one, and will not allow it to be molested. Moncrif, a clever French writer and member of the Academy, was another cat lover, and author of *Les Lettres sur les Chats.* Then come the German story-writer, Hoffman, the French poets Baudelaire, Gautier, and Victor Hugo, the historian Mérimée, and our own Edgar Poe, besides a well-known list of English writers. On the whole, the cats have no reason to be ashamed of their intimates. There have been artists who have loved this creature well enough to do much good work in drawing and painting him. Champfleury's book is illustrated by eighty excellent wood-cuts, which give us at least a hint of what has been done in this line by the Egyptians, the Romans, the Japanese; by the German Gotfried Mind, "the Raphael of cats;" by the Dutch Cornelius Wischer; by the Frenchmen, Grandville, Rouvière, and Delacroix; by the English Burbank, and several others. It is remarkable that one of the very best of these limners of the feline race is the Japanese Hok'sai, or Fo-Koa-Say, an artist of really distinguished merit, who died some fifty years since, leaving a prodigious number of sketches, many of which have reached Paris. The cats of Hok'sai are so plump and smooth and gracious, that you feel a desire to catch and fondle them. They are even more like nature than the best work of Delacroix, and they are hardly surpassed by the highly finished pieces of Mind and Wischer and Burbank.—*Atlantic Monthly.*

ADVENTURE OF KING JAMES V. OF SCOTLAND.

BEING once benighted when out hunting and separated from his attendants, he happened to enter a cottage in the midst of a moor, at the foot of the Ochil Hills, near Alloa, where, unknown, he was kindly received. In order to regale their unexpected guest, the "gudeman" (i.e. landlord, farmer) desired the "gudewife" to fetch the hen that roosted nearest the cock, which is always the plumpest, for the stranger's supper. The king, highly pleased with his night's lodging and hospitable entertainment, told mine host at parting, that he should be glad to return his civility, and requested that the first time he came to Stirling, he would call at the castle, and inquire for the "Gudeman of Ballengeich." Donaldson, the landlord, did not fail to call on the "Gudeman of Ballengeich," when his astonishment at finding that the king had been his guest, afforded no small amusement to the merry monarch and his courtiers; and, to carry on the pleasantry, he was thenceforth designated by James with the title of King of the Moors, which name and designation have descended from father to son ever since, and they have continued in possession of the identical spot till very lately.—*Campbell's Statistical Account of Scotland.*

A GEM.

ACCEPT, dear maid, this beauteous rose,
  To deck thy breast so fair;
Observe its hue, nor wonder why
  It blushes to be there!

DRINKING.

THREE cups of wine a prudent man may take:
The first of these, for constitution's sake;
The second, to the girl he loves the best;
The third and last, to lull him to his rest;
Then home to bed. But if a fourth he pours,
That is the cup of folly, and not ours:
Loud, noisy talking on the fifth attends;
The sixth breeds feuds and falling out of friends;

Seven begets blows and faces stained with gore ;
Eight, and the watch patrol breaks ope the door ;
Mad with the ninth, another cup goes round,
And the swelled sot drops senseless on the ground.

HENRY VIII. AND THE ABBOT OF READING.

A CURIOUS story is told in Fuller's Church History, which records a memorable visit of " bluff King Hal " to Reading Abbey :

As King Henry VIII. was hunting in Windsor Forest, he either casually lost, or probably wilfully losing himself, struck down, about dinner time, to the Abbey of Reading, where, disguising himself (much for delight, much for discovery unseen), he was invited to the abbot's table, and passed for one of the king's guard, a place to which the proportion of his person might properly entitle him. A sirloin of beef was set before him (so knighted, saith tradition, by this Henry), on which the king laid on lustily, not disgracing one of that place for whom he was mistaken. " Well fare thy heart (quoth the Abbot), and here in a cup of sack I remember his grace your master. I would give an hundred pounds on the condition I could feed as lustily on beef as you do. Alas ! my weak and squeezie stomach will hardly digest the wing of a small chicken or rabbit." The king pleasantly pledged him, and heartily thanked him for his good cheer ; after which he departed as undiscovered as he came thither. Some weeks after, the abbot was sent for by a pursuivant, brought up to London, clapt in the Tower, kept close prisoner, and fed for a short time with bread and water; yet not so empty his body of food, as his mind was filled with fears, creating many suspicions to himself, when and how he had incurred the king's displeasure. At last a sirloin of beef was set before him, of which the abbot fed as the farmer of his grange, and verified the proverb, that two hungry meals make the third a glutton. In springs King Henry out of a private lobby, where he had placed himself, the invisible spectator of the abbot's behaviour. " My lord (quoth the king), presently deposit your hundred pounds in gold, or else no going hence all the days of your life. I have been your physician, to cure you of your squeezie stomach, and here, as I deserve, I demand my fee for the same." The abbot down with his dust, and glad he had escaped so, returned to Reading as somewhat lighter in purse, so much more merry in heart, than when he came thence.

THE GAME OF CHESS.

A SECRET many yeares unseene,
In play at chess, who knowes the game,
First of the King, and then the Queene,
Knight, Bishop, Rooke, and so by name,
        Of everie Pawne I will descrie
        The nature with the qualitie.

THE KING.

The King himself is haughtie care,
Which overlooketh all his men ;
And when he seeth how they fare,
He steps among them now and then,
  Whom, when his foe presumes to checke,
  His servants stand, to give the necke.

THE QUEENE.

The Queen is queint, and quicke conceit,
Which makes her walk which way she list,
And rootes them up, that lie in wait
To work her treason, ere she wist :
  Her force is such against her foes,
  That whom she meets, she overthrowes.

THE KNIGHT.

The Knight is knowledge how to fight
Against his prince's enemies ;
He never makes his walk outright,
But leaps and skips, in wilie wise,
  To take by sleight a traitrous foe,
  Might slilie seek their overthrowe.

THE BISHOP.

The Bishop he is wittie braine,
That chooseth crossest pathes to pace,
And evermore he pries with paine,
To see who seekes him most disgrace :
  Such straglers when he findes astraie
  He takes them up, and throwes awaie.

THE ROOKES.

The Rookes are reason on both sides,
Which keep the corner houses still,
And warily stand to watch their tides,
By secret art to worke their will :
  To take sometime a thief unseene,
  Might mischief mean to King or Queene.

THE PAWNES.

The Pawne before the King, is peace,
Which he desires to keep at home,
Practise, the Queene's, which doth not cease
Amid the world abroad to roam ;
  To finde, to fall upon each foe,
  Whereas his mistress meanes to goe.

Before the Knight, is perill plast,
Which he, by skipping overgoes ;
And yet that Pawne can worke a cast
To overthrow his greatest foes ;
  The Bishop's prudence, pricing still
  Which way to worke his master's will.

The Rooke's poore Pawnes, are sillie swaines,
Which seldom serve, except by hap ;
And yet those Pawnes can lay their traines,
To catch a great man in a trap :
  Soe that I see, sometime a groome
  May not be sparèd from his roome.

THE NATURE OF THE CHESSE MEN.

The King is stately, looking hie ;
The Queene doth beare like majestie :
The Knight is hardie, valiant, wise ;
The Bishop prudent and precise.
  The Rookes no raingers out of raie,
  The Pawnes the pages in the plaie.

L'ENVOY.

Then rule with care, and quicke conceit,
And fight with knowledge, as with force ;
So beare a braine, to dash deceit,
And work with reason and remorse.
  Forgive a fault when young men plaie,
  So give a mate, and go your way.

And when you plaie beware of checke,
Know how to save and give a knecke,
And with a checke beware of mate ;
But chiefe, ware had I wist too late :
  Loose not the Queene, for ten to one,
  If she be lost the game is gone.

                              N. Breton, 1638.

CHARLES DICKENS.

ONE great source of Dickens' power as a novelist and humorist was his weakness as a thinker, his determination not to think, perhaps his incapacity for thinking over any complicated social or philosophical problem. We do not want Dickens to be a philosopher ; we are very glad he was not one. Had he been anything of a social philosopher, we must have lost some of the most delightful of his stories, and we should have gained just nothing in return. To criticise his works with reference to any accepted principles of social economy or psychology, would be like testing the value of Æsop or La Fontaine by an examination into the fidelity of their zoological descriptions. Dickens sincerely preached a gospel of joyousness and human kindness. His dreamland, his Utopia, would have been a world where the poor were plentifully fed in their own homes, having everything they liked to eat and drink ; where all hearths were neat, and all homes were bright ; where all wives were pretty, plump, winsome little creatures, for ever in good humour ; where Christmas was always merrily kept, and laughing girls were faithfully kissed under the mistletoe ; and above all, where the lives of children were always free, gladsome, and happy. To "a world bursting with sin and sorrow," as his own admired friend Sydney Smith described it, this was the delightful idyllic picture Dickens held up. To a world, at all events, terribly in earnest in all its characteristic tendencies, absorbed in its science, its commerce, its inventions, whose very religions seem to have lost their old-fashioned paternal geniality and sympathy with human joy, and the "last word" of whose philosophy appears only to proclaim that humanity itself is chained by materialistic and inexorable laws, rigid as the grasp of the Strength and Violence which held down the Greek poet's Prometheus—to such a world Dickens offered his bright, beautiful, fanciful, "living pictures." We are all delighted in them. They gladdened and refreshed us, not, as so many people foolishly think, because they were like our social life, but because they were so absolutely unlike it, because they withdrew us from it for a moment,—stole us away, like the children in the legends, and carried us into Fairy-land.

Daily News.

FROM "JEPHTHA," A DRAMA, BY GEORGE BUCHANAN.

(Translated from the original Latin.)

MODERATION IN PROSPERITY.

BUT ill the human mind knows to observe
The golden mean ; it swells in high success ;--
The more God's goodness hath bestowed on men,
The more security obscures their minds,
Which, swoll'n with empty haughtiness, vain pride
Greatly excites.

RETIREMENT.

Oh sweet security of lowliest lot !
Methinks he's born beneath a happy star,
Who far from turmoil spends his life remote,
Unknown, in silence, safe, and free from care.

INSTABILITY OF FORTUNE.

On no one hath so prosperous fortune shone,
That adverse may not poise with equal beam ;
The stern vicissitude of fortune tempers
The sad with prosperous, prosperous with sad.

MAN'S DISCONTENT WITH HIS CONDITION.

Comes it not mostly through our own default,
And the inconstancy of restless mind,
That we bear neither lot in stable state ?
The rich man praises the tranquillity
Of the poor cottage and its silence deep,
By warlike trump unbroken ; the slumber free
From dreams, the vigils free from vexing cares ;
The poor extol with praises without end
The gold, the purple, clients, vassals, slaves,
The royal equipage, the houses wide,
And think that only rich men can be blessed.
But balance either in its proper scale,
And neither lot is free from every trouble.
Want vexes poor men, fear the opulent ;
The rich have pleasure, and the poor few cares.
Fortune in either mingles sad with sweet ;
But that should surely be esteemed the best
Which mingles many joys with sorrows few.

SORROW AND JOY SUCCESSIVE.

Surely this lot unto our life belongs,
That sorrow must succeed to joy in turn,
As darkness does the sun,
As winter rough the gently breathing spring ;
Never so pure a pleasure is at all
That sorrow may not spoil with bitter gall.
The treach'rous levity of fortune's mood
With cruel change commingles human good.
As when with placid waves the sea still lies
Beneath the soft serene and silent skies,
The gathering storm rolls on the tempest black,
And heaps the swollen billows from afar ;
Here the wild currents of the tided main,
There wanton Caurus' blasts
The trembling bark drag through the foaming straits :
That is the very image of our life,
Which we, 'mong slaughters, tumults, thefts,
And fears of death, more terrible than death,
Spend ; but if aught of joyful chance has shone,
Swift on the speedy breath away 'tis flown,
Like evanescent light of fleeting flame,
Which 'mong dry stubble plays ;
Then in a chain unbroken, linked and slow,
Follow long trains of sorrows and of woe.

CONPENSATIONS FOR MISFORTUNE.

One, those who hunt for rich men's legacies,
Hunts in return ; and bed that barren proves

S

Of the sweet pledge of love,
Compensates with a numerous crowd of clients ;
And joys in turn with studied wile
The gaping ravens to beguile.
One would not change the cradle's murmurs bland,
And prattling plainings of the tender lip,
For Crœsus' wealth, nor for the yellow sand
Which lucid Hermus rolls along,
Underneath his wealthy wave.
But none can plan the manner of his life
So wisely, that he'll not perchance condemn
His course ten times within an hour.

HUMAN LIFE.

God whirls the affairs of men, as dust is driven
By the light whirlwind of the mobile air ;
Or in the manner of a wintry storm,
Which by the blasts of Caurus wild,
Buries the lofty hills in hail ;
Presently, where the pure torch of clear day,
Since rosy morn with pleasant light had shone,
Now wide dispersèd o'er the whitening fields,
The sun scarce seen, it melts and dies away.

DEATH OF JEPHTHA'S DAUGHTER.

And then perchance had Nature on her breathed
A beauty sweeter to behold than wont,
As if desirous, by a gift supreme,
To dignify the noble heroine's death.
As the receding splendour Phœbus pours,
Now rushing down to the Tartessian sea,
Is wont to be more grateful ; as the hue
And breath of roses in the end of spring
Are wont to hold our greedy eyes the more ;
So, standing on the utmost edge of fate,
Prepared to die, nor softly recusant,
Nor sluggish with base fear of parting breath,
The virgin all had moved, and on her drawn
The looks of all the sorrowing multitude,
Astonished to behold the wondrous sight,
And brought a solemn silence upon all.

AN IMPERIAL JOKER.

HELIOGABALUS was an expensive joker, but his guests paid for
the fun, and he might, therefore, indulge his humour without restraint
at the time, or remorse after it.   His supremely imperial joke lay in
placing a number of guests on table-couches (guests reclined and did

not sit down to dinner), which were blown up with air instead of being stuffed with wool. At a moment when the cups were filled to the brim with the choicest wine, and the guests were lifting them to their lips with anticipations of liquid Elysium, a tap was drawn beneath the carpet, and consequently down tumbled all the recliners on the floor, where they lay pell-mell, with wine spilt, goblets lost, and utter confusion prevailing, except on the face of Heliogabalus, who looked on, and indulged in laughter inextinguishable.

OLD-FASHIONED RIDDLES.

Q. IN words unnumbered I abound,
    In me mankind doth take delight ;
In me much learning still is found,
    Yet I can neither read nor write.
    A. It is a book, printed or written.

Q. With learning daily I am conversant,
    And scan the wisdom of the wisest man ;
With force I pierce the strongest argument,
    Yet know no more than it had never been.
A. It is a worm that eats through the books in a learned library.

Q. Full rich am I, yet care not who
    Doth take away from me my wealth ;
Be it by fraud, I will not see,
    Nor prosecute, though 't be by stealth.
    A. It is a coffer wherein great riches are laid up.

Q. Though I am pierced a thousand times,
    Yet in me not a hole is made ;
I notice give when Phœbus climbs
    To drowsy mortals in their bed.
    A. It is a window penetrated by the light.

Q. I'm dragged along through dirt and mire,
    O'er craggèd stones and hills about ;
And yet I neither faint nor tire,
    But rather weary those that do 't.
    A. It is a coach drawn about by horses.

Q. Five ribs I have, a breech and head,
    Four feet, and likewise a long tail :
In smoke and fire I make my bed,
    And to do service never fail.
    A. It is a gridiron.

DID YOU EVER?

DID you ever know a sentinel who could tell what building he was keeping guard over?

Did you ever know a cabman or a ticket porter with any change about him?

Did you ever know a tradesman asking for his account who had not " a bill to take up on Friday"?

Did you ever know an omnibus cad who could not engage to set you down within a few yards of any place within the bills of mortality?

Did you ever know a turnpike man who could be roused in less than a quarter of an hour, when it wanted that much of midnight?

Did you ever see a pair of family snuffers that had not a broken spring, a leg deficient, or half an inch of the point knocked off?

Did you ever know a lodging-house landlady who would own to bugs?

Did you ever know the boots at an inn call you too early for the morning coach?

Did you ever know a dancing-master's daughter who was not to excel Taglioni?

Did you ever know a man who did not think he could poke the fire better than you could?

Did you ever know a Frenchman admire Waterloo Bridge?

Did you ever know a housemaid who, on your discovering a fracture in a valuable china jar, did not tell you it was " done a long time ago," or that it was " cracked before"?

Did you ever know a man who did not consider *his* walking-stick a better walking-stick than *your* walking-stick?

Did you ever know a penny-a-liner who was not on intimate terms with Lytton-Bulwer, Captain Marryat, Sheridan Knowles, Tom Hood, Washington Irving, and Rigdum Funidos?

Did you ever know a hatter who was not prepared to sell you as good a hat for ten and sixpence as the one you've got on at five-and-twenty shillings?

Did you ever know a red-haired man who had a very clear notion of where scarlet began and auburn terminated?

Did you ever know an amateur singer without a " horrid bad cold"?

Did you ever know an author who had not been particularly ill-used by the booksellers?

Did you ever know a man who did not consider that he added ten years to his life by reading the Comic Almanac?—*Hood's Comic Annual*, 1841.

THE GRAVE.

THE grave is deep and soundless,
  And canopied over with clouds ;
And trackless, and dim, and boundless,
  Is the unknown land that it shrouds.

In vain may the nightingales warble
  Their songs—the roses of love
And friendship grow white on the marble
  The living have reared above.

The virgin, bereft at her bridal
  Of him she has loved, may weep ;
The wail of the orphan is idle,
  It breaks not the buried one's sleep.

Yet everywhere else shall mortals
  For peace unavailingly roam ;
Except through the shadowy portals,
  Goeth none to his genuine home !

And the heart that tempest and sorrow
  Have beaten against for years,
Must look for a summer morrow
  Beyond this temple of tears.—*Seewis (German).*

THE CRAFTY BUTCHER.

A BUTCHER of Caen bought a calf of a cattle-jobber in the environs ;
half a gallon of cider was to clench the bargain, and the butcher
jocosely observed in conversation, among other things, that he meant
to smuggle the calf into town in broad daylight, and to pass the *octroi,*
or customs barrier, publicly, without paying. The cattle-dealer declared
this to be impossible, and a wager was accordingly laid between him
and the butcher, who merely made this condition, that the dealer
should lend him his dog for half an hour. He put the dog into a large
sack, which he threw over his shoulder, and away he trudged into the
city. On reach ing the *octroi,* he declared he had nothing to pay, as
there was only a dog in the sack, which he had just bought, and shut
up that he might not find his way to his former master. The officers
of the *octroi* would not take this story on trust, but insisted on seeing
the dog. The butcher was therefore obliged to open his sack, and the
dog naturally availed himself of the opportunity to run away. Off
scampered the butcher after him, scolding and swearing all the way.
In a quarter of an hour he was again at the *octroi,* with the sack on his
shoulder as before. "You have given me a pretty chase," said he,
peevishly, walking through. Next day he invited the officers to partake of a veal cutlet, with which, having won the wager, he treated
them and the cattle dealer.

PLEASE TO RING THE BELLE.

I'll tell you a story that's not in Tom Moore,
Young Love likes to knock at a pretty girl's door—
So he called upon Lucy, 'twas past ten o'clock,
Like a spruce *single* man with a smart *double* knock.
Now a handmaid, whatever her fingers be at,
Will run like a *puss* when she hears a *rat*-tat ;
So Lucy ran up, and in two seconds more,
Had questioned the stranger, and answered the door.
The meeting was bliss, but the parting was woe,
For the moment must come when such comers must go ;
So she sighed and she whispered, poor innocent thing,
" The next time you come, Love, pray come with a *ring !*"

Thomas Hood.

FRANKLIN ON THE GAME OF CHESS.

CHESS is so interesting in itself as not to need the view of gain to induce engaging in it, and thence it is never played for money.   Life is a kind of chess, in which we have points to gain, and competitors or adversaries to contend with, and in which there is a great variety of good and ill events that are, in some degree, the effects of prudence or the want of it.   By playing at chess then we learn,—

1st. Foresight, which looks a little into futurity, considers the consequences that may attend an action, for it is continually occurring to the player :—If I move this piece what will be the advantage of my new situation ?   What use can my adversary make of it to annoy me ?   What other moves can I make to support it, and to defend myself from his attack ?

2nd.   Circumspection, which surveys the whole chess-board, or scene of action, the relations of the several pieces and situations, the dangers they are respectively exposed to, the probability that the adversary may take this or that move, and attack this or the other piece, and what different means can be used to avoid the stroke or turn the consequences against him.

3rd. Caution, not to make our moves too hastily.   This habit is best acquired by observing strictly the laws of the game, such as, " If you touch a piece you must move it somewhere; if you set it down you must let it stand," and it is therefore best that these rules should be observed, as the game thereby becomes more the image of human life, and particularly of war, in which if you have incautiously put yourself into a bad and dangerous position, you cannot obtain your enemy's leave to withdraw your troops and place them more securely, but you must abide all the consequences of your rashness.

And lastly, we learn by chess the habit of not being discouraged by present bad appearances in the state of our affairs, the habit of hoping for a favourable change, and that of persevering in the search of resources.

A BACHELOR SKETCH.

MARRIED people are all levelled down below the region of speculative opinions, paradoxical heterodoxes, or heterodoxical paradoxes. They speak sensibly of cookery, of the training of children, of the price of the four-pound loaf, the rise of butter, and the expense of education. They are rational ; but what do we at our symposia of darling fellow-ships ? Ah ! " there's the rub." Funny and free, then, are our bachelor revelries. We are jolly dogs, " fellows of infinite jest and most excellent fancy," who instruct the planets in what orbits to run, correct Old Time, and regulate the sun ; we mount where science guides, measure earth, weigh air, and state the tides. Every one of us rides his hobby, which he whips and spurs to the amusement of his fellows,—each of whom, when the laugh is out, mounts his wooden Rosinante, and gallops helter-skelter.

All have their charms, but charm not all alike ;
On different senses different objects strike ;
Hence different passions more or less inflame,
As strong or weak the organs of the frame.

We have all of us a species of happy madness, which we increase by our libations; and, as the blood of the grape warms our hearts, we experience the soothing effects of "the weed," as we appreciate the delicious aroma and its influences over the senses and thinking faculties (Christison concludes that " no well-ascertained ill effects have been shown to result from the practice of smoking. Dr. Pereira testifies to its healthy effects both on the mind and body. Even Dr. Prout, the highest medical authority of the day who can be cited against tobacco, only speaks of what " is said" of its deleterious effects. Locke says that "Tobacco may be neglected, but reason first recommends the trial, and custom makes it pleasant." Professor Johnstone, himself no smoker, concludes from the testimony of mankind,—for, next to salt, tobacco is the article most largely consumed by man,—" that its greatest and first effect is to assuage and allay and soothe agitation in general ; and that its after-effects are to excite and invigorate, and at the same time to give steadiness and fixity to the powers of thought")—our better nature, as it surges in our bachelor hearts, wells over towards mankind. We fight our battles o'er again, we " set the table in a roar," we laugh loud, long and heartily; we cultivate the flowers of imagination, and paint pictures until the curtain falls to our own satisfaction ; and when at length we bid adieu to this sublunary scene, we endow princely hospitals for the destitute, on whom it devolves to calm down the harpy faces of our shades by drinking to our memory on the anniversaries of our birth. Ladies fair, gentle and simple, our fate is in your hands. You can do as you like with us. You are our jury, and can give your

She mellows the landscape, and crowds the stream
With shadows that flit like a fairy dream :
Still wheeling her flight through the gladsome air,—
The Spirit of Beauty is everywhere !

Rufus Dawes (American).

'Neath the sunny beams of Beauty's glance ;
And felt the rapturous, thrilling charm
Of her young breath, coming soft and warm ;
The languid eye, and the skin like milk,
The silver whisper of trailing silk ;
The twinkling feet, 'neath the lustre's ray,
That over the well-chalked floor would play ;
The tender grasp of the white-gloved hand,
As around we went to Strauss's band ;
Ah ! those times were to us most sweet !
We don't dance now, it so hurts our feet ;
Our waists are thick, our breath is short,
We're martyrs to gout, and fond of port ;
And, alas ! prefer—how a mortal errs !
Short whist, and elderly dowagers.

Castes of Edinburgh, by John Heiton.

ANECDOTE OF FONTENELLE.

THIS remarkable man died in February, 1757, just one month before completing his 100th year. His character, both personally and literally, is admirably given by M. Grimm. Utterly without heart, generosity, or sympathy with any human being, he was extremely complaisant and amusing in general society, where he dealt out epigrams to the very last with a neatness and vivacity that was extremely engaging ; and continued to be universally acceptable, without even pretending to take an interest in anything but himself. In the whole course of his long life, it was remarked of him that he was never known either to laugh or to cry ; and he even came at last, it seems, to make a boast of this insensibility. He had a great liking for asparagus, and preferred it dressed with oil. One day, a certain *bon vivant* abbé, with whom he was extremely intimate, came unexpectedly to dinner. The abbé was very fond of asparagus also, but liked his dressed with butter. Fontenelle said that for such a friend there was no sacrifice of which he did not feel himself capable, and that he should have half the dish of asparagus which he had just ordered for himself, and that half, moreover, should be done with butter ! While they were conversing together very lovingly, and waiting for dinner, the poor abbé falls suddenly down in a fit of apoplexy ; upon which Fontenelle instantly springs up, scampers down to the kitchen with incredible agility, and bawls out to his cook with eagerness, " The whole with oil, the whole with oil, as at first !"

" Why," said Swift, " they think that you are a very little man, but a very great poet." Pope instantly retorted, with some acrimony, " And, in England, they think of you exactly the reverse."

CHARLES II. AND MILTON.

CHARLES II. and his brother James went to see Milton, to reproach him, and finished a profusion of insults with saying, "You old villain, your blindness is the visitation of Providence for your sins." "If Providence," replied the venerable bard, " has punished my sins with *blindness*, what must have been the crimes of your father, which it punished with *death?*"

PATENT BROWN STOUT.

A BREWER in a country town
    Had got a monstrous reputation;
No other beer but his went down,
    The hosts of the surrounding station,
Carving his name upon their mugs,
    And painting it on every shutter ;
And though some envious folks would utter
Hints that its flavour came from drugs,
Others maintained 'twas no such matter,
    But owing to his monstrous vat,
    At least as corpulent as that
At Heidelberg—and some said fatter.

His foreman was a lusty Black,
    An honest fellow;
But one who had an ugly knack
Of tasting samples as he brewed,
    Till he was stupefied and mellow.
One day in this top-heavy mood,
    Having to cross the vat aforesaid
(Just then with boiling beer supplied),
    O'ercome with giddiness and qualms, he
    Reeled—fell in—and nothing more said,
But in his favourite liquor died,
    Like Clarence in his butt of Malmsey.

In all directions round about
    The negro absentee was sought,
    But as no human noddle thought
That our fat Black was now Brown stout,
They settled that the rogue had left
The place for debt, or crime, or theft.
Meanwhile, the beer was, day by day,
Drawn into casks and sent away,

Until the lees flowed thick and thicker,
When, lo ! outstretched upon the ground,
Once more their missing friend they found,
As they had often done—in liquor.
" See," cried his moralizing master,
" I always knew the fellow drank hard,
And prophesied some sad disaster ;
His fate should other tipplers strike.
Poor Mungo ; there he welters, like
A toast at bottom of a tankard !"
Next morn a publican, whose tap
Had helped to drain the vat so dry,
Not having heard of the mishap,
Came to demand a fresh supply ;
Protesting loudly that the last
All previous specimens surpassed,
Possessing a much richer gusto
Than formerly it ever used to,
And begging as a special favour,
Some more of the exact same flavour.

" Zounds !" cried the Brewer, "that's a task
More difficult to grant than ask.
Most gladly would I give the smack
Of the last beer to the ensuing ;
But where am I to find a Black,
And boil him down at every brewing ?"

ECONOMICAL ADVICE.

QUIN meeting two coxcombs one day in Pall-Mall,
Observed, with regret, that they both looked unwell.
" Indeed you judge right," replied one ; "you must know
Our physician advised, and to-morrow we go
Out of town to enjoy the pure air, and to drink
Asses' milk every morning for breakfast."   " I think,
A much shorter method I could recommend,"
Said Quin very drily, " to you and your friend ;
To drink it in London."—" How so?" said the other.
" Stay at home," he replied ; " you may suck one another."

ROGERS THE POET AS A WIT.

A CRITIC annoyed Mr. Rogers in the *Quarterly Review* by asserting
that his author was a hasty writer ; yet his literary life extended over
sixty years, and the produce of his life only fills a pocket volume ; his
were hard-bound brains, and not a line he ever wrote was produced
at a single sitting.   This was well exemplified in a favourite saying of
Sydney Smith : " When Rogers produces a couplet, he goes to bed,

and the knocker is tied up, the straw is laid down, and the caudle is made, and the answer to inquiries is, that ' Mr. Rogers is as well as can be expected.' "

Captain Gronow relates that, at an evening party, at Lady Jersey's, every one was praising the Duke of B——, who had just come in, and who had lately attained his majority. There was a perfect chorus of admiration to this effect—" Everything is in his favour ; he has good looks, considerable abilities, and a hundred thousand a-year." Rogers listened to these encomiums for some time in silence, and at last remarked, with an air of great exultation, and in his most venomous manner, "Thank God, he has got bad teeth !" His well-known epigram on Mr. Ward, afterwards Lord Dudley,—

> " They say that Ward's no heart; but I deny it,
> He has a heart, and gets his speeches by it,"

was provoked by a remark made at table by Mr. Ward. On Rogers observing that his carriage was broken down, and that he had been obliged to come in a hackney-coach, Mr. Ward grumbled out in a very audible whisper, " In a hearse, I should think," alluding to the poet's corpse-like appearance. This remark Rogers never forgave ; and he is said to have pored for days over the retaliatory epigram.— *" Anecdote Lives of the Later Wits and Humorists," by John Timbs.*

THE SMOKING PHILOSOPHER.

HIS whole amusement was his pipe ; and, as there is a certain indefinable link between smoking and philosophy, my father by dint of smoking had become a perfect philosopher. It is no less strange than true, that we can puff away our cares with tobacco, when without it, they remain an oppressive burden to existence. There is no composing draught like the draught through the tube of a pipe. The savage warriors of North America enjoyed the blessing before we did, and to the pipe is to be ascribed the wisdom of their councils, and the laconic delivery of their sentiments. It would be well introduced into our own legislative assembly. Ladies, indeed, would no longer peep down through the ventilator ; but we should have more sense and fewer words. It is also to tobacco that is to be ascribed the stoical firmness of those American warriors, who, satisfied with the pipe in their mouths, submitted with perfect indifference to the torture of their enemies. From the well-known virtues of this weed arose that peculiar expression, when you irritate another, that you " put his pipe out."—*Marryat's " Jacob Faithful."*

THE BURGHER AND HIS WIFE AND THE CURFEW BELL.

A CERTAIN burgher, of staid and sober habits, and well on in years married a pretty-faced wife, who gave him a deal of concern on account of the gay and riotous manner of her life, whereby he was much disgraced in the eyes of his fellow-citizens. Instead of minding her home, she would idle through all the day, and dance and sing at night in the ale-house after a most disorderly fashion.

Now the law of that city was, that any man, woman, or child found in the streets after the sound of the curfew bell, should be locked up all night, and dragged through the city next day at the cart's tail. The burgher's wife generally contrived to escape punishment by not coming home till the morning. Sometimes she would steal away during her husband's first sleep, and, leaving the door ajar, trust to be able to regain it without being observed, by returning through back streets from the ale-house ; and for a long time she was successful. Indeed, if a watchman saw her at such times, he would pretend to look another way, for the sake of the respect in which her husband was held. When the burgher discovered her practice, he thought of a plan of reclaiming his wife. One night he made believe to have taken too much wine, and on getting to bed feigned to fall into a sound sleep. His wife quickly rose and sped off to the ale-house. No sooner was she gone than the old man came down stairs, locked and chained the door, and then went back to his room to wait his wife's return. By-and-by she came back, tried the door and found it fast. Dreading to be found in the streets, she at last summoned courage to knock.

"Go away," said the old man, looking out of the window; "I don't know you."

"Dear husband," she said, coaxingly, "let me in ; I am your wife."

"Oh, no, you are not," he answered; "my wife came to bed two hours ago. You are some disorderly jade who wants whipping. Go away, or I will call the watchman."

She begged and entreated, but in vain. Then all at once she burst out crying, and pretended to give way to despair. "You hard, cruel man," she cried, "since you have no more care for your wife than to want to see her dragged at the cart's tail in daylight before the people, I have nothing left to live for. I will not live. I will drown myself this minute in the well." She listened, but the burgher said nothing. He did not believe she would drown herself.

"I will," she cried again, and waited ; but the burgher would not undo the door.

"You are afraid to," he answered.

"You heartless brute!" she sobbed. "But I forgive you. Farewell for ever."

So saying, she took a great stone and flung it into the well with a tremendous splash, and gave a piercing scream at the same moment. Then she ran and hid herself behind the door.

Hearing the splash and the scream, the burgher made no doubt but his wife had drowned herself. He called her by name, but there was no answer. Then, blaming himself very much for his hardness of heart, he ran out of the house. But directly he came out of door, his wife ran in, and having made fast the lock and chain went up to her chamber. As soon as he found there was no woman in the well, the burgher tried to get into his house again, but the door was fast.

" Go away," said his wife, looking out of the window, and mocking him. " I don't know you."

" You wicked woman," answered he. " Let me in, for the watchmen are coming. Let me in, I pray, for I am your husband."

" Oh, no, you are not," she said ; " my husband came to bed two hours ago. You are some wicked old man who wants to be dragged at the cart's tail. Go away, or I'll call the watchman." He besought her in vain for admittance. Then the watch came up.

" Here is my husband," said the lady, " at his old tricks again. You may have thought him a very steady and sedate old person ; but every night, as soon as I am asleep, he gets up and goes off to the ale-house. All my entreaties have been vain. Take him, watchman, and put him in prison, and perhaps that will be a lesson to him."

The watchmen knew quite well that her story was untrue ; but the burgher was certainly out after curfew, and there was no help for it but to take him to jail for the night, and the next morning to drag him round the town behind a cart, like a thief and a vagabond.— *Beeton's Christmas Annual,* 1872.

SOME OF HOOK'S ESCAPADES.

IN carrying out the following mischievous trick, Hook was aided by Liston, the famous comedian. A young gentleman of Hook's acquaintance had a great desire to witness a play, and also escort a fair cousin there, but was terrified lest his going to a theatre should come to the knowledge of his father, a rigid Presbyterian, who held such places in abhorrence. He communicated his difficulties to his gay friend. " Never mind the governor, my dear fellow," was the reply, " trust to me ; I'll arrange everything—get you a couple of orders—secure places—front row ; and nobody need know anything about it." The tickets were procured and received with great thankfulness by Mr. B——, who started with his relative to the playhouse, and the pair soon found themselves absorbed in an ecstasy of delight in witnessing the drolleries of Liston. But what was their confusion, when the comedian, advancing to the footlights during a burst of laughter at one of his performances, looked round the dress-circle with a mock offended air, and exclaimed : " I don't understand this conduct, ladies and gentlemen ! I am not accustomed to be laughed at ; I can't imagine what you see ridiculous in *me ;* why, I declare (pointing at the centre box with his finger), there's Harry B——, too, and his cousin Martha J—— ; what business have they to come here and laugh at me, I should like to know ? I'll go and tell his father, and hear what *he* thinks of it !" The consternation caused to the truant couple by this unexpected address, and the eyes of the whole audience being turned on them, may be more readily imagined than described, and they fled from the house in dismay.

Passing one day in a gig with a friend, by the villa of a retired chronometer-maker, Hook suddenly reined up, and remarked to his friend what a comfortable little box that was, and they might do worse than dine there. He then alighted, rang the bell, and on being admitted to the presence of the worthy old citizen, said that he had often heard his name, which was celebrated throughout the civilized world, and that being in the neighbourhood, he could not resist the temptation of calling and making the acquaintance of so distinguished a public character.   The good man was quite tickled with the compliment, pressed his admirer and friend to stay to dinner, which was just ready, and a most jovial afternoon was spent ; though on the way home the gig containing Hook and his companion was smashed to pieces by the refractory horse, and the two occupants had a narrow escape of their lives.

In Hook's youthful days the abstraction of pump-handles and street-knockers was a favourite amusement of the young blades about town, some of whom prided themselves not a little in forming museums of these trophies.   Hook was behind no one in such freaks.   One of them was the carrying off the figure of a Highlander, as large as life, from the door of a tobacconist, wrapping it up in a cloak, and tumbling it into a hackney coach as "a friend—a very respectable man, but a little tipsy."

On being presented for matriculation to the Vice-Chancellor (St. Mary's Hall, Oxford), that dignitary inquired if he was prepared to sign the Thirty-nine Articles.   "Oh, yes," replied Hook, "forty if you like."   It required all his brother's interest with Dr. Parsons to induce him to pardon this petulant sally.

A story is told of Hook in which he improved on the well-known device related of Sheridan.   Getting into a hackney coach one day, and being unable to pay the fare, he bethought himself of the plan adopted by the celebrated wit just mentioned on a similar occasion, and hailed a friend whom he observed passing along the street.   He made him get into the carriage beside him, but on comparing notes, he found his companion equally devoid of cash as himself, and it was necessary to think of some other expedient.   Presently they approached the house of a celebrated surgeon.   Hook alighted, rushed to the door, and exclaimed hurriedly to the servant who opened it :—"Is Mr.—— at home ?   I must see him immediately.   For God's sake do not lose an instant."   Ushered into the consulting room, he exclaimed wildly to the surgeon, "Thank heaven !   Pardon my incoherence, sir ; make allowance for the feelings of a husband—*perhaps a father*—your attendance, sir, is instantly required—instantly—by Mrs. ——.   For mercy's sake, sir, be off !"   "I'll be on my way immediately," replied the medical man ;   "I have only to get my instruments, and step into my carriage."   "Don't wait for your carriage," cried the pseudo-distressed parent ; "get into mine, which is waiting at the door."   Esculapius readily complied, was hurried into the coach, and conveyed in a trice to the residence of an aged spinster, whose indignation and horror at the purport of his visit were beyond all bounds.   The poor man was glad to beat a speedy retreat, but the fury of the old maiden lady was not all he was destined to undergo, as the hackney coachman kept hold of him and mulcted him in the full amount of the fare which Hook ought to have paid.

All Hook's other escapades were, however, fairly eclipsed by the famous Berners Street hoax, which created such a sensation in London in 1809. By despatching thousands of letters to innumerable quarters he completely blocked up the entrance to the street by an assemblage of the most heterogeneous kind. The parties written to had been requested to call on a certain day at the house of a lady, residing at No. 54, Berners Street, against whom Hook and one or two of his friends had conceived a grudge. So successful was the trick, that nearly all obeyed the summons. Coal waggons heavily laden, carts of upholstery, vans with pianos and other articles, wedding and funeral coaches, all rumbled through and filled up the adjoining streets and lanes ; sweeps assembled with the implements of their trade; tailors with clothes that had been ordered, pastry-cooks with wedding cakes, undertakers with coffins, fishmongers with cod-fishes, and butchers with legs of mutton. There were surgeons with their instruments, lawyers with their papers and parchments, and clergymen with their books of devotion. Such a babel was never heard before in London ; and to complete the business, who should drive up but the Lord Mayor in his state carriage, the Governor of the Bank of England, the Chairman of the East India Company, and even a scion of royalty itself in the person of the Duke of Gloucester. Hook and his confederates were meantime enjoying the fun from a window in the neighbourhood; but the consternation occasioned to the poor lady who had been made the victim of the jest was nearly becoming too serious a matter. He never avowed himself as the originator of this trick, though there is no doubt of his being prime actor in it. It was made the subject of a solemn investigation by many of the parties who had been duped, but so carefully had the precautions been taken to avoid detection that the inquiry proved entirely fruitless.—*Chambers' Book of Days.*

THE VICAR.

His talk was like a stream which runs
    With rapid change from rocks to roses;
It slipped from politics to puns,
    It passed from Mahomet to Moses ;
Beginning with the laws which keep
    The planets in their radiant courses,
And ending with some precept deep
    For dressing eels or shoeing horses.

He was a shrewd and sound divine,
    Of loud dissent the mortal terror ;
And when by dint of page and line
    He 'stablished truth or startled error,
The Baptist found him far too deep,
    The Deist sighed with saving sorrow,
And the lean Levite went to sleep,
    And dreamt of eating pork to-morrow.

T

He wrote, too, in a quiet way,
    Small treatises and smaller verses,
And sage remarks on chalk and clay,
    And hints to noble lords and nurses ;
True histories of last year's ghost ;
    Lines to a ringlet on a turban,
And trifles for the *Morning Post*,
    And nothings for Sylvanus Urban.

He did not think all mischief fair,
    Although he had a knack of joking ;
He did not make himself a bear,
    Although he had a taste for smoking.
And when religious sects ran mad,
    He held, in spite of all his learning,
That if a man's belief is bad,
    It will not be improved by burning.

And he was kind, and loved to sit
    In the low hut or garnished cottage,
And praise the farmer's homely wit,
    And share the widow's homelier pottage.
At his approach complaints grew mild,
    And when his hand unbarred the shutter,
The clammy lips of fever smiled
    The welcome that they could not utter.

He always had a tale for me
    Of Julius Cæsar, or of Venus ;
From him I learned the rule of three,
    Cats'-cradle, leap-frog, and Quæ genus ;
I used to singe his powdered wig,
    To steal the staff he put such trust in,
And make the puppy dance a jig
    When he began to quote Augustine.

                    W. Mackworth Praed.

OTHER TIMES, OTHER MANNERS.

HARRY BAYLIS (Hood's " Hal Baylis"), a great (albeit to the world
obscure) wit and a friend of Douglas Jerrold, and Joe Allen, an accomplished artist and drawing-master at the Blue Coat School, were the
heroes of a piece of humour which under our present superfine conditions of civilization could scarcely be repeated, and would certainly
fail to be appreciated.   They used to go down on all-fours in the club-
room (in days when clubs were convivial and not stuck up), put their
heads together, and simulate the conversation of a pair of hackney-
coach horses—" prads," as these steeds were called in the slang of the
day.   Allen's remarks on the proportion of chaff to the hay in his nose-
bag, and Baylis's complaints of the rib-roasting he had endured from

the vicious savage on the box, the whole mingled with sententious reflections on men and manners, were exquisitely humorous. In the delightful "Recollections" of Mr. J. R. Planché there are frequent allusions to the mad waggeries once indulged in without shame by clever men,—waggeries which in this age of "sweetness and light" would be scouted as so much vulgar tom-foolery. Only fancy the beautiful Mrs. Rousby knocking run-away raps in Maiden Lane, Covent Garden, or Mr. H. Irving offering to ride a rhinoceros in a menagerie! Yet precisely such pranks were played by the beautiful Mrs. Inchbald and by the sublime John Kemble himself. *Autres temps, autres mœurs.—Gentleman's Magazine.*

EARLY MARRIAGES IN THE EAST.

THE most lamentable thing of all, in the domestic arrangements of these unhappy Syrian people, is the early age at which the girls are married. The Arabic journal, the *Jenneh*, made a boast one day of having seen a grandmother of *twenty* years, herself having been married before she was *ten!* Dr. Meshakah of Damascus, that venerable, white-bearded patriarch, with his little wife whom he married at *eleven* years of age, remarked that in his day young girls received no training at home ; young men who wanted wives to please them, had to marry them early, so as to educate them to suit themselves. One of the scholars in the Beyrout seminary came in at eight years of age, and remained for two years. At ten her parents sent for her, and took her away to be married. And one of the teachers records in a very artless way what carefulness they had getting her off, and sending her dolls with her !—*Charles S. Robinson.*

BEWARE!

BEWARE of a young lady who calls you by your Christian name the first time she meets you.

Beware of Port at 30s. a dozen.

Beware of a lodging-house where you are "treated as one of the family."

Beware of every "cheap substitute for silver," excepting gold.

Beware of cigars that are bought of "a bold smuggler" in the street.

Beware of a wife that talks about her "dear husband" and "that beautiful shawl" in her sleep.

Beware of a gentleman who is "up" to all the clever tricks, and "knows a dodge or two" at cards.

Beware of giving an order to a deaf man on the first night of a new piece. He is sure to laugh and applaud in the wrong places, and so cause a disturbance which may be fatal to the success of your farce

Beware of entering a French shop which has the following inscription :— "*Here they spike the English,*" unless you can speak French very correctly, or are prepared to pay for the consequences. —*Mayhew's Comic Almanac,* 1848.

THE VAGABOND IN HUMAN NATURE.

THE fresh, rough, heathery part of human nature, where the air is freshest and where the linnets sing, is getting encroached upon by cultivated fields.   Everyone is making himself and herself *useful.* Every one is producing something.   Everybody is a philanthropist. I don't like it.   I love a little eccentricity.   I respect honest prejudices. I admire foolish enthusiasm in a young head, more than wise scepticism.   It is high time that a moral game law were passed for the preservation of the wild and vagrant feelings of human nature.   Ah, me ! what a world this was to live in two or three centuries ago, when it was getting itself discovered,—when the sunset gave up America ! Then were the "Arabian Nights" common-place, enchantments a matter of course, and romance the most ordinary thing in the world. Then man was courting Nature ; now he has married her ! Yet for all that Time has brought and taken away, I am glad to know that the Vagabond sleeps in our blood, and awakes now and then.   Overlay nature as you please, here and there, some bit of rock or mound of aboriginal soil will crop out with the wild-flowers growing upon it, sweetening the air.   Genius is a vagabond ; Art is a vagabond ; Enterprise is a vagabond.   The first fine day in spring awakes the gipsy in the blood of the British workman, no matter what his profession, and incontinently he "babbles of green fields."   On the British gentleman lapped in the most luxurious civilization, and with a thousand-power, and resources of wealth at his command, descends oftentimes a fierce unrest, a Bedouin-like horror of cities and the cry of the money changer, and in a month the fiery dust rises in the track of his desert steed, or in the six months' polar midnight he hears the big wave dashing on the icy shore.

Vagabonds have moulded the world into its present shape.   Respectable people swarm in the track of the vagabond, as rooks in the furrow of the ploughshare.   Respectable people do little in the world except storing wine cellars and amassing fortunes for the benefit of spendthrift heirs.   Respectable well-to-do Grecians shook their heads over Leonidas and his three hundred when they went down to Thermopylæ. Respectable Spanish churchmen, with shaven crowns, scouted the dream of Columbus.   Respectable German folks attempted to dissuade Luther from appearing before Charles and the princes and electors of the Empire.   Nature makes us vagabonds, the world makes us respectable.   Commend me to Shakspeare's vagabonds, the most delightful in the world ; his sweet-blooded and liberal nature blossomed into all fine generosities, as naturally as an apple-bough into pink blossoms and odours.

It would be better if we could have along with our modern enlightenment, our higher tastes and purer habits, a greater individuality of thought and manner ; better that every man should be allowed to grow in his own way, so long as he does not infringe on the rights of his neighbour, or insolently thrust himself between him and the sun.   A little more air and light should be let in upon life.   I should think the world has stood long enough under the drill of Adjutant Fashion.   It

is hard work, the posture is wearisome, and Fashion is an awful
martinet, and has a quick eye, and comes down mercilessly on the
unfortunate wight who cannot square his toes to the approved pattern,
or who appears upon parade with a darn in his coat, or with a shoulder
belt insufficiently pipe-clayed. It is killing work. Suppose we try
"standing at ease" for a little?—*Alexander Smith's Dreamthorp
Essays.*

THE BOOK COLLECTOR.

THAT in this ship the chief place I govern,
By this wide sea with fools wandering,
The cause is plain and easy to discern—
Still am I busy book assembling ;
For to have plenty it is a pleasant thing,
In my conceit, and to have them aye in hand ;
But what they mean, do I not understand.

But yet I have them in great reverence
And honour, saving them from filth and ordure,
By often brushing and much diligence ;
Full goodly bound in pleasant coverture
Of damask, satin, or else of velvet pure ;
I keep them sure, fearing lest they should be lost,
For in them is the cunning wherein I me boast.
Barclay's " Ship of Fools."

[The "Ship of Fools" is a translation by Alexander Barclay, from
the German of Brandt, and was first printed in 1509.]

"A LITTLE MORE SLEEP."

THE indisposition of "lie-a-beds" to face the severity of a winter
morning is thus pleasantly pictured by Leigh Hunt in a paper in the
Indicator. He imagines one of those persons to express himself in
these terms :—" On opening my eyes, the first thing that meets them
is my own breath rolling forth, as if in the open air, like smoke out of
a cottage chimney. Think of this symptom! Then I turn my eyes
sideways and see the window all frozen over. Think of that! Then
the servant comes in. 'It is very cold this morning ; is it not?'—
'Very cold, sir.'—'Very cold indeed ; isn't it?'—'Very cold indeed,
sir.'—'More than usually so ; isn't it, even for this weather?' (Here
the servant's wit and good nature are put to a considerable test, and
the inquirer lies on thorns for the answer.) 'Why, sir,
I think it *is !* (Good creature ! There is not a better or more truth-
telling servant going.) 'I must rise, however. Get me some warm
water.' Here comes a fine interval between the departure of the
servant and the arrival of the hot water ; during which, of course, it is
of 'no use' to get up. The hot water comes. 'Is it quite hot?'—

'Yes, sir.'—'Perhaps too hot for shaving : I must wait a little ?'—
'No, sir ; it will just do.' (There is an over-nice propriety sometimes,
an officious zeal of virtue, a little troublesome.) 'Oh—the shirt—you
must air my clean shirt ; linen gets very damp this weather.'—'Yes,
sir.' Here another delicious five minutes. A knock at the door.
'Oh, the shirt—very well. My stockings—I think the stockings had
better be aired too.'—'Very well, sir.' Here another interval. At
length everything is ready, except myself. I now cannot help thinking
a good deal—who can?—upon the unnecessary and villanous custom
of shaving ; it is a thing so unmanly (here I nestle closer), so effemi-
ate (here I recoil from an unlucky step into the colder part of the bed).
No wonder that the Queen of France took part with the rebels against
that degenerate king, her husband, who first affronted her smooth
visage with a face like her own. The Emperor Julian never showed
the luxuriancy of his genius to better advantage than in reviving the
flowing beard. Look at Cardinal Bembo's picture—at Michael Angelo's
—at Titian's—at Shakspeare's—at Fletcher's—at Spenser's—at Chaucer's—at Alfred's—at Plato's. I could name a great man for every tick
of my watch. Look at the Turks, a grave and otiose people.—Think of
Haroun Al Raschid and Bed-ridden Hassan.—Think of Wortley Montague, the worthy son of his mother, a man above the prejudice of his
time. Look at the Persian gentlemen whom one is ashamed of meeting about the suburbs, their dress and appearance are so much finer
than our own. Lastly, think of the razor itself ; how totally opposed
to every sensation of bed! how cold, how edgy, how hard ! how utterly
different from anything like the warm and circling amplitude, which

> Sweetly recommends itself
> Unto our gentle senses !

Add to this, benumbed fingers, which may help you to cut yourself, a
quivering body, a frozen towel, and a ewer full of ice ; and he that
says there is nothing to oppose in all this, only shows, at any rate, that
he has no merit in opposing it."

THE BIRTHNIGHT BALL.

[At the Ball given in celebration of Queen Charlotte's birthday
(January 18, 1782), the Princess Royal, during the first country dance,
caught the fringe of her petticoat in the buckle of her shoe, which
brought the dance to an abrupt termination. This incident gave rise
to the following song, which appears in the first number of the
European Magazine for 1782, where it is entitled, " A Piece of Ingenious Levity."]

> 'TWAS at the Birthnight Ball, sir,
>   God bless our Gracious Queen,
> Where people great and small, sir,
>   Are on a footing seen.

As down the dance,
With heels from France,
A Royal couple flew,
Though well she tripped,
The lady slipped,
And off she cast her shoe.
    Doodle-doodle-do ;
    The Princess lost her shoe ;
    Her Highness hopped,
    The fiddlers stopped,
    Not knowing what to do.

Amazed at such a pause, sir,
The dancers to a man,
Eager to hear the cause, sir,
Around the Princess ran ;
    Lord Hertford, too,
    Like lightning flew,
And though unused to truckle,
    Laid down his wand,
    And lent a hand,
    The Royal shoe to buckle.
        Doodle-doodle-do, etc.

The vestal maids of honour,
Attentive to their duty,
All crowded close upon her,
The Prince surveyed their beauty,
    Admired their zeal
    For 's partner's heel,
But told them he conceived,
    Tho' *some* false steps
    Made demi-reps,
This soon might be retrieved.
        Doodle-doodle-do, etc.

The Princess soon was shod, sir,
And soon the dance went on ;
'Tis said some guardian god, sir,
Came down to get it done ;
    Perhaps 'tis true,
    Old England, too,
Might dance from night to noon,
    If slips of state,
    Amongst the great,
    Were mended half so soon.
        Doodle-doodle-do,
        Egad 'tis very true,
            Or late or soon,
            They're out of tune,
    And know not what to do.

TO ANNA.

WHAT word is that that changeth not,
  Though it be turned and made in twain ?
It is mine ANNA, God it wot,
  And eke the causer of my pain.
Who love rewardeth with disdain ;
  Yet is it loved ; what would ye more ?
It is my health, and eke my bane.
                              Sir Thomas Wyatt.

[Wyatt (1503–1541) entertained a secret passion for Anne Boleyn, but dared not openly enter into rivalry with him " who never spared woman in his lust or man in his wrath "—Henry VIII. The foregoing irregular sonnet is a specimen of Wyatt's love-verses to that unhappy lady.]

THE DOTING HUSBAND.

ONE day a sturdy peasant was at work in the fields amidst storm and rain, and went home in the evening thoroughly tired and drenched to the skin. He was met at the door by his loving wife, who had been at home all day. " My dear," said she, " it has been raining so hard that I could not fetch water, and so I have not been able to make you any soup. But now, as you are wet through, I shall be obliged to you to fetch me a couple of buckets of water : you will not get any wetter." The argument was striking ; so the good man took the buckets and fetched some water from the well, which was at a considerable distance. On reaching the house, he found his wife comfortably seated by the fire ; then, lifting one bucket after another, he poured both over his kind and considerate partner. " Now, wife," said he, " you are quite as wet as I am, so you may as well fetch water for yourself : you can't get any wetter."

FAMOUS LIBRARIES.

THE Vatican Library, according to a description lately published, contains 23,580 manuscripts, written in the various oriental and classic tongues ; and 387,000 printed volumes. The first literary curiosity is seen in the entrance-hall, being a fine papyrus inclosed in a glass case, descriptive of the funeral rites of the Egyptians. Passing down the great hall you enter the immense double gallery, celebrated for the effect of its perspective ; it is here one is surrounded by some of the first treasures extant. It being simply our purpose to notice some of its literary curiosities, we shall not allude to any others with which every niche and corner of this magnificent pile is so rife. Among the most valuable manuscripts are the following :—The Bible of the 6th century, in capital letters, comprising the oldest version of the Septuagint, and the first Greek version of the New Testament ; a Virgil of the 4th century, illuminated with 50 miniatures, and a Terence, also with illuminations ; a Seneca, a Pliny of later dates, and other classics. Here are all the Homilies of St. Gregory, of 1063, and the Four Gospels, 1128—both Byzantine manuscripts of great interest ; a Greek version of the Acts, written in gold, presented to Innocent VIII. by Charlotte, Queen of Cyprus;—a large Hebrew Bible richly illuminated, for which the Jews of Venice offered its weight in gold, with several other manuscripts, finely illuminated ; a parchment scroll of a Greek manuscript of the 7th century, 32 feet long, with miniatures, etc., and the Codex Mexicanus of immense length ;—Autographs of Dante, Tasso, Petrarch, and the annals of Cardinal Baronius, in 2 volumes. There are also to be found there several manuscripts of Luther and one of Melanchthon, 1556. Among the printed books are some of the most rare known to be extant.

The Bologna University Library comprises 80,000 volumes, and 4,000 manuscripts ; amongst other curiosities it includes a Lactantius of the 5th century ; four Evangelists in Armenian, 12th century ; the image of Michael Apostolius, a Greek exile, and protégé of Cardinal Bessarion. Cardinal Mezzofanti commenced his brilliant career at this institution ; the reigning pontiff, Gregory VI., raised him from an Abbé to the highest honours in his gift. He presents another illustrious instance of the omnipotence of genius over contending circumstances ; from the obscurest origin he has made himself master of forty-three languages, and is conversant with the best literature of most of them.

The collection at Ferrara, comprising 80,000 volumes and 1,000 manuscripts, derives its principal notoriety from some of the MSS. of Tasso and Ariosto : the latter are preserved in an apartment where the poet's arm chair, designed by himself, is deposited. The *Gerusalemme* exhibits the corrections of the ill-fated author during his cruel incarceration.

The library at Sienna, the oldest in Europe, contains, among numerous relics, some of the MS. letters of the poet Metastasio ; and we should mention that, in the 12th century, the Moors possessed about seventy public libraries,—that of Cordova contained 250,000 volumes.

THE POET BURNS AND THE MORAVIAN.

ONE Sunday morning, some time before Burns commenced author, when he and his brother Gilbert were going to the parish church of Tarbolton, they got into company with an old man, a Moravian, travelling to Ayr. It was at the time when the dispute between the Old and New Light Burghers was making a great noise in the country ; and Burns and the old man, entering into conversation, differed in their opinions about it: the old man defending the principles of the Old Light, and Burns those of the New Light. The disputants at length grew very warm in the debate, and Burns, finding that with all his eloquence he could make nothing of his antagonist, became a little acrimonious, and tauntingly exclaimed, " Oh, I suppose I have met with the apostle Paul this morning !" " No," replied the old

Moravian, coolly; " you have not met the apostle Paul, but I think I have met one of those wild beasts which he says he fought with at Ephesus ! "

APOSTOLIC HUMILITY AND PAPAL ARROGANCE.

CHRIST, for to show His humble spirit,
Did wash His poor disciples' feet :
The Pope's Holiness, I wis,
Will suffer kings his feet to kiss.
Birds had their nests, and tods [1] their dens,
But Christ Jesus, Saver of men,
In earth had not a penny-bread [2]
Whereon He might repose His head :
Albeit the Pope's excellence
Hath castles of magnificence :
Abbots, bishops, cardinals,
Have pleasant palaces royals,
Like Paradise all these pleasant places,
Wanting no pleasure of their faces.
John, Andrew, James, Peter nor Paul
Had few houses among them all :
From time they knew the verity,
They had contemn all prosperity;
And were right heartily content
Of meat and drink and abuliment. [3]
To save mankind that was forlorn,
Christ bare a cruel crown of thorn.
The Pope three crowns for the nons,
Of gold, powdered with precious stones :
Of gold and silver, I am sure,
Christ Jesus took but little cure,
And left not when He yield the sp'rit
To buy himself a winding-sheet :
But his successor, good Pope John,
When he deceased in Avignon,
He left behind him a treasure
Of gold and silver great measure,
By a just computation,
Well, five-and-twenty million,
As doth endite Palmerus ;
Read him, and thou shalt find him thus.
Christ's disciples were well known
Through virtue which was to them shown ;
But specially fervent charity,
Great patience and humility.

---

1. *Tods,* foxes.   2. *Penny-bread,* a common board.   3. *Abuliment,* habiliment —clothing.

The Pope's flocks in all regions
Are best known by their clippèd crowns.

* * * * *

Christ did command Peter to feed His sheep,
And so he did feed them full tenderly ;
Of that command they take but little keep,
But Christ's sheep they spoil piteously,
And with the wool they clothe them curiously :
Like greedy wolves they take of them their food,
They eat the flesh, and drink both milk and blood.

Sir David Lindsay of the Mount.

EXCESSIVE POLITENESS.

MR. ROWLAND HILL was always annoyed when there happened to be any noise in the chapel, or when anything occurred to divert the attention of his hearers from what he was saying. On one occasion, about three years before his death, he was preaching to one of the most crowded congregations that ever assembled to hear him. In the middle of the discourse he observed a great commotion in the gallery. For a time he took no notice of it, but finding it increasing, he paused in his sermon, and looking in the direction in which the confusion prevailed, he exclaimed, " What's the matter there ? The devil seems to have got among you !" A plain country-looking fellow immediately started to his feet, and addressing Mr. Hill in reply, said, " No, sir, it ain't the devil as is doing on it ; it's a lady wot's fainted, and she's a very fat un, sir, as don't seem likely to come to again in a hurry." " Oh ! that's it, is it ?" observed Mr. Hill, drawing his hand across his chin ; " then I beg the lady's pardon—and the devil's too !"

INQUISITIVENESS BALKED.

Villager—" Good morning, sir ; horse cast a shoe, I see. I suppose, sir, you be going to ——." Here he paused, expecting the name of the place to be supplied ; but the *Citizen* answered, " You are quite right, sir, I generally go there at this season." " Ay, hum ; do ye ? and no doubt you be come now from ——" " Right again, sir : I live there." " Oh, ay, do ye ? But I see it be a London shay ; pray, sir, is there anything stirring in London ?" " Yes ; plenty of other chaises and carriages of all sorts." " Ay, of course ; but what do folks say ?"—— " Their prayers, every Sunday." " That is not what I mean—I wish to know whether there is anything new or fresh ?" " Yes ; bread and herrings." " Anan ! you be a queer chap ! Pray, muster, may I ask your name ?" " Fools and clowns call me ' *Muster;*' but I am one of the frogs of Aristophanes, and my genuine name is Brekekekex Koax ! Drive on, postilion ! "

BEN JONSON'S GRAVE.

THE words "O Rare Ben Jonson" inscribed on the wall near Poet's Corner (in Westminster Abbey), remind us that Jonson, though not housed in the Corner, lies in the Abbey, in the north aisle of the nave ; and a curious story is told as to the grave. The Dean of Westminster rallied the poet about his burial in the Abbey vaults ; " I am too poor for that," answered Jonson; "no one will lay out burial charges on me. No, sir; six feet long by two wide is too much for me ; two feet by two will do for what I want." "You shall have it," replied the Dean, and so the conversation ended. On the poet's death a demand was made for the space promised, and a hole made in it eight feet deep, and the coffin therein deposited upright.—*Knight's Old England.*

PEPYS AND HIS DIARY.

FEW books are so entertaining as the Diary of Samuel Pepys. There seems to be no doubt that his jottings were never meant for the public, for, to secure secrecy, he wrote his daily memorabilia in a kind of shorthand; and, moreover, the style is not such as a man of his education would have employed in a work written with a view to publication. This Diary, consisting of six closely-written volumes, comprising the years 1660–69, was, along with his fine library, bequeathed by him to Magdalene College, Cambridge, where it remained practically a sealed book for more than 120 years, till, in 1825, it was given to the world under the able editorship of Lord Braybrooke, the shorthand having been deciphered by the Rev. John Smith, Fellow of that college, whose services (as well as those of the noble editor) deserve our gratitude. Since its publication, Pepys' Diary has proved a valuable quarry to the social historian, a rich mine to the student of bygone manners and customs, while to the general reader it is " a joy for ever."

The author of this oft-quoted and curious work was the son of one John Pepys, who was descended from a respectable Norfolk family, and at one time carried on the trade of a tailor. Samuel Pepys was educated at St. Paul's School, and afterwards at Cambridge. He married, at the early age of twenty-three, a young lady of fifteen. His relative and patron, Sir Edward Montague (afterwards Earl of Sandwich), procured him a clerkship in the Exchequer. He was subsequently made Clerk of the Acts ; and his integrity and business aptitude ultimately gained him the Secretaryship to the Admiralty. He represented several boroughs in Parliament, and retired into private life on the accession of William and Mary. He was born in London in 1632, and died in the year 1703.

Pepys' Diary is one of the pleasantest narratives of daily occurrences, personal, domestic, social, and political, during ten of the most eventful years of this country's history. It is a perfect repertory of highly interesting facts and delightful gossiping anecdotes relative to the times in which he lived :—the Restoration; the Dutch War; the Great Plague; the Fire of London; Charles II. and his numerous mistresses; the Duke of York; the Duke of Buckingham ; churches, theatres, actors, plays, public gardens, new fashions in dress ; in short, we have in its fascinating pages a series of quaint but graphic pictures of the manners of courtly life, and of everyday life during the licentious—or, as it is sometimes euphemistically called, "gay"—period of reaction succeeding the rigid rule of the Commonwealth ; when courtiers—who had, while monarchy was fallen on evil days, endured great privations, and whose loyalty had been tried in the furnace of persecution—when the sun of royalty once more shone on their path, like weather-beaten seamen after "getting into port," gave vent to their long pent-up passions in a thousand frivolities and vices.

Our worthy diarist draws a sad and foreboding picture of the Court shortly after the Restoration, "where," says he, "things are in very ill condition, there being so much emulation, and the vices of drinking, swearing, loose amours, that I know not what will be the end of it but confusion, and the clergy so high." And when the redoubted Dutch were sailing up the Thames, matters had not mended a whit; for "the King and Court," he laments, "were never in the world so bad as they are now for gaming, swearing, women, drinking, and the most abominable vices that ever were in the world." Writing of one of the king's mistresses, he observes : "Lady Castlemaine is fallen in love with young Jermyn [an actor], who hath lately been oftener with her than the king, and is now going to marry my Lady Falmouth. The king is mad at her entertaining Jermyn, and she is mad at Jermyn's going to marry from her ; so they are all mad ; and," adds honest Pepys, "thus is the kingdom governed !" The personal attractions of Lady Castlemaine must have been very extraordinary, for few, if any, of the "Merry Monarch's" innumerable "flames" held so long a sway over his capricious fancy. This infamous woman was passionately fond of the dice-box. "I was told," writes our gossip, "that my Lady Castlemaine is so great a gamester as to have won £15,000 in one night, and lost £25,000 in another night at play, and hath played £1000 and £1500 in a cast."

In this curious book,—in which, as has been happily remarked, Mr. Pepys "literally thought aloud,—we are made acquainted with his most secret affairs ;—his love of money-getting and money-keeping, on the one hand ; and on the other hand, in amusing contrast, his natural disposition of a *bon vivant* and a man of pleasure : his business shrewdness contrasted with his almost childish love of dress —in which may, perhaps, be traced the influence of his father's *trade!* Every addition to his own or his wife's wardrobe is minutely described, and its effect, as it appeared to his own mind, complacently recorded, as may be seen from the following extracts, culled at random :—

"This day I first began to go forth in my coat and sword, as the manner now among gentlemen is."

"This morning I put on my black cloth suit, trimmed with scarlet ribbon—very neat—with my new cloake, lined with velvett, and a new beavre, which altogether is very noble, with my black silk canons which I bought a month ago."

"After dinner, I put on my new camlett suit, the best that ever I wore in my life; the suit costing me £24."

"I being in my coloured silk suit and coat, trimmed with gold buttons, and gold broad lace round my hands, very rich and fine."

"Lord's Day—Up and put on my new stuff suit, with a shoulder belt, according to the new fashion ; and the bands of my vest and tunique laced with silk lace of the colour of my suit, and so, very handsome, to church."

"To church, and with my mourning very handsome, and new perriwig, made a great show."

Those monstrous absurdities called periwigs, although worn in the reigns of Elizabeth and James I. (Shakspeare makes Hamlet speak of a "robustious, periwig-pated fellow"), reached their climax in Mr. Pepys' time. Our gossip, of course, duly chronicles his first appearance in the new style of head-gear. Under 8th November, 1663, he writes : "To church, where I found that my coming in a periwig did not prove so strange as I was afraid it would, for I thought that all the church would presently have cast their eyes all upon me." This fashion was introduced from France, where the servile courtiers first assumed periwigs in compliment to the long wavy hair of the Grand Monarch, which, when a young child, he wore in beautiful ringlets down to his shoulders ; and it is said that on attaining manhood, the French king acknowledged the compliment by adopting the same abominable head-gear.

"But of all Mr. Pepys' fine raiment, his "cloake" probably became in his estimation almost sacred. Walking in the Park one day, a heavy shower came on, and he records : "I was forced to lend the Duke of York my cloake, which he wore through the Park." Happy Mr. Pepys ! honoured cloak ! It would, doubtless, henceforth be carefully preserved from the predatory moth and the staining mildew, and handed down as an heirloom in the family !—*W A. Clouston.*

ANSWER OF THE MUMMY.

[This "Answer" to Horace Smith's much-admired "Address to an Egyptian Mummy in Belzoni's Exhibition," is not very generally known to modern readers. It originally appeared (signed "Mummius") in the *Mirror*, of May 15, 1824, and was subsequently reprinted, slightly altered, and with the addition of two new verses—the 10th and 13th.]

CHILD of the latter days ! thy words have broken
  The spell that long hath bound these lungs of clay,
For since this smoke-dried tongue of mine hath spoken,
  Three thousand tedious years have rolled away.
Unswathed, at length, I "stand at ease" before ye,
List, then, oh, list ! while I unfold my story.

Thebes was my birthplace—an unrivalled city,
  With many gates ;—but here I might declare
Some strange, plain truths, except it were a pity
  To blow a poet's fabric into air.
Oh, I could read you quite a Theban lecture,
And give a deadly finish to conjecture !

But you would not have me throw discredit
  On grave historians, or on him who sung
The Iliad—true it is I never read it,
  But heard it read, when I was very young ;—
An old blind minstrel, for a trifling profit,
Recited parts,—I think, the author of it.

All that I know about the town of Homer
  Is, that they scarce would own him in his day,
Were glad too when he proudly turned a roamer,
  Because by this they saved their parish pay ;—
His townsmen would have been ashamed to flout him,
Had they foreseen the fuss since made about him !

One blunder I can fairly set at rest :
  He says that men were once more big and bony
Than now, which is a bouncer at the best ;
  I'll just refer you to our friend Belzoni,—
Near seven feet high,—in sooth, a lofty figure !
Now look at me, and tell me, am I bigger ?

Not half the size ; but, then, I'm sadly dwindled ;
  Three thousand years, with that embalming glue,
Have made a serious difference, and have swindled
  My face of all its beauty ; there were few
Egyptian youths more gay : behold the sequel !
Nay, smile not, you and I may soon be equal !

For this lean hand did one day hurl the lance
  With mortal aim ; this "light fantastic toe "
Threaded the mystic mazes of the dance ;
  This heart hath throbbed at tales of love and woe ;
These shreds of raven hair once set the fashion ;
This withered form inspired the tender passion !

In vain : the skilful hands and feelings warm ;
  The foot that figured in the bright *quadrille ;*
The palm of genius, and the manly form—
  All bowed at once to Death's mysterious will,
Who sealed me up where mummies sound are sleeping,
In cerecloth and in honourable keeping :

Where cows and monkeys squat in rich brocade,
  And well-dressed crocodiles in painted cases,
Rats, bats, owls, and cats in masquerade,
  With scarlet flounces and with varnished faces ;—

Men, birds, brutes, reptiles, fish, all crammed together,
With ladies that might pass for well-tanned leather !

Where Rameses and Sabacon lie down,
  And splendid Psaminis on his hide of crust ;
Princes and heroes,—men of high renown,
  Who in their day kicked up a mighty dust ;—
There swarthy mummies kicked up dust in numbers,
When huge Belzoni came to scare their slumbers.

Who'd think these rusty hams of mine were seated
  At Dido's table, when the wondrous tale
Of " Juno's hatred " was so well repeated?
  And ever and anon the queen turned pale ;
Meanwhile the brilliant gas-lights, hung above her,
Threw a wild glare around her shipwrecked lover.

Ay, *gas-lights!* mock me not ; we men of yore
  Were versed in all the science you can mention.
Who hath not heard of Egypt's peerless lore,
  Her patient toil, acuteness of invention ?
Survey the proofs : our pyramids are thriving,
Old Memnon still looks young, and *I'm* surviving !

A land in arts and sciences prolific ;
  On blocks gigantic building up her fame ;
Crowded with signs and letters hieroglyphic,
  Temples and obelisks her skill proclaim :
Yet, though her art and toil unearthly seem,
These blocks were brought *on railroads, and by steam!*

How, when, and why our people came to rear
  The pyramid of Cheops—mighty pile !—
This and the other secrets thou shalt hear ;
  I will unfold, if thou wilt stay awhile,
The history of the Sphinx, and who began it,
Our mystic marks, and monsters made of granite.

Well, then, in grievous times, when King Cephrenes—
  But ah ! what's this ? The shades of bards and kings
Press on my lips their fingers ; what they mean is,
  I am not to reveal these hidden things.
Mortal, farewell ! Till science self unbind them,
Men must e'en take these secrets as they find them !

FOOTE'S READY HUMOUR.

THE strength and predominance of Foote's humour lay in its readiness. He was one day taken into White's Club by a friend who wanted to write a note. Standing in a room among strangers, he did not appear to feel quite at ease ; when Lord Carmarthen, wishing to relieve his embarrassment, went up to speak to him, but himself feeling rather shy, merely said, "Mr. Foote, your handkerchief is hanging out of your pocket." Whereupon, Foote, looking round suspiciously, and hurriedly thrusting the handkerchief back into his pocket, replied, "Thank you, my lord, thank you ; you know the company better than I do."

At one of Macklin's absurd Lectures on the Ancients, the lecturer was solemnly composing himself to begin, when a buzz of laughter from where Foote stood ran through the room, and Macklin pompously said to the laugher, "Well, sir, you seem to be very merry there, but do you know what I am going to say now?" "No, sir," at once replied Foote ; "pray, do you?"

" A well-beneficed Cornish rector was holding forth at the dinner-table upon the surprising profits of his living, much to the weariness of every one present ; when happening to stretch over the table hands remarkable for their dirt, Foote struck in with, "Well, doctor, I for one am not at all surprised at your profits, for I see you keep the glebe in your own hands."

What exquisite humour is there in this boast of horse-flesh : "My horse, sir ! Why, I'll wager it to stand still faster than yours can gallop !"

Dining at a house where the Bishop of —— was present, Foote was in high spirits, and talked immoderately ; when the bishop, being angry at the entire usurpation of the talk by Foote, after waiting with considerable impatience, said : "When will that player leave off preaching?" "Oh, my lord," replied Foote, "the moment I am made a bishop."

Having dined at Merchant Taylors' Hall, he was so well pleased with the entertainment that he sat till most of the company had left the dinner-table. At length, rising, he said, "Gentlemen, I wish you both very good night." "*Both !*" exclaimed one of the company, "why, you must be drunk, Foote ; here are twenty of us." "I have been counting you, and there are just eighteen ; and as nine tailors make a man, I am right—I wish you *both* very good night."

Foote had attacked some pretentious person for his characteristic foible. "Why do you attack my weakest part?" asked the assailed. "Did I ever say anything about your head?" replied Foote.

Hugh Kelly was mightily boasting of the power he had as a reviewer of distributing literary reputation to any extent. "Don't be too prodigal of it," Foote quietly interposed, "or you may have none for yourself."

A conceited young fellow was attempting to say fine things before Foote, who seemed unusually grave. "Why, Foote," said the small man, "you are flat to-day—you don't seem to relish wit." "Hang it, you have not tried me yet," was the caustic reply.

Mrs. Macaulay, who wrote a sensible and trustworthy "History of England," was less fortunate in the title of a pamphlet which she also published, entitled, "Loose Thoughts." The infelicitous choice was objected to in the presence of Foote, who dryly observed that he did

U

not himself see any objection to it, for that the sooner Mrs. Macaulay got rid of her loose thoughts the better.
"Why are you for ever humming that air?" Foote asked a man without a sense of tune in him. "Because it haunts me." "No wonder," said Foote; "you are ever murdering it."—*Book of Days.*

BEAUTIFUL BOOKS.

AMONG the books collected by Horace Walpole, and sold at the famous Strawberry Hill sale, was a magnificent missal, perfectly unique, and superbly illuminated, being enriched with splendid miniatures by Raffaelle, set in pure gold and enamelled, and richly adorned with turquoises, rubies, etc. The sides were formed of two matchless cornelians, with an intaglio of the crucifixion and another Scripture subject; the clasp was set with a large garnet, etc. This precious relic was executed expressly for Claude, Queen of France; it was bought by the Earl Waldegrave at 115 guineas. Another curious and costly specimen of bibliography was a sumptuous volume, pronounced by the *cognoscenti* as one of the most wonderful works of art extant, containing the Psalms of David written on vellum, embellished by twenty-one inimitable illuminations by Don Julio Clovio, surrounded by exquisite scroll borders of the purest arabesque, of unrivalled brilliancy and harmony. Its binding was of corresponding splendour. Its date was about 1537.

Antoine Zarot, an eminent printer at Milan, about 1470, was the first on record who printed the missal. Among other works, his execution in colours of the celebrated *Missale Romanum*, in folio, afforded a beautiful specimen of the art. The MS. copy seems to have been of a most dazzling description, its original date was MCCCCX.; every leaf is appropriately ornamented with miniatures surrounded with exquisitely elaborated borders; and its almost innumerable initials, which are richly illuminated in gold and colours, render it unsurpassed by any known production of its class. It has been estimated at 250 guineas. The *Complutensian Polyglott,* otherwise known as Cardinal Ximenes, deserves a passing notice among the renowned books of bygone times. This prodigious work was commenced under the auspices of the above-named prelate in 1502, and for 15 years the labour was continued without intermission; its entire cost amounted to 50,000 golden crowns! Arnas Guillen de Broear was the celebrated printer of this stupendous work. Of the four large vellum copies, one is said to be in the Vatican, another in the Escurial, and a third was bought by Herbets, at the sale of the M'Carthy library, for 600 guineas.

About 1572 we meet with another splendid production—the *Spanish Polyglott,* printed by Cristopher Plantin. A most magnificent copy upon vellum, in the original binding, was sold in London some five-and-twenty years since for one thousand guineas! and enormous as was this price, the copy was actually wanting three out of the ten volumes—those being in the Bibliothèque Royale.

Amongst the numerous rare and costly relics contained in the library of the Vatican, is the magnificent Latin Bible of the Duke of Urbino ; it consists of two large folios, embellished by numerous figures and landscapes in the ancient arabesque, and is considered a wonderful monument of art. There are also, by the way, some autograph MSS. of Petrarch's "*Rime*," which evince to what an extent he elaborated his versification. The mutilated parchment scroll, thirty-two feet in length, literally covered with beautiful miniatures, representing the history of Joshua, ornamenting a Greek MS., bearing date about the seventh century, is, perhaps, the greatest literary curiosity of the Vatican. The *Menologus*, or Greek Calendar, illustrated by four hundred rich and brilliant miniatures, representing the martyrdom of the saints of the Greek Church ; with views of the churches, monasteries, and basilicas, is also curious, as presenting specimens of the painting of the Byzantine school at the close of the tenth century. It contains also a fine copy of the Acts of the Apostles, in letters of gold, presented by Charlotte, Queen of Cyprus, to Innocent VIII. ; an edition of Dante, exquisitely illuminated with miniature paintings by the Florentine school ; these pictures are of about the ordinary size of modern miniatures on ivory, but far surpassing them in delicacy of finish.

KING JOHN AND THE ABBOT OF CANTERBURY.

An Old Ballad.

AN ancient story I'll tell you anon,
Of a notable prince that was called King John ;
And he ruled England with main and with might,
For he did great wrong, and maintained little right.

And I'll tell you a story, a story so merry,
Concerning the Abbot of Canterbury,
How for his house-keeping and high renown,
He rode post for him to fair London town.

An hundred men, the king did hear say,
The Abbot kept in his house every day ;
And fifty gold chains, without any doubt,
In velvet coats waited the Abbot about.

" How now, father Abbot, I hear it of thee,
Thou keepest a far better house than me,
And for thy house-keeping and high renown,
I fear thou work'st treason against my crown."

" My liege," quoth the Abbot, " I would it were known,
I never spend nothing but what is my own ;
And I trust your Grace will do me no dere [harm],
For spending of my own true-gotten gear."

" Yes, yes, father Abbot, thy fault it is high,
And now for the same thou needest must die ;
For except thou canst answer my questions three,
Thy head shall be smitten from thy body.

" And first," quoth the king, " when I'm here in this stead,
With my crown of gold so fair on my head,
Among all my liege men so noble of birth,
Thou must tell me to one penny what I am worth.

" Secondly, tell me, without any doubt,
How soon I may ride the whole world about ;
And at the third question thou must not shrink,
But tell me here truly what I do think."

" Oh, these are hard questions for my shallow wit,
And I cannot answer your Grace as yet ;
But if you will give me but three weeks' space,
I'll do my endeavour to answer your Grace."

" Now three weeks' space to thee will I give,
And that is the longest time thou hast to live ;
For if thou dost not answer my questions three,
Thy lands and thy livings are forfeit to me."

Away rode the Abbot, all sad at that word,
And he rode to Cambridge and Oxenford ;
But never a doctor was there so wise,
That could with his learning an answer devise.

Then home rode the Abbot, of comfort so cold,
And he met the shepherd a-going to fold :
" How now, my lord Abbot, you are welcome home,
What news do you bring us from good King John ? "

" Sad news, sad news, shepherd, I must give,
That I have but three weeks more to live ;
For if I do not answer him questions three,
My head shall be smitten from my body.

" The first is to tell him there in that stead,
With his crown of gold so fair on his head,
Among all his liege men so noble of birth,
To within one penny of what he is worth ;

" The second, to tell him, without any doubt,
How soon he may ride this wide world about ;
And at the third question, I must not shrink,
But tell him there truly what he does think."

" Now cheer up, sir Abbot, did you never hear yet,
That a fool he may learn a wise man's wit ?
Lend me horse, and serving men, and your apparel,
And I'll ride to London to answer your quarrel.

" Nay, frown not, if it hath been told unto me,
That I'm like your lordship as ever may be ;
And if you will but lend me your gown,
There is none shall know us at fair London town."

" Now horses and serving men thou shalt have,
With sumptuous array, most gallant and brave ;
With crozier, and mitre, and rochet, and cope,
Fit to appear 'fore our father the Pope."

" Now welcome, sir Abbot," the king he did say,
" 'Tis welcome thou'rt come back to keep the day ;
For an if thou canst answer my questions three,
Thy life and thy living both saved shall be.

"And first, when thou see'st me here in this stead,
With my crown of gold so fair on my head,
Among all my liege men so noble of birth,
Tell me to one penny what I am worth."

" For thirty pence our Saviour was sold,
Among the false Jews, as I have been told ;
And twenty-nine is the worth of thee,
For I think thou art one penny worser than He."

The king he laughed, and swore by St. Bittle,
" I did not think I had been worth so little.
Now secondly, tell me, without any doubt,
How soon I may ride this whole world about ? "

" You must rise with the sun, and ride with the same,
Until the next morning he riseth again ;
And then your Grace need not make any doubt,
But in twenty-four hours you'll ride it about."

The king he laughed, and swore by St. John,
" I did not think it so soon could be done.
Now from the third question thou must not shrink,
But tell me here truly what I do think."

" Yea ! that shall I do, and make your Grace merry :
You think I'm the Abbot of Canterbury,
But I'm his poor shepherd, as plain you may see,
That am come to beg pardon for him and for me ! "

The king he laughed, and swore by the mass,
" I'll make thee Lord Abbot this day in his place."
" Now, nay, my liege, be not in much speed,
For, alack ! I can neither write nor read."

" Four nobles a week then I will give thee
For this merry jest thou hast shown unto me ;
And tell the old Abbot, when thou comest home,
Thou hast brought him a pardon from good King John !"

ALEXANDER THE GREAT LYING IN STATE.

THE funeral car of the deceased emperor sustained a vaulted golden room, eight cubits in width and twelve in length ; the dome was decorated with rubies, carbuncles, and emeralds, and embellished by four historical paintings. Above the chamber, between its ceiling and the roof, the space was occupied by a quadrangular throne of gold, ornamented with figures in relief, to which golden rings were appended, bearing garlands of flowers that were daily renewed. Above the whole was a golden crown of such dimensions that a tall man could stand upright within it ; and when the sun's rays fell on it, shone with inconceivable splendour. In the chamber lay the lifeless body of Alexander, embalmed in aromatics, and enshrined in a coffin of massive gold.

PROBLEMS RATHER DIFFICULT OF SOLUTION.

Given—A bottle of British brandy.
To Find—A gentleman to drink it.
Given—The legal fare.
To Find—A cabman who is satisfied with it.
Given—A wife and twelve children.
To Find—The man who is contented with his lot.
Given—A good flogging.
To Find—A schoolmaster who doesn't say "it hurts him a great deal more" than the boy he is flogging.
Given—Advice.
To Find—A man who will act upon it.
Given—One hundred philanthropists.
To Find—Anything they have given.
Given—A dog, a cat, and a mother-in-law.
To Find—The house that is not too hot to hold them.
Given—A railway accident.
To Find—The person whose fault it was.

Mayhew's Comic Almanac, 1848.

BIG AND LITTLE BOOKS.

A RENOWNED copy of the Koran is probably without a parallel, at least as to its size, in the annals of letters. The task of transcribing seems to have devolved on a devotee of the prophet, styled Gholam Mohgoodeen ; it might be perused by a linguist without the aid of glasses assuredly, for the characters are described as three inches long ; the book itself being a foot thick, and its other dimensions something like five feet by three. The binding was literally " in boards." It was the labour of six years.

As a set-off to the foregoing, we might refer to the no less curious piece of paper, once presented to Queen Bess, comprising the Decalogue, Creed, and Lord's Prayer, all beautifully written in the compass of a finger-nail. Glasses *were* required here, and by their aid it is said the queen could easily read the extremely minute characters. The Iliad was once written on vellum so small that a nut-shell contained it ; and an Italian monk wrote the Acts and gospel, in compass of a farthing !

STRANGE TITLES.

IN the 16th and 17th centuries, authors of religious books were very ingenious in the matter of title pages. Here are one or two : "A Footpath to Felicitie," "Guide to Godliness." "Swarme of Bees," "Plante of Pleasure and Grove of Graces." These were most rife in the days of Cromwell. There were many bordering closely on the ludicrous, such as the one styled, "A pair of Bellows to Blow off the Dust cast upon John Fry ;" and a Quaker, whose outward man the powers thought proper to imprison, published "A Sigh of Sorrow for the Sinners of Zion, breathed out of a Hole in the Wall of an Earthen Vessel, known among Men by the name of Samuel Fish." We might multiply the numbers *ad libitum;* but must content ourselves with adding one or two more. "A Reaping Hook well tempered for the stubborn Ears of the coming Crop ; or, Biscuits baked in the Oven of Charity, carefully conserved for the Chickens of the Church, the Sparrows of the Spirit, and the Sweet Swallows of Salvation." To another we have the following copious description : "Seven Sobs of a Sorrowful Soul for Sin ; or, the Seven Penitential Psalms of the Princely Prophet David, whereunto are also annexed William Humuis's Handful of Honeysuckles, and divers Godly and pithy Ditties now newly augmented."

ILLUMINATED MANUSCRIPTS.

THE earliest specimen of illuminated manuscripts is the renowned *Codex Argenteus;* it is an extremely beautiful and costly volume in the quarto form ; its leaves, which are of vellum, are stained with a rich violet colour, and the chirography executed in silver, from which circumstance it derives the latter part of its title. It is a most elaborate performance, and one of exceeding beauty : and is further remarkable as being the only specimen extant of the parent tongue from which our own language as well as some of those of northern Europe, including Germany, the Netherlands, &c., have descended. It exhibits a very close resemblance to printing also, although executed nearly ten centuries prior to its invention. This Codex was found in the Benedictine Abbey of Werden, in Westphalia, about 1517 ; it subsequently passed into the possession of Queen Christina of Sweden, then into that of Isaac Vossius, and finally was purchased by a northern count, Gabriel de la Gardie, for £250, and by him presented to the University of Upsal. This copy is said to bear great analogy to the reading of the Vulgate ; three editions of it have been printed.

About the latter part of the seventeenth century, we find reference made by Bede to a magnificent copy of the Four Gospels having been done in letters of the purest gold, upon leaves of parchment, purpled in the ground, and coloured variously upon the surface, for the decoration of the church at Ripon, at the instance of the famous Wilford ; the chronicler speaks of it as a prodigy, and we may infer from this its rarity in those times. So costly a mode of producing manuscript could not have become general in any age ; accordingly we find these magnificent specimens were expressly executed for the nobles and princes of their times or the higher dignitaries of the Church. An instance of this is to be seen in the superb Prayer-Book of a like description with the foregoing, with the addition of its binding, which was of pure ivory, studded with gems, and is yet extant, we believe, in the celebrated Colbertine library, founded by Charles the Bald. In the middle ages even the bishops bound books. With the monks it was a common employment. There were also trading binders, called *Ligatores*, and they who sold the covers were called *Scrutarii*. There are many missals now in existence with covers of solid silver gilt. Gold relics, ivory, velvet, large bosses of brass, and other expensive adornments were bestowed upon church books, and those intended for presents to royal and great personages.

Some of these manuscript copies of the Sacred Scriptures were, it is well known, further embellished with elaborately executed miniatures and paintings. To follow in the order of chronology, we next meet with the magnificent Bible, presented by his favourite preceptor Alcuin, librarian to the archbishop of York, to the great Charlemagne, *after* he had learned to read and write ; for although among the wisest men of his age, he commenced his educational course at the tender age of 45. This remarkable copy of the Bible was in folio size, richly bound in velvet ; its embellishments were of the most superb description ; its frontispiece being brilliantly ornamented with gold and colours, and its text relieved by emblematic devices, pictures, initial letters, etc. This curious relic, which was in fine preservation, was sold in London in 1836, and produced the sum of £1500.

THE END.

Butler & Tanner, The Selwood Printing Works, Frome, and London.

Price 1s., cloth.

A Book for Home and School Use that will equal anything produced.

Beeton's Pictorial Speller. Containing nearly 200 Pages, with a multitude of Engravings, and comprising—1. Several Alphabets for learning Letters and Writing. 2. A First Spelling Book or Primer, containing Words of from Two to Four Letters, Illustrated. 3. A Second Spelling Book, containing Words of from Five to Ten Letters, Illustrated. 4. Moral Tales in Short Words, Illustrated. 5. Bible Stories and Lessons in Easy Words, Illustrated. 6. Stories from English History, written for Children.

New Edition. Demy 8vo, 160 pp., cloth, gilt back and side, 1s. 6d.; or in wrapper boards, 1s.

Webster's (The Illustrated) Reader. Containing Two Hundred Lessons on General Subjects, suited to the capacity of Young Learners, with Explanatory Introduction and Questions for Examination, on the plan of Noah Webster, the Lexicographer. Embellished with numerous first-rate Engravings from Designs by eminent English and Foreign Artists.

USEFUL BOOKS FOR SCHOOLS, FAMILIES, AND SELF-LEARNERS.

Fifth Edition, Just Ready, price 3s. 6d., 364 pp., crown 8vo, half bound, linen boards, price 2s.

Dictionary (The) of Every-day Difficulties in Reading, Writing, and Speaking the English Language ; or, Hard Words Made Easy. A Complete Epitome of Valuable Explanations and Definitions of Difficult English and Foreign Words, Phrases, and Expressions, with the Correct Pronunciation of each Word.

New Edition, Just Ready. Royal 16mo, 216 pp., cloth gilt, 2s.; roan gilt, 2s. 6d.

Mackenzie's Synonyms : A Practical Dictionary of English Synonyms. Alphabetically Arranged by D. L. MACKENZIE.

One Thousand Illustrations, price 10s. 6d., half-bound

The Self-Aid Cyclopædia for Self-Taught Students. Comprising General Drawing ; Architectural, Mechanical, and Engineering Drawing ; Ornamental Drawing and Design ; Mechanics and Mechanism; the Steam Engine. By ROBERT SCOTT BURN, F.S.A.E., &c., Author of "Lessons of My Farm," &c. 690 pp., demy 8vo.

Just Published, crown 8vo, cloth, price 7s. 6d., New and Revised Edition.

A Million of Facts of Correct Data and Elementary Informa- tion in the Entire Circle of the Sciences, and on all Subjects of Speculation and Practice. Much enlarged and carefully revised and improved, and brought down to the present year. A large amount of new matter added.

Published by Ward, Lock, and Tyler.

The Lily Series.

Wrappers, 1s. each; nicely bound for Presents, 1s. 6d. and 2s.

THE design of this New Series is to include no books except such as are peculiarly adapted by their high tone, pure taste, and thorough principle to be read by those persons, young and old, who look upon books as upon their friends—only worthy to be received into the Family Circle for their good qualities and excellent characters. So many volumes now issue from the press low in tone and lax in morality that it is especially incumbent on all who would avoid the taint of such hurtful matter to select carefully the books they would themselves read or introduce to their households. In view of this design, no author whose name is not a guarantee of the real worth and purity of his or her work, or whose book has not been subjected to a rigid examination, will be admitted into "THE LILY SERIES."

1. **A Summer in Leslie Goldthwaite's Life.** By the Author of "Faith Gartney's Girlhood," "The Gayworthys," &c.
2. **The Gayworthys :** A Story of Threads and Thrums. By the Author of "Faith Gartney's Girlhood," &c.
3. **Faith Gartney's Girlhood.** By the Author of "The Gayworthys," &c.
4. **The Gates Ajar ;** or, Our Loved Ones in Heaven. By ELIZABETH STUART PHELPS.
5. **Little Women.** By the Author of "Good Wives," "Something to Do," &c.
6. **Good Wives.** By the Author of "Little Women," &c.
7. **Alone.** By MARION HARLAND, Author of "The Hidden Path," &c.
8. **I've Been Thinking.** By the Author of "Looking Round," &c.
9. **Ida May.** By MARY LANGDON.
10. **The Lamplighter.** By Miss CUMMING.
11. **Stepping Heavenward.** By the Author of "Aunt Jane's Hero."
12. **Gypsy Breynton.** By the Author of "The Gates Ajar."
13. **Aunt Jane's Hero.** By the Author of "Stepping Heavenward."
14. **The Wide, Wide World.** By Miss WETHERELL.
15. **Queechy.** By the Author of "The Wide, Wide World."
16. **Looking Round.** By the Author of "I've Been Thinking."
17. **Fabrics :** A Story of To-Day.
18. **Our Village :** Tales. By Miss MITFORD.
19. **The Winter Fire.** By ROSE PORTER.
20. **The Flower of the Family.** By the Author of "Stepping Heavenward."
21. **Mercy Gliddon's Work.** By the Author of "The Gates Ajar."

Published by Ward, Lock, and Tyler.

New Books and New Editions.

Published by Ward, Lock, and Tyler.

New Books and New Editions.

BEETON'S HUMOROUS BOOKS.

PRICE ONE SHILLING EACH.

There is but little call to laud the men who have written the books catalogued below. They have done good work—work that needs no bush; and mankind is under obligations to them for a large sum-total of enjoyment. It will be a long day before we, in England, forget the names of Thomas Hood, Albert Smith, Reach, and the Mayhews; and from America we hail, as exponents of genuine and special humour, Artemus Ward, J. R. Lowell, Bret Harte, and Charles Dudley Warner, all of whose writings will be found included in the following list,—a various and entertaining company of genial jesters and merry penmen.

London: WARD, LOCK, & TYLER, Warwick House, Paternoster Row, E.C.